Instructor's Edition

THE COMPLETE
PARAGRAPH WORKOUT BOOK

Instructor's Edition

THE COMPLETE
PARAGRAPH WORKOUT BOOK

SECOND EDITION

CAROLYN H. FITZPATRICK

University of Maryland—Baltimore County

MARYBETH B. RUSCICA

St. Vincent's College of St. John's University

D. C. Heath and Company
Lexington, Massachusetts   Toronto

Address editorial correspondence to:

D. C. Heath and Company
125 Spring Street
Lexington, MA 02173

Acquisitions Editor: Paul A. Smith
Developmental Editor: Linda M. Bieze
Production Editor: Cormac Joseph Morrissey
Designer: Jan Shapiro
Photo Researcher: Martha L. Shethar
Production Coordinator: Chuck Dutton
Permissions Editor: Margaret Roll

Cover Credit: Scott Markewitz/FPG International, Inc.

International Standard Book Number: 0-669-27451-8

Library of Congress Catalog Number: 92-71457

10   9   8   7   6   5   4   3   2   1

Preface

The second edition of *The Complete Paragraph Workout Book: A Concise Guide to the Writing Process* meets the diverse needs of student writers enrolled in college composition classes. Suitable for developmental students, this text examines the writing and reading processes for the paragraph and essay; moreover, the text provides a review of grammar and punctuation.

The Complete Paragraph Workout Book begins with the assumption that all writers must read their own prose and that of others. By incorporating certain reading skills as they write, students can become better writers and place writing in the shared social context in which it must exist. Composing employs two skills that, as Peter Elbow states, "are so different that they usually conflict with each other: creating and criticizing." As writers, students must be allowed the freedom to invent, explore, and discover ideas as they develop paragraphs or essays. As readers, students must be able to criticize their own prose in order to address an audience with a specific purpose, determine an effective rhetorical strategy, organize details, and create an appropriate tone. In addition, students must be able to criticize the prose of others to test the validity of information presented, to determine the effectiveness of rhetorical strategies, and to respond to another's message.

Too often, student writers view their prose as the end product of several hours' work. They fail to see that writing, if it is to be meaningful, must address an audience that will respond. Within this mutual social context of writer and audience, composing becomes communication, not the mere recording of words upon a piece of paper. By encouraging student writers to be aware of their own prose and that of others, we believe that these students will increase their desire and ability to communicate with others and will take necessary risks to share ideas.

To confront the two problems of creating and criticizing, *The Complete Paragraph Workout Book* integrates reading strategies and the writing process. These strategies will facilitate student writers' abilities to understand and analyze their own prose as they compose and to recognize how other writers communicate effectively, convincingly, and honestly. Examining the writing process, Part One is arranged in a developmental sequence from the introductions to the reading process ("To the Student") and the writing process (Chapter One) to a final discussion of the essay. Part One incorporates related reading strategies within each chapter on the writing process. In "Creating Topic Sentences," for example, students identify and generate topic sentences by recognizing the distinction between fact and opinion. Students also learn that the placement of a paragraph's topic sentence is determined by the writer's purpose and audience. In addition, this text provides selected readings. Throughout the book, exercises present various types of writing, from academic textbooks to prose by professional writers as well as students, to indicate the social nature of writing. In Chapters One through Eight students can explore rhetorical strategies through model paragraphs and writing assignments. These assignments will motivate students to find their own solutions to writing situations and will allow students to use their own experience to respond to the writing of others. Chapter Nine ("The Essay") reinforces the writing process and identifies reading strategies for essays. For instance, students learn to summarize, critique, and evaluate essays; they then apply these strategies to revisions of their own work. Moreover, this chapter includes a wide variety of essay writing assignments that motivate students to apply their knowledge of composing strategies to rhetorical situations. The assignments at the end of the chapter also ask students to respond to the pictures provided in this text.

A review of traditional grammar, Part Two encourages students to edit their papers carefully after they have revised drafts. These grammar chapters are keyed to editing strategies introduced for the paragraph in Chapter Five ("Revising") and for the essay in Chapter Nine of Part One. Material within the chapters of Part Two is arranged sequentially. Each chapter contains clear learning objectives and a step-by-step explanation of a particular problem. Sentence exercises immediately follow each explanation, so that students can apply their newly acquired knowledge. In addition, we encourage students to construct their own rules and sentences. Such practice in identifying concepts and in developing sentences helps students apply principles they have learned. Practice sentences follow blocks of material and allow students to test accumulated knowledge on the sentence level before they edit paragraphs and essays.

Retaining the features of its predecessor, this second edition offers new items and chapters. Numbered lists and examples make the text in Part I more accessible to students. Each chapter in Part I now contains a section on writing strategies. In this way, students begin to write immediately. Moreover, every writing strategy is enhanced by four model papers: three by professional writers (two paragraphs and an essay) and one by a student writer. Writing tips conclude each chapter and encourage students to consider the development of their skills. Each chapter also contains two checklists: one to assist students in developing their writing process and the other to develop students' ability to revise. Additions to Part II (Grammar) include chapters on confusing and misused words and other types of punctuation.

The Complete Paragraph Workout Book offers instructors and students flexibility. Since students can vary greatly in their abilities to compose and criticize, an instructor can develop an individual approach for each class by selecting from the wide variety of exercises. As they deem appropriate, instructors can employ the writing strategies in Chapters One through Eight either in the order presented or at the end of discussion of the paragraph.

Several supplements are available to assist both instructors and students who use *The Complete Paragraph Workout Book*, Second Edition. The *Instructor's Guide* prepared by Cheryl L. Ware provides course syllabi, teaching tips, revision worksheets, suggestions for additional activities for each chapter, readability levels for readings in Part I, and answers to objective exercises and reading-related questions in Part I. The *Test Book* provides reproducible diagnostic grammar tests and two post-tests for each chapter in Part II. The *Test Book* also includes a test answer key. Software, available in versions for Macintosh and IBM-compatible computers, provides students with additional practice in grammar and writing skills.

We wish to thank Paul A. Smith and Linda Bieze, our editors, as well as Cormac Morrissey, our production editor, at D. C. Heath for their guidance and support. We are also grateful for the valuable comments of reviewers: Janet M. Carnesi, State University Agricultural and Technical College at Farmingdale, New York; Domenick Caruso, Kingsborough Community College; Irene Lurkis Clark, University of Southern California; Louise Rodriguez Connal, Chaffey College; Anthony DiMatteo, New York Institute of Technology; Phyllis T. Dircks, Long Island University—C. W. Post Campus; Donnasue Farrell, Manatee Community College; Lucy Gonzales, Del Mar College; Barbara Y. Gribble, Gulf Coast Community College; Ann Johnson, Community College of Denver; Anna Katsavos, Fiorello H. LaGuardia Community College; Christopher Cole O'Hearn, Los Angeles Harbor College; Charles Piltch, John

Jay College of Criminal Justice; Pamela L. Smyth, Riverside Community College; Irwin Weiser, Purdue University; and William F. Woods, Wichita State University.

We are especially indebted to those who have kindly allowed their essays to be reprinted here: Fernando Dela Cruz, Wayde Minami, Chris Bowen, Bill Heschle, Larry Mathena, Dan Estrada, Shellie Smith, Yvonne Schaber, Regina Raffety, Tim Maher, and Ray Stolle of the University of Maryland—Baltimore County; William McCann, Mansur Shomali, Reginald Menseses, Will Baird, Thomas Lee, Matt Wolf, Joe Liberatore, Ryan Bromwell, and Doug Eppler of Loyola High School, Towson, Maryland; and Mobeen Saeed of St. Vincent's College, St. John's University.

Carolyn H. Fitzpatrick
Marybeth B. Ruscica

▼ Contents

▼ Part One: Composing: From Paragraph to Essay   23

2 Exploring Topics   63

A * indicates a student-written piece.

7 Diction   237

▼ Part Two: Grammar Review 335

6 Run-Ons 417

7 Subject-Verb Agreement 423

8 Pronoun Reference 439

To the Student

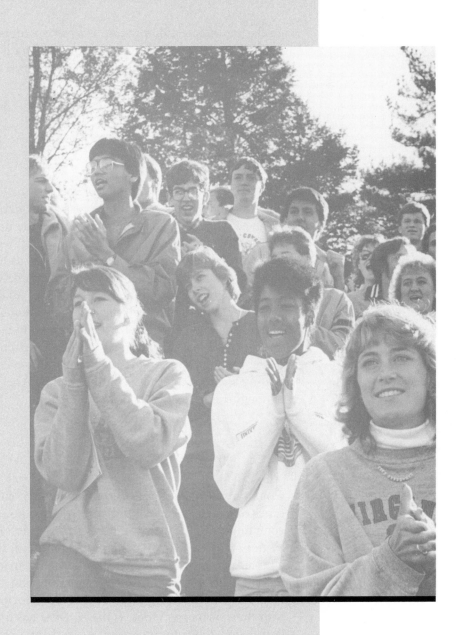

▷ **OBJECTIVES**

   1. To explore the communication process.

   2. To understand the connections between reading purpose and audience.

   3. To become an effective reader by previewing, skimming, and analyzing.

▷ **PREVIEW**

In the communication process, effective readers can understand material better, analyze a passage, synthesize new material with what they already know, and evaluate their own writing and that of others.

Effective reading gives you power. Active, analytical reading allows you to comprehend materials better, increase your knowledge, and save time and effort. As an active reader, you will analyze both the items that comprise a textbook or essay and their functions within the text. You will, for example, analyze an author's intended audience and tone as well as his or her point of view and the accuracy of the supporting details. As your analytical ability increases, you will read with greater comprehension and ease. Analytical reading also saves time, for you will not have to reread the passage to remember the material, and you will be better prepared to synthesize ideas, that is, to combine new ideas with your own knowledge. Finally, as a bonus, analytical reading can help improve your writing. In the writing process, this analytical ability will help you evaluate your own writing and that of others. Skillful reading, therefore, makes you an active reader, a thoughtful writer, and a powerful communicator.

The Communication Process

Communication, a social process, involves a sender and a receiver in an endless series of activities and roles. In effect, a sender (a speaker or writer) begins the communication process by constructing a message and sending it to an audience. With two or more people involved, communication becomes a social activity. This audience will analyze the sender's information and reconstruct the message in light of its own background, education, and experience. At that point, receivers (audience or readers) synthesize the new information presented by the sender with their own experience. If the receiver has no immediate use for this new knowledge, the communication process temporarily stops; it begins again when the receiver uses that knowledge to construct a new message. The receiver can become, in turn, a sender by communicating this new message either to the original sender or to a new audience. This action reinforces the reciprocal nature of communication. The chart on the following page depicts the complex web of elements that contributes to successful communication.

     You fill many roles when you communicate: you think, read, and write. To communicate with power, you must actively play these roles. In this chapter, you will begin to develop analytical reading skills; you will learn to think about what you read and to evaluate essays by previewing, skimming, and, in the end, analyzing them.

COMMUNICATION PROCESS ACTIVITIES

READING AS THINKING

Analytical reading is not a passive activity. Although you might believe that you can read effectively while you watch television, listen to the radio, talk with friends, or perform other tasks, you can not. You can accomplish some types of reading while you are performing other tasks. For example, you can read the directions for a recipe as you complete the instructions, and you can check the television guide as you watch a program. However, you will not retain this information.

Analytical reading allows you to remember and use what you read. Because it does so, analytical reading requires your complete concentration. In this way, analytical reading differs from the type of reading you might do when you read a billboard, a sales display, the comics in the newspaper, or even the message on your cereal box in the morning. In reading tasks like these, you do not consciously analyze the message you are receiving; often, you are simply keeping your eyes busy as you take a long trip, hunt for bargains, look for amusement, or try to awaken.

Analytical reading requires that you carefully think about the material you are reading. In effect, this type of reading demands that you enter into a dialogue with the author of the passage.

> Why did the author make a particular statement?
>
> Why did the author insist that his or her point of view was the correct one?
>
> What details did the author use to support this opinion?
>
> Are these details accurate?

By asking questions like these when you read, you become an active, effective reader.

READING PURPOSE

Usually, efficient readers have a specific purpose when they read. For example, they might read a chemistry text to understand a particular process or read a play to understand the plot and the characters' motives. Active readers know their reason for reading.

Individuals read for three major reasons: entertainment, information, and rejection.

Entertainment

When you read for *entertainment*, you want a pleasurable pastime. Consider, for example, the types of materials you read when you are on vacation. You may choose a horror story, a romance novel, a detective or mystery novel, or science fiction. You want to be scared, excited, or surprised by your material. In general, however, you will not use the material you are reading for any purpose other than daydreaming. Often, short stories, novels, and magazine articles provide your entertainment reading.

Information

When you read for *information*, you want to learn. You are interested in using the material either to acquire specific information (the current unemployment figures, for instance) or to increase your general knowledge (the biography of Abraham Lincoln, for example). Most of your academic reading falls into this category; you read newspapers, textbooks, nonfiction books, and articles for information.

Rejection

When you read for *rejection*, you judge the usefulness of the material to you. For example, if you were researching information for a term paper, you would probably scan a number of books for information. Based upon your brief reading of a piece, you would decide whether the material would be useful to your research. In this case, you would reread the piece to gain information. However, you would reject pieces that contain information you already know or that present unrelated facts. When you glance through professional journals, newsletters, newspapers, and magazine articles in search of new information, you read for rejection. You will later reread those pieces that offer information, but you will skip those pieces that do not appear informative or interesting.

Your purpose in reading influences the way you read and your reading rate or speed; therefore, you should understand your goals in reading a particular piece before you actually read it. Answers to the following questions will help you determine the types of reading you currently do and the effectiveness of your reading.

1. Why do I read? _____

_____

2. When I read, what am I trying to achieve? _____

_____

3. What is my goal when reading? _____

_____

4. Under what conditions, in what environment, do I read? _____

_____

5. How much do I remember after I have read? _____

_____

6. How long does it take me to read? _____

_____

7. How do I actually read? What is my method?_____

_____

Now, think about your answers. What do they indicate about your reading habits?

1. When I read, my purpose(s) is (are) _____

2. When I read, my goal(s) is (are) _____

3. When I read, my retention is _____

4. When I read, my rate is _____

As you have probably recognized by now, reading purpose, rate, and type are intertwined; your purpose and goal influence the type of reading you will do and the rate at which you will read.

PURPOSE AND AUDIENCE

In addition to identifying your reading goals, you must consider the characteristics of the audience for whom the material is written. Does the writer address the message to professionals in the field or to someone who wants a general overview of a situation? Is the audience unfamiliar with the material, or is it someone who requires a thorough examination of the topic? Obviously, the author's view of his or her intended audience influences style, organization, information, tone and vocabulary, and message.

A number of familiar situations confirm that an author addresses a particular audience. If you have ever received a letter from a political candidate, then you probably recognized that the message was designed to convince you of the candidate's merit. The writer might have addressed you in a friendly manner to enlist your support. Obviously, the author will present only the positive aspects of his or her career and will not include information on his or her more controversial political opinions. A letter from the candidate's opponent, however, will contain different facts and argue for a different conclusion.

Consider, too, the different audiences for whom advertisements in magazines and on television are designed. Advertisers know that their products will appeal to a section of the population if the advertisements emphasize the feature most likely to attract that group. Look, for example, at various magazines, each designed to reach a different audience; the advertisements will address the magazine's audience and its needs. The same product may, however, be advertised in a number of ways to appeal to different groups.

In textbooks, the audience's familiarity with the material obviously dictates the author's details and purpose. For instance, an advanced mathematics text is designed solely for a reader who has some experience in basic and intermediate math. The text, however, would be useless for someone who has just learned how to divide whole numbers. In the same way, some academic journals are written for professionals in particular disciplines, so their writers use the language of that field when they write for publication. These examples show that an author constructs a message for a specific audience with a specific purpose in mind.

Once you have identified the author's purpose and audience, re-examine your own reading purpose to see how your goal is affected. If the material addresses beginners and you are an expert, then you will probably read for rejection. However, if the material addresses a general audience, then you might just scan the piece for a specific detail. In other words, the author's purpose and audience influenced his or her communication and will affect your analysis of the material. Thus, identifying the author's purpose and intended audience can help you decide what *your* goal will be.

 **EXERCISE 1**

Consider your most probable purpose for reading each of the following materials. Then determine the audience for which the material was written.

	Purpose	*Audience*
1. A page in the phone book		
2. Chapter 4 in *Economics: Public and Private Choices*		
3. Business section of Sunday's newspaper		
4. "The Lottery" by Shirley Jackson		
5. Today's television schedule		

The Reading Process

To evaluate a textbook's or an essay's usefulness to you, you should employ the stages in the reading process: previewing, skimming, and analyzing.

PREVIEWING

When you begin the reading process, you preview a textbook or an essay. Previewing helps you decide whether or not a specific article, book, or chapter will provide useful information.

A **preview** is an introduction, an overview. Just as a movie preview summarizes a film's plot, characters, and action, a reading preview introduces you to the material's contents, structure, and purpose. However, the preview does not condense the entire book, chapter, or essay. Although reading the material may take an hour or more, previewing it may take only five minutes.

You preview to develop a general understanding of the material and its organization. You can then decide to reject the material if the information is not relevant or is already familiar to you, or you can decide to read the material more thoroughly. In the latter case, previewing will make your actual reading more efficient because you will already know the major topics, their relationships, and the emphasis of the piece. Although it initially requires a few extra minutes, previewing can ultimately save you time.

Since you preview to identify ideas and to begin thinking about the topic, you do not need to read the entire piece. To preview, look only at the major parts of the piece.

Source and Date

First, look at the piece's source and the date. You need to recognize any possible biases and inaccuracies. Consider, for example, two articles on whales, one published in *National Geographic* and the other in *Natural History*. Although both articles address the same topic, they will be written from different points of view and directed toward different audiences. The article in *National Geographic* will present basic information for a general audience interested in animals. In contrast, the article in *Natural History* will provide more detailed information for a professional audience educated in biology.

To test your ability to identify biases, consider the topic *health care costs*. How would the topic be treated by the *Washington Post?* To what audience would an article on this topic be directed? Consider the same topic discussed in *USA Today*. From what perspective would the article be written? What is the author's intended audience? (If you are unfamiliar with these newspapers, locate them in the library, and read several articles in each one.)

In addition, you should note the publication date to determine how current the information is. While some fields offer sound information from over several centuries of research, other fields rely upon information gathered within the past decade or even the past several months. Consider, for example, the field of computer science. Although articles from the 1940s would be interesting and valuable, they do not reflect the advances in computer technology made in just the past year. On the other hand, philosophers often return to the ancient Greeks for reflections on the nature of matter and of humankind.

Read the following titles and copyrights of books published on the care of premature infants, a field that has been transformed by improvements in technology. Which book should be used as a resource for a continuing-education course for nurses?

Born Premature, copyright 1962

Too Small, Too Soon, copyright 1991

Obviously, the book published in 1962—which has not been updated—no longer provides current information on premature infants. Doctors have learned a great deal about how to treat premature infants within the past thirty years. Therefore, researchers would gain more current information if they studied the more contemporary book.

Title and Author

Second, read the full title and subtitle of the piece. The titles will identify the subject matter and indicate how the subject will be analyzed. Also, note the author's name and any additional information provided, such as academic degrees or experience, about him or her. You may be able to tell whether the author is a recognized expert in the field and whether this analysis follows a specific author's viewpoint.

Consider these examples of titles and authors.

The Fall of the Bastille: An Insider's Account by Jean-Jacques L'Enfantant

Highlights of the French Revolution by Donald J. Pasomtory, B.A., Lecturer, Alcatraz College

Since the subtitle of L'Enfantant's book indicates that he was present during the revolution, his book would probably be more useful in discussing observers' reactions to the event. Pasomtory, however, has had the advantage of almost two hundred years of scholarship concerning the specific causes of the French Revolution. His degree (B.A.) indicates that he has completed his college education. More than likely, however, he is not a recognized expert in the field because he has not earned a graduate degree in history.

Subheadings

Third, read all the subheadings, and turn them into questions. This method provides a purpose for subsequent reading, and it will help you determine what information you, as a writer, should provide for your audience. In addition, the subheadings will allow you to determine a structure for the article and enable you to organize your facts. The following chart indicates the types of questions you could ask after you have read the subheadings in a chapter in an economics textbook.

SUBHEADINGS	QUESTIONS	INFORMATION
Real property tax	What is the real property tax? How is it calculated? What are its advantages and disadvantages?	Definition of Term
Value-added tax	What is it? How can it be implemented? How successfully does it enhance revenue?	Advantages and Disadvantages
Sales Tax	How does it affect consumption? Does it alter the buying habits of consumers?	Popular Image

Graphics

Fourth, look at charts, graphs, pictures, and other visual aids. Illustrations and tables clarify difficult material and condense information. In addition, they will alert you to the level of difficulty of the material. Consider the following chart depicting the increase in cases of tuberculosis in the United States during the last ten years.

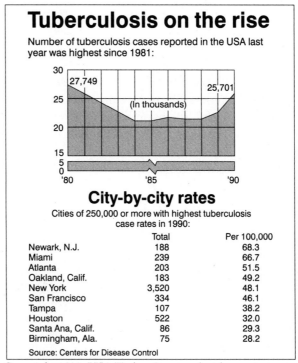

Tuberculosis on the rise

Number of tuberculosis cases reported in the USA last year was highest since 1981:

City-by-city rates

Cities of 250,000 or more with highest tuberculosis case rates in 1990:

	Total	Per 100,000
Newark, N.J.	188	68.3
Miami	239	66.7
Atlanta	203	51.5
Oakland, Calif.	183	49.2
New York	3,520	48.1
San Francisco	334	46.1
Tampa	107	38.2
Houston	522	32.0
Santa Ana, Calif.	86	29.3
Birmingham, Ala.	75	28.2

Source: Centers for Disease Control

Can you imagine trying to describe all the numbers and ratios in a paragraph? Your description would require much more space than a few inches of a newspaper column and would be far more complex for the reader to follow.

▼ **EXERCISE 2**

To practice your skill, preview the article "Beyond Rivalry," on page 13. Consider the article's usefulness if you were to write a report about the same topic for an audience with little background information in the field of family relations. Based on your preview, answer the questions below.

1. Does the source, the magazine *Psychology Today*, have any obvious biases that

   might influence the presentation of the material? _____

2. Is the information current? _____

3. Is the author an expert in the field? Does she represent a specific philosophical

   interest? _____

4. Is the organization helpful to you, or does it slow your reading? _____

5. Are there any visual aids? If so, are they useful? If not, what kinds of graphs or charts would be helpful in this article? _____

6. Finally, does the article deserve further reading? Do you think it can help you expand your knowledge? Will it be useful to you as a writer? _____

_____

If you answer *yes* to the last set of questions, then you should proceed to the next step in the reading process: skimming. However, if you reject the article as not useful, then you have finished processing the article. Although your involvement with that article has ended, the communication process has not. You can now either find another article to preview for its usefulness or rethink your approach to the entire topic.

PREVIEWING

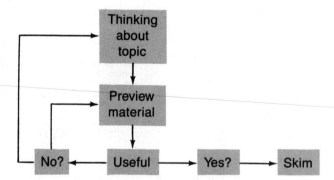

SKIMMING

Skimming allows you to grasp the essential elements of a reading selection quickly. While requiring only five to ten minutes, skimming provides you with the basic points of the topic. When you skim, you glance quickly at an article. Therefore, skimming requires speed and does not allow a detailed reading. Skimming will, however, give you an overview of an article's main idea, support, organization, and conclusions.

Purposes of Skimming

Readers skim for two purposes: information and rejection. You skim for information when your preview has convinced you of the material's usefulness but you do not have time to read the material thoroughly. By skimming the article, you can identify the main ideas and understand the author's line of reasoning. This type of skimming is valuable when you are reviewing a chapter before a class or test, doing research for a term paper, or exploring a new subject.

In addition, you can determine a source's potential usefulness by skimming it for rejection. When researching a topic, you do not read every article you can find on the topic; some will not be useful for your interests. If, after previewing, you are uncertain about an article's value, skimming can help you determine an article's worth. Then, you can reject any source that does not suit your purpose, and you can carefully read those that do. Similarly, as a professional, you must be aware of current trends and discoveries in your field, but you usually will not have the time to read every publication. Skimming will help you use your time and effort more effectively.

The Skimming Process

To skim, you must read less. Instead of reading every word in an article, you can skim for the main idea; consequently, you "finish" the article more quickly than if you had read it thoroughly. Ideally, your skimming rate should be twice your average reading speed. Skimming's advantage is this speed; its one disadvantage is decreased comprehension. You comprehend only 50 percent of a piece you have skimmed, compared to 70 to 80 percent of a piece you have read completely.

Skimming demands that you actually read—as quickly as possible—only the following parts of the material:

1. the introductory paragraphs (usually the first and second in a piece),
2. the first sentence in each following paragraph (usually the paragraph's topic sentence, identifying the paragraph's main idea), and
3. the concluding paragraphs (usually the last two in a piece).

Since you skim to determine the general lines of the author's argument, you want to recognize the main and supporting ideas in the piece. In the introduction, the author usually states a thesis, which identifies the passage's main idea. In a similar manner, the author will frequently restate this message in the conclusion; skimming the final two or three paragraphs reinforces your understanding of the thesis. Often, the body of the essay provides support for the author's main idea; consequently, by reading the first sentence in each body paragraph, you understand the essay's organization and supporting elements.

When you finish skimming a selection, you should know its contents. You should be able to discuss the author's message, even if you cannot detail the fine points of the argument. With this knowledge, you can decide whether the author's information can be used as a basis for your own writing. If so, then you should analyze the article further. However, if you have learned all the relevant material from the piece during your skimming, then there is no need to spend more time on it. You can continue your research by skimming another promising article.

▼ EXERCISE 3

To practice this skill, skim "Beyond Rivalry," on page 13. Then answer the following questions.

1. What is the author's main idea? _____

2. What arguments does she use to support the main idea? _____

_____

_____

3. What conclusion, if any, does the author draw? _____

_____

_____

4. Based on your skimming, write a short, preliminary summary of the author's

   main idea and supporting evidence. _____

_____

_____

_____

_____

5. If you were to write in response to this piece, would your intended audience

   already be familiar with this view of family relationships? Describe your

   audience. _____

_____

_____

6. Would your audience need to know this information? What, specifically,

   would the audience need to know? _____

_____

_____

7. Are you already familiar with this author's main idea and her arguments? Do

   you need to know more? _____

_____

_____

_____

The following chart illustrates the process a conscientious reader undertakes to gather information in preparation for writing.

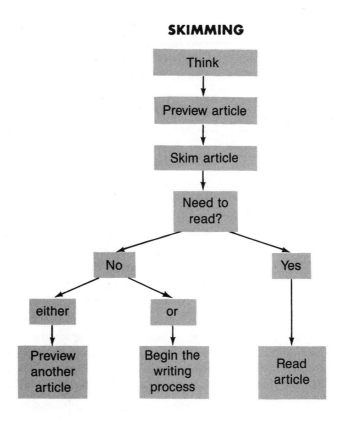

SKIMMING

> ▶ **Beyond Rivalry**
>
> ELIZABETH STARK
>
> *Mellowing and maturity allow many sisters and brothers to put aside competition and animosity in late adulthood. Elizabeth Stark, who has one younger sister, is an associate editor at* Psychology Today. *This article appeared in the April 1988 issue of that magazine.*

1   During childhood sisters and brothers are a major part of each other's lives, for better or for worse. As adults they may drift apart as they become involved in their own careers, marriages and families. But in later life, with retirement, an empty nest and parents and sometimes spouses gone, brothers and sisters often turn back to each other for a special affinity and link to the past.

2   "In the stressful, fast-paced world we live in, the sibling relationship becomes for many the only intimate connection that seems to last," says psychologist Michael Kahn of the University of Hartford. Friends and neighbors may move away, former coworkers are for-

gotten, marriages break up, but no matter what, our sisters and brothers remain our sisters and brothers.

3   This late-life bond may be especially important to the "Baby Boom" generation now in adulthood, who average about two or three siblings apiece. High divorce rates and the decision by many couples to have only one or no children will force members of this generation to look to their brothers and sisters for support in old age. And, as psychologist Deborah Gold of the Duke Center for the Study of Aging and Human Development points out, "Since people are living longer and are healthier longer, they will be more capable of giving help."

4   Despite childhoods of teasing, bickering, competition and general meanness, most of us make peace with our sisters and brothers in adulthood. But even among the friendliest sisters and brothers, some animosity may endure, or resurface. And for those still immersed in old rivalries, turning back to a sister or brother may come only after a struggle or with great reluctance.

5   Critical events can bring siblings together or deepen an existing rift, according to a study by psychologists Helgola Ross and Joel Milgram of the University of Cincinnati. Parental sickness or death is a prime example. Ross and Milgram found that siblings immersed in rivalry and conflict were even more torn apart by the death or sickness of a parent. Those siblings who had been close since childhood became closer.

6   How parents treat their children may affect how children treat each other when the parent is gone. "If parents have fostered empathy, not competitiveness or jealousy, between their children, their children will get along after their death," Gold says. But through a continuing saga of favoritism, reflected sometimes in an inequitable will, "parents can reach back from the grave, leaving a bitter legacy," Kahn warns.

7   In a study of older people with sisters and brothers, Gold found that about 20 percent said they were either hostile or indifferent toward their siblings. Reasons for the rifts ranged from inheritance disputes to animosity between spouses. But many of those who had poor relationships felt guilt and remorse. A man who hadn't spoken with his sister in 20 years described their estrangement as a "festering sore."

8   Although most people in Ross and Milgram's study admitted to some lingering rivalry, it was rarely strong enough to end the relationship. Only 4 out of the 55 people they interviewed had completely broken with their siblings and only 1 of the 4 felt comfortable with the break, leaving the researchers to ask, "Is it psychologically impossible to disassociate oneself from one's siblings in the way one can forget old friends or even former mates?"

9   If it is not impossible, it is unlikely that sisters and brothers will entirely cut the cord that binds them, according to anecdotal evidence, as well as recent research. There may be some inherent mellowing and softening in later life, Gold suggests, as people replace jealousy for a sibling's accomplishments with respect and develop

loyalty and empathy based on their shared experiences. Most siblings overcome their former resentment and hostility as they realize, in the words of one 63-year-old woman, "if you don't have family what do you have?"

10   As brothers and sisters advance into old age "closeness increases and rivalry diminishes," explains Victor Cicirelli, a psychologist at Purdue University. Most of the elderly people he interviewed said they had supportive and friendly dealings and got along well or very well with their brothers and sisters. Only 4 percent got along poorly.

11   Gold found that as people age they often become more involved with and interested in their siblings. Fifty-three percent of those she interviewed said that contact with their sisters and brothers increased in late adulthood. With family and career obligations reduced, many said they had more time for each other. Others said that they felt it was "time to heal wounds." A man who had recently reconciled with his brother told Gold, "There's something that lets older people put aside the bad deeds of the past and focus a little on what we need now . . . especially when it's brothers and sisters."

12   Another reason for increased contact was anxiety about a sister's or brother's declining health. Many would call more often to "check in" and see how the other was doing. Men, especially, reported feeling increased responsibility for a sibling; women were more likely to cite emotional motivations such as feelings of empathy and security.

13   Siblings also assume special importance as other sources of contact and support dwindle. Each of us moves through life with a "convoy" of people who supply comfort and nurturance, says psychologist Toni C. Antonucci of the University of Michigan. As we age, the size of this convoy gradually declines because of death, sickness or moving. "Brothers and sisters who may not have been important convoy members earlier in life can become so in old age," Gold says. And they do more than fill in gaps. Many people told Gold that the loneliness they felt could not be satisfied by just anyone. They wanted a specific type of relationship, one that only someone who had shared their past could provide.

14   This far-reaching link to the past is a powerful bond between siblings in later life. "There's a review process we all go through in old age to resolve whether we are pleased with our lives," Gold explains. "A sibling can help retrieve a memory and validate our experiences. People have said to me, 'I can remember some with my spouse or with friends. But the only person who goes all the way back is my sister or brother.'"

15   Older adults tend to idealize these memories, Gold found. "Selective memory has a way of highlighting certain aspects of the past, particularly positive ones," she says. But she sees no harm in this idealization and believes it fosters the reemerging desire for strong sibling ties. "It's fun reminiscing, thinking of things we used to do together. It's a warm, safe feeling," one woman told Gold.

16   Cicirelli agrees that reviewing the past together is a rewarding activity. "Siblings have a very important role in maintaining a connection to early life," he says. "Discussing the past evokes the

warmth of early family life. It validates and clarifies events of the early years." Furthermore, he has found that encouraging depressed older people to reminisce with a sister or brother can improve their morale.

17 Some of the factors that affect how much contact siblings will have, such as how near they live, are obvious. Others are more unexpected—for example, whether there is a sister in the clan. Cicirelli found that elderly people most often feel closest to a sister and are more likely to keep in touch through her. According to Gold, sisters, by tradition, often assume a caretaking and kin-keeping role,

Fame In The Family

People were always talking about psychologist Joel Milgram's older brother Stanley and his well-known experiments on obedience. For years, Milgram says, "my colleagues felt sorry for me because I had a famous brother in the same field."

Puzzled and intrigued by the assumption that having a famous sibling is a bad break, Milgram and his colleague Helgola Ross interviewed other siblings of celebrities to see if any of them felt overshadowed. Most were younger sisters of famous male artists, entertainers and politicians.

Although one woman said she felt like "a pebble next to a boulder" when compared to her famous sister, few interviewees felt outclassed. Instead, a close-up view of fame allowed many people to see it as something they could pursue and possibly attain. "My sister's success in acting," said one woman, "determined my choice to become an actress." A university professor commented that he recognized his own ability to achieve through his brother, a prominent figure in the United Nations.

Some siblings pursued fame themselves, but others rejected it, preferring a more private life. Two sisters of a distinguished writer, for example, agreed that fame in the family had fueled their own efforts in the arts, but had not increased their desire for public life.

Generally, the siblings were proud of their famous brothers and sisters, even when "twinges of envy" were acknowledged. And all saw talents and strengths in themselves that the celebrity lacked. Many mentioned their superiority at handling personal relationships. "All my life," said one woman, "I thought he was better in everything. But when his wife died, he turned to me."

Surprisingly, rivalry was not a lifelong problem, even among siblings in the same or related fields. When it was present, rivalry began long before one sibling became famous and often gave way to mutual admiration in adulthood. Milgram himself admits that "it bothered me as a kid that Stanley was so damn smart. But that bookworm turned into someone I admired who valued my accomplishments in return."

—HOLLY HALL

especially after the death of their mother. "In many situations you see two brothers who don't talk to each other that much but keep track of each other through their sisters," she says. Researchers have found that the bond between sisters is strongest, followed by the one between sisters and brothers and, last, between brothers.

18   Sisters and brothers who live near each other will, as a matter of course, see more of each other. But Cicirelli says that proximity is not crucial to a strong relationship later in life. "Because of multiple chronic illnesses, people in their 80s and 90s can't get together that easily. Even so, the sibling seems to evoke positive feelings based on the images or feelings inside."

19   Gold's findings support this assertion. During a two-year period, contact among her respondents decreased slightly, but positive feelings increased. "Just the idea that the sibling is alive, that 'there is someone I can call,' is comforting."

20   Although older people may find solace in the thought that their siblings are there if they need them, rarely do they call each other for help or offer each other instrumental support, such as loaning money, running errands or performing favors. "Even though you find siblings saying that they'd be glad to help each other and saying they would ask for help if necessary, rarely do they ask," Cicirelli points out.

21   Gold believes that there are several reasons siblings don't turn to each other more for instrumental help. First, since they are usually about the same age, they may be equally needy or frail. Another reason is that many people consider their siblings safety nets who will save them after everything else has failed. A son or daughter will almost always be turned to first. It's more acceptable in our society to look up or down the family ladder for help than sideways.

22   Finally, siblings may not turn to each other for help because of latent rivalry. They may believe that if they need to call on a brother or sister they are admitting that the other person is a success and "I am a failure." Almost all of the people in Gold's study said they would rather continue on their own than ask their sister or brother for help. But she found that a crisis beyond control would inspire "a 'rallying' of some or all siblings around the brother or sister in need."

23   Kahn has seen the same phenomenon. "When a crisis occurs, many siblings put their differences aside and help one another." He and his colleague Stephen Bank, a psychologist at Wesleyan University, have found that siblings tend to outgrow their fighting and are able to "forgive and forget" the grievances of childhood. He suspects that brothers and sisters take more verbal abuse than they deserve. "Next to mothers-in-law, siblings are the easiest relations to put down," Kahn says. "But in reality, there's a lot of smoke and not so much fire."

24   Despite the quarreling and competition many people associate with the mere mention of their sisters and brothers, most of us, Gold says, will find "unexpected strengths in this relationship in later life."

April, 1988

ANALYZING

Before you begin reading an article thoroughly, you should recognize a few important aspects about the author's perspective.

- First, an essay, a short composition, discusses one topic. The essay usually presents the author's personal perspective on the topic; the author will not examine the topic in exhaustive detail since he or she does not have the space of an entire book. Whatever its length (from a few paragraphs to several pages), the essay should be clearly written and organized; therefore, it will probably have a recognizable structure. As you skim, you should be able to see that structure. Then, with this structural pattern in mind, you will be able to organize the author's points.

- Second, an essay often presents a personal perspective. Although the author's point of view is subjective, he or she is writing to persuade you that this opinion is logically correct because it is based on reliable, objective evidence. Your preview of the material will identify any broad biases; however, the author may reveal more subtle biases that you can find only by a thorough reading. Carefully analyze the facts, statistics, and examples provided by the author. Decide whether they actually explain the main idea, provide sufficient details, and support the author's view.

- Third, an essay does not examine a topic completely. After all, an essay is not a book. Because of its comparatively short length, an essay must omit some information. Based on purpose, intended audience, and length of the essay, the author has included or excluded material. Consequently, some pertinent information may not have been given in the essay. In some cases, this information was excluded because it contradicted the author's main idea. Therefore, be aware that a completely different opinion might exist on the same topic.

By familiarizing yourself with additional evidence and opposing views, you can better evaluate the author's conclusions. In this way, you can judge for yourself whether the author presented his or her view honestly or whether the author omitted potentially contradictory information. To make such judgments, you must be well informed and familiar with your library and with research techniques.

▼ EXERCISE 4

This exercise will guide you through the entire reading process. Return to the article on page 13 that you have previewed and skimmed. Treat it as if you were unfamiliar with it. Use this reading guide to help you process the article.

1. Preview the article. Based on the title, what do you think the article will

   discuss? _____

2. Is there a perceived slant to the material? _____

    _____

3. Are any subtopics discussed? _____ If so, are they discussed in

    great detail? _____

    Is there any boxed material? How does it relate to the main topic? _____

    _____

4. Skim the article.

5. Based on your skimming, write a short, preliminary summary of the author's

    thesis and supports. _____

    _____

    _____

    _____

6. List below any words from the article with which you are not familiar. Look

    up their meanings in a dictionary and write the definitions here. _____

    _____

    _____

    _____

    _____

    _____

7. Read the article thoroughly.

8. Based on your reading of the essay, revise your preliminary summary to

    include any important information that might not have been available to

    you when you skimmed. _____

    _____

    _____

    _____

9. What is the author's main idea? _____

    _____

10. How does the author support her main idea? _____

    _____

    _____

11. Reread the conclusion carefully. What is the author's final point? _____

    _____

    _____

12. What other knowledge or experience do you have on this topic? Does your

    knowledge support or refute the author's main idea? _____

    _____

    _____

    _____

13. Before writing a paper, do you need to know more about this topic? _____

If you answered *yes* to the last question, then you need to research the topic
more. A *no* answer indicates that you have analyzed the material and are beginning to synthesize it with your own knowledge. This synthesis will make generating ideas for your own writing easier and make your communication more
effective. The following chart identifies the stages of communication as a person
assumes the varied roles of thinker, reader, and writer to become a more powerful communicator.

COMMUNICATING ABOUT A TOPIC

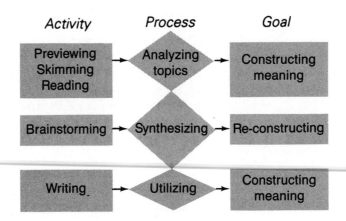

1

The Writing Process

OBJECTIVES

1. To develop a personal writing approach.

2. To understand the writing commitment.

3. To explore the entire writing process, from generating ideas to revising papers.

4. To generate ideas through prewriting.

PREVIEW

Writing is a recursive activity; it does not end with a first, or even second, draft of a paper. Throughout the entire process of writing, you can discover and explore ideas as you compose. You can use prewriting to generate and explore your ideas before you begin to write.

All of us are writers. Certainly, the ability to write well contributes to your academic success. Through term papers, essay examinations, lab reports, book reviews, and short compositions, you demonstrate your ability to analyze and synthesize material from various sources and to utilize this material to support your ideas.

Composing, however, does not end when you receive your degree; writing belongs to the larger professional and social world we share with others. In an age when we seem to use the telephone and computer more frequently than the postal service, businesses still operate primarily through the written word. Your power to write for different audiences on a number of subjects will serve you well when you enter a career. The more effectively you communicate ideas to others, the more effectively you complete professional tasks. In addition, writing itself is a social activity; through our letters, reports, papers, and articles, we communicate and share ideas with our audiences. This interchange of thought demonstrates that composing is *not* an isolated activity practiced only by creative geniuses who live in attics.

Composing begins with an individual who, in response to personal observations and reading, wishes to transmit ideas to an audience who, in turn, will react to the written words. If we were to watch a writer at work, we would observe only the external process. We would see the writer bending over blank pages or a computer terminal, recording thoughts, adding and deleting sentences and words, rearranging the order of paragraphs or even crossing them out altogether, and possibly listening to the sound of words as the writer reads a sentence or paragraph aloud. But we do not see a number of other activities: the writer's thoughts, the knowledge drawn from personal experience and research, the facts selected, the organization chosen, the words employed to convey the writer's meaning best, the sense of audience and purpose the writer has established, the discussions about the piece the writer has had with others, and the constant revisions made. This mental process defines writing, which proves to be much more than the mechanical recording of black marks upon white paper.

As you improve your composing ability, you will notice the effect your ideas, conveyed through your choice of words and details, have upon an audience. To inform, entertain, or persuade your audience, you should employ the entire composing process to explore ideas, discover details, and organize papers effectively. Through successive drafts of papers, your analytical ability will enable you to revise conscientiously.

Within the next few pages, you can compare your thoughts about writing to a number of traditional beliefs, compare your own composing method to an overview of the writing process, and begin to explore ideas through prewriting exercises. This chapter will enable you to analyze your own composing method and learn about new techniques to aid you in writing better.

Developing a Personal Writing Approach

Too many of us believe that a writer sits down at a well-lighted desk, has a steady stream of ideas and paper, and simply constructs a unified piece within a few hours. We also believe that writing is a talent one either has or lacks. Moreover, we believe that certain conditions—such as environment, equipment, methods, time limits, or proficiency with grammar—guarantee a good product. However, each writer uses a personal method of constructing a text based upon individual experiences, knowledge, preferences, and abilities.

ENVIRONMENT FOR WRITING

For example, each writer chooses a comfortable environment. Some professional writers, for instance, prefer to work at home in their libraries or workshops where they are not distracted by the bustling household. Other writers, particularly journalists, must work in an enormous room crowded with other reporters who are also rushing to complete articles for the next edition of the paper. College students select certain locations in which to write. Many choose the quiet atmosphere of the college library while others compose in the chaotic setting of a dormitory room where the television and stereo constantly compete for their attention. Unfortunately, simply being in a comfortable environment does not guarantee that a writer can generate ideas each time he or she goes there. In fact, many writers always have pens and paper with them; they know that good ideas often come when they are engaged in activities other than writing.

TOOLS FOR WRITING

We also believe that the tools we use will affect our ability to write. Some professional writers will not begin to work unless they have their favorite pen and a legal pad with them. Using a basic writing implement—a pen or pencil—many writers scrawl ideas onto scraps of paper and then draw arrows to indicate additional sentences that will be incorporated into the final copy. Other writers compose at the typewriter because they believe that seeing their ideas in print is a more effective way of recognizing the worth of the ideas rather than trying to decipher their own handwriting. These writers wish to see how something will "look" when it is finished.

Modern technology has also given us options in the equipment we use. Many people, from professional writers to students, usually "write" on video-display terminals connected to a main computer or to a personal unit. This method allows them to alter their text at any point, to rearrange paragraphs and sentences quickly, and to print successive edited copies easily rather than retyping each draft. This modern tool makes the task of writing easier, but it does not substitute for the content of the writing itself.

METHODS OF WRITING

No matter what tools a writer uses, the methods of organizing material and the time to complete an assignment can vary greatly. For instance, a newspaper reporter who has a late-breaking story must write 800 to 1,000 words within an hour or two so that the front page is complete. The reporter will probably follow an age-old formula: he or she will answer the questions "who, what, where, when, how, and why." A good journalist's lead paragraph will inform the reader of what happened, when it occurred, how it happened, where it took place, who was involved, and why it happened. The rest of the column will expand upon this basic information. At other times, when a reporter is at the scene of the event, he or she may "write" the article by calling the newspaper and dictating the story to a rewrite person. On the other hand, a feature writer for the same paper may have weeks, even months, to research and write an article. Unlike reporters, however, a novelist does not have to work under the constraints of time and space. A novelist may literally take years to perfect a book. Unlike the reporter, who must be objective and concise, a novelist may wish to withhold information from readers in order to build suspense in a detective novel, to create a mood in a romantic scene, or to develop a character or setting thoroughly.

TIME LIMITATIONS

Students face other problems with time. Ideally, students will have a week or two to compose a single essay. Within this time limit, students can easily refine and revise the assignment several times. However, less-than-ideal situations also exist. Sometimes professors assign an essay for the next class meeting, or students may procrastinate. They are then forced to compose in an evening what had been assigned for a week. Certainly, the more time a writer has to compose, the better the piece should be, but the writer cannot use lack of time as an excuse. Imagine the embarrassment of a reporter who fails to submit copy on time; the final edition of the paper will have a gaping hole unless a substitute article can be found. Consider, too, the position of a business executive who promises to submit a proposal and a bid on a product to a client by a certain date. Failure to complete the assignment will cost the company money and the executive his or her reputation.

PREOCCUPATION WITH CORRECTNESS

Finally, too many of us believe that proficiency with grammar, punctuation, and spelling is the sole standard by which our writing should be judged. Because many writers are intimidated by the red marks of a teacher's pen on their papers, they write only the types of sentences they can control and use only familiar words they can easily spell. Of course, correctness is important in writing; a writer's use of traditional grammar, punctuation, and spelling helps the reader understand the message quickly. However, during the initial process of composing, writers' insistence upon correctness frequently leads to a more serious problem: students often sacrifice their messages for mechanical correctness. When asked, for example, to analyze a particular short story, students may write only a summary of the events. Although their sentences may be correct, students do not address the assignment and instead repeat only what they already know well. Or when asked to describe a vacation, students may insist that it was interesting and exciting but fail to convey these qualities to readers. Fearing mistakes, they recite generalizations and clichés instead of making the piece original and lively. Correct grammar, punctuation, and spelling constitute a final phase of the composing process. However, writers cannot limit their messages because of their lack of knowledge in these areas. A paper that is correct grammatically but that says little new or interesting does not necessarily guarantee a good grade.

▼ EXERCISE 1

Complete the following chart by identifying advantages and disadvantages of certain environments, tools, methods, and time limits. Also, fill in your own preferences for each item. Identify which conditions you would choose for writing different types of pieces, such as letters, class papers, research reports, or lab reports. In a group, compare your answers to your fellow students' responses. What changes would you like to make?

CONDITIONS	ADVANTAGES	DISADVANTAGES

1. Environment
   a. a library
   b. a dorm room
   c. a room at your home
   d. your preference
   _____		

2. Tools
   a. pen and paper
   b. computer or word
      processor
   c. tape recorder
   d. your preference
   _____		

3. Method
   a. outline first
   b. write several drafts
   c. write one draft
   d. discuss with others
   e. your preference
   _____		

4. Time
   a. two or three hours
   b. one week
   c. two weeks
   d. your preference
   _____		

The Writing Commitment

Writing is a complex, individual activity. No particular method of composing ensures a successful paper, and writers find that, although one paper may be easily written, another requires two or three times the number of hours. Your individual experiences, knowledge, preferences, and abilities determine how you compose each piece. Moreover, composing effective prose to share with others requires time and honesty. To produce the best possible paragraph, essay, or report, you must be willing to invest time. You must generate and discover ideas, research facts, determine a purpose and audience, organize details, remove unnecessary items, verbalize complex ideas or descriptions, revise constantly, edit sentences and paragraphs, and, finally, proofread the finished piece for errors.

Composing also requires honesty. As a writer, you must work until you are satisfied with the material and alter paragraphs or ideas you find weak, unnecessary, or uninteresting. Honesty with the topic and with yourself forces you to refine your prose and to discover what you actually believe about a topic. Professional writers often admit that they don't know what they mean to say about a topic, or what their views are, until they are forced to write about it.

Beginning writers, however, usually do not take the time to consider what they believe about a topic. Given an assignment, beginning writers often cling to the first idea that comes to them and do not carefully explore other possibilities, their own knowledge of the topic, or their ideas. Too often, they begin writing with seeming ease because they assume that they know what they want to say. However, in the middle of the paper, they run out of ideas and do not know how to conclude. They are then forced to write a paper that either relies on generalizations or develops only part of the topic. More commonly, students who carelessly complete writing assignments the night before a deadline know only too well that they have not done their best work. The marks on their graded papers usually confirm the students' suspicions. In both cases, beginning writers have failed to devote any time to discovering what they want to say and to analyzing the effectiveness of their papers. Moreover, they have cheated themselves of one of the great rewards of writing—the discovery of their own ideas.

 **EXERCISE 2**

Consider the techniques you use when you compose a piece. Use the questions below to identify your preferences about writing. Be honest; do not simply repeat what teachers have told you is the "correct" method. After answering these questions, describe your writing process in a paragraph or two. Finally, compare your responses, both in the list and in the paragraphs, to those of other students. What differences do you notice? What techniques do you share with others?

1. What types of writing do you do most frequently? (Do you write personal

    letters, business letters, papers and reports for school, or journal entries?)

    _____

2. What do you usually do first when you begin a specific piece? _____

    _____

3. How many drafts do you make? How is each draft different? _____

_____

4. What do you do if you get "stuck"? _____

_____

5. How do you organize ideas? _____

_____

6. How do you determine whether details fit your topic? _____

_____

7. When do you revise? How do you revise? _____

_____

8. Do you talk with others about the piece? When do you show others your

paper? What questions do you ask them? _____

_____

9. How long do you usually spend on a piece? _____

_____

10. What determines when you are finished? _____

_____

11. What difficulties or rewards do you find when writing a piece? _____

_____

12. What is most important to you in your writing? _____

_____

_____

_____

13. What do you learn about yourself and others through your writing? _____

_____

14. How do you determine if your writing is effective? _____

_____

_____

The Writing Process: An Overview

Writing is a messy activity. Rarely do professional writers complete an essay with no errors in one sitting. Instead, they find that the writing process itself encourages them to repeat three major activities—planning, drafting, and revising—as they compose. Consider some of your own papers. Many times, you may write a sentence only to cross out some words and add others; you may even decide that one sentence is better placed in another paragraph. In other words, as you compose, you plan, draft, and revise, often all at the same time. For this reason, writing is called a recursive activity, an activity that moves ahead by repeating its actions. The chart below illustrates this recursive nature of the writing process.

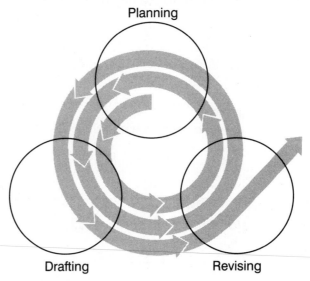

Planning

Drafting   Revising

The Recursiveness of the Writing Process

Because the writing process is recursive, do not assume that you can proceed in a straight path as you compose a paragraph. Instead, be open to discovering and incorporating new ideas as you compose.

GENERATING IDEAS

Problems with composing usually can be avoided if you pay attention to the entire composing process instead to only parts of it. If you take time at the start to generate ideas and consider them carefully, you will have a clearer idea of what you must do before you write. For example, you may be able to draw upon your own knowledge and experiences to create a sentimental description of a favorite family holiday. Sometimes your own knowledge and interests are just starting points. If you are concerned about ecology, for instance, you can use your personal experience of camping in a national park as a beginning, but eventually you must go to the library to research the topic more or interview authorities in the discipline. Usually, you generate these ideas before you organize details into a unified paper.

However, this process of invention can continue while you are composing the piece. You may often find that your original ideas need refinement, that some facts are unnecessary, and that other facts must be included. In other words, you should not cling to your first impressions. You must remain flexible as you compose. You must be willing to view the topic in several ways and to discard your original ideas if they do not support your new attitudes and discoveries. This process of invention does not always require endless hours of thought and research. As you become more experienced, you can shorten the process. Usually, when professional writers approach a topic, they quickly decide what to say and how to say it. Their familiarity with the topic, interest in it, and knowledge of writing help them to complete the piece more quickly than the writer who does not know where to begin. The final section in this chapter discusses various approaches to prewriting, the generating of ideas.

AUDIENCE AND PURPOSE

After deciding upon a topic, you must next identify your audience and purpose, for if you fail to clarify these crucial elements, the final piece will not complete its function: to communicate and share ideas with others. Examples of writers who fail to consider their audiences and purposes abound. Consider, for example, the directions for operating a household appliance or the directions for assembling a child's toy. Many of these instructions are so abstract, and the diagrams so complex, that only an engineer can comprehend them. However, these instructions are intended to help the average consumer assemble and operate the appliance or toy. The manufacturers failed to focus on that audience and purpose. As a further example of writers' failure to address audiences and purpose, contrast the two following letters by college graduates applying for jobs.

1 Dear _____ ,

I hope that you won't mind my intrusion into your busy day, but I would be so grateful if you would spare a minute to consider my application for the entry-level position of junior accountant.

While at school, I did not learn everything possible about accounting, but I took as many courses as I could. I hope you will be kind enough to teach me more about the complexities of the accounting field.

Many people have told me that I am a diligent student, so I think I would be able to learn once I am on the job. I also humbly suggest that I get along well with others in a work environment.

I sure do want the opportunity to work with your excellent company, and I promise I'll give it my all. Please accept my apology for bothering you, but I

really would be extremely appreciative if you'd call
me anytime for an interview.

> Sincerely,

2   Dear _____ ,

Do you need an expert accountant? Then, I am
your person. I just graduated from college with a
degree in accounting.

I took every available course, so I know everything there is to know. I plan to start as a senior
accountant. After all, if I am an expert, then why
should I be forced to begin as a lowly junior accountant?

I'll call you within the next few days, when my
schedule permits, so that I can set up an interview
with you. I do want to know what you can offer me.

> Sincerely,

Neither letter will secure a position or even an interview for its writer. Both authors do have a purpose in writing: they want a job with the company. However, both writers fail to identify the specific skills they could bring to the positions, and they do not provide the reader with any incentive to look further at their applications. For different reasons, both letters fail to address the intended audience: the prospective employer. In letter 1, the writer, perhaps unaware of his tone, indicates that he is insecure, subservient, and overly humble. He will not get the position because he is not confident about his own abilities. In letter 2, the writer suffers from the opposite problem: she is so overly confident that she demands a senior position in the firm. She, too, will not be hired, for several reasons. First, since she claims to know everything, she would be unwilling to learn the policies of a specific company. In addition, she lacks common courtesy; notice the way she demands an interview. She also fails to understand her potential relationship with an employer: she wants to know what the company can do for her, rather than what she can do for the company. Finally, her egotism may prove to be a source of conflict within the company. These examples clearly demonstrate the need for a writer to identify an audience and purpose.

ORGANIZING IDEAS

When writers finally commit ideas to paper, determine audience and purpose, organize facts, and construct paragraphs and sentences, they use any number of composing techniques.

For example, some writers generate thousands of words before they begin to organize and revise their material. Thomas Wolfe, the twentieth-century American author, would sometimes write 10,000 words a day. Stored in packing crates, his manuscripts could run to over 1,000,000 words, which his editor would shape into the final book.

Other writers prefer to outline all of their thoughts and then perfect each paragraph before they write the next one. Because they spend long hours selecting, organizing, and outlining their ideas completely, the act of composing allows them to revise each section as they write. Since they already know what the next paragraph will discuss, they polish each paragraph as they write it.

Occasionally, however, a writer may become overly conscious of style. Oscar Wilde, the late-nineteenth-century Irish playwright and novelist, was said to spend the morning putting a comma in and the afternoon taking it out.

Some writers organize as they write. They begin with a general idea of their facts and write the entire piece first. They then return to the piece to revise and restructure their ideas.

Finally, some professional writers complete a piece with one draft. Needless to say, their writing experience and their general knowledge make them rare exceptions, and even these writers will choose another composing process when they need to research an unfamiliar topic. Ideally, each writer chooses a composing process that best meets the needs of the individual writing task.

REVISING

Throughout the composing process, writers revise constantly. Revision requires that you be willing to rethink your original ideas. You must determine honestly when you are finished working on a project, but sometimes it is difficult to say when to stop revising. Some writers need only a few drafts. Others need piles of paper scattered around their feet. After composing a paper, some writers discard their original topics and begin an entirely different paper. Still other writers revise solely by correcting mistakes on the original draft of the paper. They incorrectly believe that "cleaning up" the first draft requires nothing more than checking spelling, punctuation, and grammar. They do not analyze what they have said and how they have said it, and they are unwilling to be honest about the worth of their writing. Hence, they fail to commit themselves to the writing process.

Of course, there is a time to stop revising. Very often, the time you have for revision is determined by the due date of the assignment, yet, no matter what the time limit, you should be satisfied with what you submit.

First Draft: Exploring the Topic

A writer usually produces a number of drafts before the piece is finished. An analysis of these drafts offers the best understanding of the composing process. After generating ideas, you might use the first draft of a paper to explore your ideas. In this exploration, you will attempt to discover a topic, identify your interests, and play with ideas. Without regard for correctness in grammar and punctuation and without concern for organization, you will put everything down on paper; in fact, you may produce more than you will actually need later in the composing process. This freedom allows you to consider a topic from many vantage points. For example, if you wish to describe a basketball game, you might approach the topic from a number of viewpoints in the first draft: you might try to see the game as a coach, a parent, a member of the team, a cheerleader, an announcer, a scout from the National Basketball Association, or a substitute player does. Although you do not need to consider every viewpoint, your consideration of a few will allow you to find what seems to be the most interesting one.

Second Draft: Focusing the Paper

In the second draft, you can begin to give direction to the paper by deciding upon a specific purpose and audience. After identifying these, you can choose those details and ideas from your first draft that support your purpose and correspond to your audience's needs. At this point, you might also make some decisions about an effective organization for the piece.

Third Draft: Organizing Ideas

The third draft focuses on organization of details selected in the second draft. You can now structure the paper into paragraphs that develop your purpose and central idea. You may also choose to revise your topic if you find that your original ideas no longer are effective, or to revise the order of paragraphs if they fail to produce the results you desire. Hence, you could construct a number of new paragraphs, alter their arrangement, or delete unnecessary paragraphs or sentences. Therefore, the third stage of drafts could actually contain any number of revisions as you work to make the piece more effective for your purpose and audience.

Final Drafts: Editing Sentences and Paragraphs

In the last drafts, you can edit sentences and paragraphs to ensure that they say what you want them to say, that your meaning is clear, that transitions help the reader understand the relationship between details and ideas, and that the paragraphs are unified. As a final check, you can proofread your piece for errors.

In each of these drafts, however, you must remain flexible and receptive to new ideas as you generate them, for it is the discovery of your own ideas that makes writing valuable for you. Certainly, too, there is not a "correct" way of constructing rough drafts; all writers create their own preferences and discover their abilities as they gain more experience through their writing.

Consider the following last drafts of a student's paper describing a softball game. Since the paper details the events of the game, the student was able to construct a time sequence for his topic. Hence, there are few changes in the placement of paragraphs, since each one describes in chronological order an aspect of the game. However, the writer does alter his material further. Where does he make changes? Why might he revise words, sentences, and paragraphs?

Take Me Out of the Ballgame
~~The Big Swing~~

ROUGH DRAFT:

Softball is a dangerous sport. It lulls its participants into thinking that it's something enjoyable and easy to play. In this contest, men in the twilight of their youth, with receding hair and falling chest, savor every moment of both the game and the beer

that inevitably follows. A sprite teenager, ~~among the~~ _with_

~~substantially padded confidence~~ _for example might_

~~middle-aged, ought to be able_ to clean up in such a

think it an easy task

league. But many take for granted, ~~as did I,~~ that

unfortunately,

softball is safe for the inexperienced populace. ~~In~~

this attitude before a game is doomed to cause

~~truth, the game of softball can lead to~~ fits of anxiety,

during afterwards

obliteration of egos, and quite frankly, pain. For me,

this realization came about in June of '85.

It all began at the

~~One summer,~~ ~~I worked at~~ Elkridge Country

where I worked as a lifeguard _when_

Club pool. One rainy day, the pool was empty. ~~The~~

immature staff members, including myself, formed

illustrious

the ~~famed~~ Elkridge Baseball League. (Generally, the

scores were held to under a hundred runs.) A home

run in this demanding sport required hitting the side

of a three-story barn with a tennis ball using a metal

Commanded

pipe as a bat. At Elkridge, I ~~had~~ numerous home run

titles and was fondly referred to by my adoring fans

as "Whipper Will" or simply "The Whip." ~~For some~~

~~unexplainable reason,~~ my confidence soared as each

a good _several_

ball slammed into the metal pipe, flew ~~at least~~ twenty-

thousand feet

five yards, and bounced off the huge barn. With my

cruising at an attitude of

ego ~~inflated,~~ it came as no surprise to me when the

manager of the pool asked if I could play softball on

play

Friday night. Knowing that I would ~~be playing~~ with

slow thirty-five-year-old men envious of my abilities,

chuckled

I ~~laughed~~ to myself and accepted. The week that

preceded

~~proceeded~~ the Friday night game overflowed with

exaggerated stories of my baseball glory days. I could

not help but let everyone know that I was an official

I continued this streak of overconfidence even up to the day

Rogers Forge Clinic All Star. I played an exhausting _of the game_

(margin notes:) Pregame, game, Post game — Categorization

(margin note:) EBL

tennis match earlier that day, ~~figuring~~ *deciding* that strength was not a requirement for softball. But ~~as time~~ *as the game neared* ~~passed,~~ anxiety about proving my big words overtook me. By gametime I realized that my boasts were unattainable, and fits of nervousness possessed me. As if an omen, the game began in a light ~~rain~~ *drizzle* on a muddy ~~field.~~ *diamond* During warmups I couldn't relax ~~my tension,~~ so the acting coach benched me for four innings. Soaked by the rain, I ~~watched~~ *peered* from the cold bench ~~as the other players ran, caught, and threw.~~ *at the not-so-old thirty-five-year-olds running, catching, and throwing*

In the top of the fifth inning, I got my chance to play. I was placed *strategically* in right field. Of course the first ~~pitch yielded~~ *batter hit* a high fly ball to right field, the place *because so I was told—nobody hits it there* where no one hits it. I charged forward under the ball preparing for my now-legendary play. In the last second, I realized the ball was sailing way over my head (to my horror.) I applied the brakes suddenly, forgetting ~~what~~ *the probable* results on wet grass. *For one embarrassing moment,* A generous portion of my body bounced across the grass as the softball rolled deep in the outfield. After the inning ended, I ~~walked~~ *strode* quickly back to the bench *on which I* ~~sulked;~~ *in my empty glove I held my grounded ego.*

Learning I was the lead-off hitter, I concentrated my disappointment in determination at the bat. All I desired to do was swing at that enormous ball with every ounce of strength that I could muster. I first scanned the outfield, and decided to push the ball to right field in my swing. With complete determination I dug each foot very securely in the mud of the batter's box, and stared coldly back at the pitcher. The ball started its ~~loping~~ *trajectory* course towards the plate. My eyes focused only on that gigantic soft-

ball ~~coming~~ *journeying* towards me. With every ounce of muscle

tensed, I drew the bat from my shoulder and whipped

it across the plate towards the ball.

Although the ball raced from my bat, I never

moved more than two feet from home plate. An

excruciating pain ripped through my knee, and

forced me crippled to the ground. ~~The next thing I~~

~~know was the envious~~

Pain

~~thirty-five year olds looked at the~~
~~popped out knee of the Sprite~~
~~teenager and shook their heads.~~
~~The game was called on account~~
~~of too many paramedics on the~~
~~field, and the once cold beer~~
~~now forgotten.~~ In the course of
this game's four and two-third
innings I had managed to invite
an ulcer with my anxiousness,
crash in the outfield on my rear
landing gear, and dislocate my
patella at home plate. So when
the grinning pool members exclaim
"You hurt your knee playing
softball?" I caution them.
Softball is a very dangerous
sport.

As the ~~the~~ thirty-five year
olds *swiftly* gathered around the ~~soft~~
fallen ~~Sprite~~ teenager, I knew
what had happened. My
knee had dislocated. any

movement on my part brought pain to my disarranged joint. The game was soon called on account of too many paramedics on the field and the once cold beer was forgotten. ~~Any softball just wasn't~~ My ordeal was finally over.

Maybe softball just wasn't my game. Maybe I had a bad day. Whatever ~~the~~ may be the cause. The facts were evident ~~that~~. In the course of four and two-thirds innings I had managed to ~~too~~ lose all self-confidence through deep anxiety, crash in the outfield on my rear landing gear and dislocate my patella at home plate.

▼ FINAL COPY:

Take Me Out of the Ballgame

Softball is a dangerous sport. It lulls its participants into thinking that it is something enjoyable and easy to play. In this contest, men in the twilight of their youth, with receding hair and falling chests, savor every moment of both the game and the beer that inevitably follows. But many take for granted that softball is safe for the inexperienced populace. A sprightly teenager with substantially padded confidence, for example, might think it an easy task to clean up in such a league. Unfortunately, this attitude is doomed to cause fits of anxiety before such a game, obliteration of egos during, and afterwards, quite frankly, pain. For me, this realization came about in June of '85.

It all began at the Elkridge Country Club pool where I worked as a lifeguard. One rainy day when the pool was empty, the immature staff members, including myself, formed the illustrious Elkridge Baseball League. A home run in this demanding sport required hitting the side of a three-story barn with a tennis ball using a metal pipe as a bat. Generally, the scores were held to under a hundred runs. At Elkridge, I commanded numerous home run titles and was fondly referred to by my adoring fans as "Whipper Will" or simply "The Whip." My confidence soared as each ball slammed into the metal pipe, flew a good twenty-five yards, and bounced off that huge barn. With my ego cruising at an altitude of several thousand feet, it came as no surprise when the manager of the pool asked if I could play softball on Friday night. Knowing that I would play with slow thirty-five-year-old men envious of my abilities, I chuckled to myself and accepted.

The week that preceded the Friday night game overflowed with exaggerated stories of my baseball glory days. I could not help but let everyone know that I was an official Rogers Forge Clinic All Star. I continued this streak of overconfidence even up to the day of the game. I played an exhausting tennis match earlier that day, deciding that strength was not a requirement for softball. But as the game neared, anxiety about proving my big words overtook me. By game time I recognized that my boasts were unattainable, and fits of nervousness possessed me. As if an omen, the game began in a light <u>drizzle</u> on a muddy <u>diamond</u>. <u>During warmups I could not relax</u>, so the acting coach benched me for four innings. Soaked by the rain, I <u>peered</u> from the cold bench <u>at the not-so-old thirty-five-year-olds running, catching, and throwing</u>.

In the top of the fifth inning, I got my chance to play. I was <u>strategically</u> placed in right field <u>because—so I was told—nobody hits it there</u>. Of course, the first <u>batter</u> <u>hit</u> a high fly ball to right field. I charged forward under the ball preparing for my now-legendary play. In the last second, <u>to my horror</u>, I realized the ball was sailing way over my head. I applied the brakes suddenly, forgetting the <u>probable</u> result on wet grass. <u>For one brief, embarrassing moment</u>, a generous portion of my body bounced across the grass as the softball rolled deep in the outfield. After the inning had ended, I <u>strode</u> quickly back to the bench <u>on which I sulked; in my empty glove I held my grounded ego</u>.

Learning I was the lead-off hitter, I concentrated my disappointment in determination at the bat. All I desired to do was swing at that enormous ball with every ounce of strength that I could muster. I first scanned the outfield, and decided to push the ball to right field in my swing. With complete determination I dug each foot very securely <u>into</u> the mud of the batter's box and stared coldly back at the pitcher. The ball started its loping <u>trajectory</u> towards the plate. My eyes focused only on that gigantic softball <u>journeying</u> towards me. With every ounce of muscle tensed, I drew the bat from my shoulder and whipped it across the plate towards the ball.

Although the ball raced from my bat, I never moved more than two feet from home plate. An excruciating pain ripped through my knee and forced me crippled to the ground. <u>As the thirty-five-year-olds swiftly gathered around the fallen teenager, I knew what had happened. My knee had dislocated. Any movement on my part brought intense pain to my quickly swelling knee. The game was soon called on account of too many paramedics on the field, and the once-cold beer was forgotten. The ordeal was finally over.</u>

<u>Maybe softball just is not my game. Maybe I had a bad day. Whatever the excuse may be, the facts are evident. In the course of four and two-third innings, I had managed to lose all self-confidence through deep anxiety, crash in the outfield on my rear landing gear, and dislocate my patella at home plate. So when the grinning pool members exclaimed, "You hurt your knee playing softball," I cautioned them. Softball is a dangerous sport.</u>

Notice the underlined passages in the final draft; these passages or words have been altered or added. While the overall structure of this essay does not change, the student does make substantial changes in the last two paragraphs, sentence structure, and wording. In particular, he incorporates changes that increase the dramatic action and irony. For instance, in the final two paragraphs, he completes the description of the end of the game and then turns to his conclusion; originally, he had covered both of these aspects in one paragraph. He incorporates humor into these final paragraphs by telling the reason the game ended suddenly: "too many paramedics on the field." His final paragraph summarizes his actions during the game ("lose all self-confidence through deep anxiety, crash in the outfield on my rear landing gear, and dislocate my patella at home plate") and returns to the statement beginning the essay ("Softball is a dangerous sport").

In some paragraphs, the student consciously alters the placement of sentences or adds them to strengthen the paragraph's unity. In the first paragraph, for example, the student reverses the placement of sentences 4 and 5; this change stresses the movement from the fact that "many take for granted that softball is safe" to his own overconfidence as he anticipates the game against much older men. In addition, in paragraph 3, he adds one sentence ("I continued this streak of overconfidence even up to the day of the game"), which not only reinforces his topic sentence but also explains his reason for playing tennis the day of the game.

Finally, the writer combines a number of sentences to add sentence variety and pertinent information, and several times he chooses more descriptive words. In the second paragraph, for example, he combines the first sentence with an added sentence to form a more complete topic sentence. In his fourth paragraph, the final sentence is expanded to include more information about his actions; rather than saying he "walked" back to the bench, he "strode." The bench, which he had just left, becomes the place where he "sulked." He also adds a final touch of irony: although he had failed to catch the fly ball, the "empty glove" now holds his "grounded ego."

▼ EXERCISE 3

Consider the changes the student made in the final draft. What further changes would have made the final draft even better? In a group, compare your answers to those of other students.

Prewriting

Prewriting, what writers do before they actually write an organized paper, can take many forms. You need this time to think about a topic, to consider it from several points of view, to examine it carefully, and to discuss it with others. Through these activities, you will begin to have a better sense of what you believe, what is important to say, and how you might say it. However, this invention—this thinking about writing—does not end when you pick up a pencil and paper. Even after committing ideas to paper, you can still add and delete facts or alter your original ideas or focus. Simply because you have constructed a certain sentence does not mean that you are required to keep it in the final draft. In other words, you should be flexible and willing to explore a topic throughout the entire writing process.

For many writers, including professionals, a blank piece of paper or a blank computer screen is intimidating because these writers believe that they must create a complete, unified piece immediately. They may stare at the paper or screen for several hours as they wait for inspiration to strike; unfortunately, their wait often wastes time. Even if they manage to write a few sentences, they may find that they have little to say about the topic because they have not identi-fied or discovered their beliefs and opinions about it. Fortunately, three prewrit-ing techniques—brainstorming, freewriting, and outlining—help writers gener-ate material quickly to get themselves started.

BRAINSTORMING

Brainstorming, quickly identifying and listing ideas at random, provides a useful starting point in the composing process. During a brainstorming session, which can take as little as ten minutes, you should record every idea and detail you can think of about a general topic. When beginning a brainstorming session, think first of personal experiences and knowledge you have about a topic and list them. Then record any interests you have in the topic that you could later research. At the end of the session, you will have generated several potential starting points and will have listed a number of ideas and points of view to consider. Examine the following results of a brainstorming session, completed in ten minutes, on the topic *baseball.*

Ideas generated for paper:
types of fans at baseball games
types of pitches thrown
heroes from years past
famous games—the 1919 World Series, for example, was rigged so that one team would win
famous clubs and their histories
changes in the game since its beginning
players' salaries and strikes
a team's commitment to a community
the revenue a franchise generates for the
   community
Little League games
the fun of a summer game with friends
parents and coaches at Little League games
the requirements for each position
the rewards of playing baseball
the scandals in baseball
different stadiums—the new domes or the old
   ballparks
the pleasure of watching a game

Of course, the writer might generate many other ideas for this paper, but this list provides a starting point. Also, for most of these ideas, the writer can draw upon personal memories of attending baseball games to create a fresh and original piece about baseball. Because a brainstorming session allows you to identify a number of ideas, it can be used at any point in the composing process when you need to generate ideas quickly.

▼ EXERCISE 4

Return to the essay "Beyond Rivalry" on page 13, and quickly review it. In a brainstorming session, record ideas for a paper about the topic of the essay. Be sure to include your personal experiences and knowledge. Also, identify areas you would like to research.

▼ EXERCISE 5

Choose three of the categories below. Complete a brainstorming session on each topic chosen. At the end of each session, place a check by those ideas you believe you could develop into a paragraph.

1. School   6. Vacations
2. Sports   7. Jobs
3. Holidays   8. Technology
4. Dates   9. Personal Heroes or Influential People
5. Family   10. Parties

FREEWRITING

After you have used brainstorming to generate ideas for a paper, you can be overwhelmed by the number and types of possible topics. Your greatest problem now is to decide which topic you can expand successfully. An efficient way to decide upon one or two possible topics is to use freewriting, since it will help you identify potential advantages and disadvantages of pursuing a topic. In addition, freewriting can generate details and allow you to explore a topic more fully than a brainstorming session would.

In a freewriting exercise, you force yourself to write continuously for ten to twenty minutes on a particular topic. Without concern for correct sentences, spelling, grammar, or punctuation, you must keep your pen moving for the required time as you record specific ideas about the topic. Sometimes, you may believe that you are moving away from the chosen topic; however, this is not the case. As its name implies, freewriting gives you freedom to explore and discover ideas. For example, if you begin a freewriting exercise on the topic *holidays*, you may begin by identifying specific holidays that are important to you. As you continue to write, however, you may find that the memory of a specific family holiday dominates your writing. Hence, you can use the details about one incident as a starting point in a paper about holidays or family celebrations. Occasionally, in a freewriting exercise, you might become "stuck" for ideas. At this point, you should repeat a key phrase or word until a new idea comes.

Writers are often pleasantly surprised when they read their finished freewriting exercises. They find that they do indeed have something to say about a particular topic. They may also find that ideas generated in the freewriting exercise are more interesting than their original topics. In either case, this method offers several advantages. First, it helps you decide whether a topic can be treated fully by using personal experience and knowledge or whether you need to research the topic before you commit ideas to paper. Second, freewriting helps generate ideas that can be used later for a more formally structured paper. Finally, freewriting can be used at any point in the composing process to provide ideas quickly and yield supporting details for a topic.

▼ EXERCISE 6

Select three subjects from Exercise 5, in which you employed brainstorming to identify topics for a paragraph. Complete a 15- to 20-minute freewriting exercise on each one. Using the list of questions below, compare your responses with those of other students.

1. What ideas did you generate?

2. Which of these ideas can be used in a paragraph?

3. What differences do you note between your freewriting and that of others?

4. What different ideas did you generate?

5. Why might these differences occur?

OUTLINING

Some writers prefer to outline their ideas after they have completed a freewriting exercise or when they believe they know the topic well enough to begin to compose. Outlines can take many forms, from the traditional Roman-numeral outlines to more visual maps and diagrams. Some writers also use tree diagrams or grids. Regardless of the form you prefer, you can use an outline to determine your interest and knowledge in a topic quickly. Below are some examples of outlines that chart a course for writers. The topic is *Summer jobs for students.*

▶ Roman-numeral outline:

I. Develops student's sense of responsibility and accomplishment
  A. Student develops good work habits
    1. Arrives on time
    2. Completes assigned tasks to best of ability
    3. Learns to work with others

  B. Student develops pride in job
    1. Rewarded by praise on job
    2. Enjoys paycheck at end of week

II. Encourages a student to understand value of money
  A. Student has own spending money
    1. No need to rely upon parents' money or allowance
    2. Can enjoy freedom of own money
  B. Student can learn to budget money wisely

▶ Map:

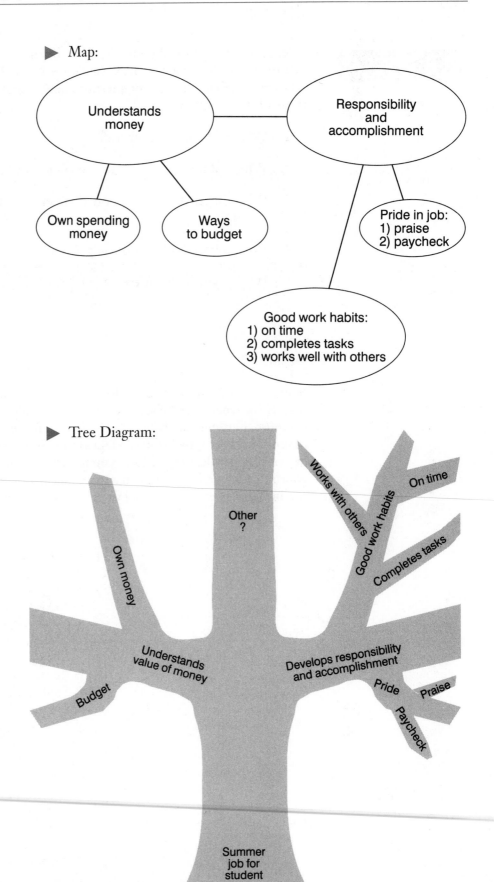

▶ Tree Diagram:

Like the other two prewriting techniques, outlining can be used at any time during the composing process because it quickly identifies the extent of ideas the writer has considered. Additionally, it is an easy way to check your organization, the relationship of your ideas to the main topic and to each other.

▼ EXERCISE 7

Select one freewriting exercise from Exercise 6. Underline the ideas you think you could use to build a paragraph. Next, organize those ideas by using one of the outlining techniques. Add new ideas as they come to mind.

▼ Writing Strategy: NARRATION

Probably the oldest strategy, narration is simply telling a story. A narration usually develops a story either by ordering events chronologically or by moving from the least important detail to the most important one in order to create suspense. Occasionally, a writer might even use a flashback, an abbreviated narration of a past event, to begin a piece or to provide necessary background information for the rest of the story.

Since narration is a frequently used technique—nearly every day we tell friends or relatives of the day's events—writers may overlook certain keys to an effective written narration. First, you must provide your reader with a clear reason for the narration. Explain the importance of the story to your audience. Second, you must provide clues for your audience about the timing of events in the narration. In speech, the phrase "and then" may be appropriate; however, in a written piece, these words quickly become monotonous.

In this section, you will have the opportunity to read and respond to four narrative pieces, three by professional writers and one by a student. As you read these pieces, analyze the chronological method each author uses to tell the story. These models will guide you later as you create your own narrative paragraph.

▶ ## An Eye-Witness's View of the San Francisco Earthquake

JACK LONDON

In this article, newspaper reporter and novelist Jack London details the events of the San Francisco earthquake of 1906, the most devastating earthquake in American history.

1   The earthquake shook down in San Francisco hundreds of thousands of dollars' worth of walls and chimneys. But the conflagration that followed burned up hundreds of millions of dollars' worth of property. There is no estimating within hundreds of millions the actual damage wrought. Not in history has a modern imperial city

been so completely destroyed. San Francisco is gone! Nothing remains of it but memories and a fringe of dwelling houses on its outskirts. Its industrial section is wiped out. Its social and residential section is wiped out. The factories and warehouses, the great stores and newspaper buildings, the hotels and the palaces of the nabobs, are all gone. Remains only the fringe of dwelling houses on the outskirts of what was once San Francisco.

2   Within an hour after the earthquake shock the smoke of San Francisco's burning was a lurid tower visible a hundred miles away. And for three days and nights this lurid tower swayed in the sky, reddening the sun, darkening the day, and filling the land with smoke.

3   On Wednesday morning at a quarter past five came the earthquake. A minute later the flames were leaping upward. In a dozen different quarters south of Market Street, in the working-class ghetto, and in the factories, fires started. There was no opposing the flames. There was no organization, no communication. All the cunning adjustments of a twentieth-century city had been smashed by the earthquake. The streets were humped into ridges and depressions and piled with debris of fallen walls. The steel rails were twisted into perpendicular and horizontal angles. The telephone and telegraph systems were disrupted. And the great water mains had burst. All the shrewd contrivances and safeguards of man had been thrown out of gear by thirty seconds' twitching of the earth crust.

4   By Wednesday afternoon, inside of twelve hours, half the heart of the city was gone. At that time I watched the vast conflagration from out on the bay. It was dead calm. Not a flicker of wind stirred. Yet from every side wind was pouring in upon the city. East, west, north, and south, strong winds were blowing upon the doomed city. The heated air rising made an enormous suck. Thus did the fire of itself build its own colossal chimney through the atmosphere. Day and night, this dead calm continued, and yet, near to the flames, the wind was often half a gale, so mighty was the suck. . . .

5   Wednesday night saw the destruction of the very heart of the city. Dynamite was lavishly used, and many of San Francisco's proudest structures were crumbled by man himself into ruins, but there was no withstanding the onrush of the flames. Time and again successful stands were made by the fire fighters, and every time the flames flanked around on either side, or came up from the rear, and turned to defeat the hard-won victory.

6   An enumeration of the buildings destroyed would be a directory of San Francisco. An enumeration of the buildings undestroyed would be a line and several addresses. An enumeration of the deeds of heroism would stock a library and bankrupt the Carnegie medal fund. An enumeration of the dead—will never be made. All vestiges of them were destroyed by the flames. The number of the victims of the earthquake will never be known.

▶ QUESTIONS   1. What is the effect of the sentence "San Francisco is gone"?

2. London refers to San Francisco both as a "modern,

imperial city" (paragraph 1) and as a "doomed city".
Explain his references.

3. Define the following words: *nabobs* (1), *lurid* (2),
cunning (3), and *enumeration* (6).

4. In the final paragraph, London repeats the phrase "an
enumeration of." Why?

5. How does London arrange the events in this piece?
What is the importance of using the events of that
Wednesday?

▶ The Calling

RUSSELL BAKER

*Russell Baker, winner of a Pulitzer Prize, explains how he
discovered the joy of writing in this passage from his
autobiography,* Growing Up.

1   The only thing that truly interested me was writing, and I knew that
sixteen-year-olds did not come out of high school and become writers. I thought of writing as something to be done only by the rich. It
was so obviously not real work, not a job at which you could earn a
living. Still, I had begun to think of myself as a writer. It was the only
thing for which I seemed to have the smallest talent, and, silly though
it sounded when I told people I'd like to be a writer, it gave me a way
of thinking about myself which satisfied my need to have an identity.

2   The notion of becoming a writer had flickered off and on in my
head since the Belleville days, but it wasn't until my third year in
high school that the possibility took hold. Until then I'd been bored
by everything associated with English courses. I found English
grammar dull and baffling. I hated the assignments to turn out
"compositions," and went at them like heavy labor, turning out lead-
en, lackluster paragraphs that were agonies for teachers to read and
for me to write. The classics thrust on me to read seemed as dead-
ening as chloroform.

3   When our class was assigned to Mr. Fleagle for third-year
English I anticipated another grim year in that dreariest of subjects.
Mr. Fleagle was notorious among City [City College, a Baltimore
high school] students for dullness and inability to inspire. He was
said to be stuffy, dull, and hopelessly out of date. To me he looked to
be sixty or seventy and prim to a fault. He wore primly severe eye-
glasses, his wavy hair was primly cut and primly combed. He wore
prim vested suits with neckties blocked primly against the collar
buttons of his primly starched white shirts. He had a primly pointed
jaw, a primly straight nose, and a prim manner of speaking that was
so correct, so gentlemanly, that he seemed a comic antique.

4   I anticipated a listless, unfruitful year with Mr. Fleagle and for a
long time was not disappointed. We read *Macbeth*. Mr. Fleagle loved

Macbeth and wanted us to love it too, but he lacked the gift of infecting others with his own passion. He tried to convey the murderous ferocity of Lady Macbeth one day by reading aloud the passage that concludes

> . . . I have given suck, and know
> How tender 'tis to love the babe that milks me.
> I would, while it was smiling in my face,
> Have plucked my nipple from his boneless gums. . . .

The idea of prim Mr. Fleagle plucking his nipple from boneless gums was too much for the class. We burst into gasps of irrepressible snickering. Mr. Fleagle stopped.

5   "There is nothing funny, boys, about giving suck to a babe. It is the—the very essence of motherhood, don't you see."

6   He constantly sprinkled his sentences with "don't you see." It wasn't a question but an exclamation of mild surprise at our ignorance. "Your pronoun needs an antecedent, don't youFsee," he would say, very primly. "The purpose of the Porter's scene, boys, is to provide comic relief from the horror, don't you see."

7   Late in the year we tackled the informal essay. "The essay, don't you see, is the . . . " My mind went numb. Of all forms of writing, none seemed so boring as the essay. Naturally we would have to write informal essays. Mr. Fleagle distributed a homework sheet offering us a choice of topics. None was quite so simpleminded as "What I Did on My Summer Vacation," but most seemed to be almost as dull. I took the list home and dawdled until the night before the essay was due. Sprawled on the sofa, I finally faced up to the grim task, took the list out of my notebook, and scanned it. The topic on which my eye stopped was "The Art of Eating Spaghetti."

8   This title produced an extraordinary sequence of mental images. Surging up out of the depths of memory came a vivid recollection of a night in Belleville when all of us were seated around the supper table—Uncle Allen, my mother, Uncle Charlie, Doris, Uncle Hal— and Aunt Pat served spaghetti for supper. Spaghetti was an exotic treat in those days. Neither Doris nor I had ever eaten spaghetti, and none of the adults had enough experience to be good at it. All the good humor of Uncle Allen's house reawoke in my mind as I recalled the laughing arguments we had that night about the socially respectable method for moving spaghetti from plate to mouth.

9   Suddenly I wanted to write about that, about the warmth and good feeling of it, but I wanted to put it down simply for my own joy, not for Mr. Fleagle. It was a moment I wanted to recapture and hold for myself. I wanted to relive the pleasure of an evening at New Street. To write it as I wanted, however, would violate all the rules of formal composition I'd learned in school, and Mr. Fleagle would surely give it a failing grade. Never mind, I would write something else for Mr. Fleagle after I had written this thing for myself.

10   When I finished it the night was half gone and there was no time left to compose a proper, respectable essay for Mr. Fleagle. There was no choice next morning but to turn in my private reminiscence of Belleville. Two days passed before Mr. Fleagle returned the

graded papers, and he returned everyone's but mine. I was bracing myself for a command to report to Mr. Fleagle immediately after school for discipline when I saw him lift my paper from his desk and rap for the class's attention.

11   "Now, boys," he said, "I want to read you an essay. This is titled 'The Art of Eating Spaghetti.'"

12   And he started to read. My words! He was reading *my words* out loud to the entire class. What's more, the entire class was listening. Listening attentively. Then someone laughed, then the entire class was laughing, and not in contempt and ridicule, but with open-hearted enjoyment. Even Mr. Fleagle stopped two or three times to repress a small prim smile.

13   I did my best to avoid showing pleasure, but what I was feeling was pure ecstasy at this startling demonstration that my words had the power to make people laugh. In the eleventh grade, at the eleventh hour as it were, I had discovered a calling. It was the happiest moment of my entire school career. When Mr. Fleagle finished he put the final seal on my happiness by saying, "Now that, boys, is an essay, don't you see. It's—don't you see—it's of the very essence of the essay, don't you see. Congratulations, Mr. Baker."

14   For the first time, light shone on a possibility. It wasn't a very heartening possibility, to be sure. Writing couldn't lead to a job after high school, and it was hardly honest work, but Mr. Fleagle had opened a door for me. After that I ranked Mr. Fleagle among the finest teachers in the school.

▶ QUESTIONS   1. Is Baker's description of Fleagle effective? Why does Baker repeat the word "prim" throughout paragraph 3?

2. Why does Baker finally want to write the student paper? What difference does this motive make in his essay? Why does Baker say that he "would write something else for Mr. Fleagle"?

3. What effect does Baker's paper have on other students?

4. Baker wrote this piece as an older man reflecting on his adolescence. What is his tone here? Would the tone have been the same if a sixteen-year-old boy had written this passage?

▶ 38 Who Saw Murder Didn't Call the Police
MARTIN GANSBERG

In this piece, written over twenty-five years ago, Martin Gansberg chronicles the last few hours of Kitty Genovese, a murder victim in New York City. The article raises a number of questions about our responsibility to others and identifies a dangerous lack of concern about the fate of others.

1   For more than half an hour 38 respectable, law-abiding citizens in Queens watched a killer stalk and stab a woman in three separate attacks in Kew Gardens.

2   Twice their chatter and the sudden glow of their bedroom lights interrupted him and frightened him off. Each time he returned, sought her out, and stabbed her again. Not one person telephoned the police during the assault; one witness called after the woman was dead.

3   That was two weeks ago today.

4   Still shocked is Assistant Chief Inspector Frederick M. Lussen, in charge of the borough's detectives and a veteran of 25 years of homicide investigations. He can give a matter-of-fact recitation on many murders. But the Kew Gardens slaying baffles him—not because it is a murder, but because the "good people" failed to call the police.

5   "As we have reconstructed the crime," he said, "the assailant had three chances to kill this woman during a 35-minute period. He returned twice to complete the job. If we had been called when he first attacked, the woman might not be dead now."

6   This is what the police say happened beginning at 3:20 A.M. in the staid, middle-class, tree-lined Austin Street area:

7   Twenty-eight-year-old Catherine Genovese, who was called Kitty by almost everyone in the neighborhood, was returning home from her job as manager of a bar in Hollis. She parked her red Fiat in a lot adjacent to the Kew Gardens Long Island Rail Road Station, facing Mowbray Place. Like many residents of the neighborhood, she had parked there day after day since her arrival from Connecticut a year ago, although the railroad frowns on the practice.

8   She turned off the lights of her car, locked the door, and started to walk the 100 feet to the entrance of her apartment at 82-70 Austin Street, which is in a Tudor building, with stores in the first floor and apartments on the second.

9   The entrance to the apartment is in the rear of the building because the front is rented to retail stores. At night the quiet neighborhood is shrouded in the slumbering darkness that marks most residential areas.

10   Miss Genovese noticed a man at the far end of the lot, near a seven-story apartment house at 82-40 Austin Street. She halted. Then, nervously, she headed up Austin Street toward Lefferts Boulevard, where there is a call box to the 102nd Police Precinct in nearby Richmond Hill.

11   She got as far as a street light in front of a bookstore before the man grabbed her. She screamed. Lights went on in the 10-story apartment house at 82-67 Austin Street, which faces the bookstore. Windows slid open and voices punctuated the early-morning stillness.

12   Miss Genovese screamed: "Oh, my God, he stabbed me! Please help me! Please help me!"

13   From one of the upper windows in the apartment house, a man called down: "Let that girl alone!"

14   The assailant looked up at him, shrugged and walked down Austin Street toward a white sedan parked a short distance away. Miss Genovese struggled to her feet.

15   Lights went out. The killer returned to Miss Genovese, now trying to make her way around the side of the building by the parking lot to get to her apartment. The assailant stabbed her again.

16   "I'm dying!" she shrieked. "I'm dying!"

17   Windows were opened again, and lights went on in many apartments. The assailant got into his car and drove away. Miss Genovese staggered to her feet. A city bus, O-10, the Lefferts Boulevard line to Kennedy International Airport, passed. It was 3:35 A.M.

18   The assailant returned. By then, Miss Genovese had crawled to the back of the building, where the freshly painted brown doors to the apartment house held out hope for safety. The killer tried the first door; she wasn't there. At the second door, 82-62 Austin Street, he saw her slumped on the floor at the foot of the stairs. He stabbed her a third time—fatally.

19   It was 3:50 by the time the police received their first call, from a man who was a neighbor of Miss Genovese. In two minutes they were at the scene. The neighbor, a 70-year-old woman, and another woman were the only persons on the street. Nobody else came forward.

20   The man explained that he had called the police after much deliberation. He had phoned a friend in Nassau County for advice and then he had crossed the roof of the building to the apartment of the elderly woman to get her to make the call.

21   "I didn't want to get involved," he sheepishly told the police.

22   Six days later, the police arrested Winston Moseley, a 29-year-old business-machine operator, and charged him with homicide. Moseley had no previous record. He is married, has two children and owns a home at 133-19 Sutter Avenue, South Ozone Park, Queens. On Wednesday, a court committed him to Kings County Hospital for psychiatric observation.

23   When questioned by the police, Moseley also said that he had slain Mrs. Annie May Johnson, 24, of 146-12 133d Avenue, Jamaica, on Feb. 29 and Barbara Kralik, 15, of 174-17 140th Avenue, Springfield Gardens, last July. In the Kralik case, the police are holding Alvin L. Mitchell, who is said to have confessed to that slaying.

24   The police stressed how simple it would have been to have gotten in touch with them. "A phone call," said one of the detectives, "would have done it." The police may be reached by dialing "O" for operator or SPring 7-3100.

25   Today witnesses from the neighborhood, which is made up of one-family homes in the $35,000 to $60,000 range with the exception of the two apartment houses near the railroad station, find it difficult to explain why they didn't call the police.

26   A housewife, knowingly if quite casually, said, "We thought it was a lover's quarrel." A husband and wife both said, "Frankly, we were afraid." They seemed aware of the fact that events might have been different. A distraught woman, wiping her hands in her apron, said, "I didn't want my husband to get involved."

27   One couple, now willing to talk about that night, said they heard the first screams. The husband looked thoughtfully at the bookstore where the killer first grabbed Miss Genovese.

28   "We went to the window to see what was happening," he said, "but the light from our bedroom made it difficult to see the street."

The wife, still apprehensive, added: "I put out the light and we were able to see better."

29   Asked why they hadn't called the police, she shrugged and replied: "I don't know."

30   A man peeked out from a slight opening in the doorway to his apartment and rattled off an account of the killer's second attack. Why hadn't he called the police at the time? "I was tired," he said without emotion. "I went back to bed."

31   It was 4:25 A.M. when the ambulance arrived to take the body of Miss Genovese. It drove off. "Then," a solemn police detective said, "the people came out."

▶ QUESTIONS

1. What is the unstated thesis?

2. What details does Gansberg choose to include? Is there a particular slant to this piece? What is it? How does Gansberg support his point of view?

3. The neighbors gave many excuses for not helping Kitty Genovese. What were they? Were any of the excuses valid?

4. What is the tone of this piece? How does Gansberg achieve this tone?

5. The last sentence of the article is "Then . . . the people came out." Explain the purpose of this sentence.

▶ # The All-American Job

JOE LIBERATORE

In this student paper, Mr. Liberatore narrates the events of a typical day at his job at a fast-food restaurant.

1   It's called a job. The most challenging aspect is trying to arrive on time. Fortunately, the first hour allows ample opportunity to wake up. When I feel secure about my consciousness, though, the initial rush of customers mercilessly strikes. As my attitude towards the customers turns sarcastic, the manager wisely sends me on break. When business becomes slow, I gladly focus on the conversation of my fellow

crew members. Every Sunday I serve breakfast at the Golden Goalposts and attempt to survive through eight hours of madness called a job.

2   The most challenging aspect of this job is trying to arrive on time. "It's 6:30 A.M.," warns the radio announcer. I'm late! I dart from the bed in a frenzy and jump into my dingy brown uniform. Trying not to stumble, I creep into my parents' bedroom and steal the car keys. I scurry out to the car and battle against the stalling engine. The first rays of sun guide my lonely journey to the Golden Goalposts. Blindly, I search for my time card and punch the clock precisely at 7:00 A.M.

3   The first hour offers few customers and invites the opportunity to wake up. Immediately, I brew three pots of coffee in order to smell the eye-opening aroma. My first customer jokes about my sluggishness, but I am proud that the dreaded thought of early work hours had no influence over my activities last night. Then I break a full coffee pot. This blunder results in a thirty-minute cleaning on my part. Only the similar condition of the manager allows such ineptitude to go unquestioned.

4   Now that I feel secure about my consciousness, the early church service lets out, and the rush begins. The food supply dwindles, and I notify the grill team to begin working again. Customers start complaining that I am not keeping up with the "30 seconds or less" policy which is advertised on the far left wall behind a large plant. I sacrifice quality, cleanliness, and value for service speed. Each child

screams for a "Fast Goalpost" racecar until the parent submits out of embarrassment. The manager's threats anger me to the point where I begin to put forth no effort. As soon as one rush is handled, another quickly follows, and I am trapped at the counter for three continuous hours of service.

5   Just as I reach the point of sarcasm in dealing with my customers, the manager wisely sends me on break. Only the absence of food for twelve hours compels me to eat the food I serve to hundreds of people. Being an experienced crew person, I choose to eat only that which has been personally prepared. I retreat to the crew room downstairs and attempt to eat amid the puddles from broken water pipes. I fiddle with the black-and-white television set which has no antenna and rotate the tuning dial of the stereo which receives every station except my favorite. In a span of fifteen minutes in my estimation, the time clock tells me that my thirty-minute break has expired. I punch back in and now must recover from my break.

6   Seeing that the rate of customers has fallen considerably, I focus on the various conversations among the other crew members. I particularly enjoy the competition of the grill team as each relates his impressive story concerning last night's parties. I cannot resist the temptation to ridicule the plight of the Cavel Hall football team in the presence of a student from that school. My attempt to impress the gorgeous brunette with my humor not only fails but

also attracts the attention of an outgoing blonde whom I dislike. The presence of the manager now eliminates all the conversations among the crew who give the appearance of working.

7   As the time of my departure arrives, I cleverly impress the manager with a sudden outburst of work which convinces her to send me home early, the wish of every crew member. As I strut back to punch out, I quickly glance at the broken coffee pot in the sink. I hurl a "Fast Goalpost" across the room before picking up my time card. Bolting down to the crew room, I retrieve the name tag which I had left during the break. Beaming at the jealous glares of the grill team, I depart, noticing the long lines of people forming at the counter. The sun is blinding. The car starts on the first try, and I drive away with the Golden Goalposts in my mirror. On the way home, I repeat my promise to find another job soon.

▶ QUESTIONS   1. What is Liberatore's opinion of his job? What alerts you to these feelings?

2. What is the busiest time at his job? What details does Liberatore include in his narration of this busy time?

3. Why does Liberatore want to find another job?

▼ PARAGRAPH ASSIGNMENTS

1. Usually, the first week of a semester is an exhilarating, challenging time for students. Recount your first-week experiences for a group of college-bound high-school seniors. In order to predict your audience's concerns and expectations, recall what you knew and wondered about as a high-school senior. What would you have liked to know about the first week of the semester before you experienced it?

2. Doing something for the first time—whether it is skiing, taking a trip alone, or driving your own car—is unique. Narrate a personal first experience. Consider several different audiences before you begin. Finally, identify one audience and purpose.

3. Choose an exciting or terrifying adventure that you remember well. (You might want to consider an event ranging from a trip in a raft down a river to an amusement-park ride.) Select an audience for your paragraph, and narrate this adventure.

4. If you work, narrate a typical day on the job for your employer. Be sure to include your regular activities and any unusual events.

▼ Writing Tips

Use any of the three prewriting techniques whenever you need to generate ideas quickly. You can use these techniques to write and revise a paragraph, complete an essay examination, record a labo atory experiment, or describe a computer program.

After you have written your paragraph, check it carefully for fragments. See Chapter 4 in Part II for a discussion of fragments.

▼ Writing Process Checklist

Use the following questions to improve your understanding of the writing process.

1. What prewriting strategy did you use to generate ideas for this paragraph?

   _____

   _____

2. How did your audience and writing purpose influence the words you used?

   _____

   _____

   _____

   _____

   _____

   _____

3. How did you decide to organize your paragraph? Why?

   _____

   _____

   _____

   _____

   _____

4. How many drafts of this paragraph did you write? What was your revision purpose for each draft?

   _____

   _____

   _____

   _____

   _____

▼ Narration Checklist

Use the following questions to revise your narration.

1. What is the point of your narration? That is, why are you telling this story? Where do you make this point clear to your readers?

_____

_____

_____

_____

_____

2. What details did you include in your narration? Can any of these be omitted or changed?

_____

_____

_____

_____

3. How did you organize this paragraph? What words or phrases help the reader follow your story?

_____

_____

_____

_____

4. If your proofreading revealed fragments, how did you correct them?

_____

_____

_____

_____

2

Exploring Topics

► **OBJECTIVES**

1. To identify paragraph topics.

2. To use details to discover paragraph topics.

3. To generate paragraph topics.

4. To narrow paragraph topics.

5. To explore composing through description.

► **PREVIEW**

The topic of a paragraph is its main idea. The topic identifies the specific idea you will discuss and tells the reader your purpose for writing the paragraph.

Ranging in length from a journalist's single sentence to an essayist's twenty sentences, paragraphs share a common feature: they usually develop only one main idea. The main idea of a paragraph, the **topic** indicates the specific idea a writer will explore and alerts the reader to an author's purpose. Without a narrowed paragraph topic, writers tend to ramble and generalize for their readers, who will be unable to determine the purpose of the paragraph.

Identifying Topics

Identifying a topic gives an audience its first clue to the writer's purpose in the paragraph. Without an identifiable topic, a paragraph fails to communicate with its audience. Try to identify the topic of the following paragraph.

> As with many other things in life, this, too, is a process; it has a beginning, middle, and end. All of the steps must be followed in sequence, or the end product will be useless; it will not be a "finished" product, merely an end one. Obviously, such an outcome would be a disappointment. It would be a waste of time, effort, and energy, and it is something to be avoided at all costs.

This paragraph has no topic. It does not convey the writer's reason for discussing a process since the writer's audience has no idea what that process might be. If anything, the paragraph obscures the writer's meaning and indicates the writer's unwillingness to communicate with the audience.

A topic can be either **specific** (precise) or **general** (broad) depending upon the context into which it is placed. The topic *cars*, for example, could be specific if the writer described different means of transportation; on the other hand, the same topic could be general if the writer identified various makes and models of automobiles. The ladder of abstraction on the following page represents this concept.

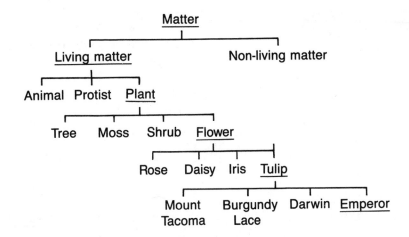

Follow the underlined topics through the chart; notice that the most general term is *matter*, and the most specific one is the *Emperor tulip*. However, items in the middle of the chart can be either specific or general, depending on their context. For example, the term *flower* can be specific when you compare it to the term *matter*:

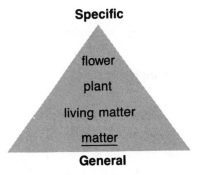

However, *flower* can be general if you compare it to a particular *type* of flower:

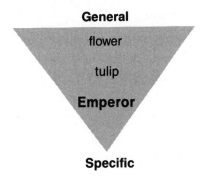

To identify a topic effectively, you should be able to classify ideas as either general or specific.

▼ **EXERCISE 1**

Read the following lists of topics closely, and decide whether the topics are becoming more general or more specific. Complete each list by adding either specific details or general terms.

▶ Example: education   (a general term)

school

elementary

Fourth grade

4th grade teacher   (a specific example)

1. penny

   coin

   currency

   _____

   _____

2. communication

   written communication

   book

   _____

3. neighborhood

   house

   room

   _____

   _____

4. vacation

   travel

   ship

   cruise

   _____

5. M-16

   rifle

   weapon

   _____

6. entertainment

   singers

   Country-and-Western singers

   _____

   _____

Discovering Topics

Some writers prefer to discover what they might say about a *general* topic by writing first; they then analyze their details to determine a *specific* topic for the paragraph. Other writers use ideas generated in several journal entries to discover a paragraph topic. These two methods, as well as brainstorming for topics, require the classification of ideas into general and specific topics. Such classification is the same skill writers use to identify paragraph topics from a list of details or from a paragraph itself. To practice that classification skill, identify the topic of the following paragraph by analyzing its specific details.

> Business people typically keep a close watch on *demographics*—the age, sex, income, education, and other key characteristics of the nation's people. The reason is that any significant change in demographics can dramatically alter consumer purchases. The rest of this century will see an increasingly larger middle-aged and elderly population as those who were born in the postwar "baby boom" in the late 1940s reach maturity. As you might expect, this demographic change will have a big effect on a number of different businesses, including the recording and motion picture industries, hospitals, apparel, and so forth. The expected slowdown in U.S. population until 2000 has caused Procter and Gamble to search for products besides those bought by consumers.

> (from William Rudelius and W. Bruce Erickson, *An Introduction to Contemporary Business*)

Now, look at some possible topics of this paragraph:

1. If you came up with the topic *decrease in population*, your response is *too specific*. The probability of a decline in the U.S. population is mentioned in the paragraph, but only as one of many details. Therefore, as a topic, it represents too little information from the paragraph and is too specific to be the paragraph topic.

2. Other topics might be inappropriate for the opposite reason. For example, the topic *demographics* would be *too broad* in the context of this paragraph. This topic includes too much information, more than is actually given in the paragraph itself. It raises readers' expectations of a more general discussion than actually occurs. (Consider, too, that a detailed treatment of demographics would require far more space than a paragraph allows.)

3. The topic *businesses' interests in changing demographics* is *appropriate* since the paragraph discusses why business people are concerned with changing demographics. The following specific details from the paragraph support this topic: aging population affects businesses; changes in people's characteristics can alter their purchases; and overall decline in population requires that new products be created for consumers. Thus, by identifying and listing specific details, you can discover a paragraph's topic.

▼ EXERCISE 2   Identify and list the specific details in each of the following paragraphs. Determine a paragraph topic that identifies the main idea in the paragraph.

1. Marketing people help create and bring about exchanges by performing certain functions. Some organizations may stress one function or another. Manufacturers take responsibility for transporting goods to convenient locations. Advertisers alert the public to the product's availability. Retailers are responsible for the details of the final exchange. Some functions—such as providing information, setting a price, and assuming risk—may be shared by many marketers. The point to keep in mind is that someone must perform these functions in order for an exchange to occur.

(from Daniel J. Rachman, *Marketing Today*)

Specific Details _____

_____

_____

Topic _____

2. Many Europeans, from Karl Marx to Hitler, have been deluded by the so-called materialism of the Americans. It seems incomprehensible to them that in a country where there seems to be only a difference of appreciation between the methods of the robber barons and those of the gangsters, the faith of the people as a whole in the validity of democratic ideals should remain intact. It is a fact that in no other civilized nation—and up to a very recent past—has the power of money given more impunity and caused more injustice than in America. But it is also a fact that in no other nation have these abuses caused less moral damage to the nation as a whole.

(from Raoul de Roussy de Sales, "The Idea of Happiness," in *The Saturday Review Treasury*)

Specific Details _____

_____

_____

Topic _____

3. Prior to the Industrial Revolution in the early 1800s, American colonists depended on trade with England for everything from tea to textiles. After the Revolutionary War, the country was forced to become more self-sufficient. Soon mills and factories were being built, and a new era of production began. The Civil War spurred the growth of industry and mass production even further. When the war was over, factories turned from making armaments to producing consumer goods. With a seemingly limitless supply of customers and boundless natural resources, the first Industrial Age business philosophy was developed—the production concept.

(from Daniel J. Rachman, *Marketing Today*)

Specific Details _____

_____

_____

Topic _____

4. The great error in Rip's composition was an insuperable aversion to all kinds of profitable labor. It could not be from the want of assiduity or perseverance; for he would sit on a wet rock, with a rod as long and heavy as a Tartar lance, and fish all day without a murmur, even though he should not be encouraged by a single nibble. He would carry a fowling-piece on his shoulder for hours together, trudging through woods and swamps, and up hill and down dale, to shoot a few squirrels or wild pigeons. He would never refuse to assist a neighbor, even in the roughest toil, and was a foremost man at all country frolics for husking Indian corn, or building stone-fences; the women of the village, too, used to employ him to run their errands, and to do such little odd jobs as their less obliging husbands would not do for them. In a word, Rip was ready to attend to anybody's business but his own; but as to doing family duty, and keeping his farm in order, he found it impossible.

(from Washington Irving, "Rip Van Winkle")

Specific Details _____

_____

_____

Topic _____

5. What is in a handful of sand? poets have queried. The scientists have been able to answer that question with some assurance. These sand detectives can even tell a person where on the beach he picked up the sand in his shoes. No one should walk on the dunes of our beaches today—they are the natural guardians of our beach—but if anyone did, the sand between his toes could easily be identified under a microscope. Dune sand is smaller than the sand of the rest of the beach. If we study this closely, we shall find dune sand's surface and edge are rough because on the dunes they have been subjected to a fierce weathering of storms. We'll find salt too among the sand grains, in contrast to the uniform sand of the beach. Sand does not lie and, because it has such a high percentage of quartz, it is almost ineradicable. The pirates wind, water, and glaciers cannot destroy quartz. They can grind it smaller and smaller, but the quartz remains in sand.

(from Robert and Seon Manley, *Beaches*)

Specific Details _____

_____

_____

Topic _____

Generating Topics

Have you ever experienced the following situation? Toward the end of your English class, your instructor informs you that a paper on the topic of your choice is due in two days. You immediately panic and think, "But I don't know what to write about!" During the next day, you consider and discard many ideas because you believe that they are just not "right." Finally, late that evening, now desperate to produce a paper, you place a title on a blank piece of paper and stare out the window for the next hour. No ideas come to you as you constantly remind yourself that the finished paper is due tomorrow. As a last resort, you reach for another piece of paper and write down a topic you have used many times before—*a student's responsibilities in school*—even though you know you have no new insights to offer on this topic. Slinging words on paper, you promise yourself that you will revise the paper before class. The next morning, however, you oversleep and rush to get to class on time. You grudgingly submit the paper to your instructor.

In a sense, you have cheated yourself of one of writing's great rewards: the discovery of new ideas. Because you believed that some ideas were not "right" since they did not fit a preconceived notion that a paragraph could be written easily in one draft, you failed to explore what were possibly more interesting topics for both you and your audience.

Few situations can intimidate writers as much as having a blank piece of paper on the desk, being alone in a room with only their own thoughts as guides, and knowing that they must write a paper. Where, then, do writers begin? Most writers admit that it is easier to write about themselves since they know the subject well and usually find their own experiences interesting. However, nearly every subject imaginable can be a topic for a paragraph if writers carefully consider their personal experiences, knowledge, and interests. Therefore, writers usually begin with what they know—either from personal experience or study—or with a topic they wish to investigate more.

INTEREST

Certainly, the more interested you, as a writer, are in a subject, the more interesting you can make it for your audience. Writing about personal experiences makes the final piece an individual one and often gives you more control over the paragraph since you can visualize the event and draw upon memories of it for specific details. For example, if you were asked to describe a holiday, then you should first consider the ones your family celebrates regularly. This process leads you to synthesize ideas from your background. The combination of ideas you know from your general background and from experience can be incorporated into your writing. For example, what makes the holiday important? Which family members do you see only on that holiday? How is the holiday celebrated? What rituals or customs does the family follow? Is the holiday celebrated at a particular place? Are certain foods and decorations used only at this time? Was one particular holiday more memorable than others? Has your attitude changed toward that holiday? All of these ideas will be interesting to others who either remember similar holidays or wish to learn about other cultures and ethnic groups. By asking questions like these in a brainstorming session, you can easily generate many ideas for a paragraph.

INFORMATION

Some paragraphs, however, require more knowledge than you already possess. Hence, you will not be able to synthesize ideas, since you lack background information. In such cases, you must research and analyze a topic by reading more about it in the library, interviewing authorities in the field, conducting experiments, or observing a particular event or location. However, even for a paragraph topic that demands research, you can synthesize personal experience into the piece by following your own interests.

For instance, if you were asked to describe the effects of inflation on the American economy, you could research a recent period of inflation to obtain specific facts about unemployment and productivity. You also could interview people who were affected by the rise in prices. You might even begin this paper with the story of a middle-class family that suffered greatly under inflation. By using a family's hardships as examples, you give life to otherwise dry statistics. Similarly, if you want to know more about the Great Depression of the 1930s, then you could begin your research by interviewing relatives who lived through that troubling decade. Whatever the assigned topic, you must begin with what you know and what you want to know. If you do this, then you will be interested in the topic and will convey your enthusiasm to your audience.

QUESTIONING

If you have difficulty generating paragraph topics, then use the questions reporters ask when they investigate a story: what, why, who, how, where, and when. These questions can guide you in your investigation of a topic.

1. What are your interests in the topic?

   What do you know from personal experience about the topic?

   What do you want to know about the topic?

   What is the history or development of the topic?

   What one item makes this topic interesting?

   What can you tell others about the topic?

2. Why is the topic important?

   Why should others know about this topic?

   Why did an event take place?

3. Who should know about this topic?

   Who are important people connected with this topic?

   Who helped discover, invent, or promote this topic?

4. How did an event take place?

How has the topic had an impact on others?

How is the topic related to everyday life?

5. Where did this event take place? (Is the location important?)

Where does one find information about the topic?

6. When did an event occur? (What is its historical setting?)

When is knowledge of this topic important?

▼ **EXERCISE 3**

In a brainstorming session, use the questions reporters ask to generate five specific paragraph topics for each of the following general topics. Compare your responses with other students' topics. What does the variety of responses indicate about paragraph topics?

1. Family Life

2. Shopping Malls

3. Neighborhoods

4. Movies

5. Students

Narrowing Topics

Too often, writers choose paragraph topics that are too general; in other words, they choose topics that they cannot develop adequately in paragraphs because the topic is too broad. With a broad topic, writers are forced to make only general statements about the topic in their paragraphs. Contrast the following two paragraphs on the topic *education.*

1. Education is a necessity for all Americans. One must be able to deal with society, and education allows one to do this. In grade school, students are taught the basics of reading, writing, and mathematics. In high school, students develop their skills in these areas and gain additional knowledge. In college, students focus on one particular subject which will prepare them for careers. Therefore, education provides Americans with basic knowledge and prepares students for future employment.

2. A liberal-arts education prepares college students for a career and for the rest of their lives. After graduates have entered the work force, they will call upon their liberal-arts education frequently. Their ability to analyze and synthesize

information, gained from countless hours in history, literature, and sociology classes, will be valued in middle- and upper-management positions. Their flexibility in approaching problems, developed in various academic fields, will enable them to confront problems which resist traditional and time-worn solutions and to provide innovative answers. Their skill in communicating ideas, refined in writing and speech classes, will make them desirable candidates for a position. Moreover, knowledge acquired in liberal-arts courses will serve them well in life. Courses in psychology and sociology will give them insight into human behavior and needs. Courses in economics, political science, and history will make them more informed citizens, with the ability to analyze political events. Courses in literature, art, and music will provide them with life-long interests. For these reasons, colleges should encourage students to enroll in liberal-arts classes.

In paragraph 1, the broad topic *education* forces the writer to make obvious statements about the value of education in American society and the types of knowledge students gain at each school level. The writer has not provided his readers with specific examples of the differences in levels of education or with specific examples of courses of study that will increase students' knowledge. For example, what does "gain additional knowledge" mean? Does it suggest that students will study subjects other than the basics of reading, writing, and mathematics? Or does it mean that students will be able to pursue individual interests through athletics, music, drama, or any other organizations the school might sponsor? The writer is too vague about the value of education, and his paragraph attempts to cover too many aspects of formal education in the United States. The topic *education* could generate thousands of ideas that could be developed in paragraphs, essays, journal pieces, and books. Hence, as this paragraph shows, the topic *education* is far too general to be covered adequately in a paragraph. In addition, this writer leaves his reader with questions about the topic. Certainly, there is no sense of the audience this paragraph is addressing; after all, most Americans do know these general statements about education. The paragraph also lacks a purpose; the writer does not indicate *why* education is a necessity for Americans. The writer implies that different school levels provide students with basic skills for everyday life and prepare them for careers; however, the writer fails to explain why this knowledge is important to Americans.

In contrast, paragraph 2 focuses on specific benefits of a liberal-arts education in college. The writer gives examples of how different liberal-arts courses relate to a student's career and personal interests. Hence, the writer has narrowed the original topic of *education* sufficiently so that he can explore ideas completely in the paragraph. Readers do not expect to read more about the topic, nor do they question the author's meaning. In addition, a specific audience is addressed in the paragraph. In his last sentence, the author urges college administrators and advisors to encourage students to enroll in liberal-arts classes for the reasons he has cited. The author's purpose is clear in his first sentence: liberal-arts classes benefit students. Therefore, the paragraph successfully develops the writer's purpose.

① why is ed. necessary ?

① why is knowledge imp. to Americans

EVALUATING TOPICS

A paragraph topic is too general if you can think of several subtopics for it. Consider the following topics: *advertising, American politics, antiques,* and *national parks.* Each topic naturally leads to other, more specific, topics. For instance, *American politics* encourages readers first to question which century or decade the writer will focus on. Readers will also question which level—national, state, or local—the writer will discuss. Therefore, the topic is too general and must be narrowed before the writer develops a paragraph. However, a topic can be too specific if there is little for you to explore. For example, *the number of students who eat in the campus cafeteria* is too specific. One or two sentences listing the number of students would support this topic adequately. Hence, this topic cannot be developed in a paragraph. Yet you could easily turn this narrow topic into a possible paragraph topic if you consider other aspects of it. For example, the topic *student dissatisfaction with the food quality in the campus cafeteria* could provide material for a well-developed paragraph.

LOGICAL REDUCTION

To narrow a topic logically, you should be able to identify stages of subtopics. Consider the following example of how a topic is narrowed through various stages, each more specific than the last, until it is a suitable topic for a paragraph.

General Topic: *American History*

Specific Topic of American History: *The Civil War*

Specific Topic of The Civil War: *The Gettysburg Battlefield*

Specific Topic of The Gettysburg Battlefield: *Exhibits for Visitors at Gettysburg*

Specific Topic of Exhibits for Visitors at Gettysburg: *The Display of Equipment Used by Field Soldiers at Gettysburg*

For each specific topic, the writer chose one aspect of the preceding topic. From all of American history, the writer chose to discuss the Civil War. From this topic, she chose one particular battle. From her knowledge of Gettysburg, she selected the aspect of exhibits for twentieth-century visitors to the Gettysburg battlefield. Of the many displays in the visitors' center and on the battlefield, the writer concentrated on a single display.

Analyze the following reduction of a general topic. Is this topic narrowed in a logical manner? Or did the writer skip stages of reduction?

General Topic: Media

Reduction 1:   Radio

Reduction 2:   Advertising on radio

Reduction 3:   Advertising on television

Reduction 4:   Cost of advertising

Reduction 5:   Different advertisements for specific audiences

Actually, the writer has generated several topics to develop. However, his final topic is not part of a logical reduction. For example, *Advertising on television* is not logically a subtopic of *Advertising on radio.* Nor is it clear which topic the writer will finally develop or how he narrowed the topic. In fact, the list approximates a brainstorming session more than it suggests a reduction of a general topic to a specific paragraph topic.

▼ EXERCISE 4

Label each set of topics from 1 for the most general to 5 for the most specific. Make sure that your stages of development are logical and that each topic really narrows the one before it.

▶ Example:

  __4__ Training procedures for race horses

  __2__ Horses

  __1__ Animals

  __3__ Race Horses

  __5__ Training a race horse for its first race

1. _____ Dramatic television programs

 _____ *L.A. Law*

 _____ Weekly plots on *L.A. Law*

 _____ Television

 _____ Diversity of plots each week on *L. A. Law*

2. _____ Egyptians' contributions to geometry

 _____ Contributions of Egypt

 _____ Ancient civilizations

 _____ Egypt in the Pharaohs' times

 _____ Scientific contributions of Egyptians

3. _____ Revival of musicals in the 1980s

 _____ Broadway plays

 _____ Theater

 _____ Musicals on Broadway

 _____ Reasons for the revival of older Broadway musicals in the 1980s

4. _____ Effects of oil spills

_____ Environment

_____ Pollution in the environment

_____ Effect of pollution

_____ Effect of oil spills on aquatic life

5. _____ Mark Twain's stories

_____ American writers

_____ Humor in Mark Twain's novels

_____ Mark Twain

_____ Humor in Mark Twain's *Tom Sawyer*

▼ EXERCISE 5

For each general topic below, use logical reduction to create a more specific topic that could be developed in a paragraph. Show the stages of your reduction.

1. Athletes

Reduction 1 _____

Reduction 2 _____

Reduction 3 _____

Reduction 4 _____

Reduction 5 _____

2. Music

Reduction 1 _____

Reduction 2 _____

Reduction 3 _____

Reduction 4 _____

Reduction 5 _____

3. A town or city

Reduction 1 _____

Reduction 2 _____

Reduction 3 _____

Reduction 4 _____

Reduction 5 _____

4. A vacation spot   Reduction 1 _____

                         Reduction 2 _____

                         Reduction 3 _____

                         Reduction 4 _____

                         Reduction 5 _____

5. Part-time or   Reduction 1 _____
   summer jobs
                         Reduction 2 _____

                         Reduction 3 _____

                         Reduction 4 _____

                         Reduction 5 _____

Identifying Audience and Purpose

The discovery of a paragraph topic does not end with selecting a reduced topic. What you write and how you present it depend on two conditions: audience and purpose. If you were to describe a recent trip to another college campus, then you would certainly choose the facts you present and alter the manner in which you present these facts to suit different audiences. Your parents, for example, would be interested in the size of the campus, its population, its academic facilities, and its reputation. Your best friend, however, might want more specific impressions about classes, programs in certain majors, the professors, and the social life on campus. Hence, in each situation, your letter would present different facts, have a different purpose, and vary greatly in the language used. We tend to tell people in authority fewer specific details than we tell close friends. In addition, our language becomes more formal when we speak with those in authority and more colloquial with peers. In most cases, your letter to your parents about the campus visit would be more formal and contain fewer details than the letter to your close friend. (You might, for instance, omit the details of a late-night dorm party or the antics of a professor in class in a letter to your parents.) When you write, you must capitalize on this natural ability to present a single topic in different ways to diverse audiences.

THE SIGNIFICANCE OF AUDIENCE AND PURPOSE

Daily Life

Consider the importance of audience and purpose in the types of writing all of us must do. When we write to communicate ideas, observations, experiences, and skills to others, we must consider that our audience may be people who differ greatly in educational background, their interest in the topic, the time they have to read our message, and their social and cultural experiences. Therefore, as much as possible, you must be able to visualize a specific audience and determine the purpose of your message to the audience. In each case, you must be able to explain, describe, and argue so that each member of a specific audience will comprehend your message fully.

College Life

In college, you constantly write lab reports, essays, and research papers. Each type of writing indicates to professors how well you have comprehended concepts, theories, or practices. However, each piece differs according to audience and purpose. For instance, a lab report should contain only objective information—information you gained through observation of a chemical process, the dissection of a frog, or any other experiment. On the other hand, essays and research papers often require that you begin with your own ideas and support them with facts gathered from books, experiments, or individuals. In both cases, you must consider your audiences. If you were asked to write an analytical paper about Shakespeare's play *Hamlet*, then you cannot simply submit a summary of the play's events; the professor already knows the play well. Instead, the professor expects you to analyze particular passages and discuss themes or symbols that occur in the work.

Business Life

Writing is not limited to college assignments, however. Even in this age of electronic communication—when the telephone and electronic mail seem to be more efficient and faster than letters—written communication is the means by which the business world operates. As a college graduate, you will begin your job search with a résumé and a cover letter of application mailed to a prospective employer. Your ability to write well will be judged long before an employer invites you for an interview. Once you begin work, you will write letters, memos, proposals, and reports to others. In each writing situation, your ability to communicate effectively will save the company time, money, and embarrassment. In addition, if you write well, then you will find that your chances for promotion are enhanced if you can address different audiences and convey your purpose.

BENEFITS OF IDENTIFYING AUDIENCE AND PURPOSE

Unfortunately, beginning writers often ignore their audiences and purposes. When they receive an assignment, they usually write the piece without sufficient reflection. The final product is sometimes flat, contains only generalizations, and lacks direction; in fact the paper may bore both the writer and the reader. However, if these writers will take the time to identify their audience and purpose, then their message will be focused, and the language and tone will be appropriate for the audience.

Consider the following topics designed for specific audiences and purposes. Note that one general topic can yield several specific topics for different audiences.

GENERAL TOPIC	AUDIENCE	PURPOSE
1. College Life	a. High-school seniors	Discuss how to make the transition from high school to college
	b. Parents	Describe the college's facilities and housing for students
	c. Friends	Describe the campus's social activities
2. Politics	a. College students	Encourage students to support one candidate by voting
	b. Members of a particular political party	Convince them to give money to the party's effort
	c. Supporters	Tell them how to promote their candidate
3. Law	a. Law students	Explain the ethics of their profession
	b. Police academy students	Describe methods of enforcing laws
	c. Criminal suspect	Define the suspect's rights under the law

QUESTIONS TO HELP IDENTIFY AN AUDIENCE AND PURPOSE

To identify your audience and purpose, think first of a specific person to whom you would address a topic; consider also what you would want this writing to accomplish. If you cannot identify a specific member of an audience, then ask the following questions to create a potential audience.

1.   Who would be most interested in the topic?

2.   What might this person already know about the topic? (What pieces of information must be included? What items can be omitted?)

3.   What is this person's educational background? What are his or her social and cultural interests?

4.   How old is this person? What might be his or her political concerns?

5.   Is this person sympathetic or hostile to the topic? (How would you handle each response?)

In addition to identifying an audience, you must decide what the purpose of the paper is. Ask these questions to pin down your purpose.

1.   Do you want to explain, compare and contrast, define, classify, motivate, persuade, describe, narrate, or argue?

2. How do you want your audience to respond? Do you want your readers to agree with your argument, enjoy the humor of a story, feel sympathy, follow your directions, understand a problem and possible solutions, or alter their behavior?

Answers to both of these questions will provide you with a better sense of your audience and purpose in writing.

▼ EXERCISE 6

For each topic below, several audiences are listed. List a likely purpose for a paragraph addressed to each audience.

1. Topic: **Drugs**

Audience	Purpose
a. teenagers	_____
b. parents	_____
c. city police officers	_____

2. Topic: **Student Athletes**

Audience	Purpose
a. college administrators	_____
b. high-school players	_____
c. college coaches	_____

3. Topic: **Urban Poverty**

Audience	Purpose
a. city council members	_____
b. social workers	_____
c. someone on welfare	_____

▼ EXERCISE 7

List two different audiences and purposes for each paragraph topic.

General Topic	Audience	Purpose
1. Social Organizations	_____	_____
	_____	_____

General Topic	*Audience*	*Purpose*
2. Rural Areas		
3. Pets		
4. Peer Pressure		
5. Education		

▼ Writing Strategy: DESCRIPTION

Description, one of the most frequently used strategies, appears in nearly every type of writing: news articles, technical manuals, novels and short stories, personal essays, business reports, and research papers. Descriptions can provide a reader with specific physical characteristics of people, places, or things; therefore, descriptions give an audience a sharp visual image. In addition, descriptions can make abstract concepts, such as religion or beauty, concrete by providing specific details. The generalization that childhood is a pleasant time can be made more specific if the author describes specific childhood experiences. Moreover, description can make statistics more meaningful and interesting.

Descriptions require specific details. It is not enough to note that a sunset is beautiful, a house lavish, or a landfill ugly; you must help the reader *visualize* the place, person, or object being described. By providing specific details—that the sunset filled the western sky with streaks of red and purple, that the house with its Grecian columns and antique furniture illustrates a life of wealth, and that the landfill houses battered, rusted cars—you make abstract, subjective statements concrete. By choosing appropriate details, you can provide an *objective* description at the same time that you include, through word choice, a *subjective* assessment of the topic. For instance, in a description of an Appalachian coal-mining town, you could choose to use only those details that portray such a place as barren, isolated, and depressing. In contrast, another writer could choose to characterize the people as industrious individuals who retain their own culture amid the uniform housing, unemployment, and hardship.

Although a seemingly easy rhetorical strategy, description demands that you consider point of view and scale. Through **point of view,** you choose a dominant pattern by which the paper will be organized. For example, a building or a person can be described from top to bottom or from bottom to top, or a landscape or room can be described from left to right or right to left. Whatever dominant pattern you choose, you must be consistent, for without consistency in point of view, you are likely to lose your reader. In addition, you must consider

scale. A harbor, for example, requires different descriptions when viewed from an observation platform on the twentieth floor of a building than when viewed from street level. Again, you must be consistent if your reader is to have an accurate visual image.

Finally, when organizing details for a longer description, you should consider major features of the person, place, or object for possible topic sentences in the piece's body paragraphs. For instance, a description of the view from a mountain's crest might demand four topic sentences for body paragraphs for views to the north, east, south, and west. In a description of a person, a dominant impression of a major physical feature could control the piece. In the pieces that follow, pay particular attention to the visual images and the writers' choices of details.

▶ A Building in Upper Harlem

CLAUDE BROWN

In his autobiography Manchild in the Promised Land, *Claude Brown describes a childhood filled with youth gangs, reformatories, and intermittent formal education that led eventually, however, to Harvard University. In his book* The Children of Ham, *from which this paragraph is taken, Brown writes about the experiences of black youth today.*

There is a building in upper Harlem on a shabby side street with several other buildings that resemble it in both appearance and condition. "This building" is in an advanced state of deterioration; only cold water runs through the water pipes, the rats here are as large as cats. The saving grace of this building might very well be the erratic patterns of the varied and brilliant colors of the graffiti which adorn it internally and externally from basement to roof. This building has no electricity in the apartments, but the electricity in the hallway lamp fixtures is still on. Some of the apartments have garbage piled up in them five feet high and that makes opening the door a very difficult task for those whose nasal passages are sufficiently insensitive to permit entry. In some of the apartments and on the rooftop, the garbage and assorted debris are piled only one or two feet high, and the trash has been there so long that plant life has generated. The most rapid tour possible through this building will necessitate boiling oneself in a hot tub of strong disinfectant for a couple of hours, and even then this astonishingly formidable breed of lice will continue to make its presence felt throughout a long itchy night. This building is adjacent to a fully occupied tenement whose inhabitants are families, some of which include several children. This building has a few steps missing from the staircase above the second floor and there are no lightbulbs in the hallway; it's a very unsafe place for trespassers, even during the day. This building's last family of tenants was emancipated several weeks ago; they hit the numbers and moved to the Bronx, shouting "Free at last, free at last; thank God for the number man." Prior to their liberation, the "last family" had lived a most unusual existence. Somebody had to be at home at all times to protect the family's second-hand-hot television from becoming a third-hand-hot television; there were too many junkies in and out who used the vacant apartments to stash their loot until they could "down" it and who also used some of the apartments for sleeping and as "shooting galleries." For protection, the last family had a large, vicious German shepherd. This dog was needed for the rats as well as the junkies. A cat would be no help at all. The sight of the rats in this building would give any cat smaller than a mountain lion instant heart failure. The last family considered itself fortunate, despite the many unpleasant, unhealthy and unsafe aspects of its residence. "We ain't paid no rent in two years. I guess the city just forgot that we was here or they was just too embarrassed to ask for it," said the head of the last family. This building has holes in the walls large enough for a man to walk through two adjacent apartments. This building has holes in the ceilings on the fourth and fifth floors, and when it rains, the rain settles on the floor of a fourth-story apartment. This building is not unique, there are many others like it in the ghettos of New York City; and like many others . . . this building is owned by the City of New York.

▶ QUESTIONS 1. What is the overwhelming impression conveyed by this paragraph?

2. What details directly contribute to that impression?

3. Define *saving grace* and *formidable*.

4. Why would New York City be too "embarrassed" to demand rent payments?

▶ # The Turtle

JOHN STEINBECK

John Steinbeck is a twentieth-century American writer famous for his short stories and novels. His sympathy for poor and downtrodden individuals shines through his realistic writings. This selection is taken from Steinbeck's Grapes of Wrath, *a book about the plight of poor Oklahoma farmers during the Depression.*

The sun lay on the grass and warmed it, and in the shade under the grass the insects moved, ants and ant lions to set traps for them, grasshoppers to jump into the air and flick their yellow wings for a second, sow bugs like little armadillos, plodding restlessly on many tender feet. And over the grass at the roadside a land turtle crawled, turning aside for nothing, dragging his high-domed shell over the grass: His hard legs and yellow-nailed feet threshed slowly through the grass, not really walking, but boosting and dragging his shell along. The barley beards slid off his shell, and the clover burrs fell on him and rolled to the ground.

His horny beak was partly open, and his fierce, humorous eyes, under brows like fingernails, stared straight ahead. He came over the grass leaving a beaten trail behind him, and the hill, which was the highway embankment, reared up ahead of him. For a moment he stopped, his head held high. He blinked and looked up and down. At last he started to climb the embankment. Front clawed feet reached forward but did not touch. The hind feet kicked his shell along, and it scraped on the grass, and on the gravel. As the embankment grew steeper and steeper, the more frantic were the efforts of the land turtle. Pushing hind legs strained and slipped, boosting the shell along, and the horny head protruded as far as the neck could stretch. Little by little the shell slid up the embankment until at last a parapet cut straight across its line of march, the shoulder of the road, a concrete wall four inches high. As though they worked independently the hind legs pushed the shell against the wall. The head upraised and peered over the wall to the broad smooth plain of cement. Now the hands, braced on top of the wall, strained and lifted, and the shell came slowly up and rested its front end on the wall. For a moment the turtle rested. A red ant ran into the shell, into the soft skin inside the shell, and suddenly head and legs snapped in, and the armored tail clamped in sideways. The red ant was crushed between body and legs. And one head of wild oats was clamped into the shell by a front leg. For a long moment the turtle lay still, and then the neck crept out and the old humorous frowning eyes looked about and the legs and tail came out. The back legs went to work, straining like elephant legs, and the shell tipped to an angle so that the front legs could not reach the level cement plain. But higher and higher the hind legs boosted it, until at last the center of balance was reached, the front tipped down, the front legs scratched at the pavement, and it was up. But the head of wild oats was held by its stem around the front legs.

▶ QUESTIONS
1. What is the topic sentence? Where is it located?

2. What is Steinbeck's perspective? Does the scale change in the piece? If so, where?

3. What is Steinbeck's tone? What particular words suggest the tone?

▶ The Buffalo Stampede
ZANE GREY

The author of many Western stories, Zane Grey narrates this account of men caught in a stampede. Consider his use of images and the emotion he conveys throughout this piece.

1   As he turned back I looked out upon the vast prairie. Near at hand it was faintly moonlit and I imagined I could see distinctly at least half a

mile. I made out telegraph poles standing like dark sentinels all of that distance but beyond that from where the growing sound came, it seemed opaque and ghostly. In my state of mind, imagination could conjure up anything; but I made stern effort to stem my agitation and be cool. Outwardly, no doubt, I succeeded.

2   When I turned back to follow Shaw, the two oil-soaked wagons burst into flames and a great space all around us was brightly lighted. The faces of the men were no longer dark. Bare-headed and pale-faced, with burning eyes fixed on the prairie, they looked only in the one direction. Shaw herded them back even with the point of the wedge and lined them up on each side just in the lee of the two front wagons. If the herd split around these obstacles the buffalo would pass on each side of the men and of the wedge. If not—! Shaw lined me up beside him on the inside and he faced forward, rifle ready, with a shout that strangely sounded like a whisper:

3   "Shoot when I shoot an' keep on shootin!"

4   I knew, because his voice sounded so faintly, that the stampede was almost upon us, but I actually did not hear anything on the instant. When I took out my watch to make out the time by moonlight my hand trembled so that I could hardly discern the hands. It was eight-thirty. The next move I made was to peer ahead, transfixed, with my feet riveted to the ground, sure that I was about to live the supreme moment of my life.

5   Then out there on the moonlit prairie I saw something. It moved. It was black. It was like the torrential flow of an ocean behind which there were unknown leagues of pushing waves. The fire, catching the top of the canvas wagons, flared up brighter. That oncoming wave swallowed up the moonlit space. Then I recognized the shaggy front of a buffalo herd in stampede. It had a straight front and extended as far as I could see on both sides, and surely for miles and miles.

6   I became aware that I was rocking on my feet. The ground had become unstable. It was shaking under me. On the moment, when I ceased to be aware of an engulfing tremendous pressure, I knew that it had been the roar of this avalanche and that I could no longer hear it. I was deafened. There was no sound. I knew there was no sound because when Shaw raised his rifle in a signal for us all to fire there was no report following the belching of red flame and smoke. Even reports of all the heavy guns in unison could not be heard.

7   Shaking as one with the palsy I imitated Shaw and rapidly emptied my rifle straight into the front of this rebounding black juggernaut with its myriad of shiny horns and fiery green eyes. But shaking though I was, unsteady on my pins, I could shoot and I could see.

8   And suddenly the center of that advancing line sustained a staggering shock and disintegrated, huge black shaggy forms hurdling high to fall and slide and others as if by magic taking their places until the augmenting pile encroached upon the burning wagons, bumping them to send aloft showers of sparks from the burning canvas. My faculties, my blood, almost my heart itself, had stopped with that first shot—the unbearable suspense—the suspension of thought until it became certain that the buffalo herd had split and the rolling black sea of the stampede was passing on to each side of us. I almost fainted then. This was a little too much for a tenderfoot.

9   Seeing Shaw reload his rifle, I did likewise with fingers that were all thumbs. His rifle was blazing flame before I had finished reloading. We were in the thick of something so supremely terrible that I became an automaton, reacting like a machine. I shot methodically, regulating my shooting and reloading to Shaw and the other men. My eyes were assailed by a fury of action, a maelstrom of churning buffalo, endless and boundless.

10   In time, coming to reload again, I found all the ammunition in one pocket gone and had recourse to the other. One by one I inserted shells into my rifle with nervous fingers and shot ahead. The bright flare of the burning wagons had died down. There was not so much light. Only the wagon beds were blazing. A column of smoke rolled aloft a few yards to merge into the solid canopy of dust. My sight grew dim from exhaustion or terror or from the thickening of the atmosphere. For long I gazed through a haze with smarting eyes. The huge pile of buffalo on each side of the wagons grew apace to right and left, widening the barricade of dead bodies in front of our wedge.

11   Actually to hear once more seemed unreal and unbelievable. But my ears were filled with thundering din and it diminished to a roar. As my hearing returned I began to come out of the state under which I had labored. That trembling of the earth under my feet began to lessen. The men had ceased shooting. The dust clouds seemed thinner. I became aware of Shaw's arm under mine, probably supporting me. Again the great volume of thundering rumble was registered by my ears. It was receding. It was behind us. The hideous streaming black nightmare on each side of us had passed by, the earth between my feet ceased to rock and became solid again, the dust clouds roared away as if sucked into a vacuum created by the moving herd. The stampede was over.

▶ QUESTIONS   1. Grey suggests that sound is the dominant sensory impression of a buffalo stampede. Cite examples of other sensory details.

2. What comparisons does Grey employ to describe the herd of buffalo?

3. Does the fact that the stampede took place at night enhance the quality of suspense in the piece?

4. Define the following words: *riveted (paragraph 4), juggernaut (7), myriad (7), maelstrom (9), and canopy (10).*

Paradise Can Be a Concentration Camp
Regina Raffety

In this student piece, Regina Raffety describes a favorite childhood site. However, her perceptions of the place have changed greatly.

1   People sometimes wish they were children again, so some try to recapture or visit their childhood in the later years of their lives. Some return to places once explored and frequented as a young child. Whether it would be one's own bedroom closet or tree-house, everyone had, at one point, a place to go as a child to vacation from the "real" world. To many people's dismay, these personal paradises usually change, physically and perceptually, as time goes by. As a child living in Germany, I invented a completely new world in a massive forest near my home; however, the actual physical appearance and the way I feel about the forest have changed dramatically from the time of my childhood innocence to my early adulthood.

2   During my adolescent years the forest overflowed with beauty. The trees, which towered miles over my head, were filled with leaves of all different kinds. At one point the trees formed a tunnel by joining limbs and branches over my favorite path. It was like walking under a sea that had every shade of green ever imagined, and when the wind blew it was

like listening to the waves of an ocean. This majestic forest was also bountiful, for at the entrance stood a great chestnut tree, and scattered throughout the rest of the forest were cherry trees, crab apple trees, and big, thick raspberry and blackberry bushes, but only the great chestnut tree had a good season every year. As well as these fruits, there were pine cones as big as a little kid's head scattered all over the ground where they had fallen. Not too far into the forest was a clear, blue, small stream that only minnows could survive in. Farther into the woods were a couple of cleared out spaces that were relatively close together and a little larger than football fields. These clearings were like oceans of long sea-green grass and dandelions. The sound of birds singing, quick glimpses of deer, squirrels meandering about, and sometimes people passing by riding horses always kept me company.

3   The forest also served as a place of fun and adventure for me. On the hotter days of the year I would wait hours on top of a smooth rock that was right over the stream for a school of several hundred minnows to swim by. When a school did swim by, I would jump in the middle of them, and get as many in my hand as I could before I would let them go. Sometimes I would venture where there were not any paths to walk on. This is how I found the vast clearings. It was here that I would bring my dog to play and run around, and where I would bring my little friends for picnics and games like stuck-in-the-mud.

Although I often played in the woods by myself, I never felt like I was alone. I suppose it was because I never experienced fear which would cause me to want companions; and no matter what, I always felt free and happy in the woods. Here, I was able to create different worlds, and no one was around to spoil it for me.

4   Unfortunately, in my late teens my childhood paradise was completely shattered by Germany's dark history when a German relative sent me a news article. The article not only had recent pictures of the parts of the forest that I spent most of my childhood in, but it also revealed that the large, bountiful clearings were a concentration camp during World War II. Now, at the entrance of the forest, right next to the great chestnut tree, stands a large memorial to the Jews who lost their lives in these woods, my playground. Even though the forest apparently still physically looks the same, with the exception of the memorial, it does not feel the same. I can only imagine the piles of bones that were scattered around the forest where Jews suffered painful and agonizing deaths. All the fun I had in that forest is now an embarrassment, for it is hard to except that I danced and played on people's graves as a child.

5   My paradise did not take the usual deterioration of being either completely destroyed or converted into something else. Instead, my perception of my paradise was destroyed by its horrid past. I can no longer feel good about my childhood playground

because where I played and had so much fun was the
same place where so many suffered through torture,
the loss of family, and their own painful deaths.

▶ QUESTIONS   1. What is Raffety's main idea? Where is it located?

2. In paragraph 2, Raffety states that "the forest overflowed with beauty." This statement is very broad. What details in the paragraph describe this beauty?

3. Why was this forest hideaway so appealing to Raffety as a child?

4. How have Raffety's perceptions changed about this forest? What caused this change?

▼ PARAGRAPH
ASSIGNMENTS

1. Steinbeck describes the turtle's actions as it moves toward the road. In a similar fashion, describe one activity of a person or an animal in a particular location (for example, someone painting a room, washing dishes, or studying for a test, or an animal at play).

2. Think of tourists visiting your area for the first time. Besides the usual attractions, what would you suggest they visit? Describe the site to demonstrate that it is a "must-see," even if usually overlooked, attraction.

3. Describe a social, cultural, or athletic event, such as an ethnic festival, a high school or college football game, or a college dance. This piece will appear in your school's newspaper; therefore, your audience will be your peers. Determine a purpose for the description before you begin writing.

4. Describe for a local city council the condition of a section of town that should be rehabilitated. Your purpose will be to persuade the city council members that the project is worthwhile.

▼ WRITING TIPS

Think about your reason for writing. What are you trying to accomplish with this paragraph? Have you made your purpose clear?

Also, consider your audience. How much information do your readers need in order to understand your message? You should not deluge them with facts, but neither should you be stingy with necessary details.

Finally, check your verb tense (See Part II, Chapter 1). Make sure that the time frame is consistent throughout your paragraph.

▼ Paragraph Topic Checklist

1. Have you narrowed the topic of your paragraph?

   _____

   _____

2. Is the paragraph directed to a specific audience? What identifies the audience?

   _____

   _____

   _____

   _____

   _____

   _____

3. Can you state your purpose for writing this paragraph? How
   do you want your audience to respond?

   _____

   _____

   _____

   _____

   _____

   _____

▼ Description Checklist

1. Have you used specific details to create a visual image?

   _____

   _____

   _____

2. Have you used descriptive verbs that give a visual impression?

   _____

   _____

   _____

3. Does your paragraph have a topic sentence that supports the description?

   _____

   _____

   _____

4. What is the tone of your description?

   _____

   _____

   _____

5. Does your paragraph create a dominant visual or emotional impression? What is it?

   _____

   _____

   _____

Creating Topic Sentences

3

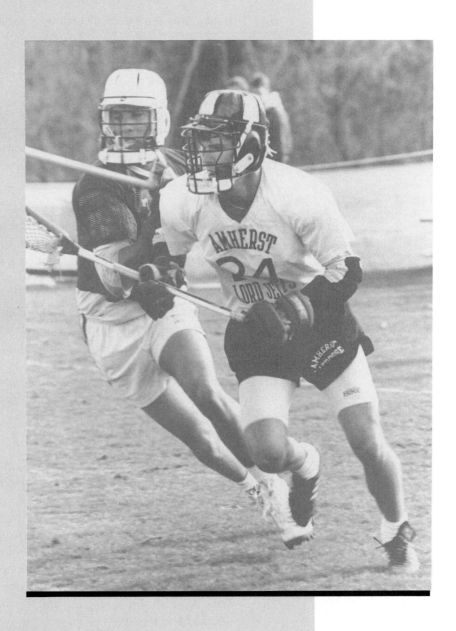

▶ **OBJECTIVES**

1. To identify controlling ideas in topic sentences.

2. To identify facts and opinions.

3. To generate topic sentences.

4. To locate topic sentences in paragraphs.

5. To place topic sentences according to their functions in paragraphs.

6. To explore composing through process analysis.

▶ **PREVIEW**

A topic sentence states the main idea of a paragraph to your reader. The topic sentence defines your opinion, predicts your discussion, and controls the way in which you develop the paragraph. A topic sentence presents a controlling idea that offers an opinion about or limits the topic.

A **topic sentence** states the main idea of a paragraph. It is the sentence in the paragraph that tells your audience the subject (topic) of the paragraph and the controlling idea (the statement you want to make about the topic). Therefore, the topic sentence *defines* your opinion, *predicts* what you will discuss in the paragraph, and *controls* the development of the paragraph.

Every paragraph you write should contain a topic sentence stating the main idea of the paragraph. Usually the first sentence of a paragraph, the topic sentence, promises your reader that you will discuss a specific topic within the paragraph and thereby helps your readers to predict the outline of the discussion. In effect, the topic sentence limits what you can argue, explain, define, or describe within a certain paragraph and, thus, controls the development of the paragraph.

Consider these paragraphs:

1.   So Grant and Lee were in complete contrast, representing diametrically opposed elements in American life. Grant was the modern man emerging; beyond him, ready to come on the stage, was the great age of steel and machinery, of crowded cities and a restless burgeoning vitality. Lee might have ridden down from the old age of chivalry, lance in hand, silken banner fluttering over his head. Each man was the perfect champion of his cause, drawing both his strengths and his weaknesses from the people he led.

2.   Each man had, to begin with, the great virtue of utter tenacity and fidelity. Grant fought his way down the Mississippi Valley in spite of acute personal discouragement and profound military handicaps. Lee hung on in the trenches at Petersburg after hope itself had died. In each man there was an indomitable quality . . . the born fighter's

refusal to give up as long as he can still remain on his feet and lift his two fists.

(both from Bruce Catton, "Grant and Lee: A Study in Contrasts")

In the first paragraph, the topic sentence is the first one; it informs readers that the author intends to contrast two Civil War generals, Grant and Lee, as opposites in war and in character. The author also suggests that their differences were representative of separate elements in the America of the 1860s. The rest of the paragraph then describes each man's character.

In the second paragraph, the topic sentence, again the first one, notes a comparison between Grant and Lee: both men were loyal and dedicated. The author then supplies specific examples of separate campaigns to support his topic sentence.

Both of these paragraphs appear in a longer essay and develop only a small portion of the comparisons and contrasts between the men. However, notice that both topic sentences are more general than the sentences that follow. From these examples, you should conclude that, although a topic sentence narrows a limited topic for a paragraph-length discussion, the topic sentence is more general than the specific details that support it. Therefore, the topic sentence has two functions:

1. it unifies the paragraph, and

2. it organizes the ideas contained in the paragraph.

The Controlling Idea

A topic sentence unifies and organizes through its **controlling idea,** usually located in the sentence's predicate. The controlling idea offers an opinion or sets limits to the topic; it is the statement that the author wants to make about the topic. Because this idea states the point of the paragraph, it limits the discussion. Authors know that they must support that stated opinion or explain the given limit. With this goal in mind, they choose only those details that will help them validate their opinion and thereby ensure a *unified* paragraph. They then present those facts in a logical manner and thereby organize their paragraph.

Therefore, topic sentences contain two major parts: a subject that identifies the topic and a controlling idea, a word or phrase, that identifies the writer's opinions or limitations.

	subject	controlling idea

▶ Example: Each new scientific *development* has *many benefits* for the average consumer.

In this sentence, *development* is the subject of the sentence; it is also a narrowed topic suitable for a paragraph. The controlling idea is *many benefits.* In the body of the paragraph, the writer will list and explain some major advantages of scientific discoveries.

How do you discover the controlling idea? That requires a two-step process.

1. Locate the topic. Look at the subject of the sentence and determine whether it is the topic under discussion.

2. Then, ask yourself, what statement is the author making about the topic? What is he or she trying to prove? You will probably find the answer in the verb part of the sentence. The answer is the controlling idea.

▼ EXERCISE 1

Circle the controlling idea in each topic sentence below.

1. Contemporary fads indicate a great deal about Americans' images of themselves.

2. Training a pet requires time, patience, and determination.

3. Urban crime has created many problems for residents of large cities.

4. Foreign travel increases one's knowledge of other cultures, languages, and customs.

5. Classical music offers several rewards to its listeners.

6. Television game shows promise their participants instant wealth and fame.

7. Americans' fascination with games has many far-reaching effects.

8. The senator listed five reasons for her popularity.

9. Stereo systems can be expensive to buy, complex to operate, and enjoyable to use.

10. Raising children is a difficult task.

Be careful to phrase your controlling idea clearly. Some words may be inadequate because they are vague and open to interpretation by your reader. Analyze this topic sentence:

Gone with the Wind is the greatest movie ever made.

The controlling idea of this sentence is *greatest movie ever made*. What does *greatest* mean? Does the writer mean that he enjoyed the movie? Did he enjoy the movie for a particular reason, such as the acting, the dialogue, or the settings? Can he actually compare this movie, a historical romance, to every movie made? How, in fact, could he compare the value of *Gone with the Wind* to a movie like *Casablanca* or *Field of Dreams?* This controlling idea is poorly written because it gives the reader an inadequate message of what the writer means.

To correct an inadequate controlling idea, you could make one of the following revisions.

1. You could provide a more specific word or phrase to replace the vague controlling idea.

   Revision: For its theme of survival, *Gone with the Wind* is one of the best-remembered movies of all time.

2. You could qualify your statement by limiting your controlling idea.

   Revisions: *Gone with the Wind* captivates audiences with its characters and theme.

   Gone with the Wind creates an imperfect vision of the South before, during, and after the Civil War.

NOTE: Be particularly careful with words such as *good, bad,* or *interesting.* Each of these words is certainly open to a reader's interpretation of what may be good, bad, or interesting within a specific context.

▼ EXERCISE 2

Identify the controlling idea in each topic sentence below. If the controlling idea is adequate, place an *A* in the blank next to the sentence. If the controlling idea is inadequate, place an *I* in the blank. Correct all inadequate controlling ideas by using one of the two methods discussed above.

_____ 1. In the past ten years, women have made outstanding contributions to businesses.

_____ 2. Unlike Europeans, Americans use the word *friend* to describe many types of acquaintances.

_____ 3. Jury selection is an arduous process.

_____ 4. Millions of Americans enjoy running because it promotes good muscle tone and cardiovascular fitness.

_____ 5. The Orient Express, the famous train that connected Paris and Istanbul, offered a nice journey to its passengers.

_____ 6. Many advertising slogans have become part of our everyday speech.

_____ 7. The new XLT personal computer is a fascinating piece of equipment.

_____ 8. Americans are interested in purchasing good cars.

_____ 9. World War II brought many changes to Americans.

_____10. Most students prefer multiple-choice tests over essay tests.

In each of the following paragraphs, note how the topic sentence unifies and organizes the paragraph. Each paragraph works because the author was guided by the controlling idea and used only those details that directly contributed to the paragraph's intended message.

▶ Paragraph 1:   [In this paragraph, Henry David Thoreau describes the night he spent in a Concord, Massachusetts, jail for failing to pay his poll, or voting, tax.]

It was like travelling into a far country, such as I had never expected to behold, to lie there for one night. It seemed to me that I never had heard the town-clock strike before, nor the evening sounds of the village; for we slept with the windows open, which were inside the grating. It was to see my native village in the light of the Middle Ages, and our Concord was turned into a Rhine stream, and visions of knights and castles passed before me. They were the voices of old burghers that I heard in the streets. I was an involuntary spectator and auditor of whatever was done and said in the kitchen of the adjacent village-inn—a wholly new and rare experience to me. It was a closer view of my native town. I was fairly inside of it. I never had seen its institutions before. This is one of its peculiar institutions; for it is a shire town. I began to comprehend what its inhabitants were about.

(from Henry David Thoreau, *"Civil Disobedience"*)

In this paragraph, the topic sentence is the first one. *It* (Thoreau's night in jail) is the topic, and *travelling into a far country*, the idea of a new and unusual experience, is the controlling idea. For the paragraph to be unified, the details must demonstrate that spending his first night in jail was a remarkable experience for Thoreau. Notice how these details accomplish this task:

1. "heard town clock" and "evening sounds of the village" as if for the first time

2. medieval references (the Rhine, knights and castles, old burghers), and

3. "involuntary spectator" and "auditor" as a "new and rare experience"

Because the details support and enlarge upon the topic and because they explain the controlling idea, this paragraph is unified.

▶ Paragraph 2:   The return of Halley's Comet has caused quite a stir. The news media report on its progress daily and offer suggestions for the best viewing times and places. The sale of binoculars and telescopes has soared, all with the purpose of getting a better look at this once-in-a-lifetime visitor. Comet tee-shirts, coffee mugs, and key chains are being sold. Cruises to the southern hemisphere at prime viewing times have been organized. Scientists have cleaned all their instruments and devised various experiments in the hope of learning more about occasional celestial visitors. After all the commotion and promotion, not catching a glimpse of this astral pilgrim would be a great disappointment.

Again, the topic sentence is the first one: "The return of Halley's Comet has caused quite a stir." The topic is the reappearance of the comet, and the controlling idea is the sensation it is causing. Among the supporting details are these:

1. daily media reports

2. soaring sales of telescopes and binoculars and various souvenirs

3. cruises to likely viewing areas

Again, each of the details directly contributes to the controlling idea; consequently, the paragraph is unified.

▼ EXERCISE 3

Underline the topic sentence in the following paragraphs. Then write the topic and the controlling ideas. Finally, list the details that support the controlling idea.

1.   The rocket engine has overcome these disadvantages. Rockets do not depend upon the atmosphere to supply the oxygen they need for combustion. Instead, they carry their own supply. The liquid oxygen, or oxygen-rich compound, makes possible the combustion of the fuel. The liquid fuel and the liquid oxygen mix together in the combustion chamber to produce hot exhaust gases. These gases are hurled at very great speeds from the nozzle of the combustion, and the rocket engine moves by reaction.

(from Foundations Physical Science)

Topic _____

Controlling Idea _____

Supporting Details _____

_____

_____

_____

_____

2.   As the weeks went by, my [Dr. Watson's] interest in him [Sherlock Holmes] and my curiosity as to his aims in life gradually deepened and increased. His very person and appearance were such as to strike the attention of the most casual observer. In height he was rather over six feet, and so excessively lean that he seemed to be considerably taller. His eyes were sharp and piercing, save during those intervals of torpor to which I have alluded; and his thin, hawk-like nose gave his whole expression an air of alertness and decision. His chin, too, had the prominence and squareness which mark the man of determination. His hands were invariably blotted with ink and stained with chemicals, yet he was possessed of extraordinary delicacy of touch, as I frequently had occasion to observe when I watched him manipulating his fragile philosophical instruments.

(from Arthur Conan Doyle, *"A Study in Scarlet"*)

Topic _____

Controlling Idea _____

Supporting Details _____

_____

_____

_____

_____

▼ EXERCISE 4

The following sets of sentences are rearranged versions of paragraphs. From each set, select the sentence that controls and organizes the entire paragraph—in other words, select the paragraph's topic sentence. Circle its letter.

1. a. The city taxes tickets, parking, and concessions, and businesses close to the ball park—hotels, bars, and restaurants especially—note an increase in patronage.

   b. Also, citizens just seem to have more pride in their city—and perhaps about themselves—when there is a franchise, especially a successful one, performing at the ball park.

   c. A major-league sports franchise aids a city tremendously.

   d. Moreover, the city receives national coverage through the media as the city's name is mentioned in conjunction with that of its team.

   e. This franchise, for example, can generate a great deal of money.

2. a. For example, this exercise improves the body's cardiovascular system, for the heart and lungs come to operate more efficiently.

   b. Jogging proves beneficial in several ways.

   c. The jogger knows that he has gained control of his life and is doing what is best for him.

   d. Moreover, jogging increases the body's endurance; the legs, especially, grow stronger through repeated use.

   e. In addition, the discipline that jogging requires increases one's self-esteem.

3. a. With the aid of a catalog and a course schedule, a student must first determine the courses she wishes to take and the times she wishes to take the courses.

   b. Next, the student must meet with her advisor to make sure that she has selected courses that will fulfill college requirements.

   c. Finally, the student presents the amended schedule to the registrar only to be told that two of her five courses are already filled.

   d. The most difficult part of a freshman's first week at college may be the registration process.

   e. This process of creating a schedule can be especially exasperating if a student must also plan hours for a part-time job.

4. a. The oversized head measures 110 square inches and encloses a "sweet spot" 3-1/2 times larger than traditional rackets.

   b. Before playing tennis, a person obtains the best equipment available on the market just as the professionals do.

   c. Framed in 60 percent graphite and 40 percent fiberglass for power and control, the high-performance instrument slices through the wind with its new aerodynamic design.

   d. Since the professional tennis player never appears in a tournament without a reserve racquet, the person has to buy several custom-made racquets costing $200 each.

   e. Padded with foam to prevent blisters, the handle is wrapped with genuine calfskin leather to assure a strong grip.

5. a. From the mirror-covered ceiling hung reflective balls reminiscent of 1970s discothéques.

   b. The inside of the tavern was something straight from an interior decorator's worst nightmare.

   c. Each table had four chairs made of aluminum frames with red vinyl cushions that almost, but not quite, matched the walls.

   d. The walls of the 50 x 100 foot room were covered with maroon velvet and decorated with art work of dubious quality.

   e. Along one wall was the bar itself, and evenly distributed about the room were twenty-odd formica tables of differing shapes and sizes.

Identifying Facts and Opinions

As discussed earlier, the topic sentence states your opinion about the topic. Examine the following sentence. Does it offer an opinion?

> At Milbrook University, 80 percent of the full-time students commute to campus daily.

This sentence does *not* offer an opinion about the general topic of college students who commute to campus. Instead, the writer simply states a fact. While facts are useful as supporting ideas, they do not create topic sentences because nothing more can be said about a factual statement. This topic sentence is not adequate.

A **fact** is a statement that can be definitively and objectively proven or disproven by using sensory evidence. An **opinion** is a personal belief concerning what one thinks is true or valid; it can never be absolutely proven or disproven. A factual statement can be shown to be false, but an opinion can be changed only because it is shown to be invalid. In other words, a fact is objective; an opinion is subjective.

Examine these sets of facts and opinions:

Fact: The Pacific Ocean is the largest body of water on the earth.

Opinion: The Indian Ocean is best for surfing.

Fact: Thomas A. Edison received the first patent for an incandescent light bulb.

Opinion: Thomas Edison's inventions propelled humankind into the modern era.

Fact: Whales are actually mammals, more closely related to humans than to sharks.

Opinion: Killing whales should be prohibited.

Each of the above facts can be proven true. All of the oceans can be measured to see which one is the largest. Patent Office records can be searched to see who first patented the light bulb. Scientists can study the genetic make-up of whales, sharks, and humans to determine their genetic similarities. Because objective means are used to prove or disprove those statements, they are facts.

Each of the opinion statements represents a personal point of view. Whereas one person may, on the other hand, like surfing in the Indian Ocean, another may prefer the Mediterranean Sea. Similarly, although Mr. Edison's inventions changed America's lifestyles, not everyone would agree that they served as a catalyst for modernity. Finally, some nations need whale meat as a source of protein for their people, so they would resent any interdiction against whaling. Since neither side in the dispute can be absolutely proven true or false, right or wrong, these are opinion statements. An opinion should be supported by facts, but it is not itself a fact.

▼ **EXERCISE 5**

Read each of the following statements carefully. If the statement can be proven or disproven by using objective evidence, write *Fact* in the blank to the left. If the statement reveals a personal viewpoint that cannot be absolutely proven or disproven, write *Opinion* in the blank.

_____ 1. New York City has the best Chinese restaurants.

_____ 2. NASA announced that it will redesign the space shuttle's booster rockets.

_____ 3. The first day of spring is the vernal equinox.

_____ 4. State law requires that all children, up to the age of six, use seat belts or safety seats while riding in cars.

_____ 5. If we rank the income of medical specialists, pediatricians are among the lowest-paid doctors.

_____ 6. Toddlers are contrary and fractious.

_____ 7. McDonald's is more popular than Roy Rogers.

_____ 8. A college degree has become worthless; one needs an MBA to get a good job.

_____ 9. Orchids are difficult plants to grow.

_____ 10. No one has yet patented a black tulip.

To correct a topic sentence that does not express an opinion, reconsider the original topic. Since most topics can be developed in several ways, you should be able to create another topic sentence that *will* include an opinion. Use the previous example, with the general topic of college commuters, as the basis of a brainstorming session. Here are a few possibilities:

> commuter and travel time
> advantages of living off-campus or at home
> the school's responsibility to commuters
> the economic responsibilities of the commuter
> the disadvantages of commuting

Any of these ideas could be developed into a valid topic sentence:

1.   During the day, Milbrook University must provide more activities for commuters.

2.   Commuting to college has many advantages.

3.   Commuters face many problems as they travel to and from school.

Note sentences 2 and 3. Besides offering opinions (commuting is advantageous or commuting is problematical), these topic sentences also state limits: *many* advantages, *many* problems. So a topic sentence can limit the topic even as it offers an opinion, or it can simply limit the topic by listing causes, effects, steps in process, stages of development, or characteristics. Examine the following topic sentences. Do they offer opinion or limitation?

> Many college students choose to major in computer science for three reasons.

> To change a flat tire correctly and safely, you must complete four tasks.

Both topic sentences limit the writers' discussions to either the three reasons or the four tasks. Although the writers have not expressed an opinion, they have classified and enumerated essential elements and, thus, have limited the topics further.

▼ EXERCISE 6

Identify the topic sentences that offer either an opinion or a limitation by placing a (√) next to them. Identify the factual statements by placing an (X) next to them. Consider ways to turn the factual statements into topic sentences. For each factual statement, generate one topic sentence that offers an opinion and one that limits the topic.

_____ 1. Pollution can take many forms.

_____ 2. Americans watch an average of four hours of television each day.

_____ 3. Man O'War won the Preakness in 1920.

_____ 4. The board game Trivial Pursuit requires many hours to play.

_____ 5. Mountain climbers must prepare themselves physically and mentally for each climb.

_____ 6. Candidates for the police academy must have a high school diploma and pass physical and aptitude tests.

_____ 7. Although retirement promises great rewards, many senior citizens face adversity, diminishing abilities, and financial hardships.

_____ 8. Many clothing fashions reappear every twenty years or so.

_____ 9. Because it has many untapped resources, Alaska offers great opportunities.

_____ 10. American government has become increasingly bureaucratic.

Generating Topic Sentences

As you learned earlier, one topic can often yield several topic sentences. When you write, you must choose the one you believe you can develop adequately in a paragraph. Generally it is best to choose the one you are most interested in, wish to research, or know about through personal experience or observation. For example, the general topic *agriculture* could be narrowed to the more limited topic *farmers in the United States.*

Here are several possible topic sentences:

1. To succeed financially, farmers must use modern technology, including computers.

2. Many environmental factors can cause financial ruin for American farmers.

3. To be a farmer, one must know the land, work hard, and know sound business practices.

4. Cotton farmers in the South face three major problems each year.

5. For many reasons, thousands of farmers face bankruptcy each year.

The choice of which to write about in a paragraph depends on the interests and knowledge of the writer.

▼ EXERCISE 7

Limit each of the following general topics , and write *three* topic sentences for each limited topic. Try to write at least one opinion topic sentence and one limiting topic sentence in each category. Circle the controlling idea in each topic sentence and underline the topic.

1. General Topic: **Camping**

   Limited Topic: _____

   Topic Sentence 1. _____

   Topic Sentence 2. _____

   Topic Sentence 3. _____

2. General Topic: **Computers**

   Limited Topic: _____

   Topic Sentence 1. _____

   Topic Sentence 2. _____

   Topic Sentence 3. _____

3. General Topic: **Sports**

   Limited Topic: _____

   Topic Sentence 1. _____

   Topic Sentence 2. _____

   Topic Sentence 3. _____

4. General Topic: **Cities**

Limited Topic: _____

Topic Sentence 1. _____

Topic Sentence 2. _____

Topic Sentence 3. _____

Discovering Topic Sentences

Sometimes, as a result of a prewriting exercise or a first draft, you may develop an organized and unified paragraph that lacks a topic sentence. In other words, instead of writing the topic sentence first and then generating supporting ideas, you may have developed all the details but not have written a topic sentence. Here is an example:

> At first, the car proceeded down the road at 20 mph. Then, its speed increased suddenly to 55 mph, and it moved from the left lane into the middle one without signaling any intention to change. As the car's speed continued to increase, it moved erratically from the middle lane to the left lane and then quickly across the road to the right lane. At that point, the speed dropped dramatically to 15 mph, and the car began to drift slowly to the right. After its tires hit the curb, the car began to weave between the middle and right lanes until ultimately it was straddling the broken white line. There it came to a full stop.

There is no specific sentence in this paragraph that gives the reader the topic and the controlling idea. Obviously, comprehending the paragraph will be easier for your audience if you do provide a topic sentence. Since the topic sentence is not yet written, you must somehow develop one. But how would you do it? The following process will help you organize the information you have generated so that you can formulate an appropriate topic sentence.

Developing a Topic Sentence from Detail Sentences

1. What is the whole paragraph about?

    _____ a car _____

    (The answer is the paragraph's **topic.**)

2. What details about the topic have you stated?

    _____ 20 mph- increase to 55 _____

    _____ lane change - no signal _____

    _____ speed increase - erratic movement _____

    15 mph drifting and weaving across lanes

full stop in middle of road

(The answers are the **significant details.**)

3. What do the details tell about the topic? What conclusion can be drawn?

The driver can't control the car.

(The answer is the **controlling idea.**)

4. Formulate your conclusion into a topic sentence.

The driver can be classified as Driving while Intoxicated).

The last sentence is your first attempt at writing a topic sentence for that paragraph. The next step in the writing process is to reformulate the topic and controlling idea; try to generate a more sophisticated, less bare-boned, topic sentence, one that will appeal more to your reader's interest.

▼ EXERCISE 8

Develop a topic sentence for the following paragraphs.

1. "Run" can mean a fast means of personal locomotion; it can also refer to a flaw in a woman's stocking. In a more serious mood, a run on a bank can deplete its financial resources. To the baseball fan, a run can mean the difference between a win or a loss.

What is the whole paragraph about?

_____

(*topic*)

What information about the topic are you given?

_____

_____

_____

(*significant details*)

What do the details tell you about the topic? What conclusion can be drawn?

_____

_____

(*controlling idea*)

Formulate your conclusion into a topic sentence.

_____

Rewrite the above topic sentence, making it more appealing to your audience.

_____

2. George Washington was beloved by his troops and, living among them, shared their suffering at Valley Forge. The people's love for the man continued through his presidency. Andrew Jackson invited thousands of the "common folk" to his inaugural ball, and, although they destroyed the furniture in the White House, no one was injured. Ticker-tape parades for the president-elect were common, and President John F. Kennedy even strolled down Fifth Avenue. However, more recent presidents have been the victims of assassination attempts, and any venture off the White House grounds worries the Secret Service.

What is the whole paragraph about?

_____

(*topic*)

What information about the topic are you given?

_____

_____

_____

_____

(*details*)

What do the details tell you about the topic? What conclusion can you draw?

_____

_____

(*controlling idea*)

Formulate your conclusion into a topic sentence.

_____

Rewrite the above topic sentence; be sure it either limits the topic or expresses an opinion.

_____

Strategies for Placing the Topic Sentence

As you have probably noticed, the topic sentence is usually the first sentence in the paragraph. But it does not have to be. Take another look at the paragraph in exercise 3 about Sherlock Holmes's appearance. Which sentence in that paragraph is the topic sentence? The second one is. If the topic sentence does not have to be first, then where else in the paragraph can it be? It can be anywhere; its placement depends on its purpose in the paragraph. You, the writer, must decide on the best placement based on what you want the topic sentence to accomplish.

PLACEMENT: FIRST SENTENCE

When the topic sentence is the first sentence in the paragraph, it *introduces* the details that support or explain the controlling idea. Such a paragraph could be diagrammed as an inverted triangle:

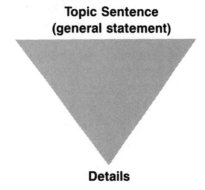

Topic Sentence
(general statement)

Details

The triangle narrows from the broad topic statement to the individual, specific details. You immediately tell your reader what the whole paragraph is about. You make it easy for the reader to skim your writing, and you forestall any possible misinterpretation of your message.

Practice this strategy by locating the topic sentence in the following paragraph. On the following page write the sentence on the given line; then, underline the topic and circle the controlling idea. In the column to the right, diagram the paragraph.

Registration is an impossible process. The first step requires a student to see his or her advisor for a heart-to-heart talk about career choices, academic options, and schedules. Of course, all of that must be completed in the allotted ten minutes, or else the other one hundred student advisees become annoyed. Then, even if the student/advisor combination does manage to arrive at a mutually satisfactory arrangement, the odds are overwhelming that one, some, or all of the courses will be closed by the time the student actually arrives at the registration desk. That forces a reenactment of the whole scenario, beginning at the end of the line.

Topic Sentence: _____   Paragraph Diagram

_____

_____

PLACEMENT: LAST SENTENCE

Read this paragraph carefully and answer the questions that follow.

> I should premise that I use this term [Struggle for Existence] in a large and metaphorical sense, including dependence of one being on another, and including (which is more important) not only the life of the individual, but success in leaving progeny. Two canine animals in a time of dearth may be truly said to struggle with each other over which shall get food and live. But a plant on the edge of a desert is said to struggle for life against the drought, though more properly it should be said to be dependent on the moisture. A plant which annually produces a thousand seeds, of which on an average only one comes to maturity, may be more truly said to struggle with the plants of the same and other kinds which already clothe the ground. . . . In these several senses, which pass into each other, I use for convenience' sake the general term of Struggle for Existence.

(from Charles Darwin, "The Struggle for Existence" in *The Origin of Species*)

1. What is the whole paragraph about?

_____

(*topic*)

2. What information about the topic does the author provide?

_____

_____

(*details*)

3. You know the topic and details of the paragraph now. What is the author saying about the topic? What message is he trying to convey? (Look at what the details tell you about the topic.)

_____

_____

(*controlling idea*)

4. Which sentence in the paragraph conveys that same message?

_____

(*topic sentence*)

In this paragraph, the topic sentence is the last one in the paragraph. There, it can *summarize* all the preceding details. It should be diagrammed as an upright triangle, with the details at the top, and broadening to the base—the general statement.

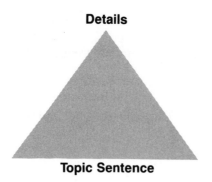

Details

Topic Sentence

Practice this strategy by using the above example as a model to locate the topic sentence in the following paragraph, and then diagram the paragraph.

> Old people see their life's savings erode and fear that they will be reduced to penury. The middle-aged have trouble meeting their expenses, much less saving for retirement. Recent college graduates receive seemingly phenomenal salaries, but soon realize that they cannot afford to marry and form a family unit. In addition, businesses cannot accurately forecast their profits and expenses. Overall, inflation affects us, one and all.

1. What is the whole paragraph about?

_____

(*topic*)

2. What information about the topic does the author provide?

_____

_____

_____

_____

_____

(*details*)

3. What message is suggested?

_____

_____

(controlling idea)

4. State the topic sentence.

_____

5. Diagram the paragraph here.

PLACEMENT: FIRST AND LAST SENTENCES

In a third strategy, the topic sentence , worded differently, appears in two places, usually at the beginning and end of the paragraph. When using this format, the writer *introduces* the reader to the general statement, supports and explains it, and then *summarizes* it. In effect, the author is trying to ensure that the reader gets the message. As a writer, you will probably use this placement when your audience is unfamiliar with the material and the material is difficult. By repeating the main idea, you reinforce the message for your readers and give them another opportunity to comprehend it. This type of paragraph is diagrammed in an unusual way:

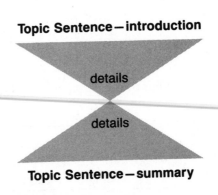

Topic Sentence—introduction

details

details

Topic Sentence—summary

Here is an example of this strategy in a paragraph:

"Body Language" can be used, both consciously and unconsciously, to project a message beyond the spoken word. A mother wagging her finger at a child knowingly reinforces the serious intent of her words. Likewise, standing with arms akimbo projects power and stolidity. In contrast, standing with arms folded across the chest is a defensive posture; someone who stands that way unconsciously labels himself the weaker individual. Similarly, a slight frown implies impatience, no matter how honeyed the tone. *Therefore, be aware of the ways the body can be used to reinforce a spoken message; furthermore, be wary of the ways it can defuse the impact of verbal statements.*

The first and last sentences are both topic sentences.

Practice this strategy by locating the topic sentence or sentences in the following paragraph, and then diagram the paragraph.

What then is the American, this new man? He is either a European, or the descendant of a European, hence that strange mixture of blood, which you will find in no other country. I could point out to you a family whose grandfather was an Englishman, whose wife was Dutch, whose son married a French woman, and whose present four sons have now four wives of different nations. He is an American, who, leaving behind him all his ancient prejudices and manners, receives new ones from the new mode of life he has embraced, the new government he obeys, and the new rank he holds. He becomes an American by being received in the broad lap of our great Alma Mater. Here individuals of all nations are melted into a new race of men, whose labours and posterity will one day cause great changes in the world. Americans are the western pilgrims, who are carrying along with them that great mass of arts, science, vigour, and industry which began long since in the east; they will finish the great circle. The Americans were once scattered all over Europe; here they are incorporated into one of the finest systems of population which has ever appeared, and which will hereafter become distinct by the power of the different climates they inhabit. The American ought therefore to love this country much better than that wherein either he or his forefathers were born. Here the rewards of his industry follow with equal steps the progress of his labour; his labour is founded on the basis of nature, self-interest, can it want a stronger allurement? Wives and children, who before in vain demanded of him a morsel of bread, now, fat and frolicsome, gladly help their father to clear those fields whence exuberant crops are to arise to feed and to clothe them all; without any part being claimed, either by a despotic prince, a rich abbot, or a mighty lord.

Here religion demands but little of him; a small voluntary salary to the minister, and gratitude to God; can he refuse these? The American is a new man, who acts upon new principles; he must therefore entertain new ideas, and form new opinions. From involuntary idleness, servile dependence, penury, and useless labour, he has passed to toils of a very different nature, rewarded by ample subsistence.—This is an American.

(from J. Hector St. John, "What Is an American?" in *Letters from an American Farmer*)

1. Topic:

_____

2. Details:

_____

_____

_____

_____

_____

3. Topic Sentence(s):

_____

_____

_____

_____

4. Location:

_____

5. Paragraph Diagram:

PLACEMENT: MIDDLE OF THE PARAGRAPH

Finally, you may place the topic sentence in the middle of the paragraph. There, it serves as a *transition* between the details given at the beginning and end of the paragraph. This placement is effective when the topic sentence has two parts to it, two controlling ideas. Here is an example:

> A mother wagging her finger at her child knowingly reinforces the serious intent of her words. Likewise, standing with arms akimbo projects power and stolidity. *As can be seen, "body language" can be used, both consciously and unconsciously, to project a message beyond the spoken word.* Standing with arms folded across the chest is a defensive posture; someone who stands that way unconsciously labels himself the weaker individual. Similarly, a slight frown implies impatience, no matter how honeyed the tone.

As you can see, this paragraph has been rearranged slightly by moving the topic sentence to the middle. Consequently, the diagram for this paragraph has changed; it is now a diamond:

details

Topic Sentence

details

When the topic sentence is in the middle of a paragraph, it can be difficult to locate because it is hard to skim a paragraph for the topic sentence. Your reader might overlook your main idea because it is buried in a mountain of details. However, this placement strategy is especially useful with complex, two-part controlling ideas. When your message is complex and you want to assure that the reader organizes your facts and interprets your opinion correctly, it is helpful to place the topic sentence in the middle of the paragraph.

To practice this strategy, read the following paragraph carefully. Underline the topic sentence and then diagram the paragraph.

> Houses are being burglarized even with the occupants at home. Purses and necklaces are snatched on the street with no hope of catching the thieves. Parked cars frequently "lose" their hubcaps and stereos. Because the populace feels unsafe in the neighborhood, auxiliary police forces are formed. Their function is to serve as the "eyes" and "ears" of the regular police force. Auxiliary officers do not attempt to stop crimes; they simply observe and report. They do not carry weapons, and they have no greater authority than any other civilian.

Diagram:

The chart below summarizes the placement strategies for topic sentences, the purposes of those placements, and their effects on your audience.

PLACEMENT STRATEGY	PURPOSE	EFFECT
beginning of paragraph	introduces supporting details	reader understands main idea immediately
end	summarizes supporting details	reader sees the proof for your position first
beginning and end	introduces and summarizes supporting details	reinforces difficult material for your reader
middle	provides transition from details that support one controlling idea to details that support the other controlling idea	supports and organizes a two-part controlling idea for your reader

▼ **EXERCISE 9**

Refer to the topic sentences you wrote for Exercise 7. Beneath each one, indicate a possible purpose and placement for it in a paragraph.

▼ **EXERCISE 10**

1. Choose a subject with which you are very familiar. Assume that your reader is unfamiliar with the material and finds it difficult to understand; write a paragraph about that subject.

2. Write a paragraph expressing your point of view on a current controversy. Be sure to state your supporting details first, and your topic sentence last, because your reader is skeptical and not likely to read material contrary to his or her opinion.

▼ Writing Strategy: PROCESS ANALYSIS

A process analysis explains to a reader how to do a task or how something works. Hence, writers use two types of process analyses as organizational strategies: a **directional** process analysis provides a set of instructions for the reader, and an **informational** process analysis explains the steps in an operation. For example, in a directional process analysis, a writer may describe how to operate a computer or calculator, how to serve a tennis ball, how to apply to college, or how to build a deck. An informational process analysis, however, might explain in a sequence of steps how a telephone works, how the heart pumps blood throughout the body, or how a microwave oven cooks food.

To provide either type of process analysis, you must consider the audience's knowledge of the process and tailor the analysis to meet the audience's needs. It would be inappropriate, for instance, for a computer expert to explain to novices, in computer jargon, how a word-processing system works. In the same fashion, it would be inappropriate for the computer expert to explain in simple language how an advanced computer works to those who are familiar with computers.

In addition, you must set forth *in chronological order* all the steps of the process or the instructions. While this may be obvious, many of us forget the difficulties we had when we first tried to water ski or to ride a bike. When we write, we often omit necessary steps or stages simply because they seem so obvious to us. These steps, however, are *not* obvious to anyone who is just learning. Always be sure that you include all the information someone needs to perform the task, and in the correct sequence.

▶ Lenses

ANNIE DILLARD

Annie Dillard, winner of a Pulitzer Prize for her autobiography Pilgrim at Tinker Creek, *explains the difficulties of using a microscope in this selection, from a collection of essays,* Teaching a Stone to Talk: Expeditions and Encounters.

1   You get used to looking through lenses; it is an acquired skill. When you first look through binoculars, for instance, you can't see a thing. You look at the inside of the barrel; you blink and watch your eyelashes; you play with the focus knob till one eye is purblind.

2   The microscope is even worse. You are supposed to keep both eyes open as you look through its single eyepiece. I spent my childhood in Pittsburgh trying to master this trick: seeing through one eye, with both eyes open. The microscope also teaches you to move your hands wrong, to shove the glass slide to the right if you are following a creature who is swimming off to the left—as if you were operating a tiller, or backing a

trailer, or performing any other of those paradoxical maneuvers which require either sure instincts or a grasp of elementary physics, neither of which I possess.

3   A child's microscope set comes with a little five-watt lamp. You place this dim light in front of the microscope's mirror; the mirror bounces the light up through the slide, through the magnifying lenses, and into your eye. The only reason you do not see everything in silhouette is that microscopic things are so small they are translucent. The animals and plants in a drop of pond water pass light like pale stained glass; they seem so soaked in water and light that their opacity has leached away.

4   The translucent strands of algae you see under a microscope— Spirogyra, Oscillatoria, Cladophora—move of their own accord, no one knows how or why. You watch these swaying yellow, green, and brown strands of algae half mesmerized; you sink into the microscope's field forgetful, oblivious, as if it were all a dream of your deepest brain. Occasionally a zippy rotifer comes barreling through, black and white, and in a tremendous hurry.

(Dillard, Annie. *Teaching a Stone to Talk: Expeditions and Encounters.*
New York: Harper and Row, 1982. pp. 104–5.)

▶ QUESTIONS   1. What difficulties did Dillard face as she learned to use a microscope?

2. What are the steps involved in looking through a microscope?

3. How does a microscope work?

4. Define the following words: *purblind* (1), *paradoxical* (2), *translucent* (3), and *mesmerized* (4).

How Dictionaries Are Made
S. I. HAYAKAWA

*S. I. Hayakawa is a leading rhetorician. He has also been
president of a university and a U.S. senator.*

1   It is widely believed that every word has a correct meaning, that we learn these meanings principally from teachers and grammarians (except that most of the time we don't bother to, so that we ordinarily speak "sloppy English"), and that dictionaries and grammars are the supreme authority in matters of meaning and usage. Few people ask by what authority the writers of dictionaries and grammars say what they say. I once got into a dispute with an English woman over the pronunciation of a word and offered to look it up in the dictionary. The English woman said firmly, "What for? I am English. I was born and brought up in England. The way I speak *is* English." Such self-assurance about one's

own language is not uncommon among the English. In the United States, however, anyone who is willing to quarrel with the dictionary is regarded as either eccentric or mad.

2   Let us see how dictionaries are made and how the editors arrive at definitions. What follows applies, incidentally, only to those dictionary offices where firsthand, original research goes on—not those in which editors simply copy existing dictionaries. The task of writing a dictionary begins with the reading of vast amounts of the literature of the period or subject that the dictionary is to cover. As the editors read, they copy on cards every interesting or rare word, every unusual or peculiar occurrence of a common word, a large number of common words in their ordinary uses, and also the sentences in which each of these words appears, thus:

> pail
> The dairy *pails* bring home increase of milk
> > Keats, *Endymion*
> > I, 44–45

3   That is to say, the context of each word is collected, along with the word itself. For a really big job of dictionary writing, such as the *Oxford English Dictionary* (usually bound in about twenty-five volumes), millions of such cards are collected, and the task of editing occupies decades. As the cards are collected, they are alphabetized and sorted. When the sorting is completed, there will be for each word anywhere from two or three to several hundred illustrative quotations, each on its card.

4   To define a word, then, the dictionary editor places before him the stack of cards illustrating that word; each of the cards represents an actual use of the word by a writer of some literary or historical importance. He reads the cards carefully, discards some, re-reads the rest, and divides up the stack according to what he thinks are the several senses of the word. Finally, he writes his definitions, following the hard-and-fast rule that each definition *must* be based on what the quotations in front of him reveal about the meaning of the word. The editor cannot be influenced by what *he* thinks a given word *ought* to mean. He must work according to the cards, or not at all.

5   The writing of a dictionary, therefore, is not a task of setting up authoritative statements about the "true meanings" of words, but a task of *recording*, to the best of one's ability, what various words have *meant* to authors in the distant or immediate past. *The writer of a dictionary is a historian, not a lawgiver.* If, for example, we had been writing a dictionary in 1890, or even as late as 1919, we could have said that the word "broadcast" means "to scatter" (seed, for example), but we could not have decreed that from 1921 on, the most common meaning of the word should become "to disseminate audible messages, etc., by radio transmission." To regard the dictionary as an "authority," therefore, is to credit the dictionary writer with gifts of prophecy which neither he nor anyone else possesses. In choosing our words when we speak or write, we can be *guided* by the historical record afforded us by the dictionary, but we cannot be *bound* by it, because new situations, new experiences, new inventions, new feelings, are always compelling us to give new uses to old words. Looking under a "hood," we should ordinarily have found, five hundred years ago, a monk; today, we find a motorcar engine.

▶ QUESTIONS

1. What is Hayakawa's main idea? Where is it located?

2. What kind of process analysis is this piece? Defend your choice.

3. Why does Hayakawa believe that it is important that we understand how dictionaries are made? What assumptions do we make about dictionaries? Why are these assumptions accurate or inaccurate?

4. Why must writers of dictionaries use words only within the contexts of sentences? What does this suggest about language?

Desperation Writing
PETER ELBOW

A noted author and teacher, Peter Elbow identifies the ways in which writers can overcome the anxiety they may feel during the writing process.

1   I know I am not alone in my recurring twinges of panic that I won't be able to write something when I need to, I won't be able to produce coherent speech or thought. And that lingering doubt is a great hindrance to writing. It's a constant fog or static that clouds the mind. I never got out of its clutches till I discovered that it was possible to write something—not something great or pleasing but at least something usable, workable—when my mind is out of commission. The trick is that you have to do all your cooking out on the table: your mind is incapable of doing any inside. It means using symbols and pieces of paper not as a crutch but as a wheel chair.

2   The first thing is to admit your condition: because of some mood or event or whatever, your mind is incapable of anything that could be called thought. It can put out a babbling kind of speech utterance, it can put a simple feeling, perception, or sort-of-thought into understandable (though terrible) words. But it is incapable of considering anything in relation to anything else. The moment you try to hold that thought or feeling up against some other to see the relationship, you simply lose the picture—you get nothing but buzzing lines or waving colors.

3   So admit this. Avoid anything more than one feeling, perception, or thought. Simply write as much as possible. Try simply to steer your mind in the direction or general vicinity of the thing you are trying to write about and start writing and keep writing.

4   Just write and keep writing. (Probably best to write on only one side of the paper in case you should want to cut parts out with scissors—but you probably won't.) Just write and keep writing. It will probably come in waves. After a flurry, stop and take a brief rest. But don't stop too long. Don't think about what you are writing or what you have written or else you will overload the circuit again. Keep writing as though you are drugged or drunk. Keep doing this till you feel you have a lot of material

that might be useful; or, if necessary, till you can't stand it any more—even if you doubt that there's anything useful there.

5   Then take a pad of little pieces of paper—or perhaps 3 × 5 cards—and simply start at the beginning of what you were writing, and as you read over what you wrote, every time you come to any thought, feeling, perception, or image that could be gathered up into one sentence or one assertion, do so and write it by itself on a little sheet of paper. In short, you are trying to turn, say, ten or twenty pages of wandering mush into twenty or thirty hard little crab apples. Sometimes there won't be many on a page. But if it seems to you that there are none on a page, you are making a serious error—the same serious error that put you in this comatose state to start with. You are mistaking lousy, stupid, second-rate, wrong, childish, foolish, worthless ideas for no ideas at all. Your job is not to pick out *good* ideas but to pick out ideas. As long as you were conscious, your words will be full of things that could be called feelings, utterances, ideas—things that can be squeezed into one simple sentence. This is your job. Don't ask for too much.

6   After you have done this, take those little slips or cards, read through them a number of times—not struggling with them, simply wandering and mulling through them; perhaps shifting them around and looking through them in various sequences. In a sense these are cards you are playing solitaire with, and the rules of this particular game permit shuffling the unused pile.

7   The goal of this procedure with the cards is to get them to distribute themselves in two or three or ten or fifteen different piles on your desk. You can get them to do this almost by themselves if you simply keep reading through them in different orders; certain cards will begin to feel like they go with other cards. I emphasize this passive, thoughtless mode because I want to talk about desperation writing in its pure state. In practice, almost invariably at some point in the procedure, your sanity begins to return. It is often at this point. You actually are moved to have thoughts or—and the difference between active and passive is crucial here—to *exert* thought; to hold two cards together and *build* or *assert* a relationship. It is a matter of bringing energy to bear.

8   So you may start to be able to do something active with these cards, and begin actually to think. But if not, just allow the cards to find their own piles with each other by feel, by drift, by intuition, by mindlessness.

9   You have now engaged in the two main activities that will permit you to get something cooked out on the table rather than in your brain: writing out into messy words, summing up into single assertions, and even sensing relationships between assertions. You can simply continue to deploy these two activities.

10   If, for example, after that first round of writing, assertion-making, and pile-making, your piles feel as though they are useful and satisfactory for what you are writing—paragraphs or sections or trains of thought—then you can carry on from there. See if you can gather each pile up into a single assertion. When you can, then put the subsidiary assertions of that pile into their best order to fit with that single unifying one. If you *can't* get the pile into one assertion, then take the pile as the basis for doing some more writing out into words. In the course of this writing, you may produce for yourself the single unifying assertion you were looking for;

or you may have to go through the cycle of turning the writing into assertions and piles and so forth. Perhaps more than once. The pile may turn out to want to be two or more piles itself; or it may want to become part of a pile you already have. This is natural. This kind of meshing into one configuration, then coming apart, then coming together and meshing into a different configuration—this is growing and cooking. It makes a terrible mess, but if you can't do it in your head, you have to put up with a cluttered desk and a lot of confusion.

11   If, on the other hand, all that writing *didn't* have useful material in it, it means that your writing wasn't loose, drifting, quirky, jerky, associative enough. This time try especially to let things simply remind you of things that are seemingly crazy or unrelated. Follow these odd associations. Make as many metaphors as you can—be as nutty as possible—and explore the metaphors themselves—open them out. You may have all your energy tied up in some area of your experience that you are leaving out. Don't refrain from writing about whatever else is on your mind: how you feel at the moment, what you are losing your mind over, randomness that intrudes itself on your consciousness, the pattern on the wallpaper, what those people you see out the window have on their minds—though keep coming back to the whateveritis you are supposed to be writing about. Treat it, in short, like ten-minute writing exercises. Your best perceptions and thoughts are always going to be tied up in whatever is really occupying you, and that is also where your energy is. You may end up writing a love poem—or a hate poem—in one of those little piles while the other piles will finally turn into a lab report on data processing or whatever you have to write about. But you couldn't, in your present state of having your head shot off, have written that report without also writing the poem. And the report will have some of the juice of the poem in it and vice versa.

▶ QUESTIONS   1. What is one aspect of writing that causes people to panic?

2. List the steps to overcome this problem.

3. What is Elbow's tone? What words achieve that tone?

4. Define the following terms: *hindrance* (1), *comatose* (5), *invariably* (7), *deploy* (9), and *metaphor* (11).

▶ Writing a Paper
Tim Maher

In this student paper, Tim Maher explains the process he uses to compose.

The process of writing a paper for me is long and many times frustrating. To write a paper that I am comfortable with and happy to hand in requires a lot of patience, which most times I do not have. The mere thought of having to write a paper seems to drain the patience from me immediately. Many times I feel that, through lack of patience or frustration, I skip through the process and pay little attention to important points. I will attempt to outline my writing process. My first step is choosing a topic. Many times I am given a topic by one of my teachers. Sometimes this assignment makes the selection process easier, but there are times when the given topic is of no interest to me, and I have no desire to write about it. When I am not given a topic, I try to think about something related to what I am studying that would be enjoyable to write about. It usually takes a day or two before I have decided on my topic. After I have made the decision on the topic, I then begin to gather as much information as possible about the subject. I may do research in the library, read over class material, or talk to the teachers. As I am completing research, I try to think of different ideas I would like to present in the paper and their organization. This is often a very frustrating process because I have either so many ideas that I can not organize them skillfully or too few to make the paper substantial. I then try to create an outline. Many times, the outline is extremely rough because I normally will start the outline and then begin writing the paper concurrently. Often the outline and first draft of the paper become one product, which gives me a good idea of the length and general idea of the paper as well as the structure I want to use. After I have written several drafts, I begin to write the final one. Usually

I write at least two drafts from the outline or rough

copy. The first is usually for proofreading purposes,

and it gives me a chance to change items. I then

write the last copy and hope that I have been critical

enough that the paper is thorough and enjoyable.

▶ QUESTIONS   1. What is Maher's topic sentence? Where does he place it?

2. How many steps does Maher list in this analysis of his writing process?

3. What details does Maher include under gathering information on this topic?

▼ PARAGRAPH ASSIGNMENTS

For each assignment below, identify a specific audience that will perform a task or understand a process. Identify, also, the skills that the audience will need to perform this task or understand this process. Finally, create a purpose for the readers: why should they learn how to complete the task or understand the process?

1. Provide a directional process analysis for one of the following tasks:

   planning a large party

   eating an ice cream cone (or any other food, such as tacos, spaghetti, or barbequed ribs)

   enrolling in college

   applying for a part-time job

2. In a paragraph, explain your writing process. Be sure to include specific details about the steps you follow and examples from previous papers.

▼ WRITING TIPS

Often it is easier to write a draft of a paper first, and then create a topic sentence with a controlling idea. Therefore, check your freewriting exercises and first drafts carefully for ideas that emerge. Use these to create a topic sentence for the paragraph.

Edit your paper carefully for run-on sentences. Check Chapter 6 in Part II for a detailed discussion of run-ons.

▼ Topic Sentence Checklist

1. Does the topic sentence of your paragraph have a specific controlling idea?

    _____

    _____

    _____

2. Does the topic sentence state your opinion about the topic, or does it limit the topic?

    _____

    _____

    _____

    _____

    _____

3. Did you develop the topic sentence of the paragraph from the details?

    _____

    _____

    _____

    _____

4. Where have you placed the topic sentence? Is it in the best location to introduce, summarize, reinforce, or be a transition between the developing details of the paragraph?

    _____

    _____

    _____

    _____

▼ Process Analysis Checklist

1. Does your process analysis present directions or information?

    _____

    _____

    _____

2. What is the purpose of your process analysis? Who is the intended audience? What might the audience already know about this process? How will this information affect your presentation?

    _____

    _____

    _____

3. How is the process analysis explained? What separate units of activity comprise this procedure? How do these units organize your paper?

    _____

    _____

    _____

4. After reading the process analysis, can someone other than you now perform the task or explain the operation? Have you listed all necessary items and actions, in the proper order?

    _____

    _____

    _____

5. If you found any fragments, comma splices, or run-ons as you proofread your paper, how did you correct them? (See Part II, Chapters 4–7.)

    _____

    _____

    _____

Organizing Details

4

▶ OBJECTIVES

1. To recognize unified paragraphs.

2. To identify and create primary support sentences.

3. To identify and create secondary support sentences.

4. To draw conclusions and make judgments.

5. To explore composing through classification.

▶ PREVIEW

A unified paragraph develops only one idea; it does not contain irrelevant or unnecessary information. Primary support sentences directly develop a topic sentence's controlling idea. Secondary support sentences provide specific examples, descriptions, or explanations for primary support sentences. Conclusions are opinions based on the information presented in the paragraph.

After exploring ideas and discovering a topic in early drafts, you should develop an organizational strategy for the generated material that will best suit your purpose and audience. Writers who record only their first impressions create disorganized paragraphs that ignore their audiences. Their readers are then forced to organize material as they read and to ignore statements that do not contribute to the paragraph's development. Such lack of courtesy reveals these writers' unwillingness to communicate with their audiences. You can avoid this problem, however, if you create unified paragraphs in which all of the supporting sentences develop the controlling idea of the topic sentence.

Using material generated by prewriting techniques and by initial drafts, you can select those items that best support your topic sentence. To make the material more accessible for an audience, you can organize details to reflect major ideas (primary support sentences) and minor ideas (secondary support sentences). **Primary support sentences** directly develop the controlling idea in the topic sentence. **Secondary support sentences** may contain a specific example or illustration, specific description, or explanation of the primary support sentences. Selected according to the audience's needs and your purpose, these details provide a well-organized paragraph that is accessible to your readers.

Unity

In a paragraph, you may explain, narrate, or describe a particular event or idea. However, you should develop only one idea in a paragraph. If, for example, you have promised the reader that you will discuss the importance of computers in high-school math classes, then you are committed to that idea only. Information describing the physical appearance of the computers, their operations, their use in other academic subjects, or personal experiences or ability with computers would be inappropriate in this paragraph. A reader could correctly question your inclusion of such details, since they do not develop the topic you promised: the importance of computers in high-school math classes.

If, in your paragraph, you present material you promised the reader in your topic sentence, then the paragraph will be unified. However, if you include random sentences that do not develop your topic sentence, then the paragraph is not unified and ignores its audience. To illustrate this point, consider the following example of a unified paragraph.

In a slender, five-and-a-half-foot body, my forty-six-year-old uncle hoped for better conditions in the barrio. His eyes squinted in the bright sun like a hawk's eyes seeing prey from a distance. But unlike the hunter's eyes, my uncle's eyes were narrowed permanently because of insufficient light after dark; because electricity was scarce in the area, gasoline lamps were used. His back also curved slightly and forced his shoulders to be ahead of him when he walked, for lack of indoor plumbing had made him bend down to pump water from an outdoor well. Furthermore, standing on a dusty dirt road, he favored his left leg because long journeys on foot to other parts of the barrio left him with a bad leg. Although life in the barrio had left its physical marks upon him, my uncle continued to believe that life there could be better.

In this paragraph, the student describes his uncle's hope for better conditions by detailing how life in the barrio has affected him physically. Each physical problem, from the narrowed eyes to the bad leg, has its origin in the barrio. Contrast the next student's paragraph with the one above.

The best strategy of dieting is not to decrease weight in a short period of time, as in a fad diet, but to commit oneself to a program of food reduction and exercise. To lose weight and keep it off, one has to exercise while dieting. The dieter must also watch his intake of calories. However, this type of weight loss requires more time than a fad diet. At a certain

point, weight loss levels off, and one remains at a

constant weight for a brief period of time. This is

called a plateau in weight loss, but eventually one

begins to lose weight again. As soon as the dieter

acquires the habit of eating correctly and exercising

while dieting, then the dieter can maintain a constant

weight.

This student's paragraph is not unified because the student includes a definition of *plateau* used in the specific context of dieting. However, the paragraph has promised the reader a description of the proper way to diet. Moreover, the writer fails to include sufficient information about the process of losing weight. The reader does not know the quantity or types of food a dieter should eat, nor does the reader know what types of exercise are most beneficial to dieters. Therefore, the information given in the paragraph is too general to be of use to the reader.

▼ EXERCISE 1

In each of the following paragraphs, underline the topic sentence, and then identify the sentence or sentences that do *not* support the topic sentence. Write their numbers in the blanks provided.

_____ 1. (1) Although weddings are for the bride and groom, parents and other relatives often determine the formality and size of the wedding. (2) If the bride and groom want a small, simple wedding, they frequently find that their parents insist upon inviting all of the relatives down to third cousins twice removed and friends from decades ago. (3) The guest list, once set at thirty, has now grown to over three hundred. (4) In addition, the simple ceremony, with the bride in a plain white dress and the groom in a suit, has now been transformed into a formal occasion. (5) The bride now wears a long white gown with a ten-foot train, and the groom sports a tuxedo. (6) Many conflicts can occur when the bride and groom want one type of ceremony and the parents want another. (7) Many parents want to use the occasion to repay old social obligations and to insure that their offspring receive many gifts. (8) The wedding party now includes seven bridesmaids, seven ushers, a ring bearer, and a flower girl. (9) The informal reception now takes place in a rented hall with a caterer and an orchestra. (10) Perhaps parents feel obligated to provide the best for their children on their wedding days; however, the wishes of the bride and groom should be respected. (11) It's their wedding.

_____ 2. (1) Being an only child has several advantages. (2) The child receives the full attention of both parents. (3) Certainly, this attention can benefit the child as she goes through school; both parents support her efforts completely. (4) At holidays, the only child is showered with gifts from both parents and grandparents. (5) Often, the parents will include the child in their social plans, so the child becomes adept at handling social situations at an early age. (6) Also, the child is taken to "adult" places: restaurants, museums, movies, and plays. (7) Many only children are overachievers; they must be the best at everything they do, so they become overly ambitious and studious. (8) Being around adults so often, the child actually is never given a chance to be a child. (9) Moreover, an only child must learn to be self-reliant and creative. (10) Unless there are neighborhood children her age, the only child relies upon her own imagination for games and activities. (11) As the child becomes more self-reliant, she is given more responsibility and freedom. (12) Therefore, the only child benefits from the attention her parents give her.

_____ 3. (1) Football's advantages outweigh its disadvantages. (2) As the sport's detractors like to point out, and as all athletic directors clearly know, football is expensive. (3) To outfit a player for practice costs over $200, with the helmet and face mask requiring the largest investment. (4) Game uniforms add an additional expense, as do such items as two- and seven-man sleds and blocking dummies. (5) Football's critics also dwell upon the possibility of serious injury by stressing the vulnerability of the head and neck. (6) Only boys who stand six feet tall and weigh over 180 pounds should play football. (7) While both arguments contain elements of truth, they do not prove conclusive. (8) Careful maintenance and judicious purchasing can decrease equipment costs. (9) Moreover, successful football programs can often generate more money than they spend. (10) Many college coaches are paid more than the presidents of the universities. (11) Also, while it is impossible to remove completely the risk of injury—from football or from any other contact sport—the incidence of injury can be reduced through the teaching of safe blocking and tackling techniques. (12) Football's detractors—and a number of them seem never to have played the game—fail to appreciate the mental discipline which the sport requires. (13) Even Howard Cosell's book on his adventures with football is entitled *I Never Played the Game*. (14) Played properly, football in no way proves to be a contest between Neanderthals but rather a sport that requires a mixture of strength, speed, and mental acuity. (15) As the players know, the camaraderie raised through mutual hard work makes the sport a most rewarding one. (16) The following scene is a familiar one: on a crisp, fall afternoon, before a brightly dressed, noisy, and appreciative crowd, the coach calls the correct play; the defenders are knocked to the ground, and the back speeds into the end zone as the referee raises his hands signalling a touchdown. (17) At times such as these, the expense, self-denial, and possibility of injury matter little, if at all.

_____ 4. (1) America's geographical diversity has encouraged many American writers to celebrate their regional cultures. (2) In New England, Henry D. Thoreau recorded life in Concord, Massachusetts, and described his travels in Maine and on Cape Cod. (3) Louisa May Alcott also depicted the village of Concord in her classic *Little Women*. (4) The lives of New

England farmers were immortalized in Robert Frost's poems. (5) Alexander Solzhenitsyn, the Russian novelist, lives in Vermont. (6) In the South, William Faulkner and Thomas Wolfe captured the essence of small southern towns like Oxford, Mississippi, and Asheville, North Carolina. (7) Faulkner also travelled to Los Angeles during the 1930s to write screen plays for the movies. (8) In the Midwest, Sherwood Anderson and Willa Cather described the loneliness of rural communities. (9) In the West, Jack London and John Steinbeck provided an accurate portrayal of California. (10) Jack London also wrote *Call of the Wild*, a story based in Alaska. (11) America has, indeed, proven to be a fertile ground for its native writers.

_____ 5. (1) Movies often reflect attitudes Americans hold. (2) For example, in the 1950s, when Americans enjoyed immense economic prosperity and domestic tranquility, many Westerns were made. (3) John Wayne, the archetypal Western hero, portrayed a strong, moral, silent man who always held high principles. (4) In his films, Wayne usually won the love of a beautiful girl, but she was not his goal throughout the movie. (5) Instead, he saved ranchers from evil bankers who threatened to foreclose and settlers from marauding bands of belligerent Indians. (6) In sharp contrast, films from the mid-1960s to the late 1970s offered heroes who seemed tortured by the political turmoil of the times. (7) This was not seen in the 1942 film *Casablanca*. (8) In the film *The Deer Hunter*, the protagonist Nick enlisted in the Army to fight in Vietnam. (9) Instead of the glorious military victory he anticipated, he found that the war, filled with death and destruction, lingered on long after the last American assault. (10) War films in the 1940s always showed the Americans as victors. (11) In the 1980s, however, America returned to a stronger economy and was led by a president who advocated self-reliance and strength. (12) Ronald Reagan won by a landslide in the 1984 election. (13) These beliefs were evident in our movies. (14) For instance, in the *Rocky* series, Rocky Balboa moves from the underdog in a championship fight to the heavyweight champion of the world through his determination and perseverance. (15) In the *Rambo* movies, Sylvester Stallone creates a Vietnam vet, trained in guerrilla warfare, who single-handedly destroys a town in *First Blood* and who rescues American prisoners of war from Southeast Asian communists in the second *Rambo* film. (16) Hence, American attitudes toward ourselves and our country are often apparent in our films.

Primary Support Sentences

After generating ideas by brainstorming, freewriting, or composing a first draft, you need to select and organize those ideas that best develop your purpose, stated in the topic sentence, and that best address your audience's background, knowledge, and need for information. An effective method of organizing is to identify major details, or primary support sentences.

Primary support sentences directly develop the controlling idea in a topic sentence. To develop the controlling idea, primary support sentences might provide explanations, descriptions, definitions, illustrations and examples, causes or effects, points of comparison and contrast, or reasons for an argument. Consider the following topic sentence:

> As a hobby, photography provides many benefits for the amateur.

The controlling idea is "many benefits." Therefore, the primary support sentences should enumerate the types of benefits photography offers. Now, examine these three primary support sentences:

1. Photography helps record many family events.

2. Photography allows individual artistic expression.

3. Photography can become a lucrative hobby.

Each of these sentences identifies a specific benefit of photography as a hobby. Certainly, each sentence needs further explanation—about the types of family events one might record, about the methods of artistic expression, and about the monetary reward of the hobby—but these primary support sentences give readers a clear indication of the types of benefits the hobby provides.

Analyze the following paragraph about a model office for a high-school yearbook staff. Identify the topic sentence, its controlling idea, and the primary supports.

> The model yearbook staff works in a spacious, well-equipped office. Within this large office, several long tables line the walls to provide ample work space. In addition to plenty of work space, the ideal yearbook office has ample room for storage in the form of both numerous filing cabinets and a walk-in closet. This spacious office houses outstanding modern equipment. On one long table, there rest both several electronic typewriters and a state-of-the-art computer and printer. To one side of the office, a door leads to the yearbook staff's newly equipped darkroom.

- The topic sentence is *The model yearbook staff works in a spacious, well-equipped office.*

- The controlling idea is *spacious, well-equipped office.*

- The primary support sentences are (1) *Within this large office, several long tables line the walls to provide ample work space.* (2) *In addition to plenty of work space, the ideal yearbook office has ample room for storage in the form of both numerous filing cabinets and a walk-in closet.* (3) *This spacious office houses outstanding modern equipment.*

Each primary support sentence describes what a "spacious, well-equipped office" should have. The first two primary support sentences give examples of the spacious office by describing ample work and storage space. The third primary support sentence defines the "well-equipped office" as having "outstanding modern equipment." The writer then gives specific examples—the typewriters, computer and printer, and the darkroom—of the modern equipment the office has. Thus, each primary support sentence helps develop the controlling idea in the topic sentence.

▼ EXERCISE 2

In the following paragraphs, underline the topic sentence, circle the controlling idea, and number the primary supports.

1.   While in high school, the lazy student reflects his attitude by the way he studies, acts, and dresses. I know a student, for example, who does no homework at all; he foolishly wastes his free study periods in the cafeteria with others like himself. His actions also reflect his slothful attitudes. When walking between classes, he moves slowly and speaks with everyone; as a result, he is always late for his next class. After his last class, he jumps into his car and rushes out of the parking lot with the car radio blaring; his only desire is to leave school quickly. He cares neither about what he gets on his report card nor about his appearance during school hours. His shirttail always hangs out, and he has no problem wearing stripes with plaids. His hair is rarely combed, and his shoelaces are untied.

2.   Besides being destructive to one's health, smoking can also be destructive to one's property. Over the years, smoking can result in property damage that will cost several thousands of dollars. For example, the carelessly dropped hot ash or spark, as well as the burning cigarette left on the edge of an ash tray, can do considerable damage to both furnishings and clothing. Furniture may be marred by a burn, and clothing can be spotted with holes from ashes or sparks. Moreover, the destructive effect smoking has on property inadvertently can affect one's health and life. For instance, a smoldering mattress, the result of a careless smoker's unnoticed spark, can itself produce enough smoke to cause the death of the bed's occupant through smoke inhalation. A house fire, the result of a carelessly extinguished cigarette, can lead to serious burns or death of the occupants of the house. Also, a carelessly dropped cigarette can destroy an entire ecological system and its wildlife. Anyone who thinks the effects of smoking on property are minimal should think again.

3.   When I moved into my apartment, I had to assume the household chores my parents had previously done for me. One of my first tasks was learning to push a vacuum cleaner. But about six weeks ago, the motor in my vacuum died. During this month and a half, the carpet went uncleaned. The carpet got so dirty that I was forced to make a decision: either borrow a vacuum cleaner or allow the carpet to walk out the door on its own. So recently, I decided to pay my parents a visit and borrow their cleaner. I am sure I made the right decision; this fifteen-minute cleaning job made a noticeable difference in my carpet's appearance. I have also learned to clean the bathroom, mop the floor, and wash the windows. Although none of these chores are enjoyable, they are all done at regular intervals. For example, the bathroom fixtures are cleaned every two weeks, and the kitchen floor is mopped once a month. Finally, the windows are cleaned once every six months. Living on my own has taught me new responsibilities.

4.   The role-playing game Dungeons and Dragons has been blamed by some for causing violent behavior, devil worship, and even suicide among its players. Critics claim that the game's violent nature—players imagine that they are medieval heroes who confront and destroy various monsters—encourages players to be more aggressive in real life. Opponents of the game also assert that the game, rather than being mere entertainment, is actually a form of mind control that alters the player's personality; they believe that the game's "occult" nature leads some players to devil worship. Moreover, critics claim that the game has led some players to commit suicide. Supposedly, the player becomes so involved with the game that he can no longer distinguish between fantasy and reality. According to the game's critics, a participant, believing that he will be brought back to life in the game, may kill himself. However, such claims are poorly supported by facts.

5.   Other people support the position that Dungeons and Dragons is actually beneficial to players. According to its advocates, the game encourages players to use their imaginations and logic while they are finding solutions to problems they encounter during the course of the game. Proponents argue that this imaginative role-playing helps players to develop more mental flexibility and that the players, consequently, are more able to find solutions to real-life problems. Also, since the game relies upon a numerical rating system for combat, magic, characters, and other aspects, the players develop their mathematical skills and their abilities to work with and understand numbers. Hence, two distinct skills are developed by the game: inventive problem-solving and mathematical ability.

▼ **EXERCISE 3**

To understand the relationship between a topic sentence and its primary supports, read each pair of topic sentences. Then read the list of primary supports. In the blank to the left of each primary support, write the letter of the supported topic sentence.

1.

A	*B*
The use of corporal punishment must be curbed.	Spanking is still a time-honored form of discipline.

_____ a. Physical abuse by anyone against anyone cannot be tolerated.

_____ b. Children have been spanked for years, and no one is harmed by it.

_____ c. Some children need quick reminders of who is in charge.

_____ d. Corporal punishment merely condones the use of violence to solve problems.

_____ e. It is better to punish physically and quickly than to withdraw love and affection.

2.

A	B
Properly used, the grading system benefits students.	Improperly used, grades can harm students.

_____ a. Grades rank a student against his or her peers and thereby foster competition.

_____ b. Tests measure the ability to take tests, not knowledge gained or information acquired.

_____ c. A poor grade can indicate which areas need to be studied.

_____ d. Grades are an indication of progress and improvement.

_____ e. Grades can't predict success or failure because they do not measure motivation and interest.

3.

A	B
The concept of comparable worth has generated a great deal of controversy.	Feminists believe equal pay for work of comparable value is an idea whose time has come.

_____ a. Many business and manufacturing associations have voiced opposition to it.

_____ b. Opponents argue that it will build another layer of bureaucracy.

_____ c. Even the federal judiciary is divi8ed: some judges have mandated it, others have thrown the suits out of court.

_____ d. Why should nurses be paid less than truck drivers when nurses have even greater responsibilities?

_____ e. The marketplace has traditionally been dominated by men who tend to see their occupations as more valuable.

_____ f. The issue will not be settled easily or quickly.

4.

A	B
Many researchers believe that cancer is a self-induced disease.	Cancer does not have to be a death sentence.

_____ a. Skin cancer is almost 100 percent curable if caught in its early stages.

_____ b. Leukemia victims now live many years with their disease in remission.

_____ c. Stress definitely puts an extra load on the body by decreasing its chances of repelling harmful agents.

_____ d. Known carcinogens such as tobacco can and should be eliminated from one's lifestyle.

_____ e. Gene splicing offers the hope of eliminating many causes of cancer.

_____ f. Poor or inappropriate diet contributes to specific kinds of cancer.

_____ g. Radiation therapy and chemotherapy can now eradicate the disease, not just prevent its spread.

5.

A	B
Some students believe that they should take only courses in their majors during college.	Educators encourage students to take courses in a number of disciplines.

_____ a. In highly technical fields, such as computer science and engineering, students should concentrate on acquiring knowledge they will need later on the job.

_____ b. Since many students attend college to learn a profession, additional courses not related to their majors are unnecessary.

_____ c. Many business executives value the graduate who took a number of different types of courses in college, since this graduate can approach problems in various ways.

_____ d. Courses in psychology, English, sociology, and history can prepare a student for a number of professional fields.

_____ e. The student who learns about different fields is better prepared to change careers if he or she wishes.

_____ f. In some majors, taking courses in a number of disciplines can add extra semesters to a student's college education.

CREATING PRIMARY SUPPORTS

When you want to create primary support sentences, try brainstorming for ideas about your topic sentence and its controlling idea. This method will give you ideas for several primary support sentences, probably more than you will need for the adequate development of the controlling idea. Choose the best primary support sentences for your paragraph; for example, you might choose the most important examples from a list to support a topic sentence. Consider the following example.

▶ Topic Sentence: Many first-semester college students are not prepared for the rigors of college life.

▶ Brainstorming: poor study habits
lack of self-discipline
lack of academic preparation in high school
lack of a workable schedule
lack of a place to study
can't handle complete freedom away from
   parent's watchful eyes
unprepared to live with a roommate
failure to take responsibility for themselves
unable to deal with different types of people
too many temptations in the form of parties or
   sports
first time away from home

▶ Primary Supports: 1. Many students are not prepared academically
   for the demands of college courses.
2. Many students did not develop good study
   habits in high school.
3. Some students are tempted by the social life
   on a college campus rather than by the
   intellectual activities.
4. Some students have never before had complete responsibility for themselves.

These four primary support sentences will develop the paragraph adequately. In addition, the statements are broad enough that the writer will be able to incorporate other details from the brainstorming session. For example, the last primary support about the lack of complete responsibility could also include the idea about the lack of self-discipline. Moreover, these four primary support sentences list major reasons why first-semester college students might not be prepared to do well in college.

Would the writer want to use all of the ideas from his brainstorming session? More than likely, he would not. If the writer tried to include all of the ideas he developed during the brainstorming session, then his paragraph would be extremely long, and he probably would not develop each idea thoroughly.

UNIFIED PARAGRAPHS

To create a unified paragraph, you must also make sure that the primary support sentences develop only the topic sentence you have chosen. In other words, if you commit to one idea in the topic sentence, then you cannot include tangential material even if it's related. You have promised to discuss one topic; you must adhere to the promise you made to the reader in the topic sentence. Consider the following example.

▶ Topic Sentence: Before purchasing a dog, one should consider
several matters carefully.

▶ Primary Supports: 1. The amount of space in an apartment or
house is important.

2. The buyer must consider the animal's purpose in the household.
3. The buyer should also consider the breed, its size, and its temperament.
4. Great Danes are often cute puppies but become large dogs.

Do all of these primary supports develop the topic sentence? Which one does not? Why?

▼ EXERCISE 4

Carefully read each topic sentence and the primary support sentences below it. Place an *X* by those primary support sentences that do *not* develop the topic sentence. Replace the faulty primary supports with ones of your own.

1. **Topic Sentence:**   Recent high-school graduates should not rush to enroll in college immediately.

   Primary Support 1:   Working for a year or two gives a teenager time to experience the business world.

   Primary Support 2:   Colleges are anxious to reverse a trend toward declining enrollments.

   Primary Support 3:   Working a while and saving money enable the student to choose a more expensive college; the choice of schools is not limited by finances.

   Primary Support 4:   A "young adult" of twenty is much more likely to appreciate the benefits of a college education than is a "teenager."

2. **Topic Sentence:**   Board games for adults have risen in popularity lately.

   Primary Support 1:   Grown-ups prefer to beat a peer rather than a computer.

   Primary Support 2:   Board games are a social activity; couples can compete with one another.

   Primary Support 3:   Because they require strategy and knowledge rather than eye-hand coordination, such games are more suited to the over-30 age group.

   Primary Support 4:   Trivial Pursuit has started a new craze.

3. **Topic Sentence:**   House plants add beauty to a house and provide a hobby for the grower.

   Primary Support 1:   House plants can be used effectively to decorate a home or apartment.

   Primary Support 2:   Cacti do not always grow well in humid environments.

   Primary Support 3:   Growing plants is a relaxing hobby.

4. **Topic Sentence:**   A child should have a pet.

   Primary Support 1:   By caring for a pet, a child learns responsibility.

   Primary Support 2:   A child gains companionship and affection from the pet.

Primary Support 3:	Pets can be expensive.
5. **Topic Sentence:**	Good study skills are important for success in college.
Primary Support 1:	Good students know the value of taking good lecture notes.
Primary Support 2:	Conscientious students read their textbooks carefully, underline important concepts, and outline the chapter.
Primary Support 3:	Students do not need to read everything an instructor assigns.

▼ EXERCISE 5

For each topic sentence below, use brainstorming to create as many supporting details as you can. Identify a specific audience and purpose for each topic sentence. Finally, select from your list of details those that best support the topic sentence according to the audience and purpose you named; write those primary supports in the space provided.

1. College students should/should not be required to take at least a basic course on computers.

_____

_____

_____

Audience: _____ Purpose: _____

2. Owning a car can be expensive.

_____

_____

_____

Audience: _____ Purpose: _____

3. Selecting a college requires careful consideration of many factors.

_____

_____

_____

Audience: _____ Purpose: _____

4. Sex education courses should/should not be required in high schools.

_____

_____

_____

Audience: _____ Purpose: _____

5. High-school students should/should not be required to pass competency tests in writing, reading, and mathematics before they graduate from high school.

_____

_____

_____

Audience: _____ Purpose: _____

Secondary Support Sentences

Secondary support sentences explain and illustrate the primary support sentences by giving examples or descriptions. Consider the following paragraph.

> As a hobby, photography provides many benefits for the amateur. First, photography helps the amateur record many family events. Next, photography allows artistic expression. Finally, photography can become a lucrative hobby for the amateur.

Is this paragraph adequately developed? No, it is not. Although the paragraph contains a topic sentence with a controlling idea and three primary supports, it does not answer all of the questions readers might have if they are considering photography as a hobby. For example, the first primary support might be clear to readers; most readers could easily think of examples of family events that would be captured on film. However, the second primary support, "allows artistic expression," and the third, "can become a lucrative hobby," need far more explanation than the writer provides. Certainly readers would want to know more. What might be an example of artistic expression in film? How does one begin to use photography artistically? How can photography be lucrative? What steps should the amateur take to make money with this hobby? Since the paragraph fails to answer the readers' questions, it fails to fulfill the promise made to readers in the topic sentence: to explain the benefits of the hobby. The paragraph merely *lists* the benefits.

Analyze the following paragraph. How does it differ from the one above? Does it answer the essential questions a reader might have?

> As a hobby, photography provides many benefits for the amateur. First, photography helps the amateur record many family events. For example, photographs capture important family celebrations, such as a wedding, the birth of a baby, a family reunion, or a family member's graduation. Snapshots also record daily events, such as a baby's first steps, the antics of children or pets, or a child's growth.

Moreover, these pieces of film give us a glimpse into family history; pictures of grandparents and great-grandparents remind us of our heritage. Next, photography allows artistic expression. Because photography is more than the mere capturing of a moment of time, the photographer can use many devices to create the mood or emotion he or she wants to convey. The amateur photographer begins to learn more about composition of elements in the photograph, light, and color to create the effect he or she seeks. For example, with black and white film, the photographer can create dramatic juxtapositions of shadow and light. The photographer also begins to recognize that the same setting, taken from different angles, yields many different interpretations. Finally, photography can become a lucrative hobby for the amateur. The amateur who develops skill with the camera can submit photos for contests to gain either monetary prizes or public recognition of this ability. The amateur may wish to publish some shots in a local newspaper; for example, these shots may accompany a travel article about a local historical landmark. By photographing weddings or portraits of friends and associates, the amateur can also expand this hobby into a part-time business. These benefits make photography more than just owning a camera.

The additional sentences illustrating the primary supports are *secondary support sentences*. The paragraph now offers more development of the controlling idea, and it answers many questions that readers might have.

THE PARAGRAPH OUTLINE

By creating primary and secondary supports, the writer has actually developed a basic outline for the paragraph. This outline ensures that the writer will fulfill his or her promise to the reader to develop the paragraph completely. Were you to outline the paragraph above, it would appear as the one that follows.

> ▶ Topic Sentence: As a hobby, photography provides many benefits for the amateur.

I. Primary Support 1: First, photography helps the amateur record many family events.

   A. Secondary Support 1A: For example, photographs capture important family celebrations, such as a wedding, the birth of a baby, a family reunion, or a family member's graduation.

   B. Secondary Support 1B: Snapshots also record daily events, such as a baby's first steps, the antics of children or pets, or a child's growth.

C. Secondary Support 1C: Moreover, these pieces of film give us a glimpse into family history; pictures of grandparents and great-grandparents remind us of our heritage.

II. Primary Support 2: Next, photography allows artistic expression.

A. Secondary Support 2A: Because photography is more than the mere capturing of a moment of time, the photographer can use many devices to create the mood or emotion he or she wants to convey.

B. Secondary Support 2B: The amateur photographer begins to learn more about composition of elements in the photograph, light, and color to create the effect he or she seeks.

C. Secondary Support 2C: For example, with black and white film, the photographer can create dramatic juxtapositions of shadow and light.

D. Secondary Support 2D: The photographer also begins to recognize that the same setting, taken from different angles, yields many different interpretations.

III. Primary Support 3: Finally, photography can become a lucrative hobby for the amateur.

A. Secondary Support 3A: The amateur who develops skill with the camera can submit photos for contests to gain either a monetary prize or public recognition of this ability.

B. Secondary Support 3B: The amateur may wish to publish some shots in a local newspaper; for example, these shots may accompany a travel article about a local historical landmark.

C. Secondary Support 3C: By photographing weddings or portraits of friends and associates, the amateur can also expand this hobby into a part-time business.

▶ Concluding Sentence: These benefits make photography more than just owning a camera.

Each primary support is followed by secondary supports, which further illustrate and explain the primary support. If you examine primary support 2 and its secondary supports, then you will see that, in addition to supports that directly develop the primary support, some sentences actually develop each other more specifically. For example, secondary support 2B lists the types of devices to create a mood; moreover, secondary supports 2C and 2D further explain how light and composition might be used artistically. Each secondary support, however, does develop its corresponding primary support sentence.

As you can see, outlines are extremely helpful at this point in the writing process:

- First, they allow you to determine if you have adequate support for your ideas. If you create only primary supports, your lack of specific details will be revealed in your outline.

- Second, outlines allow you to determine if every sentence performs its function. For example, after you have identified the controlling idea, then you can quickly check your primary supports to ensure that they develop only the controlling idea of your topic sentence. Also, you can ensure that your secondary supports are more specific than your primary supports and that the secondary supports do further illustrate the primary supports.

- Finally, outlines allow you to identify sentences that do not contribute to the paragraph's unity. You can then replace these irrelevant sentences with others that adhere to your controlling idea.

As you outline your ideas, you will find that ideas do not require a specific number of primary supports. In the same manner, every primary support does not have to be followed by the same number of secondary supports. Therefore, retain some flexibility in the organization you choose. Of utmost importance to you is the ability to address a specific audience and to develop a paragraph so that it presents your purpose in writing. Hence, use only those details, both primary and secondary, that best support your main idea, develop your purpose, and address your audience. Do not be bound by a set system with a certain number of supports.

▼ EXERCISE 6

In each of the paragraphs that follow, identify and label the topic sentence (TS), the controlling idea (CI), the primary supports (PS), the secondary supports (SS), and the concluding sentence (CS).

1. ____(1) Although American society provides no formal rite of passage from childhood to adulthood, several informal rites exist. ____(2) An adolescent's first date, for example, is one such informal initiation into the adult world.

____(3) The first date is usually filled with expectation, excitement, and anxiety as both parties adopt more mature attitudes and prepare for the date.

____(4) Getting a driver's license also proves that a teenager is almost an adult.

____(5) To new drivers, licenses represent the freedom to go places on their own without a chaperon. ____(6) For parents, the license represents the teenager's acceptance of responsibility and independence. ____(7) Also, a teenager's first job indicates a willingness to develop new skills and assume new responsibilities. ____(8) The teenager must make sure to arrive on time and be prepared to work; he or she also will learn how to budget money from the job. ____(9) Although there are few formal celebrations for these activities, each informal rite marks the teenager's movement into the adult world.

2. ____(1) Of the many differences between college and high school, perhaps the most important is the students' degree of independence. ____(2) While students are in high school, parents often assume more responsibility than students for their performance, motivation, and attendance at school. ____(3) For example, parents provide a comfortable environment in which students can relax; students, in fact, may do little to clean their rooms or the house. ____(4) Parents may provide the extra money that students need. ____(5) Parents encourage students by asking about the school day and grades. ____(6) Parents may also discuss with teachers the students' abilities and progress to ensure that they are receiving the correct support at home. ____(7) However, in college, all of this changes for students. ____(8) Students must force themselves to rise at 7:00 a.m. for that 8:00 a.m. class. ____(9) They must also prepare their own breakfasts, wash their clothes, and clean their dorm rooms. ____(10) College students must determine a schedule for study time. ____(11) With no one to remind them of homework and assignments, students must assume the responsibility themselves. ____(12) They must take the responsibility of discussing any academic difficulties with their instructors. ____(13) In other words, college students are on their own while high-school students have others to monitor them.

3. ____(1) Most of us believe that only housewives watch soap operas; however, many other types of people comprise the legions who watch the daytime and nighttime dramas. ____(2) Many students enjoy soap operas. ____(3) The

proof of their loyalty is readily available; one need only look into television rooms in student centers and dorms each day between noon and 4 o'clock. ____(4) In addition, many executives are rumored to be faithful fans. ____(5) Perhaps their interest lies in the advertisement of their products during this prime viewing time. ____(6) Certainly, too, millions of Americans who watch the nighttime soaps break the stereotype of soap-opera watchers. ____(7) For example, during that memorable summer when J. R. Ewing's life was in danger on *Dallas*, many sophisticated adults speculated about the identity of J. R.'s attacker. ____(8) With their intrigue, sophisticated fashions, and melodramatic plots, soap operas are no longer aimed at only one segment of the population.

4. ____(1) Many of the books children enjoy are actually not children's books at all. ____(2) *The Adventures of Huckleberry Finn*, long considered to be a companion book to *The Adventures of Tom Sawyer*, is far more than the adventures of the orphan Huck and his friend Jim on the Mississippi River. ____(3) The book actually exposes the insidious way that Southern society defended slavery as a legal and moral obligation. ____(4) However, young readers too often comprehend only the great adventures described in the book; they rarely understand Mark Twain's attacks upon the institution of slavery. ____(5) Another children's classic, *Gulliver's Travels*, has been made into a cartoon that regularly appears on Saturday morning television. ____(6) The book really provides a biting social and political satire of England in the eighteenth century; however, few children recognize this message. ____(7) Moreover, *Robinson Crusoe*, the tale of a man on a deserted island, imparts religious and economic comments about humankind and our universe. ____(8) Unfortunately, many people read these books only once—when they are young—and fail to appreciate the books' true messages and worth.

5. ____(1) Christmas has become too commercialized within the past two decades. ____(2) First, we begin to anticipate the holiday months before its

arrival. ____(3) Stores now decorate their spaces with elves and reindeer just after Halloween. ____(4) Before Thanksgiving, Santas arrive at department stores, not in sleighs, but in helicopters. ____(5) Television and magazine advertisements with Christmas themes begin at least six to eight weeks before December 25. ____(6) Second, Christmas is celebrated with gifts and material possessions, not family gatherings and religious feeling. ____(7) We are all encouraged to purchase presents for everyone—from Johnny's grade-school teacher to the box boy at the local supermarket. ____(8) Children, for whom the holiday remains a magical time, count their blessings in the number of gifts they receive, not in the messages of peace and good will. ____(9) Retailers, moreover, make sure that we spend plenty of money; early in December, dire predictions of a poor retail year suggest that everyone will suffer economically unless we hurry to spend money during the last few weeks of the year. ____(10) Perhaps a solution to all of this commercialization would be to ban the purchase of presents; instead, only homemade presents would be given, and families would focus on their own happiness together rather than on material blessings.

▼ EXERCISE 7

Each of the following set of sentences forms a unified paragraph. Renumber the sentences in the correct order and label the topic sentence (TS), the primary supports (PS), and the secondary supports (SS).

1. ____   1. The same is true for typhoons and monsoons.

   ____   2. Blowing hot and dry as it sweeps down the side of a mountain, it can quickly wither lush crops and destroy a farmer's dreams.

   ____   3. A cool, light breeze can bring welcome relief from summer's heat and humidity.

   ____   4. Some types of wind are harmful because of their speed and strength.

   ____   5. The wind, an infrequently researched aspect of our environment, is a friend to humanity, but it can also be an enemy.

   ____   6. Hurricanes cause millions of dollars worth of damage each year and sometimes take lives.

_____ 7. One of the signs of approaching autumn is the wind rustling through the leaves high on a tree.

_____ 8. Twisters or tornadoes bring fear to the hearts of Midwesterners.

_____ 9. The foehn is one such wind.

_____ 10. Sailors fear the absence of wind; they know the dangers of being becalmed.

_____ 11. Other winds are hated because they are lifeless; all they carry is hot air.

2. _____ 1. This requires paper, paper, and more paper.

_____ 2. The world is drowning in paper—not people, not pests, but paper.

_____ 3. In school, students make copies of notes, rather than take their own.

_____ 4. The demand for "copies" has outstripped the need for those reprints a thousandfold.

_____ 5. Reports devour paper, too.

_____ 6. Everyone wants a copy of whatever has been deemed important, necessary, useful, or top secret.

_____ 7. Superiors demand reports.

_____ 8. They no longer want to be "kept informed"; they want twenty typed pages of details, statistics, and examples.

_____ 9. In government, the IRS requires triplicates.

_____ 10. In business, memos circulate widely, and each recipient makes a personal copy "for the files."

3. _____ 1. Public opinion surveys seem to indicate that Americans are quickly becoming a semi-literate people.

_____ 2. While that statement may be true, it can quickly be rendered harmless by pointing to the large numbers of periodicals and newspapers published in the United States.

_____ 3. That is an acceptable percentage.

_____ 4. Someone must read them.

_____ 5. Much publicity has been given to statistics that proclaim that almost one-quarter of the population is functionally illiterate—i.e., unable to read a newspaper or comprehend a job application.

_____ 6. Another nail in the coffin of the literate American is the statement that "fewer than 20 percent of Americans read at least three books last year."

_____ 7. Of course, no attention is paid to the flip side of those statistics: 75 percent of Americans can read and write.

4. _____ 1. Finally, there must be jobs.

_____ 2. With an adequate academic background (it does not have to be brilliant or even outstanding), a poor person can step onto the ladder of success.

_____ 3. Self-respect is of primary importance.

_____ 4. Without it, there is no hope, no goal, no purpose.

_____ 5. The cycle of poverty must be broken, and it can be done.

_____ 6. He or she can begin the climb.

_____ 7. A finely honed mind and a willing spirit need a work area.

_____ 8. Without academic skills, a person is doomed to rely on brawn, not brains, and a life of poverty quickly robs the body of its strength.

_____ 9. Education, jobs, and self-respect will enable the poor to cast aside their chains and rise from the bottom of society.

_____ 10. There can be belief in a better future.

_____ 11. They must not be stifled but should be encouraged to create and grow.

_____ 12. Of course, incentive and motivation are useless without the proper tools.

_____ 13. Their creativity and development will benefit all of society, not just the poor.

_____ 14. With it, there is a reason to strive and to seek improvements.

_____ 15. Self-respect provides incentive and motivation.

5. _____ 1. Best of all, the window allowed the soft morning sunlight to shine through; the sunshine matched the pale yellow walls.

_____ 2. A ceramic lamp sat on the desk; its base was a baseball player who was the embodiment of a young Little Leaguer like me—oversized uniform, wide-eyed stare, and a boyish grin.

_____ 3. A double window faced the front lawn and offered a spacious view of full-bodied spruces and spindly white pines.

_____ 4. At first glance, the bedroom I shared as a child with my brother seems too small to hold two growing boys; however, the room suited me fine, and it had the right features.

_____ 5. The bed consisted of four carved posts, two mattresses—one four feet above the other—and a simple three-step ladder that I used to reach the top bunk.

_____ 6. Beneath the window was a three-drawer desk marked with wounds inflicted by my pocket knife.

_____ 7. Then there was the bunk bed, a space-saving monstrosity that occupied a prominent position against the wall across from the desk.

_____ 8. These features created a sanctuary for a young boy.

▼ EXERCISE 8

Choose one of the paragraph topics below. Brainstorm for ideas, and then write a first draft to explore the topic. After you have identified your topic, audience, and purpose, select details that would best support your topic sentence. Finally, compose your paragraph. To check your ability to organize effectively, share your paper with two or three other students in a group. For each paper, identify the supports in the paragraph and discuss their relationships to the topic sentence.

1. a movie you saw recently

2. a nearby recreational spot or amusement park

3. parents and discipline

4. problems of working and going to school simultaneously

5. a problem that needs to be solved in your community or at your school

Conclusions

CONCLUDING SENTENCES

Since each paragraph acts as a complete unit and is self-contained, the last sentence in the paragraph should offer some conclusion to the reader. If the last sentence does not conclude the paragraph, then conceivably the paragraph remains open, and more information could be added. Therefore, paragraphs should have concluding sentences. The concluding sentence can perform one of three functions:

1. It can restate the topic sentence.

2. It can restate the topic sentence and summarize the primary supports.

3. It can offer a logical conclusion based upon information provided in the paragraph. (This type of concluding sentence is often introduced by one of the following words or phrases: *therefore, as a result, as a consequence, thus,* or *consequently.*)

Any one of these methods will work well as a final sentence in a paragraph.

However, students often use another method which does *not* work: a concluding sentence that introduces new material. If you conclude with new information—information that you did not cover in the paragraph and information that you will not have time or space to develop—then you have broken your promise to discuss only one topic in the paragraph. In this situation, you have not completed the paragraph, and the reader is left to wonder what importance the new material might have on the paragraph. Consider the following paragraph, and analyze the concluding sentence.

> Because corporal punishment might leave psychological scars, parents should be very wary about using spanking or slapping as a means of correcting a child's behavior. First, a child often becomes resentful of the parent who administers the punishment. Very often, the child will seek revenge upon the offending parent by withholding affection or by refusing to speak to that parent. Second, a child who is punished physically may become anxious around other adults because he fears that they too will inflict pain if he misbehaves. In this case, a child may become distrustful of all adults and become withdrawn. Certainly, this child will not mature emotionally as he should. Third, a child may believe that inflicting physical pain is an acceptable way of dealing with situations and people he doesn't like. The child might become belligerent towards his peers and turn into a bully who intimidates those who are weaker. *Therefore, parents should consider other means of disciplining a child.*

The concluding sentence in this paragraph tells parents to consider other means of disciplining a child; however, it does not discuss those means. While readers might understand the possible consequences of corporal punishment, they would need more information about different ways to discipline a child. Because this concluding sentence actually offers new information, but no discussion of the information, it is inadequate. However, here are three sentences that could conclude the paragraph:

1. A **restatement** of the topic sentence:

   > Parents should be careful about administering corporal punishment because it may damage the child psychologically.

2. A **summary** of the topic sentence and the primary supports:

   > Because physical punishment can cause a child to grow resentful, anxious, or belligerent, parents should be cautious about administering corporal punishment.

3. A **logical conclusion** of the paragraph:

   > Therefore, parents should consider the consequences of physical punishment before they discipline a child who misbehaves.

▼ EXERCISE 9 | Create each of the three types of concluding sentences for each of the following paragraphs. Identify the audience that would best appreciate each conclusion. Also, check (√) the conclusion you believe is most effective. Be prepared to explain its effectiveness.

1.   Founded in 1910, the organization of Boy Scouts gives valuable benefits to its members. The typical Scout learns lasting values. For example, many former Scouts still remember the Scout's code well: "A Scout is trustworthy, loyal, helpful, friendly, courteous, kind, obedient, cheerful, thrifty, brave, clean, and reverent." Certainly, these are admirable virtues upon which a young man builds character. In addition, the organization provides its members with companionship. Many young boys learn how to deal with others through competition and through united efforts. Finally, a boy learns about the world around him. While tying knots seems to be the staple knowledge of Boy Scouts, many learn about science, the environment, citizenship, and survival.

Restatement: _____

_____ Audience: _____

Summary: _____

_____ Audience: _____

Logical Conclusion: _____

_____ Audience: _____

2.   Although cowboys have long since disappeared from the American West, a new breed of men has taken their place in contemporary America—the truck driver. Like the cowboy, the trucker is always on the move and usually far from home. The typical trucker will cover thousands of miles and cross several states as he delivers goods throughout the country, and he will do this in a week's time. Because his business requires constant motion, a trucker usually drives twelve to fourteen hours a day for ten out of fourteen days. Truckers share another characteristic with cowboys; they are fiercely independent. Many truckers prefer to own their own rigs, select their shipping contracts, and rely upon their own initiative to make a living rather than work for a company. Their independence is easily proven: truckers resist an easy stereotype. Some truckers have little formal education; others have doctorates. Some truckers are from blue-collar working families; others are from white-collar, upper-income families. Look at their trucks also. Even trucks that were identical on the assembly line are not identical by the time their owners equip them.

Restatement: _____

_____ Audience: _____

Summary: _____

_____ Audience: _____

Logical Conclusion: _____

_____ Audience: _____

3.   During the 1920s, many American writers chose to live in Europe for various reasons. First, European countries, particularly France, offered more artistic freedom and a larger intellectual community than the United States did. Regularly enforced in the United States, censorship was rarely in evidence in Europe. In addition, the large colony of expatriates in France offered a congenial intellectual atmosphere to many Americans, such as F. Scott Fitzgerald and Ernest Hemingway. Second, Europe was exciting and inexpensive. For those writers too young to have served in the Great War, Europe was filled with adventure. Writers could easily travel to many countries and experience new cultures. Because the American dollar was strong after World War I, a poor writer who would have lived meagerly in New York or Chicago could live comfortably in France or Spain. In addition, many small literary magazines could be published for much less in Europe than in the United States. Third, European countries allowed more personal liberty than the America of the 1920s. While Americans could not drink alcohol because the Eighteenth Amendment prohibited the sale and consumption of alcoholic beverages, Americans in Paris could enjoy whatever they wanted to drink. The rules of personal conduct, so rigid in the United States, were more relaxed in Europe.

Restatement: _____

_____ Audience: _____

Summary: _____

_____ Audience: _____

Logical Conclusion: _____

_____ Audience: _____

4.   Completed in 1809, Monticello reflects many of Thomas Jefferson's interests. Architecturally, the house is a masterpiece. It is topped with a dome—one of the first American houses to have one—and has skylights. Because Jefferson did not want the view of his lawn spoiled, many of the dependencies—the kitchen, the stables, the ice house, and other sections— were built into the sides of hills and connected to the main house by a series of corridors. Jefferson's inventiveness can easily be seen inside the house. Above the front door hangs a seven-day clock, driven by weights and pulleys, that still keeps time. Dumbwaiters helped carry wine from the cellar to the dining room and saved the servants from climbing many flights of stairs. Finally, the contents of the rooms tell us about the man himself. In his library are over 6,000 books, many in other languages. (Jefferson could read six languages.) Also, bookstands are located in every room of the house so that Jefferson could read during each spare moment.

Restatement: _____

_____ Audience:_____

Summary: _____

_____ Audience:_____

Logical Conclusion: _____

_____ Audience:_____

5.   The country homes of the British aristocracy offer more than retreats from urban living; they display centuries of art and history. Many of the gentry collected paintings and sculpture; aristocrats in past centuries were patrons of the arts. Therefore, the private collections of paintings and sculpture are some of the best in the world. Landscapes by Constable and portraits by Gainsborough grace the halls and drawing rooms of some country homes. In addition, because families lived in the houses for generations, attics and even kitchens and dining rooms contain priceless examples of past centuries. Attic trunks with Victorian clothing and central halls guarded by empty suits of armor give specific examples of the treasures these houses hold.

Restatement: _____

_____ Audience:_____

Summary: _____

_____ Audience:_____

Logical Conclusion: _____

_____ Audience:_____

DRAWING LOGICAL CONCLUSIONS

When writing a final sentence that offers a logical conclusion, you must be sure that the last sentence is based on the facts given in the paragraph. After all, a conclusion is an opinion formed after thought and investigation. As the final, logical result of the reasoning process, a conclusion ends all further reasoning; therefore, the conclusion must pull together all available facts and then state where those facts have led the audience. When it does all that, the conclusion is considered **valid.** The conclusion is **invalid** when it merely offers another fact or when it is not based on the given information. Examine these examples:

1.   Susie has two dogs, a cat, two doves, and a rabbit for pets. When she was only seven years old, she found a sick duck, nursed him back to health, and then released him. Since then, she has doctored snakes, turtles, and hamsters. From the age of twelve, she has spent most of her free time at the racetrack, not in the grandstands, but in the stables, and has befriended the horses and cared for them.

▶ Invalid
Conclusion:

Her dogs are called Zeb and Zack. (This simply provides another fact; it does not offer a result.)

▶ Valid
Conclusion:

Susie likes animals. (Nowhere in the paragraph is that statement made, but it is the logical result of all the information given.)

2. No neurosurgeon has ever seen or touched a mind, yet when certain parts of the human brain are injured or destroyed, certain aspects of the mind are also damaged or annihilated.

▶ Invalid
Conclusion:

Most neurosurgeons are males. (This may or may not be true, but the sex of the doctor has nothing to do with the point of the sentence.)

▶ Valid
Conclusion:

The mind is located within the skull cavity. (That the mind is situated in the brain is the only logical conclusion to be drawn from these facts.)

Therefore, you as the writer must remember to edit your paragraphs and check your concluding sentences carefully. If you want to offer a conclusion, make sure the sentence states a logical result and not just another fact.

▼ EXERCISE 10

Carefully read the following paragraphs and the pair of sentences that follows each. Write *C* next to the sentence that is a valid conclusion based on the evidence given. Write *F* next to the factual statement. Then check (√) the one that would be more appropriate as the last sentence in the paragraph.

1. The movie *Bad Days* uses stock characters: the shy, bumbling bank clerk and the prostitute with a heart of gold. The typical improbable situation develops; he falls in love with her and wants to bring her home to meet his parents. What this movie lacks in plot and character it does not make up for in special effects or action. Both seem to be based on C-grade movies from the 1950s. In addition, *Bad Days* was obviously shot on a studio's back lot, one that had been allowed to fall into disrepair.

    ____ This movie will not win an Oscar for anything.

    ____ The plot is the standard "boy-meets-girl-and-falls-in-love."

2. Within two hours the patient's temperature rose to 104°F and stayed there; nothing brought it down. Body fluids were lost in great quantities and were not replaced because of severe vomiting and diarrhea. Then the patient became lethargic and unconcerned about his illness; he was content to just lie in bed. Finally, he even stopped asking for water.

_____ The patient had a high fever.

_____ The patient required immediate medical care and should have been
rushed to an emergency room.

3.   The nature of the refugee issue has been transformed in very
fundamental ways over four decades. It has grown from a continental to a
global problem, from one that could be kept at a distance to one that may be
very near. The world's refugee population has expanded manyfold. It has
changed from a transient to a semi-static population. Assistance requirements
have multiplied. Any crisis anywhere can now produce refugees everywhere.
The resulting problems now need close and urgent attention.

(from W. R. Smyser, "Refugees: A Never-Ending Story," Foreign Affairs)

_____ There are more refugees today than there were forty years ago, and
they are displaced for a greater variety of reasons.

_____ Americans must be awakened to the dangers inherent in the world-wide
refugee problem.

4.   House hunting is an arduous task. Everyone begins the assignment with a
mental image of the "perfect house." Slowly, parts of that image are gnawed
away by the realities of money, location, availability, and luck. Too often, after
combing the real estate ads and arriving on the doorstep of the fourth open
house for that day, one learns that a bid on the "almost-perfect" house was
accepted fifteen minutes ago.

_____ Cost and neighborhood affect the purchase of a house.

_____ People rarely buy their dream house.

5.   Despite many suggestions to the contrary, few students study in a quiet
atmosphere. Although they may have been told that quiet enhances
concentration and prevents distraction, students seem to feel that quiet is
unnatural and enervating. Consequently, they study in groups, with music
blaring in the background, while munching on popcorn and peanuts.

_____ Many students have poor study habits.

_____ Listening to music distracts a student from studying.

MAKING JUDGMENTS

Closely related to conclusions are judgments. Just as you must review the given
information and decide whether a conclusion is valid, so you must examine facts,
make comparisons and contrasts, and think critically about any stated opinions
when you make a judgment. A **judgment** is an evaluation; it is a decision about
the merits of a given situation.

When you write, you must be careful to use facts, not judgments, to
support your controlling idea. It is very easy to include judgments rather than
facts in your paragraph as secondary supports; therefore, you must read and

reread carefully to ensure that your audience is not being misled by your statements. Analyze the difference between these two statements:

▶ Fact: Hemingway won the Nobel Prize for Literature.

▶ Judgment: Hemingway deserved to win the Nobel Prize.

That Hemingway won the Nobel Prize is a fact—it can be checked. That he was a worthy recipient of the prize is a judgment made after one has evaluated Hemingway's writing and the writings of his contemporaries. The statement that he deserved to win is a judgment. What is the difference between these next two sentences?

▶ Fact: Koko the gorilla was taught to use sign language.

▶ Judgment: Primates have the capacity for meaningful nonverbal communication.

No one denies that Koko was able to manipulate her fingers to form the symbols used in sign language; that is a fact. Whether that finger play represented meaningful nonverbal communication is a judgment, based on a review of this experiment, interviews with Koko's trainer, and an evaluation of the evidence.

▼ EXERCISE 11

Read each pair of sentences below. Write *F* next to the factual statement and *J* next to the judgment.

1. a. ＿＿＿ New York City has more Chinese restaurants per capita than any other American city.

   b. ＿＿＿ Little Lotus in Chinatown is the best Chinese restaurant.

2. a. ＿＿＿ The Sanitation Department has hired 1,000 additional workers.

   b. ＿＿＿ The "Clean Streets" campaign is a failure.

3. a. ＿＿＿ A college education is an absolute necessity in today's society.

   b. ＿＿＿ Less than 25 percent of the population has a college degree.

4. a. ＿＿＿ Teenagers believe that an MBA is a guaranteed ticket to success.

   b. ＿＿＿ Enrollment in graduate business programs has increased by 8 percent in each of the last three years.

5. a. ＿＿＿ Whales are the largest species of mammal still extant.

   b. ＿＿＿ Whaling must be prohibited; it is an abomination.

There are two situations in which judgment statements may be made: (1) your audience may render a judgment concerning the validity of your opinion (in this case, you will probably never know how you rated), or (2) you may present an evaluation of the preceding topic in the final sentence.

▼ EXERCISE 12

Read each of the following paragraphs carefully. Then write *J* next to the judgment statement and *F* next to the factual one, and circle the better concluding sentence.

1.   The coach had three rows of seats, each calculated to hold three persons, and as we were only six, we had, in the phrase of Milton, to "enhabit lax" this exalted abode, and, accordingly, we were for some miles tossed about like a few potatoes in a wheelbarrow. Our knees, elbows, and heads required too much care for their protection to allow us leisure to look out of the windows; but at length the road became smoother, and we became more skillful in the art of balancing ourselves, so as to meet the concussion with less danger of dislocation.

   (from Frances Trollope, *Domestic Manners of the Americans*)

   a._____ The stage coach traveled on rough roads.

   b. ____ The stage coach was an uncomfortable means of transportation.

2.   The cars were very full, and were not able to seat all the passengers. Consequently, according to the usages of American etiquette, the gentlemen vacated the seats in favour of the ladies, who took possession of them in a very ungracious manner as I thought. The gentlemen stood in the passage down the centre. At last all but one had given up their seats, and while stopping at a station another lady entered.

   (from Isabella Lucy Bird, *The Englishwoman in America*)

   a._____ Good manners required a gentleman to relinquish his seat to a lady.

   b. ____ The men of the nineteenth century were more courteous toward and considerate of women than are their twentieth-century counterparts.

3.   On board this steamboat, there were two young gentlemen, with shirt collars reversed as usual, and armed with very big walking sticks; who planted two seats in the middle of the deck, at a distance of four paces apart; took out their tobacco boxes; and sat down opposite each other, to chew. In less than a quarter of an hour's time, these hopeful youths had shed about them on the clean boards, a copious shower of yellow rain; clearing, by that means, a kind of magic circle, within whose limits no intruder dared to come, and which they never failed to refresh and re-refresh before a spot was dry. This being before breakfast, rather disposed me, I confess, to nausea; but looking attentively at one of the expectorators, I plainly saw that he was young in chewing, and felt inwardly uneasy, himself. A glow of delight came over me at this discovery; and as I marked his face turned paler and paler, and saw the ball of tobacco in his left cheek quiver with his suppressed agony, while yet he spat, and chewed,

and spat again, in emulation of his older friend, I could have fallen on his neck and implored him to go on for hours.

(from Charles Dickens, *American Notes and Pictures From Italy*)

a._____ Tobacco chewing is an offensive and vulgar habit.

b. ____ One of the tobacco chewers was inexperienced at chewing.

4.   Lawyers are so numerous in all our populous towns, that I am surprised they never thought before of establishing themselves here: they are plants that will grow in any soil that is cultivated by the hands of others; and when once they have taken root they will extinguish every other vegetable that grows around them. The fortunes they daily acquire in every province, from the misfortunes of their fellow-citizens, are surprising! The most ignorant, the most bungling member of that profession, will, if placed in the most obscure part of the country, promote litigiousness, and amass more wealth without labour, than the most opulent farmer, with all his toils. They have so dexterously interwoven their doctrines and quirks with the laws of the land, or rather they are become so necessary an evil in our present constitutions, that it seems unavoidable and past all remedy. What a pity that our forefathers, who happily extinguished so many fatal customs, and expunged from their new government so many errors and abuses, both religious and civil, did not also prevent the introduction of a set of men so dangerous! In some provinces, where every inhabitant is constantly employed in tilling and cultivating the earth, they are the only members of society who have any knowledge; let these provinces attest what iniquitous use they have made of that knowledge.

(from J. Hector St. John, *Letters from an American Farmer*)

a._____ Men could live together in harmony if there were no lawyers.

b. ____ Lawyers are educated people.

5.   Singular as it may appear to you, there are but two medical professors on the island [of Nantucket]; for of what service can a physic be in a primitive society, where the excesses of inebriation are so rare? What need of galenical medicines, where fevers, and stomachs loaded by the loss of the digestive powers, are so few? Temperance, the calm of passions, frugality, and continual exercise, keep them healthy, and preserve unimpaired that constitution which they have received from parents as healthy as themselves; who in the unpolluted embraces of the earliest and chastest love, conveyed to them the soundest bodily frame which nature could give. But as no habitable part of this globe is exempt from some diseases, proceeding either from climate or modes of living; here they are sometimes subject to consumptions and to fevers. Since the foundation of that town no epidemical distempers have appeared, which at times cause such depopulations in other countries; many of them are extremely well acquainted with the Indian methods of curing simple diseases, and practice them with success. You will hardly find anywhere a community, composed of the same number of individuals, possessing such uninterrupted health, and exhibiting so many green old men, who show their advanced age by the maturity of their wisdom, rather than by the wrinkles of their faces; and this is indeed one of the principal blessings of the island, which richly

compensates their want of the richer soils of the south; where iliac complaints and bilious fevers grow by the side of the sugar cane, the ambrosial ananas, etc. The situation of this island, the purity of the air, the nature of their marine occupation, their virtue and moderation, are the causes of that vigour and health which they possess.

(from J. Hector St. John, *Letters from an American Farmer*)

a._____ Only two doctors practiced medicine on Nantucket Island during the late eighteenth century.

b. _____ Nantucket was a healthy place to live during the 1700s.

▼ Writing Strategy: CLASSIFICATION

Classification is an everyday activity. Consider the way that most individuals shop for groceries: first, they determine their needs and then group items under such categories as meats, vegetables, and household supplies. They may even arrange their shopping lists to reflect the design of their favorite supermarket. Without this classification of items, shoppers could wander down aisles for hours as they determine what to purchase and where to find each item. Classification requires that items be separated into broad categories; then, specific items are assigned, according to their inherent characteristics, to these broad categories. In brainstorming sessions, you begin to classify ideas and details into categories that will help you develop a paragraph. You might also divide details into groups according to their connections with the topic sentence. Hence, you classify items that support a topic sentence and items that explain the main supports in more detail.

Classification requires that your categories do not overlap. For example, if you classify students by their majors, then you should not include a category identifying their political preferences. In addition, because a classification seeks to divide items into meaningful groups, try to avoid stereotypes and generalizations. In a survey of students' political preferences at your school, for instance, it would be inappropriate to suggest that all students share the same political preferences.

As you read the selections that follow, consider the ways in which the writer uses classification. For example, in "Three New Yorks," E. B. White identifies three different views of the same city; each view is seen by a different group of people, such as suburban commuters or city dwellers, who understand the city only in terms of their immediate relationship to it.

▶ Three New Yorks
E. B. WHITE

A long-time essayist and contributor to The New Yorker *magazine, E. B. White explains how three groups of people view New York.*

There are roughly three New Yorks. There is, first, the New York of the man or woman who was born here, who takes the city for granted and accepts its size and its turbulence as natural and inevitable. Second, there is the New York of the commuter—the city that is devoured by locusts each day and spat out each night. Third, there is the New York of the person who was born somewhere else and came to New York in quest of something. Of these three trembling cities the greatest is the last—the city of final destination, the city that is a goal. It is this third city that accounts for New York's high-strung disposition, its poetical deportment, its dedication to the arts, and its incomparable achievements. Commuters give the city its tidal restlessness, natives give it solidity and continuity, but the settlers give it passion. And whether it is a farmer arriving from Italy to set up a small grocery store in a slum, or a young girl arriving from a small town in Mississippi to escape the indignity of being observed by her neighbors, or a boy arriving from the Corn Belt with a manuscript in his suitcase and a pain in his heart, it makes no difference: each embraces New York with the intense excitement of first love, each absorbs New York with the fresh eyes of an adventurer, each generates heat and light to dwarf the Consolidated Edison Company.

▶ QUESTIONS
1. The topic sentence is the first sentence. Does the author provide sufficient support for it? Explain.

2. The author structures this paragraph by using three groups of elements. Locate the groups and explain his organization.

3. What is the tone of the paragraph?

▶ Whales

RACHEL CARSON

A noted naturalist, Rachel Carson classifies the different types of whales.

Eventually the whales, as though to divide the sea's food resources among them, became separated into three groups: the plankton-eaters, the fish-eaters, and the squid-eaters. The plankton-eating whales can exist only where there are dense masses of small shrimp or copepods to supply their enormous food requirements. This limits them, except for scattered areas, to arctic and antarctic waters and the high temperate latitudes. Fish-eating whales may find food over a somewhat wider range of ocean, but they are restricted to places where there are enormous populations of schooling fish. The blue water of the tropics and of the open ocean basins offers little to either of these groups. But that immense, square-headed, formidably toothed whale known as the cachalot or sperm whale discovered long ago what men have known for only a short time—that hundreds of fathoms below the almost untenanted surface waters of these regions there is an abundant animal life. The sperm whale has taken these deep waters for his hunting grounds; his quarry is the deep-water population of squids, including the giant squid Architeuthis, which lives pelagically at depths of 1500 feet or more. The head of the sperm whale is often marked with long stripes, which consist of a great number of circular scars made by the suckers of the squid. From this evidence we can imagine the battles that go on, in the darkness of the deep water, between these two huge creatures—the sperm whale with its 70-ton bulk, the squid with a body as long as 30 feet, and writhing, grasping arms extending the total length of the animal to perhaps 50 feet.

▶ QUESTIONS

1. What is the basis for Carson's classification of whales?

2. Which of the three types of whales suffers most for its food? Give specific examples of the struggle.

3. Define the following words: *untenanted, writhing, temperate,* and *formidably.*

4. Evaluate the concluding sentence. Would you change it or add another? If so, why?

Friends, Good Friends—and Such Good Friends
JUDITH VIORST

Contemporary poet, essayist, and newspaper columnist, Judith Viorst discusses the different types of friends women have.

1 Women are friends, I once would have said, when they totally love and support and trust each other, and bare to each other the secrets of their souls, and run—no questions asked—to help each other, and tell harsh truths to each other (no, you can't wear that dress unless you lose ten pounds first) when harsh truths must be told.

2 Women are friends, I once would have said, when they share the same affection for Ingmar Bergman, plus train rides, cats, warm rain, charades, Camus, and hate with equal ardor Newark and Brussels sprouts and Lawrence Welk and camping.

3 In other words, I once would have said that a friend is a friend all the way, but now I believe that's a narrow point of view. For the friendships I have and the friendships I see are conducted at many levels of intensity, serve many different functions, meet different needs and range from those as all-the-way as the friendship of soul sister mentioned above to that of the most nonchalant and casual playmates.

4 Consider these varieties of friendship:

5 1. Convenience friends. These are the women with whom, if our paths weren't crossing all the time, we'd have no particular reason to be friends;

a next-door neighbor, a woman in our car pool, the mother of one of our children's closest friends or maybe some mommy with whom we serve juice and cookies each week at the Glenwood Co-op Nursery.

6   Convenience friends are convenient indeed. They'll lend us their cups and silverware for a party. They'll drive our kids to soccer when we're sick. They'll take us to pick up our car when we need a lift to the garage. They'll even take our cats when we go on vacation. As we will for them.

7   But we don't, with convenience friends, ever come too close or tell too much; we maintain our public face and emotional distance. "Which means," says Elaine, "that I'll talk about being overweight but not about being depressed. Which means I'll admit to being mad but not blind with rage. Which means I might say that we're pinched this month but never that I'm worried sick over money."

8   But which doesn't mean that there isn't sufficient value to be found in these friendships of mutual aid, in convenience friends.

9   2. Special-interest friends. These friendships aren't intimate, and they needn't involve kids or silverware or cats. Their value lies in some interest jointly shared. And so we may have an office friend or a yoga friend or a tennis friend or a friend from the Women's Democratic Club.

10   "I've got one woman friend," say Joyce, "who likes, as I do, to take psychology courses. Which makes it nice for me—and nice for her. It's fun to go with someone you know and it's fun to discuss what you've learned, driving back from the classes." And for the most part, she says, that's all they discuss.

11   "I'd say that what we're doing is *doing* together, not being together," Susanne says of her Tuesday-doubles friends. "It's mainly a tennis relationship, but we play together well. And I guess we all need to have a couple of playmates."

12   I agree.

13   *My* playmate is a shopping friend, a woman of marvelous taste, a woman who knows exactly *where* to buy *what*, and furthermore is a woman who always knows beyond a doubt what one ought to be buying. I don't have the time to keep up with what's new in eyeshadow, hemlines and shoes and whether the smock look is in or finished already. But since (oh shame!) I care a lot about eyeshadow, hemlines and shoes, and since I don't *want* to wear smocks if the smock look is finished, I'm very glad to have a shopping friend.

14   3. Historical friends. We all have a friend who knew us when . . . maybe way back in Miss Meltzer's second grade, when our dad was out of work for seven months, when our brother Allie got in that fight where they had to call the police, when our sister married the endodontist from Yonkers and when, the morning after we lost our virginity, she was the first, the only friend we told.

15   The years have gone by and we've gone separate ways and we've little in common now, but we're still an intimate part of each other's past. And so whenever we go to Detroit we always go to visit this friend of our girlhood. Who knows how we looked before our teeth were straightened. Who knows how we talked before our teeth were straightened. Who knows how we talked before our voice got unBrooklyned. Who knows what we ate before we learned about artichokes. And who, by her presence, puts us in touch with an earlier part of ourself, a part of ourself it's important never to lose.

16   "What this friend means to me and what I mean to her," says Grace, "is having a sister without sibling rivalry. We know the texture of each other's lives. She remembers my grandmother's cabbage soup. I remember the way her uncle played the piano. There's simply no other friend who remembers those things."

17   4. Crossroads friends. Like historical friends, our crossroads friends are important for *what was*—for the friendship we shared at a crucial, now past, time of life. A time, perhaps, when we roomed in college together; or worked as eager young singles in the Big City together; or went together, as my friend Elizabeth and I did through pregnancy, birth and that scary first year of new motherhood.

18   Crossroads friends forge powerful links, links strong enough to endure with not much more contact than once-a-year letters at Christmas. And out of respect for those crossroads years, for those dramas and dreams we once shared, we will always be friends.

19   5. Cross-generational friends. Historical friends and crossroads friends seem to maintain a special kind of intimacy—dormant but always ready to revived—and though we may rarely meet, whenever we do connect, it's personal and intense. Another kind of intimacy exists in the friendships that form across generations in what one woman calls her daughter-mother and her mother-daughter relationships.

20   Evelyn's friend is her mother's age—"but I share so much more than I ever could with my mother"—a woman she talks to of music, of books and of life. "What I get from her is the benefit of her experience. What she gets—and enjoys—from me is a youthful perspective. It's a pleasure for both of us."

21   I have in my own life a precious friend, a woman of 65 who has lived very hard, who is wise, who listens well; who has been where I am and can help me understand it; and who represents not only an ultimate ideal mother to me but also the person I'd like to be when I grow up.

22   In our daughter role we tend to do more than our share of self-revelation; in our mother role we tend to receive what's revealed. It's another kind of pleasure—playing wise mother to a questing younger person. It's another very lovely kind of friendship.

23   6. Part-of-a-couple friends. Some of the women we call our friends we never see alone—we see them as part of a couple at couples' parties. And though we share interests in many things and respect each other's view, we aren't moved to deepen the relationship. Whatever the reason, a lack of time or—and this is more likely—a lack of chemistry, our friendship remains in the context of group. But the fact that our feeling on seeing each other is always, "I'm so glad she's here" and the fact that we spend half the evening talking together says that this too, in its own way, counts as a friendship.

24   (Other part-of-a-couple friends are the friends that came with the marriage, and some of these are friends we could live without. But sometimes, alas, she married our husband's best friend; and sometimes, alas, she *is* our husband's best friend. And so we find ourself dealing with her, somewhat against our will, in a spirit of what I'll call *reluctant* friendship.)

25   7. Men who are friends. I wanted to write just of women friends, but the women I've talked to won't let me—they say I must mention man-woman friendships too. For these friendships can be just as close and as

dear as those that we form with women. Listen to Lucy's description of one such friendship:

26   "We've found we have things to talk about that are different from what he talks about with my husband and different from what I talk about with his wife. So sometimes we call on the phone or meet for lunch. There are similar intellectual interests—we always pass on to each other the books that we love—but there's also something tender and caring too."

27   In a couple of crises, Lucy says, "he offered himself, for talking and for helping. And when someone died in his family he wanted me there. The sexual, flirty part of our friendship is very small, but *some*—just enough to make it fun and different." She thinks—and I agree—that the sexual part, though small is always *some*, is always there when a man and a woman are friends.

28   It's only in the past few years that I've made friends with men, in the sense of a friendship that's *mine*, not just part of two couples. And achieving with them the ease and trust I've found with women friends has value indeed. Under the dryer at home last week, putting on mascara and rouge, I comfortably sat and talked with a fellow named Peter. Peter, I finally decided, could handle the shock of me minus mascara under the dryer. Because we care for each other. Because we're friends.

29   8. There are medium friends, and pretty good friends, and very good friends indeed, and these friendships are defined by their level of intimacy. And what we'll reveal at each of these levels of intimacy is calibrated with care. We might tell a medium friend, for example, that yesterday we had a fight with our husband. And we might tell a pretty good friend that this fight with our husband made us so mad that we slept on the couch. And we might tell a very good friend that the reason we got so mad in that fight the we slept on the couch had something to do with that girl who works in his office. But it's only to our very best friends that we're willing to tell all, to tell what's going on with that girl in his office.

30   The best of friends, I still believe, totally love and support and trust each other, and bare to each other the secrets of their souls, and run—no questions asked—to help each other, and tell harsh truths to each other when they must be told.

31   But we needn't agree about everything (only 12-year-old girl friends agree about *everything*) to tolerate each other's point of view. To accept without judgment. To give and to take without ever keeping score. And to *be* there, as I am for them and as they are for me, to comfort our sorrows, to celebrate our joys.

▶ QUESTIONS 1. What is Viorst's thesis? Where is it stated?

2. Why does Viorst include comments from other women? Do these comments strengthen or hinder her classifications?

3. Describe the difference between historical friends and crossroads friends.

4. Is Viorst's classificatton sound? Does she combine some groups? Why would this combination be effective?

▶ # Students and Their Shoes
MOBEEN SAEED

In this essay, Mobeen Saeed distinguishes students on the basis of their footwear.

1   The types of shoes individuals wear can provide insights into their personalities. The students here can be divided into three categories based on their foot gear. The first group, a specialized minority, is the sneaker-wearers. The largest group is the penny-loafers or, in other words, the casual-shoe wearers. The last and smallest group is the dress-shoe wearers.

2   The "sneakers" are more commonly known as the athletes. Most of these students attend college on athletic scholarships. They can usually be seen wearing jogging pants. They almost always look as if they are prepared to work out for hours on end. This specialized group's home-away-from-home is the gym. There, each member prepares for an upcoming game or competition. All the "sneakers" must stay in shape; therefore, they are health-conscious eaters. To satisfy their appetites, the "sneakers" go to Samson Cafeteria where they can choose from a variety of salads and vegetable dishes. The "sneakers" are a small, but visible, group on campus.

3   The "penny-loafers" are the majority of students. These are the people who come to the five-hundred acre campus in comfortable walk-

ing shoes. This group is fundamentally so diverse that its shoe apparel is one of the few things its members have in common. The "penny-loafers" can be found in every corner of the campus, from the library to the lounge. A few wear jeans and t-shirts. Some look like they dressed themselves while sleepwalking, while others make an effort to adorn themselves. The "penny-loafers" also differ in their food preferences. Many don't have time for a leisurely lunch, so they go to the Center to grab something. Others go to the Terrace to enjoy a quiet, relaxed meal. "Penny-loafers" seem to be everywhere on campus.

4   The last category is the "dress-shoes." These students stand out in a crowd. Male "dress-shoes" come to school in Italian leather shoes, cuffed shirt, and tie. Female "dress-shoes" are adorned with jewelry, silk blouses and two-inch heels. Each "dress-shoe" has a select group of friends; they do not associate with "sneakers" or "penny-loafers." These students will rarely be found in a cafeteria. They almost always go off campus to eat. Another name for these students is "preppie."

5   Few outsiders realize that college students can be classified according to their footwear. Although students can be "sneakers," "penny-loafers," or "dress-shoes," they are all students, working hard to earn their degrees and graduate.

▶ QUESTIONS

1. What is the author's main idea? Where is it located?

2. How does she support her point of view? What connections does she make between students and their shoes?

3. Are her categories all-inclusive? Can you add anything to them?

▼ PARAGRAPH
ASSIGNMENTS

1. As E. B. White does, classify the ways people might view your city or town. Present this information to someone who is moving into the area so that she or he can understand the variety your city has to offer.

2. Before financial speculators commit themselves to a project, they demand market research to prove the profitability of the investment. Therefore, classify shoppers at a local mall to show your financial backers that your proposal, a more up-scale mall, is needed.

3. Whales can be typed by the foods they eat. Can people? Observe students in the cafeteria; notice what, how much, and how often they eat. Then write about your observations. Can you create categories of student eaters? Regard this assignment as a report to the food service manager, who is considering changing the cafeteria's menu and ambience.

▼ WRITING TIPS

Try visualizing your writing. See in your mind's eye your main proposals and their inter-relationships. Use any method—mapping, outlining, creating a tree—that suits you and your style. Make sure that your major concepts are adequately supported and that there are enough details to explain your point of view thoroughly.

Carefully edit your paragraph for fragments. Read each item that has been punctuated as a sentence to determine whether or not it is a complete thought. (For more information on fragments, see Part II, Chapter 4.)

▼ Organization Checklist

1. Have you listed separate categories in primary support sentences?

   _____

   _____

2. What specific supports have you given for each category?

   _____

   _____

   _____

   _____

3. What type of concluding sentence did you use?

   _____

   _____

   _____

   _____

4. Did you try to draw any logical conclusions? If so, are they valid?

   _____

   _____

   _____

   _____

5. Did you make any judgments? If so, did you support them sufficiently by the information given?

   _____

   _____

   _____

   _____

▼ Classification Checklist

1. What is the basis for your classification?

     _____

     _____

     _____

     _____

     _____

2. Is the classification consistent?

     _____

     _____

     _____

     _____

     _____

3. Did you divide the topic into distinct categories? Do any
    categories overlap?

     _____

     _____

     _____

     _____

     _____

4. Does the classification include stereotypes? Can you omit
    these?

     _____

     _____

     _____

     _____

5

Revising

▶ **OBJECTIVES**

1. To revise a paragraph effectively.

2. To edit a paragraph effectively.

3. To proofread a paragraph effectively.

4. To explore composing through illustration by example.

▶ **PREVIEW**

When you revise, you re-examine the purpose, audience, topic sentence, and organization in your paragraph. When you edit, you reread your paragraph to polish your sentences for a final draft of the paragraph. When you proofread, you carefully review the final draft to correct minor errors.

Throughout the composing process, writers constantly revise their ideas, tone, purpose, and organization. Through revision, they explore ideas, discover insights, and gain more control over their paragraphs. Revision includes three major stages: revising for content and structure, editing sentences, and proofreading the final draft. This chapter presents many strategies you can use to revise, edit, and proofread your work.

Revision Strategies

Too often, writers consider the process of writing completed once they have produced a first draft of a paragraph; they do not take the time to analyze what they have written or how they have stated ideas. If they do revise, then they tend to look only for obvious grammatical and mechanical errors; they do not examine the content and the organization of the paper. However, by revising, writers can develop a paragraph more fully and logically and can make it more effective.

Most professional writers admit that all writing is actually rewriting. In other words, revision is the key to effective writing, writing that both communicates the ideas the author wishes to state and receives the response the writer desires from an audience. To accomplish these goals, you must revise, or re-see, your paper. Revision focuses on a paper's content and structure. At this stage, do not worry about grammar, punctuation, or word choice. You can check these items later when you edit.

Revision can take many forms. Your choice of a revision strategy is determined by your own writing process. Below are several different revision strategies. Practice each one to learn its benefits.

1. You can produce three or four drafts of a paper, each with a different goal, before the paper is completed. (See "The Writing Process: An Overview" in Chapter 1 in Part I for information on stages of drafts.)

2. You can outline your paper by using a traditional outline, map, or diagram. This method will point to problems in your development of ideas.

3. You can gloss the entire paper. In this revision strategy, you write a one- or two-word summary beside each idea in your paper. This method quickly identifies any problems with unity and development. In addition, use the following questions to assist in your analysis of your paragraph or longer paper.

    a. What is your main point? Where is it located?

    b. What develops or supports this main idea? Why or why not is this development effective? What information needs to be included or omitted?

    c. How are supports organized? What makes this organization effective for your audience?

    d. What are the two best features of the paper?

    e. What needs to be changed to make this piece more effective?

4. You can also choose to analyze your first or second draft for specific weaknesses in organization, details, and transitions. In each case, because there are too many areas to check and analyze at one time, you should revise in stages. The following checklist will guide you in this revision strategy.

    I. *Purpose* (See "Identifying Audience and Purpose" in Chapter 2 in Part I.)

        A. What is your purpose in writing? Do you wish to explain, narrate, describe, or persuade?

        B. How is your purpose clearly evident to your readers?

        C. What identifies the purpose in your paragraph?

        D. How does the entire paragraph support your purpose?

    II. *Audience*

        A. Who is your intended audience?

        B. What are some characteristics of this audience?

        C. What in the paragraph identifies your audience?

        D. How do you want your audience to respond to the paragraph? What in the paragraph will lead the audience to this response?

    III. *Topic Sentence* (See Chapter 3 in Part I.)

        A. Does the paragraph have a topic sentence? Where is it?

        B. How does the topic sentence predict, control, and obligate?

        C. Does the topic sentence have a controlling idea?

        D. What makes the controlling idea specific? Does it avoid vague words?

IV. *Organization* (See Chapter 4 in Part I.)

   A. How is the paragraph organized? Does this organization support your purpose?

   B. Does the paragraph have primary support sentences? Do the primary support sentences directly develop the topic sentence?

   C. Are the primary support sentences arranged in the most effective order? Should they be arranged in another manner?

   D. Did you choose primary support sentences that will best address your audience's needs and knowledge? Do these primary support sentences represent the best examples, descriptions, or arguments to develop the topic sentence? Or can you think of other supports now?

   E. Does the paragraph contain secondary support sentences? Do these secondary support sentences provide additional information about the primary support sentences? Are the secondary support sentences specific?

   F. Do these secondary support sentences represent the best examples and explanations possible for the primary support sentences? If they do not, then can you now think of more effective ones?

V. *Transitions* (See "Transitional Words and Expressions" in Chapter 6 in Part I.)

   A. What are the transitions between sentences and ideas?

   B. What makes these transitions appropriate? Do they represent the types of relationships you wish to stress?

   C. Can the reader easily follow the ideas presented in the paragraph?

▼ EXERCISE 1

Russell Baker, a Pulitzer Prize winner in journalism, wrote the following essay. You should recognize the story as an old favorite. However, Baker has taken some liberties with the language of the original story; he has rewritten the story for a contemporary audience. Identify the contemporary language and types of characters Baker has created. After you have finished reading the story, create a different purpose in telling the story, and rewrite it to address a different audience. State your audience and purpose; also, identify the language you will use to reach this audience. (You might consider rewriting the piece for an audience of business executives, college professors, teenagers, advertising executives, or computer specialists, or you might consider creating your own audience.) This exercise will help you identify and address specific audiences by altering the details you present and the level of language you use.

Little Red Riding Hood Revisited

In an effort to make the classics accessible to contemporary readers, I am translating them into the modern American language. Here is the translation of "Little Red Riding Hood":

Once upon a point in time, a small person named Little Red Riding Hood initiated plans for the preparation, delivery and transportation of foodstuffs to her grandmother, a senior citizen residing at a place of residence in a forest of indeterminate dimension.

In the process of implementing this program, her incursion into the forest was in mid-transportation process when it attained interface with an alleged perpetrator. This individual, a wolf, made inquiry as to the whereabouts of Little Red Riding Hood's goal as well as inferring that he was desirous of ascertaining the contents of Little Red Riding Hood's foodstuffs basket, and all that.

"It would be inappropriate to lie to me," the wolf said, displaying his huge jaw capability. Sensing that he was a mass of repressed hostility intertwined with acute alienation, she indicated.

"I see you indicating," the wolf said, "but what I don't see is whatever it is you're indicating at, you dig?"

Little Red Riding Hood indicated more fully, making one thing perfectly clear—to wit, that it was to her grandmother's residence and with a consignment of foodstuffs that her mission consisted of taking her to and with.

At this point in time the wolf moderated his rhetoric and proceeded to grandmother's residence. The elderly person was then subjected to the disadvantages of total consumption and transferred to residence in the perpetrator's stomach.

"That will raise the old woman's consciousness," the wolf said to himself. He was not a bad wolf, but only a victim of an oppressive society, a society that not only denied wolves' rights, but actually boasted of its capacity for keeping the wolf from the door. An interior malaise made itself manifest inside the wolf.

"Is that the national malaise I sense within my digestive tract?" wondered the wolf. "Or is it the old person seeking to retaliate for her consumption by telling wolf jokes to my duodenum?" It was time to make a judgment. The time was now, the hour had struck, the body lupine cried out for decision. The wolf was up to the challenge. He took two stomach powders right away and got into bed.

The wolf had adopted the abdominal-distress recovery posture when Little Red Riding Hood achieved his presence.

"Grandmother," she said, "your ocular implements are of an extraordinary order of magnitude."

"The purpose of this enlarged viewing capability," said the wolf, "is to enable your image to register a more precise impression upon my sight systems."

"In reference to your ears," said Little Red Riding Hood, "it is noted with the deepest respect that far from being underprivileged, their elongation and enlargement appear to qualify you for unparalleled distinction."

"I hear you loud and clear, kid," said the wolf, "but what about these new choppers?"

"If it is not inappropriate," said Little Red Riding Hood, "it might be observed that with your new miracle masticating products you may even be able to chew taffy again."

This observation was followed by the adoption of an aggressive posture on the part of the wolf and the assertion that it was also possible for him, due to the high efficiency ratio of his jaw, to consume little persons, plus, as he stated, his firm determination to do so at once without delay and with all due process and propriety, notwithstanding the fact that the ingestion of one entire grandmother had already provided twice his daily recommended cholesterol intake.

There ensued flight by Little Red Riding Hood accompanied by pursuit in respect to the wolf and a subsequent intervention on the part of a third party, heretofore unnoted in the record.

Due to the firmness of the intervention, the wolf's stomach underwent ax-assisted aperture with the result that Red Riding Hood's grandmother was enabled to be removed with only minor discomfort.

The wolf's indigestion was immediately alleviated with such effectiveness that he signed a contract with the intervening third party to perform with grandmother in a television commercial demonstrating the swiftness of this dramatic relief for stomach discontent.

"I'm going to be on television," cried grandmother.

And they all joined her happily in crying, "What a phenomena!"

▼ EXERCISE 2

Use the questions in the revision checklist to analyze the following student paragraph. At what points should there be revision? Make specific suggestions about the types of revision the writer should make. Compare your answers to those of other students. Finally, revise the paragraph yourself.

Some people who enjoy skiing go to extremes and buy all kinds of expensive equipment to make themselves look professional. The skier starts with buying an expensive pair of skis, bindings, boots, and poles. He buys Rossignol skis with the best pair of Marker bindings. Next, the skier purchases Scott poles and Nordica rear-entry boots making sure that the entire package is color coordinated. This package runs anywhere from six hundred to seven hundred dollars. Furthermore, his looks are taken too seriously. The person purchases a Rossignol hat, Smith double-lens goggles, a Roffe powder jacket with matching Roffe stretch pants, and the appropriate color of Rossignol gloves. Also, the skier must buy a slalom ski sweater which has padded shoulders and elbows. His entire wardrobe totals approximately six hundred dollars. If he were not so serious about skiing, he would wear blue jeans, any winter coat, and rent skis, boots, and poles.

▼ EXERCISE 3

Choose a paragraph of your own to revise. With the assistance of other students and the revision checklist, decide what revisions would make the paragraph more effective. List the necessary revisions, and then revise the paragraph.

Editing Strategies

In editing a paragraph, you must concentrate upon the individual sentences to ensure that they are concise, effective, and correct. Like revision, editing can best be accomplished in stages. Begin by reading the paragraph aloud. Often this simple act of reading aloud will alert you to potential problems. If some sentences are not easily understood when the paragraph is read aloud, then you will know that you must edit those particular sentences. The following are several stages by which you can easily edit a paper. Notice that in editing, you should focus on meaning before you focus on correctness.

I. *Clarity*

   A. Do sentences mean what they say? Or are they ambiguous?

   B. Have you used the correct words to describe your meaning? Check unfamiliar words in the dictionary.

II. *Coherence* (See Chapter 6 in Part I.)

   A. Do you use pronouns to achieve coherence? Are any pronouns ambiguous in their reference?

B. Do you use synonyms? Are the synonyms accurate?

C. Do you use limited repetition to achieve coherence?

D. Do you use sentence combining to achieve coherence?

III. *Diction* (See Chapter 7 in Part I.)

A. Do you avoid vague words and use specific ones instead?

B. Do you avoid slang, jargon, and regional expressions?

C. Do you use clichés? If so, can you rephrase?

D. Do you create a specific, identifiable tone through word choice?

E. Are key terms clearly defined? Is this tone appropriate for your intended audience?

IV. *Style* (See Chapter 8 in Part I.)

A. Are sentences wordy?

B. Do you use active voice and descriptive verbs?

C. Do you subordinate ideas effectively?

D. Are sentences varied in structure? Or are they all the same type?

V. *Correctness*

A. Are there any fragments, run-ons, or comma splices? (See Chapters 4, 5, and 6 in Part II.)

B. Do subjects and verbs agree in number? (See Chapter 7 in Part II.)

C. Are there any unnecessary shifts in verb tense? (See Chapters 1 and 2 in Part II.)

D. Are there any unnecessary shifts in point of view?

E. Are your pronouns correct in case, number, and gender? (See Chapter 8 in Part II.)

F. Have you checked marks of punctuation? Are commas, semicolons, colons, and other marks of punctuation used correctly? (See Chapters 9, 10, 11, and 12 in Part II.)

G. Are words properly spelled? (See any good dictionary or Chapter 13 in Part II.)

▼ EXERCISE 4

Edit the following two student paragraphs for sentence problems. Use the editing checklist as a guide. Compare your responses with those of other students. Did you identify the same problems? Did you make the same alterations? With your classmates, discuss which changes are the most effective.

1.   Having lived my entire life in a house

located at the western part of Maryland, I adapted

to the weather and the lifestyle of the residents. However, when I graduated from high school, I decided to spend my summer with friends working at Ocean City. For the first time I was living on my own in an apartment without my parents, older brothers, and sisters. So, spending a summer working at Ocean City caused my lifestyle and responsibilities to change. Going from a dependent life to an independent one at age eighteen caused my lifestyle to change. First, I went from going to school and working part-time in a small bakery in the mall to a full-time waitress at Lombardi's Italian Restaurant. Now, I was working from five in the afternoon until two in the morning everyday or from twelve in the afternoon to ten at night. Also, one would think that an Italian restaurant at the ocean would not be busy, however, this was not the case. Furthermore, I started to enjoy lying on the beach in the sun as much as I like skiing down a mountain. Another part of my lifestyle freedom affected. First of all, I was able to come and go as I pleased since I did not have my parents around to watch over me. Since I did not have a curfew I arrived at my apartment anywhere from one o'clock A.M. to seven o'clock A.M. Also, being on my own enabled me to invite friends over anytime I wanted for example if I had the night off I would call up some people to come over and have a party. Along with these freedoms I could dress anyway I wanted without my parents, brothers, or sisters telling me to change. My living conditions were affected by my move to the ocean. I went from my two-bed, two-closet bedroom to sharing a two bed, two closet bedroom with three girls. Having no parents to pick up after me, I realised it would not get done unless I did it. Hence I learned how to do laundry, clean the bathroom, and vacuum however these chores did not get done as often as I would have liked them to because of working late, partying late, and being too tired. I also had to learn how to cook. A summer away from parents and pressures gave me a chance to see how I was going to handle moving away to college. I believe without this summer at the beach I would have had a hard time adjusting to college life.

2. San Diego California and Rockville, Maryland are two cities that are separated by many miles and differ in several ways. One difference between these two cities is their variety of seasons. Summer and Fall are the only two seasons a year San Diego really has. The summers last through early March to late November with the temperature fluctuating between 80 degrees and 101 degrees fahrenheit. The Fall season lasts from early December to late February with large amounts of rainfall. During this dreary season, the temperature does not reach below 30 degrees. However, Rockville has four distinct seasons: Spring, Summer, Winter, and Fall. Spring, the most beautiful season of all, last from March to late May. During the summer season, which lasts from

June to August, the humidity ranges from 70-80%.
The Fall season lasts from late August to late
November, with pleasantly cool winds. Winter, the
snow-filled season, is cold but gratifying. In addition the distance traveled for entertainment is
another difference. In San Diego, the distance to
and from entertainment is much less that that of
Rockville. LaJolla Shores Beach located twenty
minutes away from downtown San Diego.
McDonalds, the favorite hangout of high school
students, is five minutes away from Mt. Carmel
High School, which I attended, also the worldwide
known San Diego Zoo is only an half hour away
from the vacinity of Mt. Carmel High. On the other
hand, Rockville is three hours away from Ocean
City beach. The regular high school hangout,
McDonalds, is fifteen minutes from Magruder High
School, and at times it seems like forever to get
there. Furthermore, the National Zoo is an hour
and a half away, a considerable distance to drive.
Besides the seasons and distances, the attitudes of
people differ immensely between San Diego and
Rockville the people of San Diego posses a very
"laid-back" attitude. They go about their daily lives
in an unrushed manner. Work projects and punctuality are second priority to recreation and social
activities. On the contrary, people of Rockville are
much more rushed and tend to put work as their
number one priority. Trivial incidences upset and
aggrevate Rockville inhabitants, which create a

very tense atmosphere. The seasons, distances,

and attitudes are just some of the differences

between the two cities one should always keep in

mind.

▼ EXERCISE 5

Return to the paragraph that you revised in Exercise 3, and edit it now for sentence-level problems. Ask others to assist you, and compare your answers with theirs.

Proofreading Strategies

After writers have revised and edited a paragraph, they produce a clean copy for submission. Since students tend to be rushed in this last stage, they often over-look typing errors (such as transposed letters in words), the omission of words, and stray marks of punctuation. Therefore, always proofread the final copy for these errors. You can easily make corrections in pen and insert words neatly. (Most instructors will accept final copies with some corrections on them.) Use the following guidelines for proofreading the final copy.

I.   Is each word spelled correctly? (Very often when writers proofread too quickly, they anticipate what they will see and overlook simple spelling or typing errors. To break this pattern of anticipation, read the paper backwards. In this way, you can isolate each word and easily check its spelling.)

II. Are any words omitted or repeated? (Again, writers anticipate what they meant to say and misread what is on the paper. Read each sentence aloud slowly and carefully. Listen closely to the words. Are there any omissions or repetitions?)

III. Are there stray marks of punctuation? (Isolate each sentence by placing pieces of paper around it; then, read the sentence carefully.)

▼ EXERCISE 6

Read the following final draft of a student paragraph carefully. Proofread it and make any necessary corrections here. Correct neatly, as if the paper were to be handed in.

Competitiveness is very influential to students

because it encourages the student and it imporves the

quality of student's work. Most importantly, the

competitive spirit encourages the student to work. Though the years, humans have always tried to do better than their peers. Hunters competed with each other to see who shoots the greatest number of deer or catches the most fish, so everyone has this natural instinct of competition between other individuals. This natural instinct is the whole idea for using competition in schools. Students are constantly trying to do better then each other, and teachers encourage this so that everyone tries to improve his standing in the class. As a result, students who work at their grades will improve. In additoin, as a consequence of being challenged, quality in the work becomes an important issue. To insure a high grade, students want their work to be the best it can be. The student may spend hours and hours reading English papers to insure perfection. Furthermore, neatness is very important because it makes the instructor's job easier and, thus, gives the student a advantage over students who are sloppy writers. With this drive for perfection, a sense of pride in accomplishments accurs. Recieving a paper back from a teacher with no mistakes makes the student feel that the few extra hours of work payed off. In the long run, students are better off when they are challenged to suceed.

 ▼ EXERCISE 7

Make a final copy of your edited paragraph from Exercise 5. Using the questions to guide you, proofread the copy carefully and make any necessary corrections.

▼ Writing Strategy: ILLUSTRATION BY EXAMPLE

In this section, you will have the opportunity to analyze another organizational strategy. In addition to the reading selections that demonstrate this technique and the writing assignments that will guide your exploration of this strategy, you will be asked to use the revision techniques in this chapter to revise and edit two student paragraphs. This activity will help you to revise more effectively when you develop your own paragraphs.

Illustration by example means exactly that: the supporting sentences provide examples for the main idea of the paragraph. For instance, if you wished to explain that the registration process at college is complex and frustrating, then your supports would identify examples of frustrating and complex situations. Or, if you wished to explain that living on campus has several advantages, then you would list the advantages for your reader. You determine how the paragraph will be structured. You can move from the least important example to the most important one, or you can reverse this order. In addition, you could move in a chronological order or even in an order determined by geographical distance or area. In other words, the structure of the piece is determined by the purpose and audience *you* select.

▶ **The Commuter**

E. B. WHITE

In this paragraph, E. B. White, the famous essayist and stylist, explains the plight of commuters who work in New York City.

The commuter is the queerest bird of all. The suburb he inhabits has no essential vitality of its own and is a mere roost where he comes at day's end to go to sleep. Except in rare cases, the man who lives in Mamaroneck or Little Neck or Teaneck and works in New York, discovers nothing much about the city except the time of arrival and departure of trains and buses, and the path to a quick lunch. He is desk-bound, and has never, idly roaming in the gloaming, stumbled suddenly on Belvedere Tower in the Park, seen the ramparts rise sheer from the water of the pond, and the boys along the shore fishing for minnows, girls stretched out negligently on the shelves of the rocks; he has never come suddenly on anything at all in New York as a loiterer, because he has had no time between trains. He has fished in Manhattan's wallet and dug out coins but has never listened to Manhattan's breathing, never awakened to its morning, never dropped off to sleep in its night. About 400,000 men and women come charging onto the island each weekday morning, out of the mouths of tubes and tunnels. Not many among them have ever spent a drowsy afternoon in the great rustling oaken silence of the reading room of the Public Library, with the book elevator (like an old water wheel) spewing out books onto the trays. They tend their furnaces in Westchester and in Jersey but have never seen the furnaces of the Bowery, the fires that burn in oil drums on zero winter nights. They may work in the financial district downtown and never see the extravagant plantings of Rockefeller Center—the daffodils and grape hyacinths and birches and the flags trimmed to the wind on a fine morning in spring. Or they may work in a midtown office and may let a whole year swing round without sighting Governors Island from the sea wall. The commuter dies with tremendous mileage to his credit, but he is no rover. His entrances and exits are more devious than those in a prairie-dog village, and he calmly plays bridge while buried in the mud at the bottom of the East River. The Long Island Rail Road alone carried forty million commuters last year, but many of them were the same fellow retracing his steps.

▶ QUESTIONS   1. What does White suggest commuters miss by not living in the city?

2. What is the tone of the piece?

3. In the first sentence, White likens a commuter to a bird. Where is this metaphor continued? What other metaphors does White include in the piece?

4. Define the following words: *gloaming, ramparts, spewing,* and *devious.*

Sharks

PHILIPPE COUSTEAU

Philippe Cousteau, son of explorer/oceanographer Jacques Cousteau, discusses his adventures swimming with sharks.

In the Mediterranean, sharks are rare and cause few accidents. But their very rarity confers a peculiar solemnity on each encounter. My "first" sharks, at Djerba, were Mediterranean and impressed me unduly, because I had not expected to see them. On the other hand, in the Red Sea, where it is practically impossible to dive among the reefs of the open sea without being surrounded by sharks, coexistence was inevitable and my companions and I very soon became imprudent, almost unaware of their presence. I even sensed in our team the beginnings of a certain affectation of disdain for these inoffensive prowlers, a tendency to feign ignorance of them, to speak of them only in jest. I argued against this form of snobbishness because it could become dangerous, but I was vulnerable to it myself. It is intoxicating for an awkward and vulnerable creature, such as a diver becomes the instant he drops beneath the surface of the water, to imagine himself stronger than a creature far better armed than he. It was in this climate of excessive vanity and confidence in the early years that I dived myself and allowed others to dive, without protection, in the most dangerous waters. On the reef of Joaõ Valente, in the

Cape Verde Islands, we jostled or pulled on the tails of animals over twelve feet in length, incomparably more powerful and competent than we awkward intruders with steel bottles on our backs, our field of vision limited by the masks we wore, and caricatures of fins on our feet. The day at João Valente when Dumas and I glimpsed in the distance the pale silhouette of a great white shark (the species that all specialists qualify as a man-eater), we were frozen with terror and instinctively drew closer together. We had seen him before he saw us. But as soon as he became aware of our presence, it was he who was seized with panic; emptying out his intestines, he disappeared with a single flick of his tail. Later, in the Indian Ocean, the same incident occurred on two separate occasions. And each time, the violent emotion brought on in us by the appearance of the great white shark gave way to an unjustified sensation of triumph when he fled at the mere sight of us. Each of these unusual encounters provoked great excitement among us, and with it an excessive confidence in ourselves and a consequent relaxation of security measures.

▶ QUESTIONS   1. What is the topic sentence of the paragraph? Why is it placed there?

2. How does Cousteau compare divers to sharks?

3. The initial reaction of Cousteau and Dumas to sharks is replaced by another emotion. Identify both reactions, and explain their significance.

4. What does Cousteau reveal about himself as he details the encounters with sharks?

▶ ## The Boons of Civilization
H. L. MENCKEN

Journalist, editor, philologist, and literary critic, H. L. Mencken was called the most powerful private citizen of the United States during the 1920s. In this humorous piece, written in 1931, Mencken examines the consequences of contemporary inventions.

1   "What we call progress," says Havelock Ellis, "is the exchange of one nuisance for another nuisance." The thought is so obvious that it must occur now and then even to the secretary of the Greater Zenith Booster League. There may be persons who actually enjoy the sound of the telephone bell, but if they exist I can only say that I have never met them. It is highly probable that the telephone, as it stands today, represents more sheer brain power than any other familiar invention. A truly immense ingenuity has gone into perfecting it, and it is as far beyond its progenitor of 1880 as a battleship is beyond Fulton's *Clermont*. But all the while no one has ever thought of improving the tone of its bell. The sound

remains intolerably harsh and shrill, even when efforts are made to damp it. With very little trouble it might be made deep, sonorous and even soothing. But the telephone engineers let it remain as it was at the start, and millions of people suffer under its assault at every hour of the day.

2 The telephone, I believe, is the greatest boon to bores ever invented. It has set their ancient art upon a new level of efficiency and enabled them to penetrate the last strongholds of privacy. All the devices that have been put into service against them have failed. I point, for example, to that of having a private telephone number, not listed in the book. Obviously, there is nothing here to daunt bores of authentic gifts. Obtaining private telephone numbers is of the elemental essence of their craft. Thus the poor victim of their professional passion is beset quite as much as if he had his telephone number limned upon the sky in smoke. But meanwhile his friends forget it at critical moments and he misses much pleasant gossip and many an opportunity for vinous relaxation.

3 It is not only hard to imagine a world without telephones; it becomes downright impossible. They have become as necessary to the human race, at least in the United States, as window glass, newspapers or aspirin. Every now and then one hears of a man who has moved to some remote village to get rid of them, and there proposes to meditate and invite his soul in the manner of the Greek philosophers, but almost always it turns out that his meditations run in the direction of Rosicrucianism, the Single Tax, farm relief, or some other such insanity. I have myself ordered my telephone taken out at least a dozen times, but every time I found urgent use for it before the man arrived, and so had to meet him with excuses and a drink. A telephone bigwig tells me that such orders come in at the rate of scores a day, but that none has ever been executed. I now have two telephones in my house, and am about to put in a third. In the years to come, no doubt, there will be one in every room, as in hotels.

4 Despite all this, I remain opposed to the telephone theoretically, and continue to damn it. It is a great invention and of vast value to the human race, but I believe it has done me, personally, almost as much harm as good. How often a single call has blown up my whole evening's work, and so exacerbated my spirit and diminished my income! I am old enough to remember when telephones were very rare, and romantic enough to believe that I was happier then. But at worst I get more out of them than I get out of any of the other current wonders: for example, the radio, the phonograph, the movie, and the automobile. I am perhaps the first American ever to give up automobiling, formally and honestly. I sold my car so long ago as 1919, and have never regretted it. When I must move about in a city too large for comfortable walking I employ a taxicab, which is cheaper, safer and far less trouble than a private car. When I travel farther I resort to the Pullman, by long odds the best conveyance yet invented by man. The radio, I admit, has potentialities, but they will remain in abeyance so long as the air is laden and debauched by jazz, idiotic harangues by frauds who do not know what they are talking about, and the horrible garglings of ninth-rate singers. The phonograph is just as bad, and the movie is ten times worse.

5 Of all the great inventions of modern times the one that has given me most comfort and joy is one that is seldom heard of, to wit, the thermostat. I was amazed, some time ago, to hear that it was invented at least a

generation ago. I first heard of it during the War of 1914–18, when some kind friend suggested that I throw out the coal furnace that was making steam in my house and put in a gas furnace. Naturally enough, I hesitated, for the human mind is so constituted. But the day I finally succumbed must remain ever memorable in my annals, for it saw me move at one leap from an inferno into a sort of paradise. Everyone will recall how bad the coal was in those heroic days. The patriotic anthracite men loaded their culm-piles on cars, and sold them to householders all over the East. Not a furnaceman was in practice in my neighborhood: all of them were working in the shipyards at $15 a day. So I had to shovel coal myself, and not only shovel coal, but sift ashes. It was a truly dreadful experience. Worse, my house was always either too hot or too cold. When a few pieces of actual coal appeared in the mass of slate the temperature leaped up to 85 degrees, but most of the time it was between 45 and 50.

6   The thermostat changed all that, and in an instant. I simply set it at 68 degrees, and then went about my business. Whenever the temperature in the house went up to 70 it automatically turned off the gas under the furnace in the cellar, and there was an immediate return to 68. And if the mercury, keeping on, dropped to 66, then the gas went on again, and the temperature was soon 68 once more. I began to feel like a man liberated from the death-house. I was never too hot or too cold. I had no coal to heave, no ashes to sift. My house became so clean that I could wear a shirt five days. I began to feel like work, and rapidly turned out a series of imperishable contributions to the national letters. My temper improved so vastly that my family began to suspect senile changes. Moreover, my cellar became as clean as the rest of the house, and as roomy as a barn. I enlarged my wine-room by 1000 cubic meters. I put in a cedar closet big enough to hold my whole wardrobe. I added a vault for papers, a carpenter shop, and a praying chamber.

7   For all these boons and usufructs I was indebted to the inventor of the thermostat, a simple device but incomparable. I'd print his name here, but unfortunately I forget it. He was one of the great benefactors of humanity. I wouldn't swap him for a dozen Marconis, a regiment of Bells, or a whole army corps of Edisons. Edison's life-work, like his garrulous and nonsensical talk, has been mainly a curse to humanity: he has greatly augmented its stock of damned nuisances. But the man who devised the thermostat, at all events in my private opinion, was a hero comparable to Shakespeare, Michelangelo or Beethoven.

▶ QUESTIONS   1. The author gives examples of inventions he could live without, actually could live better without. What are they? Why does he dislike them?

2. Explain Mencken's opinion of the thermostat.

3. Define the following words: *limned (2)*, *vinous (2)*, *boons (7)*, and *usufructs (7)*.

4. Since Mencken is so grateful for gas furnaces and thermostats, why can he not remember the inventor's name? Why is the inventor not as famous as Marconi, Morse, Bell, and Edison?

▶ # Do Something Different: Go Back in Time
RAY STOLLE

In this student paragraph, Ray Stolle explains the experience of attending the Maryland Renaissance Festival, an annual event that recreates a lively English village in the 1600s.

Upon arriving at the entrance of the Maryland Renaissance Festival, one feels that he is about to experience something different and exciting. The permanent location of the festival is surrounded completely by a stout, wooden wall that seems to guard something sacred and secret. With cheerful companions in tow, and once given leave to pass beyond the guard-tower entrance, a day of many and different activities, events, and encounters lies just ahead. The interior of the Renaissance Festival is set up like a little English town, with literally scores of shops, amusements, and food vendors. Hoards of merchants sell any souvenir imaginable. Blacksmiths sell swords and armor, woodworkers their handicrafts, glassblowers trinkets, and clothiers clothes (Renaissance style, of course). Proprietors of amusements, games, and other tests of skill offer distraction in exchange for a bit of your money. Archery, Frankish axe throwing, darts, and a Jacob's ladder, among other things, are at the ready to entertain and challenge, and sometimes, even offer a prize. Accompanying the many stores and shops are half a dozen stages and other specialized areas where planned events take place. Throughout the entire day, different performances rotate from stage to stage and begin at intervals of every couple of hours. Accompanied by musicians, these performances are usually in the form of short plays that commonly either mock some Shakespearean piece, such as the hilarious <u>MacBeth in Twenty Minutes or Less,</u> or deal with some other Renaissance theme in a humorous way. Other shows feature magicians, a human chess match, jousting tournaments, and a wrestling match at the "mud pit." Maybe the most interesting aspect of the festival is the amount and diversity of the different "characters" seen wandering about the fairgrounds. Jugglers, beggars, rogues, town watchmen, and others, all in period costumes, roam the grounds at will. Even the Queen, her court, and her guards occasionally parade by. Overall, these wandering vagabonds and miscreants add a final touch that makes the Renaissance Festival uniquely different. At other fairs and festivals, it is possible to avoid the attractions, events, and atmosphere if one wishes, but at the Renaissance Festival, they come after you. For a different and enjoyable experience, I highly recommend attending the Maryland Renaissance Festival.

▶ QUESTIONS

1. What is Stolle's topic sentence? Where is it located? Does it fulfill the requirements of a topic sentence?

2. How is the piece developed? What primary support statements are included to guide readers?

3. What specific details are included in secondary support statements to provide examples?

4. What is the tone of the piece? How does Stolle achieve this tone?

Using the techniques discussed in this chapter, revise the following drafts of two student paragraphs. Apply all of the guideline questions about revising and editing to each paragraph; then, write and proofread a final draft of each.

1. The serious amatear tennis player must look like a tennis player and wear the identical garmets the proffessionals wear in tournaments. Because they have a place to carry tennis balls. The white shorts with oversized pockets are an integral part of the players game. A tennis bag is also necessary to carry the equipment the player brings. Made of waterproof canvas the bag has to be large enough to hold all the gear and more important, it has to have a sporty design and the name of a well known racket manufacturer on it. The serious amateur tennis player acquired the "tennis look" before they step onto the court. The two balls fit snuggly in each front pocket a person possesses a total of five balls including the one in his hand. He appears deformed because of the protusions created by the balls, so that number of balls allow the game to be played continually. The players don't have to chase every ball they smash over the fence. Another important piece of clothing is the white collered shirt with colorful design stretched across the chest. Somehow, the amateurs wearing the same kind of shirt that John McEnroe wore when he won the Wimbledon title transfers John's abilities to the neophyte. The shirt gives the person an inflated sense of confidence: he feels that he can beat Jimmy Connors with his eyes closed. A last important garmet is the terrycloth

headband. The headband gives the impression that the player has been sweating from running back and forth over the court. Although he has yet to hit the ball over the net. The headband also keeps his hair from interferring with his eyesight when he searches for the balls that flew over the fence. Although clothes do not make the tennis player, many amateurs must believe they do.

2.   Building a fire properly require a good deal of preparation and a lesser amount of expertise. Above all, make certain that the flue in your fireplace or wood stove is clear and is drafting well. if this flue is blocked, then the smoke from the fire will fill your room with acrid fumes. It is recommended that your chimney be cleaned once a year by a sweep, simply check the classified ads for the name of a professional. Next, try to make certain that your wood is seasoned and dry for the best burning. This wood can be purchased—prices vary across America—or you can cut it yourself. As Henry David Thoreau remarked, you get warm twice when you chop your own wood. Now, consider your kindling: twigs of any sort of dry wood which has been gathered from your own yard, bark fallen from your logs, or uniform, small sticks that can be purchased commercially. Finally, keep a pile of old newspapers, preferably those with no color photographs, for they produce noxious fumes when burning. Once you have gathered this material, you are ready to build your

fire. Ball up several newspapers and shove them under the grate then begin to layer your kindling, papers and logs. On the grate first place your kindling, preferably in a crisscross pattern. Place two or three logs vertically on the kindling, and stuff the space between the logs with more newspaper. This is your first layer, reverse the procedure for your second: that is, the next set of logs should be layed horizontally, and then vertically again. Above all, make certain that the spacing of the logs provides air pockets for the fire to draft. If the fire has been laid properly, you need only to touch a match to the newspaper on the bottom to start a roaring blaze. You need none of the other pathetic devices I have witnessed: a frantic householder dangerously squirting lighter fluid into the fireplace, the strongest son pumping bellows, or a family praying in unison to Vulcan, the god of fire. At a cost lower than either gas or oil, you now have an attractive source of heat, the spot, above all others, for the family to gather, the dog to lie, or for the solitary person to commune with a good book.

▼ PARAGRAPH ASSIGNMENTS

1. E. B. White is critical of the commuter, for he seems to believe that commuters miss much of the essential character of the city. White does not write from a commuter's viewpoint. Respond to White by identifying in a paragraph the advantages of commuting to a large urban area. Be specific about the commuter's location, lifestyle, and the city to which he or she commutes.

2. If you agree with White, who was a city dweller when he wrote *The Commuter*, then identify the advantages of living in a large city. In a paragraph, be specific

about the city and its resources; also, identify a clear purpose and audience for the piece.

3. Does it make a difference where one lives while attending college? For a group of high-school seniors, identify in a paragraph the advantages of living at home or the advantages of living on campus.

4. Ray Stolle provided an explanation of the adventures awaiting visitors at a Renaissance Festival. For your local newspaper, write a piece that explains the attractions of a local festival, amusement park, sporting event, or concert.

5. Very often others see us more clearly than we see ourselves. Our emotions affect our ability to describe our characteristics objectively. Choose an outstanding trait of an individual, perhaps a close friend or family member, and describe the trait so the person can view it objectively. Support your description with ample details and examples. Determine a specific purpose for your paragraph.

6. Cousteau explains that he often took unnecessary chances while diving in shark-infested waters. Although he was aware of the potential danger, he felt confident that he would not be attacked. Describe a similar situation that you have faced. When have you taken unnecessary risks? Why did you take them? What was the outcome? Would you repeat the incident now? Specify an audience who could profit from your experience, and determine a specific purpose for your paragraph.

7. What modern inventions are now necessities for you? In a paragraph, illustrate why you could not live without two or three modern inventions. Create an audience and purpose for your piece.

▼ WRITING TIPS

Revision can take place at any point in the writing process; this flexibility is the major characteristic of the effective writer. However, for a complete revision, use the separate stages of the revision process as you approach drafts of papers.

Edit your paper carefully for comma usage. Check Chapters 9 and 10 in Part II for rules on commas.

▼ Revision Checklist

1. List two revisions you made during the writing process. How did you determine what to revise? What changes did you make?

   _____

   _____

   _____

   _____

   _____

2. List any grammatical or punctuation problems you found during editing. How did you correct these?

   _____

   _____

   _____

   _____

   _____

3. List any typing errors you found during proofreading. How did you find them?

   _____

   _____

   _____

   _____

   _____

▼ Illustration Checklist

1. What is your topic sentence? Where is it located?

    _____

    _____

    _____

    _____

    _____

2. How do the major examples support the topic sentence?

    _____

    _____

    _____

    _____

    _____

3. How do specific details develop each example?

    _____

    _____

    _____

    _____

    _____

4. What is the structure of the paragraph? How are examples
    organized? What makes this organization effective?

    _____

    _____

    _____

6

Achieving Coherence

OBJECTIVES

1. To write a coherent paragraph using pronouns, synonyms, limited repetition, sentence combining, and transitional words and expressions.

2. To explore composing through comparison/contrast.

PREVIEW

Coherence is the logical connecting of ideas. You may use a number of techniques to link your ideas smoothly and logically.

Paragraphs require **coherence,** the logical connection of ideas, so that the reader can easily recognize the links between sentences and ideas. Coherence also helps the reader visualize the relationships among several concepts. You can achieve coherence in your writing in several different ways:

1. by using pronouns

2. by using synonyms

3. by using limited repetition

4. by combining sentences

5. by using transitional words and expressions

By developing coherence in their work, writers improve several aspects of their work simultaneously:

1. They show the relationship between ideas and sentences.

2. They avoid needless repetition of the same words.

3. They reinforce key concepts.

4. They avoid simplistic and wordy sentences.

A paragraph without coherence can be somewhat boring and difficult to read; in effect, its readers must connect ideas and sentences themselves, because the writer has failed to do so. Consider the following paragraph, which lacks coherence.

Henry Louis Mencken was born in Baltimore. He had a long, tumultuous, and eclectic career. He played a variety of roles. Edgar Allan Poe was a great literary critic. Mencken also was a truly American literary critic. Mencken struggled for freedom of expression. This helped change the course of American literary history. Mencken was a newspaperman. He wrote literally thousands of columns for the Baltimore *Herald* and the Baltimore *Sun.* His newspaper work was also syndicated in papers around the country. He covered everything in his columns. He wrote about art, economics, politics, food, heavyweight championship fights, and the Scopes trial in Tennessee. From 1914 to 1933, Mencken edited two monthly magazines. They were the *Smart Set* and the *American Mercury*. He wrote about language in his study *The American Language*. The philological work ran to four editions and two supplements. His autobiographical trilogy, the *Days* books, sold well and entertained generations of readers. Mencken estimated that he wrote ten million words for publications over his career. His career lasted for half a century. His writing generated a critical response of more than one million words. He declared joyfully that most of these words were derogatory. Few, if any, American authors have proven as prolific or as colorful as th s Baltimorean. He never went to school a day beyond the age of fifteen.

The paragraph has rather basic sentence structure: most of its sentences are simple or compound. (Simple sentences have one independent clause; compound sentences have two or more independent clauses. See "Sentence Types" in Chapter 8, Part I.) Moreover, the author needlessly repeats names and words, makes no connection between sentences, and fails to reinforce key concepts. Below, analyze the same paragraph, rewritten, using several methods to achieve coherence.

Throughout his long, tumultuous and eclectic career, Henry Louis Mencken, a Baltimorean, played a variety of literary roles. After Edgar Allan Poe, Mencken proved to be the next truly American literary critic. As a critic, Mencken's struggle for freedom of expression helped to change the course of American literary history. Mencken the newspaperman wrote literally thousands of columns in which he covered everything from art to economics, from politics to food, from a heavyweight championship fight to the Scopes trial in Tennessee. In addition to his newspaper work, Mencken edited two monthly magazines, the *Smart Set* and the *American Mercury*, from 1914 to 1933. Moreover, Mencken was a philologist; his highly respected philological study, *The American Language*, ran to four editions and two supplements. His efforts as a writer did not end there; his winsome autobiographical trilogy, the *Days* books, sold well and entertained generations of readers. Mencken once estimated that, over a career that lasted half a century, he wrote ten million words for publication. These words generated a critical response of more than one million words, the majority of which, he joyfully declared, were highly derogatory. Few, if any, American authors have proven as prolific or as colorful as this Baltimorean who never went to school a day beyond the age of fifteen.

The revised paragraph, with ten sentences compared to the original's twenty-four, is far more interesting and lively. In addition, readers can easily understand the relationship between ideas. Compare the two paragraphs to identify the writer's revisions. The writer used five techniques to achieve coherence in the revision: pronouns, synonyms, limited repetition of key ideas, transitional words and expressions, and sentence combining.

Pronouns

The constant repetition of nouns in the same sentence or paragraph can become monotonous. However, a writer can easily improve the coherence in a sentence or paragraph by using pronouns, words that replace nouns. Consider this example:

> New York is a marvelous city because New York offers many different types of attractions for tourists.

Now consider this revision of the same sentence.

> New York is a marvelous city because it offers many different types of attractions for tourists.

The pronoun *it* has replaced the noun *city* which, in turn, has been identified as New York. The pronoun eliminates the unnecessary repetition of the name of the city.

RULES FOR PRONOUN USE

Although using pronouns to achieve coherence is relatively easy, be sure to follow these rules governing their use:

1. A pronoun can replace a noun if the noun has been named or identified previously. A pronoun must refer to a specific **antecedent,** the noun the pronoun will replace. If the antecedent is missing, then the reader will be unable to identify the word the pronoun has replaced. Consider this example:

    > It was too large.

    What word does the pronoun *it* replace? What could the sentence possibly describe? There are literally thousands of nouns that could be the antecedent. If this sentence were placed in the middle of a paragraph, then perhaps the reader could identify the antecedent. However, as an opening sentence in a paragraph, it would be inappropriate unless the writer were attempting to build suspense or had identified the antecedent in the title of the paragraph.

2. The antecedent of the pronoun cannot be ambiguous. Consider the following example:

    > Hannah told Liza that she should have completed her assignment.

Because the sentence has two possible meanings, the antecedent is unclear or ambiguous. Therefore, make sure that the pronoun has a direct antecedent. In this sentence, it is unclear whether the pronouns *she* and *her* replace the noun *Hannah* or the noun *Liza*. The sentence could have one of two meanings:

> Hannah told Liza, "I should have completed my assignment."

(The pronouns *I* and *my* replace the noun *Hannah*.)

> Hannah told Liza, "You should have completed your assignment."

(The pronouns *You* and *your* refer to the noun *Liza*.)

3. Pronouns must agree in gender, number, and case with the nouns they replace. It is usually easy to identify the correct gender and number that the pronoun must follow. For example, the pronoun *he* is obviously inappropriate as a replacement for the noun *Elizabeth*. Also, the pronoun *they* could not be a substitute for the noun *car*. It is more difficult, however, to determine the correct case for the pronoun. Consider this example:

> Helen told Sam a secret that must be confidential between she and him.

In this sentence, the pronouns *she* and *him* act as objects of the preposition *between* and should be in the objective case. However, the pronoun *she* is not in the objective case; it is in the nominative case. Therefore, the pronoun *she* is incorrectly used. The sentence should be revised to say *between her and him*.

THE CASE OF NOUNS AND PRONOUNS

Pronouns and nouns are used in three cases: the nominative, the objective, and the possessive.

Nominative

The **nominative case** is used for subjects (the actors in a sentence) and predicate nominatives (the nouns or pronouns following linking verbs). For instance, in the following sentences, a pronoun in the nominative case substitutes for the subject.

Marsha wrote a paper.

She received an "A" from her teacher.

In the above sentences, *Marsha* is the antecedent for the pronoun *she;* the pronoun is in the nominative case, since it is the subject of the second sentence. In the following example, a pronoun in the nominative case acts as a predicate nominative.

The speaker is *Tom.*

The speaker is *he.*

In these sentences, the pronoun *he* replaces its antecedent *Tom.* The pronoun is in the nominative case because it is a predicate nominative. The linking verb *is* (present tense of *to be*) makes the noun after the verb equivalent to the subject; therefore, the noun must be in the same case as the subject.

Objective

The **objective case** is used for direct and indirect objects and for objects of prepositions. A direct object receives the action of the verb; an indirect object tells to whom or for whom an action is done. For example, in the following sentences, a pronoun in the objective case acts as direct object.

Harris brought the *roses.*

Harris brought *them.*

In these sentences, the pronoun *them* replaces the antecedent *roses.* The pronoun *them* is the direct object of the verb *brought;* it tells what Harris brought. In the next example, an objective case pronoun is the indirect object.

Jerry gave his *mother* a birthday present.

Jerry gave *her* a birthday present.

In these sentences, the pronoun *her* replaces its antecedent *mother.* The pronoun *her* is the indirect object in the sentence; it tells to whom Jerry gave a present. In addition, the objective case is used for objects of the preposition, nouns that follow prepositions, such as *by, to, from,* or *around.* In the following sentences, a pronoun in the objective case acts as the object of the preposition.

Jason gave a travel brochure to *Alex.*

Jason gave a travel brochure to *him.*

In these sentences, the pronoun *him* replaces its antecedent *Alex.* The pronoun *him* is the object of the preposition *to.*

Possessive

The **possessive case** is used to show ownership. Look at the following examples:

The zoo needed animals for *its* exhibit.

The engineer argued that *her* proposal was the most cost-effective one.

In the first sentence, the pronoun *its* shows the zoo's ownership of the exhibit. In the second sentence, the pronoun *her* shows that the engineer wrote the proposal. In both sentences the possessive pronouns save space and avoid repetition. Without these pronouns, you would have to write "zoo's exhibit" and "engineer's proposal."

The following chart will help you determine which pronouns are appropriate in each case.

| PERSON | NOMINATIVE CASE | | OBJECTIVE CASE | | POSSESSIVE CASE | |
	SINGULAR	PLURAL	SINGULAR	PLURAL	SINGULAR	PLURAL
First	I	we	me	us	my, mine	our, ours
Second	you	you	you	you	you, yours	you, yours
Third	he she it	they	him her it	them	his her, hers its	their, theirs

AVOIDING SEXIST (GENDER-SPECIFIC) LANGUAGE

One problem you may face with pronouns is the traditional use of a masculine, singular pronoun to substitute for an indefinite pronoun, such as *each, everyone, someone, somebody,* and *anybody,* or for a noun that does not identify gender, such as *student, driver, employee,* or *lawyer.* Certainly, this usage ignores women in the audience, as the following sentence demonstrates:

Once the *student* has completed the registration process, *he* should report to *his* academic advisor.

This sentence, which you might read in a college catalog, would be appropriate only at an all-male institution. It is not appropriate in a catalog that addresses both men and women. There are a number of methods you can use to avoid sexist language; each has its own advantages and disadvantages.

1. Use both masculine and feminine pronouns when you refer to both men and women:

   Once the student has completed the registration process, *he or she* should report to *his or her* academic advisor.

   This tactic, however, can be awkward if you use it in a lengthy passage. In addition, this usage calls attention to itself throughout the passage and may interrupt your readers needlessly.

2. Alternate masculine and feminine pronouns throughout a passage:

> Once the student has completed the registration process, *he* should report to *his* academic advisor. Finally, *she* should return to the bursar's office to pay *her* bill.

This usage, however, can be confusing to readers.

3. Use only nouns, rather than pronouns, in a passage:

> Once *the student* has completed the registration process, *the student* should report to *the student's* academic advisor.

This method can become repetitive for your reader.

4. Use plural pronouns and plural nouns:

> Once the *students* have completed the registration process, *they* should report to *their* academic advisors.

This method allows you to include everyone in your discussion and avoids the problem of being repetitive and confusing for your reader.

5. Finally, choose alternative terms for words that specifically identify men or women:

Rather than:		Choose:	
	mailman		mail carrier
	postman		postal clerk
	chairman		chairperson
	fireman		firefighter
	policeman		police officer

This method of avoiding gender-specific language is also effective if you have to write a letter to someone you do not know. For example, rather than saying "Dear Sir," you could address the person by title, "Dear Personnel Manager."

▼ **EXERCISE 1**   Supply the correct pronoun to replace the noun in parentheses.

▶ Example: The car needs a tune-up;  (the car's) engine isn't operating properly.

1. Tony ran to catch the bus, but _____ (Tony) was too late.

2. Faith explained to _____ (Faith's) sister that _____ (Faith and the sister) could not go to the movies.

3. Mark Twain earned a great deal of money from his writing; however, because

   _____ (Twain) made poor investments, _____ (Twain) was

   forced to give lectures at the end of his career in order to make money.

4. The professor returned the students' papers; _____ (the professor)

   was pleased that the class had worked diligently on the assignment.

5. Thomas Jefferson is well known as the author of the Declaration of

   Independence; however, many people do not recognize the extent of

   _____ (Jefferson's) talents. _____ (Many people) do not know

   _____ (Jefferson) was an inventor, scientist, architect, and educator.

6. Everyone must complete _____ (everyone's) own work.

7. The house was in terrible condition: _____ (the house) needed a new

   roof, new floors, and a fresh coat of paint. _____ (The house's)

   previous owners had not maintained _____ (the house) properly.

8. The dog waited patiently by the entrance of the building for _____

   (the dog's) master, but it was over an hour before _____ (the master)

   returned.

9. The jury made _____ (the jury's) decision about the case after long

   days of debate among _____ (the jury's) members.

10. The basketball team was ready for the championship game; the players knew

    what parts _____ (the players) were to play in this effort.

Synonyms

If an author uses the same word constantly, then readers will lose interest.
Analyze the effect the repetition of the word *jogging* has in this example:

> Jogging can be beneficial to one's health. Jogging
> helps to reduce tension and can aid in weight reduction.
> Jogging also helps strengthen the cardiovascular system.
> Jogging, moreover, can help develop muscle tone. There-
> fore, jogging provides excellent benefits.

The repetition of *jogging* as the subject of each sentence is monotonous. Consider some of the synonyms for this word: *light running, this exercise,* and *this sport*. Analyze the effect of these synonyms in the following revised paragraph.

> Jogging can be beneficial to one's health. This sport helps to reduce tension and can aid in weight reduction. This exercise also helps strengthen the cardiovascular system. Moreover, this activity can help develop muscle tone. Therefore, jogging provides excellent rewards.

Notice how the synonyms easily replace the repetitious word *jogging*. In addition, the demonstrative pronoun *this* refers to jogging and increases the coherence of the paragraph. Certainly, the use of synonyms can keep sentences more lively than does the repetition of one word.

Synonyms replace not only single nouns but also long phrases and sentences. Consider this example:

> The cast and crew of the play worked twenty-four hours straight to prepare for the show's opening. Because of their diligence and perseverance, the first night was a success.

In the second sentence, the words *their diligence and perseverance* replace the entire first sentence.

In addition to synonyms, the words *there* and *here* can provide quick replacements for the names of places that have already been identified. Analyze the following example:

> In London, the group visited many historical places. There, the members of the group enjoyed the fine theaters and restaurants, too.

The word *There* refers to London and provides coherence without the unnecessary repetition of the city's name.

▼ EXERCISE 2

Provide synonyms for the italicized words in each of the following sentences .

▶ Example: After long hours of waiting, we finally entered the *National Gallery of Art*. ~~Here~~), we would view the exhibit of Ansel Adams's photographs and the exhibit on the treasure houses of Britain.

1. Although we tend to group all of the *painters* in the French Impressionist

   school together, these _____ had quite different styles.

2. Each *teacher* had an individual approach to education, but each _____

   was successful at conveying knowledge to her students.

3. The *ground hog* is supposed to forecast the last six weeks of winter. If _____ sees his shadow, then we can expect another six weeks of cold weather. If _____ does not, then spring will arrive soon.

4. My *car* seems to have a personality of its own. _____ will not start if the temperature drops below 30 degrees, and its engine produces various groans if it is called upon to climb steep hills.

5. The ski patrol planned to meet at *Bear Mountain* for its annual convention. _____, the members would review first-aid procedures, discuss safety measures for skiers, and practice emergency drills.

6. The *interstate highway system* connects many states; because of _____, we can travel from coast to coast in only several days.

7. The young soldier *could not clean his rifle properly, complete the obstacle course, or stay in line for marches;* because of his _____, he was transferred to permanent kitchen duty.

8. Hank *studied for five days for his chemistry examination.* His _____ was rewarded; he earned an "A" on the examination.

9. Lee and Grant met at *Appomattox Court House.* _____, the Civil War ended.

10. The first settlers in the New World were *extremely brave* to face an entire continent alone. Their _____ helped to create a new country.

Limited Repetition

For short pieces of three or four sentences, repetition of key terms or phrases is inappropriate. Because the piece is so brief, the repetition would add monotony, not coherence. However, for longer paragraphs, repetition, used wisely, can very effectively reinforce main concepts. Several methods of repetition can be used: repeating major words or phrases, repeating specific structures, and repeating metaphors. (Because repetition of metaphors requires length, this last method is more effective in essays than in paragraphs.)

Repetition of key words or phrases is most effective when the writer has a specific purpose in mind. For example, in a paragraph on the rights and privileges of Americans, the repetition of the word *freedom* could reinforce the concept that these rights and privileges are a result of the guaranteed freedom Americans enjoy.

Finally, repetition of specific structures not only reinforces primary ideas, but also provides transitions in a paragraph. For example, in the revised sample paragraph on the literary roles H. L. Mencken played, the prepositional phrases beginning with the word *as*—*as a critic* and *as a writer*—name the different roles Mencken played; moreover, these phrases, placed at the beginning of the sentences, provide transitions for the reader.

▼ EXERCISE 3

Underline the key words or phrases and specific structures that are repeated in the following paragraphs.

1.   To those old allies whose cultural and spiritual origins we share, we pledge the loyalty of faithful friends. United, there is little we cannot do in a host of new cooperative ventures. Divided, there is little we can do—for we dare not meet a powerful challenge at odds and split asunder.

To those new states whom we welcome to the ranks of the free, we pledge our word that one form of colonial control shall not have passed away merely to be replaced by a far more iron tyranny. We shall not always expect to find them supporting our view. But we shall always hope to find them strongly supporting their own freedom—and to remember that, in the past, those who foolishly sought power by riding the back of the tiger ended up inside.

To those peoples in the huts and villages of half the globe struggling to break the bonds of mass misery, we pledge our best efforts to help them help themselves, for whatever period is required—not because the Communists may be doing it, not because we seek their votes, but because it is right. If a free society cannot help the many who are poor, it cannot save the few who are rich.

(John F. Kennedy, *Inaugural Address*)

2.   "Call this a govment! why, just look at it and see what it's like. Here's the law a-standing ready to take a man's son away from him—a man's own son, which he has had all the trouble and all the anxiety and all the expense of raising. Yes, just as that man has got that son raised at last, and ready to go to work, and begin to do suthin' for *him* and give him a rest, the law up and goes for him. And they call *that* govment! That ain't all nuther. The law backs that old Judge Thatcher up and helps him to keep me out o' my property. Here's what the law does. The law takes a man worth six thousand dollars and upards, and jams him into an old trap of a cabin like this, and lets him go around in clothes that ain't fitted for a hog. They call that govment! A man can't get his rights in a govment like this. Sometimes I've a mighty notion to just leave the country for good and all. Yes, and I *told* 'em so; I told old Thatcher so to his face. Lots of 'em heard me, and can tell what I said. Says I, for two cents I'd leave the blamed country and never come anear it agin. Them's the very words. I says, look at my hat—if you call it a hat—but the lid raises up and the rest of it goes down till it's below my chin, and then it ain't rightly a hat at all, but more likely my head was shoved up through a jint o' stove-pipe. Look at it, says I—such a hat for me to wear—one of the wealthiest men in this town if I could git my rights."

(from Mark Twain, *The Adventures of Huckleberry Finn*)

3.   Four score and seven years ago, our fathers brought forth on this continent, a new nation, conceived in Liberty, and dedicated to the proposition that all men are created equal.

Now we are engaged in a great civil war; testing whether that nation, or any nation so conceived and so dedicated, can long endure. We are met on a great battlefield of that war. We have come to dedicate a portion of that field as a final resting-place for those who here gave their lives that that nation might live. It is altogether fitting and proper that we should do this.

But, in a larger sense, we cannot dedicate—we cannot consecrate—we cannot hallow—this ground. The brave men, living and dead, who struggled here have consecrated it, far above our poor power to add or detract. The world will little note, nor long remember, what we say here, but it can never forget what they did here. It is for us the living, rather, to be dedicated here to the unfinished work which they who fought here have thus far so nobly advanced. It is rather for us to be here dedicated to the great task remaining before us—that from these honored dead we take increased devotion to that cause for which they gave the last full measure of devotion; that we here highly resolve that these dead shall not have died in vain; that this nation, under God, shall have a new birth of freedom; and that government of the people, by the people, for the people, shall not perish from the earth.

(Abraham Lincoln, *The Gettysburg Address*)

Sentence Combining

Beginning writers sometimes believe that a sentence can contain only one piece of information. Consequently, they produce sentences like the following ones:

> Inez is an exceptional child. She has many talents. She can dance and sing. She loves to tell jokes.

Notice how each sentence adds one more piece of information. This method results in a number of simple sentences that lack coherence. The following revisions use sentence combining to provide coherence:

> With her many talents—singing, dancing, and telling jokes—Inez is an exceptional child.

> Inez is an exceptional child because she has many talents, such as singing, dancing, and telling jokes.

Both revisions are far more effective than the initial sentences because they are coherent and because they indicate the relationships of ideas to each other.

WAYS TO COMBINE SENTENCES

There are six easy ways to combine sentences:

1. Join adjectives and other modifiers.

2. Use appositives.

3. Develop relative-pronoun clauses.

4. Create participles.

5. Coordinate ideas.

6. Subordinate ideas.

These six techniques are explained with examples in the following outline.

I. Adjectives and other modifiers can be joined in one of two ways.

   A. Create a list of adjectives joined by commas.

   ▶ Example: Harriet is kind. She is also considerate and amenable.

   ▶ Combination: Harriet is kind, considerate, and amenable.

   B. Place two adjectives after a noun to modify it, and enclose the adjectives within commas.

   ▶ Example: The teenager approached the microphone. He was lanky and nervous.

   ▶ Combination: The teenager, lanky and nervous, approached the microphone.

II. Appositives—nouns or noun phrases—rename or define another noun.

   ▶ Example: She is a corporate lawyer for an international firm. Ms. Thomas is also a scuba diver.

   ▶ Combination: Ms. Thomas, a corporate lawyer for an international firm, is also a scuba diver. (In this sentence, the noun phrase, *a corporate lawyer for an international firm*, is an appositive that states Ms. Thomas's occupation.)

   Ms. Thomas, a scuba diver, is a corporate lawyer for an international firm. (In this sentence, the noun phrase, *a scuba diver*, is an appositive that defines Ms. Thomas's hobby.)

III. A relative-pronoun clause can act in the same manner as an appositive. It gives additional information about a noun by renaming it, defining it, or describing it. Beginning with *who, which, that, whose,* or *whom*, a relative-pronoun clause is a dependent clause—a group of words with a subject and a verb that cannot stand alone.

   ▶ Example: Because of the decline in oil prices, the local refinery has closed. The refinery employed five thousand workers.

▶ Combination: Because of the decline in oil prices, the local refinery, which employed five thousand workers, has closed. (The relative-pronoun clause, *which employed five thousand workers,* describes the noun *refinery.*)

IV. Present and past participles act as adjectives to modify a noun. Because they are formed from verbs, they carry the actions and visual images of verbs. (A present participle is formed by adding *ing* to the base form of the verb. A past participle is usually formed by adding *ed* to the base form of the verb.)

▶ Example: Tim was walking down a dark street. A man approached him. The man was wearing a mask.

▶ Combination: While walking down a dark street, Tim was approached by a masked man. (This sentence contains a participial phrase, *While walking down the street,* which modifies the noun *Tim,* and a participle, *masked,* which modifies the noun *man.*)

V. Coordination forms compound sentences, which contain two or more independent clauses. (An independent clause has a subject and a verb and can stand by itself as a complete sentence.) Compound sentences are formed in one of three ways.

A. Add a comma and a coordinate conjunction. There are seven coordinate conjunctions: *for, and, nor, but, or, yet,* and *so.*

Here are the relationships the seven coordinate conjunctions express:

> *For* shows cause.
> *And* shows addition.
> *Nor* shows a negative choice.
> *But* shows contrast or contradiction.
> *Or* shows a choice.
> *Yet* shows contrast.
> *So* shows effect.

B. Add a semicolon (;). The use of the semicolon implies that the relationship between the sentences is clear. For example, the second sentence may define or give an illustration of the first sentence.

C. Add a semicolon and an adverbial conjunction, followed by a comma. There are four main adverbial conjunctions: *however, moreover, nevertheless,* and *therefore.* Here are the relationships the four adverbial conjunctions express:

> *However* shows contrast or contradiction.
> *Moreover* shows addition.
> *Nevertheless* shows contrast.
> *Therefore* shows result.

▶ Example: Her long hours in the gym were rewarded. She won the gold medal in gymnastics.

▶ Compound-Sentence Combinations:

Her long hours in the gym were rewarded, for she won the gold medal in gymnastics. (The coordinate conjunction *for* indicates that winning the gold medal was the reward for the long hours in the gym.)

Her long hours in the gym were rewarded; she won the gold medal in gymnastics. (The semicolon indicates that the two sentences are equal. The second sentence describes the reward of the long hours of practice.)

She won the gold medal in gymnastics; therefore, her long hours in the gym were rewarded. (The adverbial conjunction *therefore* shows that her long hours in the gym were rewarded as a consequence of winning the gold medal.)

VI. Subordination forms complex sentences, which contain one independent clause and one or more dependent clauses. The dependent clause adds information and is subordinate to the independent clause because the independent clause contains the most important information in the sentence.

▶ Example:

The holiday recess was completed. The members of Congress returned to work on Capitol Hill.

▶ Combination:

After the holiday recess was completed, the members of Congress returned to work on Capitol Hill. (In this sentence, the dependent clause, *After the holiday recess was completed,* is not as important as the independent clause, *the members of Congress returned to work on Capitol Hill.* However, the dependent clause does tell when the members returned, so it adds more information to the sentence.)

Dependent clauses are usually preceded by subordinate conjunctions. Here is a partial list of subordinate conjunctions:

after	*because*	*than*	*when*
although	*before*	*unless*	*wherever*
as	*if*	*until*	*while*

▼ EXERCISE 4

Combine each set of sentences that follows to form one sentence, and write it on the blank. Use whatever sentence-combining method seems to be most effective. Identify the methods you use.

1. The hunter raised his gun.
   The hunter was dressed in bright orange clothing.
   The deer trotted into sight.

   _____

   _____

   Sentence-combining method _____

2. One industrious friend made popcorn.
   The rest of us sat and talked in front of a fire.
   The fire was crackling and popping.

   _____

   _____

   Sentence-combining method _____

3. At the edge of the swamp, the geese rested quietly.
   They broke into flight.
   A car approached.

   _____

   _____

   Sentence-combining method _____

4. Many nations in Africa face the effects of prolonged droughts.
   Industrial countries are offering aid to these victims of famine.
   Two industrial countries are the United States and England.

   _____

   _____

   Sentence-combining method _____

5. Travel to European countries offers Americans a chance to see other countries.
   Americans are able to experienceddifferent cultures.

   _____

   _____

   Sentence-combining method _____

6. The judge prepared to announce her decision.
   The defendant squirmed in his chair.
   He knew that the judge had found him guilty.

   _____

_____

Sentence-combining method _____

7. Many banks failed during the Great Depression.
    Franklin D. Roosevelt instituted the Federal Deposit Insurance
      Corporation.

    _____

    _____

Sentence-combining method _____

8. San Francisco is a vibrant, exciting city.
    It has the Golden Gate Bridge and a magical Chinatown.

    _____

    _____

Sentence-combining method _____

9. Women have made gains over the past few decades.
    The gains are in employment and economic opportunities.
    These changes are being appreciated by a new generation of women.

    _____

    _____

Sentence-combining method _____

10. *The Glass Menagerie* portrays the conflicts within a fragile family.
    The play is by Tennessee Williams.
    The play has long been a favorite of American theatergoers.

    _____

    _____

Sentence-combining method _____

11. The Sunbelt area is growing.
    It is the fastest growing area in the United States.
    The Sunbelt states offer mild climates and industrial expansion.
    The states offer a lower cost of living than the Northeast or the Midwest.

    _____

    _____

Sentence-combining method _____

12. Paul Newman's acting career has spanned three decades.
    He has directed films.
    He has started a food company.
    He has created a camp for children.

    _____

    _____

    Sentence-combining method _____

13. On Halloween night, many of our friends enjoy old movies.
    The movies star Vincent Price.
    They read stories by Edgar Allan Poe.

    _____

    _____

    Sentence-combining method _____ _____

14. Many urban areas are experiencing a new type of homesteader.
    The middle and upper classes are returning to the hearts of cities.
    They are purchasing old homes.
    They carefully restore the homes.

    _____

    _____

    Sentence-combining method _____

15. The great beauty of the American Southwest inspired Georgia O'Keeffe.
    Georgia O'Keeffe is a painter.
    She produced many impressionistic paintings of the desert's landscape.

    _____

    _____

    Sentence-combining method _____

16. Americans are concerned about fitness.
    Health clubs are enjoying a robust sales year.
    Businesses are enjoying a robust sales year.
    The businesses sell athletic equipment.

    _____

    _____

    Sentence-combining method _____

17. The rock band prepared to play its first song.
The crowd roared its appreciation.

_____

_____

Sentence-combining method _____

18. The Orient Express was one of the most famous trains in the world.
The Orient Express epitomized luxury and comfort.

_____

_____

Sentence-combining method _____

19. On the shores of Walden Pond, Henry David Thoreau built a small cabin.
The cabin became the setting of one of the most famous books.
The books were in American literature.
The book was called *Walden*.

_____

_____

Sentence-combining method _____

20. Many teenagers die each year in automobile accidents.
The accidents involve drunk drivers.
Most states have raised their legal drinking age to 21.

_____

_____

Sentence-combining method _____

Transitional Words and Expressions

Transitional words and expressions indicate to the reader the specific types of relationships between sentences or ideas. These words or expressions mark the passage for readers so that they can easily understand how the writer links ideas. Analyze the relationship indicated by the transitional word *because:*

> Because the weather forecaster predicted torrential rains, we cancelled our beach trip.

In this sentence, the word *because* indicates a reason or cause. In this case, the reason that "we cancelled our beach trip" was the weather forecaster's prediction of rain. If the sentence did not contain the word *because*, then the reader would be forced to infer that the prediction of rain caused the change in plans. Hence, writers include transitions not only for their readers' benefit but also for clarity. Without transitions, readers can only guess, perhaps incorrectly, about the relationships between ideas.

Study the chart below and on the following page; it indicates the types of relationships that each word or expression stresses. Notice that sometimes a transition can indicate two or three different types of relationships. To decide which transition to use, examine the stated ideas and the relationship that they suggest. Although this chart gives you several options for transitional words, it does not include all transitions. As you discover others, add them to the list.

RELATIONSHIP	TRANSITIONAL WORDS AND EXPRESSIONS	
Addition	again	in addition
	also	likewise
	and	moreover
	as well as	next
	further	similarly
	furthermore	too
Cause	because	for this reason
	for	since
Chronology	after	in the meantime
	always	meanwhile
	at last	next
	before	soon
	briefly	suddenly
	currently	then
	finally	until
	first (second, etc.)	when
	frequently	
Comparison	all	both
	and	like
	as	similarly
Conclusion	finally	therefore
	hence	thus
	so	to conclude
Contrast	although	nevertheless
	but	on the contrary
	conversely	on the other hand
	despite	though
	difference	unlike
	even so	yet
	however	
Effect	as a result	so
	consequently	then
	for that reason	therefore
	hence	thus
	resulting	

RELATIONSHIP	TRANSITIONAL WORDS AND EXPRESSIONS	
Emphasis	above all	indeed
	especially	in fact
Example	for example	specifically
	for instance	such as
	in other words	to illustrate
Importance	finally	least
	first	next
	last	primarily
List	finally	moreover
	first	next
	furthermore	second
	last	third
Repetition	again	in summary
	as stated before	to reiterate
	i.e. (that is)	to repeat
Space	above	forward
	adjacent to	here
	alongside	in front of
	among	next to
	around	on top of
	below	over
	beside	there
	between	under
	beyond	where
	down	
Summary	finally	on the whole
	in brief	overall
	in short	

▼ **EXERCISE 5**

In the following sentences, underline the transitional words and expressions. Identify the type of relationship they stress, and write it in the blank.

1. The crowd gasped in delight as the Thunderclouds performed their aerial

   maneuvers._____

2. Because the weatherman had predicted snow showers, each child arrived at

   school in leggings and boots._____

3. After limiting your topic, you should develop a thesis sentence._____

4. The construction industry began to expand when interest rates declined to the single-digit level for the first time in seven years._____

5. Furthermore, real estate agents experienced a sharp rise in their incomes._____

6. The sales figures for this year remained flat despite a 10 percent increase in catalog sales._____

7. Overall, the company's performance this year was disappointing._____

8. The support staff will be cut by one quarter as a direct consequence of the poor sales figures._____

9. There will be a freeze on hiring until our profit margins exceed 1 percent._____

10. To repeat, sales must improve, or the company will soon face bankruptcy._____

▼ EXERCISE 6   Provide transitional words or phrases that indicate the relationship in parentheses.

▶ Example: Jane went to the dance; _**but**_ Hank decided
                                    (contrast)
to see a movie.

1. _____ his car was extremely old and in poor condition, Gerald
        (cause)
decided to purchase a new one.

2. Making a cake requires several steps. _____, you must purchase the
                                              (chronology)
ingredients the cake requires. _____, you must combine the
                                    (chronology)
ingredients in the correct order. _____, bake the cake at the correct
                                      (chronology)
temperature for the required time. _____, let the cake cool, and then
                                        (chronology)
frost it.

3. We had planned the perfect summer vacation at the beach; _____, the
                                                              (contrast)
weather was unseasonably cool and wet.

4. We have explored and used almost every inch of our country;

    _____, there are few true wilderness areas left.
       (effect)

5. _____ acid rain can occur several hundred miles from the source
       (cause)

    of pollution, we must legislate stricter pollution limits.

6. _____ the hockey team won every game in its regular season, it
       (contrast)

    was unable to win the championship game.

7. A vegetable garden provides fresh vegetables for the family;

    _____, it provides a productive hobby for the gardener.
       (addition)

8. Many occupations are dangerous; _____, police officers risk
                                        (example)

    their lives every day.

9. _____ the Industrial Revolution began in England in the 1830s,
       (contrast)

    it did not begin in America until after the Civil War.

10. The circus makes adults feel like children again; _____, there
                                                          (result)

    are frequently more adults than children in the audience.

USING TRANSITIONS

In a paragraph, you may use any number of transitions as you develop the topic
sentence. Some transitions, though, are particularly suited to the types of support
you might include. For example, when you are developing a series of steps that
will direct the reader in performing an action, then transitions indicating
chronology, importance, and enumeration (listing) would be appropriate for
primary support sentences. In the same fashion, if you construct a paragraph that
moves from the least important idea to the most important one, then transitions
indicating importance would identify the primary supports. In addition, transitions that suggest examples would often identify secondary support sentences
since these secondary supports usually illustrate, describe, or explain the primary
supports.

   Analytical readers can often identify the dominant pattern of development in a paragraph by studying the transitions a writer employs. For example, if
a paragraph's topic sentence promises the reader a discussion of the effects of
inflation, then transitions that indicate cause and result will appear frequently.
Although the paragraph will not contain only one type of transition (for example,
cause and result), one pattern will dominate. Therefore, be alert to an overall
pattern of development in paragraphs.

▼ EXERCISE 7

Circle the transitions used in each of the following paragraphs, and identify the relationships they stress. In the paragraph, also underline the supports that the transitions introduce. Finally, write the dominant pattern of organization for the entire paragraph in the blank.

1. As a hobby, gardening is not the tranquil, bucolic exercise that promoters claim. Instead there are many problems and frustrations associated with "getting to know nature." First, Mother Nature does not smile and shed her warmth on the gardener during November and March, the prime months for planting bulbs and readying the soil. Spending hours on your knees digging in hard, cold soil is guaranteed to cause more arthritis than any tennis game ever could. Second, raking and hoeing the garden to prepare the soil are not the back-strengthening exercises recommended by the orthopedist. In fact, they are not recommended by anyone, other than your worst enemy. Then, once the soil is prepared and everything is planted, the real problems arrive: drought, flood, heat, and insects. There is nothing more frustrating than watching hours of back-breaking effort float away on a storm-produced stream or shrivel under record-breaking sunshine. In short, for tranquility, you should try a nice, quiet game of poker; at least then you can gamble away the proceeds of many hours of work in just two hours.

    Dominant Pattern: _____

2. Then the man drowsed off into what seemed to him the most comfortable and satisfying sleep he had ever known. The dog sat facing him and waiting. The brief day drew to a close in a long, slow twilight. There were no signs of a fire to be made, and, besides, never in the dog's experience had it known a man to sit like that in the snow and make no fire. As the twilight drew on, its eager yearning for the fire mastered it, and with a great lifting and shifting of forefeet, it whined softly, flattened its ears down in anticipation of being chidden by the man. But the man remained silent. Later, the dog whined loudly. And still later it crept close to the man and caught the scent of death. This made the animal bristle and back away. A little longer it delayed, howling under the stars that leaped and danced and shone brightly in the cold sky. Then it turned and trotted up the trail in the direction of the camp it knew, where were the other food-providers and fire-providers.

    (from Jack London, *"To Build a Fire"*)

    Dominant Pattern: _____

3.   While the method of direct payments makes certain that those suffering most from the anguish of unemployment will receive direct aid, its total effect may be less than public spending in the form of public works. If the individual is given a direct payment, the bulk of the payment is spent for consumption. This increases the level of economic activity to some degree, provided the funds received do not come at the expense of consumption and investment elsewhere in the economy. Even if the individual is employed on a simple project such as leaf raking for the sake of respectability, the total effect is not much greater. The capital needed to put a group of individuals on such a job is limited to rakes, shovels, wheelbarrows, and perhaps a few trucks. Furthermore, the spending of a direct income payment primarily for consumer goods may have no greater effect than decreasing excess inventories of consumer goods.

(from Thomas J. Hailstones, *Basic Economics)*

Dominant Pattern:_____

4.   One of the many devastating effects of inflation on the middle class is the precipitous rise in tuition costs. As a direct consequence of annual tuition increases of 15 to 20 percent, more and more students must combine schooling and working in order to be able to afford their education. Without the job, they cannot pay for school, yet, with the job, they have neither the time nor the energy required by school. After students have attended classes for five hours and worked for another five hours, homework commands little, if any, interest or effort. When homework done in a slipshod manner becomes the norm, grades suffer. Then, teachers must face students who do not know the material because they have not studied it. The final result is that the teacher becomes a remediator, a reviewer of basic skills, instead of an instructor in new materials. Therefore, despite the widespread belief in the value of working, there are instances when it is more advantageous for a student *not* to work.

Dominant Pattern:_____

5.   More people should donate blood; giving blood is truly giving life. Unfortunately, too many adults have retained their childhood fear of needles, so they refuse to face the blood technicians. Or, people don't understand the donating procedures, and this fear of the unknown prevents them from helping other human beings. Perhaps if the prospective donors knew all the uses to which their pint of blood is put and all the people who are helped by it, then

they would be more willing to give fully of themselves. The whole blood is used, of course, but so are blood products. The pint can be separated into its components, and each part given to an ill person. Platelets help those whose bodies cannot resist infection; the red cells help those whose respiratory systems do not function properly. In addition, the white cells are used to help leukemia patients, and the blood serum provides needed fluids. When adults realize the multiple recipients of their gift, each one will be eager to donate at least four times a year.

Dominant Pattern: _____

▼ EXERCISE 8

Provide coherence in the following student paragraphs by using the five methods discussed in this chapter: pronouns, transitional words and expressions, synonyms, limited repetition, and sentence combining. Identify the methods you use.

1. The ideal office for a high school yearbook staff would be spacious and well equipped; however, the office of Hammon High School's yearbook, *The Village*, is not ideal. The space resembles a broom closet. It used to be one. During the winter months, the office reaches near-Arctic temperatures. It lacks any form of heating. The only thing that permits the habitation of the office in the winter is the size. Its close proximity forces staff members to work together in a small area. The office contains three wooden desks. They are dilapidated. They leave very little room for movement. Because it is a closet, the space naturally lacks a storage closet. All pertinent papers and materials are crammed into two filing cabinets. The office lacks any sophisticated equipment. Two typewriters collect dust on the hard, cold floor of the office. The typewriters are broken. Editors must use outmoded computers in Wheeler Hall. They use the aging facilities of the Art Department's darkroom. These working conditions are not ideal.

2. In the eighteen years I lived with my parents, I had never done the laundry; washing my clothes for the first time was a new experience. The first time I performed the chore I emptied the entire contents of the hamper into the washer. I poured the detergent on top. I started the machine. I left to run a few errands. I returned twenty minutes later to check on the machine's progress. Soap suds were pouring out the top and down the sides of the machine. I ignored the mess. I let the machine complete the wash cycle. The wash cycle was complete. I transferred the laundry into the dryer. I set the timer on the machine. I pushed the start button. When the dryer was finished, I removed the wash. To my surprise,

what had been white was hot pink. This was a costly error. It made me realize that the laundry should be separated before washing. Whites go with whites into hot water. Colors are washed in cool water. Fortunately, I have improved my technique. Since that first experience, I have not destroyed any more clothing.

3. Travelers can take an airplane or an ocean liner to a seaside destination; there are differences between the two in the way the travelers' time is spent. If travelers take the airplane, then they must arrive at the airport on time. They must check their baggage and board the plane. They have no time for extra sightseeing. Their main objective is to reach their destination quickly. They can relax later. While they are on the plane, they may be treated to a movie and a dinner. Those are the only luxuries. Travelers on an ocean liner spend their time differently. Once they are on board, there are many diversions for them. An ocean trip takes a long time. The ship is designed to cater to its passengers. There is a swimming pool. There are many activities the travelers can select. They can see movies, read at their leisure, enjoy nightclubs, and attend dances. They must relax. The ocean trip becomes a vacation in itself. The travelers arrive at an island refreshed. They can see the sights for a few days and return to their ship for the voyage home. Both ways of travel take vacationers to a specific location. They differ in the way the vacation is spent.

▼ EXERCISE 9

In a paragraph of your own, provide coherence within sentences and throughout the entire paragraph by using the five methods discussed in this chapter. After you have revised the paragraph, elicit responses and suggestions from a group of writers. What makes your revisions effective? How do they add coherence to the paragraph? How are the relationships of ideas clearly identified for your audience?

▼ Writing Strategy: COMPARISON/CONTRAST

You compare and contrast items each day when you shop for clothing, food, appliances, or cars. When you decided to attend college, you had already compared the advantages of a college education to the advantages of immediate full-time employment. In addition, you compared the costs, academic reputations, admissions standards, locations, and campus activities of different colleges. As you compared these items, you began to classify colleges by their contrasts, their differences. You might have even created a chart to aid you in identifying the particular characteristics of several colleges. Throughout this entire process, you analyzed a great number of items by comparing and contrasting.

As an organizational strategy, comparison-contrast paragraphs require a complete analysis of the two items by the writer. Since most readers will anticipate the obvious comparisons and contrasts between the items, you must move to more subtle differences, ones that are not quickly apparent to readers, to demonstrate the similarities and differences. For example, if you were to compare and contrast two restaurants, one fast-food and the other French, some differences are quite obvious: the French restaurant will cost more; the dinner will take longer at the French restaurant; you will have more options about food at the French restaurant; and you will be required to dress more formally there and to use your best table manners. Therefore, if you stress these differences in a paragraph, you may bore the reader who is familiar with both types of restaurants. In this case, you should reconsider your original topic; you might instead compare two fast-food restaurants or contrast two French restaurants. By doing this, you will indeed be able to offer your readers something new: an analysis of the more subtle differences between two eating establishments. For example, although many fast-food restaurants have similar menus, their products, decor, and service vary. Preparation of dishes in a French restaurant can vary because of the chefs' talents and training.

To organize your analysis effectively, present all of the information about one item first; then present information about the second item in the same sequence as you presented points in the first. Examine the subject-by-subject comparison of two restaurants below.

I. Topic Sentence: Unlikely as it may seem, differences do exist between Joe's Burgers and the County Drive-In.

II. Joe's Burgers

   A. Interior decorations

   B. Types of burgers

   C. Service

   D. Costs

III. County Drive-In

   A. Interior decorations

   B. Types of burgers

   C. Service

   D. Costs

IV. Conclusion

By using the subject-by-subject structure, you give the reader a complete analysis of one restaurant before you begin the second analysis. Your audience will be able to distinguish the differences easily since they have already read a description of the first place.

Oranges: Florida and California
John McPhee

An orange is not always the same, claims John McPhee in this analysis of oranges from the East and West Coasts.

An orange grown in Florida usually has a thin and tightly fitting skin, and it is also heavy with juice. Californians say that if you want to eat a Florida orange you have to get into a bathtub first. California oranges are light in weight and have thick skins that break easily and come off in hunks. The flesh inside is marvelously sweet, and the segments almost separate themselves. In Florida, it is said that you can run over a California orange with a ten-ton truck and not even wet the pavement. The differences from which these hyperboles arise will prevail in the two states even if the type of orange is the same. In arid climates, like California's, oranges develop a thick albedo, which is the white part of the skin. Florida is one of the two or three most rained-upon states in the United States. California uses the Colorado River and similarly impressive sources to irrigate its oranges, but of course irrigation can only do so much. The annual difference in rainfall between the Florida and California orange-growing areas is one million one hundred and forty thousand gallons per acre. For years, California was the leading orange state, but Florida surpassed California in 1942, and grows three times as many oranges now. California oranges, for their part, can safely be called three times as beautiful.

▶ QUESTIONS 1. Enumerate the differences between the two oranges.

2. To what cause does McPhee attribute the differences between the oranges?

3. Why are California oranges "three times as beautiful" as Florida oranges?

His Talk, Her Talk
Joyce Maynard

In these paragraphs, Maynard explores the ways in which men and women tell stories.

1.   I don't want to reinforce old stereotypes of bubble-headed women (Lucy and Ethel), clinking their coffee cups over talk of clothes and diets while the men remove themselves to lean on mantels, puff on cigars and muse about world politics, machines and philosophy. A group of women talking, it seems to me, is likely to concern itself with matters just as

pressing as those broached by my husband and his friends. It might be said, in fact, that we're really talking about the same eternal conflicts. Our styles are just different.

2   When Steve tells a story, the point is, as a rule, the ending, and getting there by the most direct route. It may be a good story, told with beautiful precision, but he tells it the way he eats a banana: in three efficient chews, while I cut mine up and savor it. He can (although this is rare) spend 20 minutes on the telephone with one of his brothers, tantalizing me with occasional exclamations of amazement or shock, and then after hanging up, reduce the whole conversation for me to a one-sentence summary. I, on the other hand, may take three quarters of an hour describing some figure from my past while he waits—with thinly veiled impatience—for the point to emerge. Did this fellow just get elected to the House of Representatives? Did he die and leave me his fortune?

▶ QUESTIONS   1. Who are Lucy and Ethel?

2. In one important way the conversations of males and females are similar. What is the one similarity?

3. How do the conversational styles of males and females differ? Explain.

▶ Two Views of the River
MARK TWAIN

American novelist, steamboat pilot, journalist, and humorist, Mark Twain (Samuel Clemens) discusses the differences between innocence and experience in the specific context of piloting a steamboat. His conclusions, however, extend to other professions as well.

1   Now when I had mastered the language of this water and had come to know every trifling feature that bordered the great river as familiarly as I knew the letters of the alphabet, I had made a valuable acquisition. But I had lost something, too. I had lost something which could never be restored to me while I lived. All the grace, the beauty, the poetry, had gone out of the majestic river! I still kept in mind a certain wonderful sunset which I witnessed when steamboating was new to me. A broad expanse of the river was turned to blood; in the middle distance the red hue brightened into gold, through which a solitary log came floating, black and conspicuous; in one place a long, slanting mark lay sparkling upon the water; in another the surface was broken by boiling, tumbling rings, that were as many-tinted as an opal; where the ruddy flush was faintest, was a smooth spot that was covered with graceful circles and radiating lines, ever so delicately traced; the shore on our left was densely wooded and the somber shadow that fell from this forest was broken in

one place by a long, ruffled trail that shone like silver; and high above the forest wall a clean-stemmed dead tree waved a single leafy bough that glowed like a flame in the unobstructed splendor that was flowing from the sun. There were graceful curves, reflected images, woody heights, soft distances, and over the whole scene, far and near, the dissolving lights drifted steadily, enriching it every passing moment with new marvels of coloring.

2   I stood like one bewitched. I drank it in, in a speechless rapture. The world was new to me and I had never seen anything like this at home. But as I have said, a day came when I began to cease from noting the glories and the charms which the moon and the sun and the twilight wrought upon the river's face; another day came when I ceased altogether to note them. Then, if that sunset scene had been repeated, I should have looked upon it without rapture, and should have commented upon it inwardly after this fashion: "This sun means that we are going to have wind tomorrow; that floating log means that the river is rising, small thanks to it; that slanting mark on the water refers to a bluff reef which is going to kill somebody's steamboat one of these nights, if it keeps on stretching out like that; those tumbling 'boils' show a dissolving bar and a changing channel there; the lines and circles in the slick water over yonder are a warning that that troublesome place is shoaling up dangerously; that silver streak in the shadow of the forest is the 'break' from a new snag and he has located himself in the very best place he could have found to fish for steamboats; that tall dead tree, with a single living branch, is not going to last long, and then how is a body ever going to get through this blind place at night without the friendly old landmark?"

3   No, the romance and beauty were all gone from the river. All the value any feature of it had for me now was the amount of usefulness it could furnish toward compassing the safe piloting of a steamboat. Since those days, I have pitied doctors from my heart. What does the lovely flush in a beauty's cheek mean to a doctor but a "break" that ripples above some deadly disease? Are not all her visible charms sown thick with what are to him the signs and symbols of hidden decay? Does he ever see her beauty at all, or doesn't he simply view her professionally and comment upon her unwholesome condition all to himself? And doesn't he sometimes wonder whether he has gained most or lost most by learning his trade?

▶ QUESTIONS   1. What is Mark Twain's main idea? Where is it stated?

2. List the major differences between the two views of the river. What structural device does the author use to indicate the differences in each paragraph?

3. In addition to the differences in interpretation of the sunset, what other rhetorical device does Mark Twain use to distinguish the two views?

4. What accounts for the differences in the scenes of the river?

▶ ### Lives Beyond the Beltway
Doug Eppler

In this student essay, Doug Eppler explores the differences between the city in which he studies and the town in which he lives.

1   The distance between two lives is twenty-seven miles. Between my city life in Baltimore and my rural life in New Freedom, Pennsylvania, there lie twenty-seven miles of Interstate 83. There exists the difference between the pulsing lights of a thriving city and the warm glow of a setting country sun. Shuttling between them, I see the differences in the settings, the people, and the lifestyles. Daily glimpses of these distant points show me two different lives—mine.

2   For at least seven hours a day, I live in Baltimore, Maryland, America's charm city. My schooling there affords me ample exposure to the beat of the city. It moves fast. Glimpses are all that I get: a new skyscraper here, more parking there, a new mall rising, corner stores falling. A national hub, Baltimore draws America to her. She flaunts her national sports figures while she hides her detrimental statistics. Figures, human and numerical, rise and fall with the trends. In the eyes of the nation, Baltimore shines and is shunned and shines again. Twenty-four hours mean the difference between front page on the *Sun* and fish wrappings downtown. Baltimore waits for no man.

3   No man waits in Baltimore. The "City That

Reads" is a city of speed. To be home in this active city is to be uninterested, for the city never closes. Quitting time begins the night life. Weekends fill with plans for parties, concerts, ballgames, or movies. Movie premieres and happy hours draw vibrant crowds. Highways and byways regurgitate their mechanical users. Life in Baltimore often drives me from exhilarated energy to nearly insane confusion.

4   With my car I escape. Back on 83, I begin a half-hour metamorphosis. I watch as buildings melt into rolling hills, malls become forests, and pavement dissolves to dust. I am home in my other life—New Freedom. Gliding across sparse rural roads, I relax at the sight of rolling hills and majestic trees. Unlike her urban sister, New Freedom decorates herself solely with nature. A local farmer's abandoned coop embraces the local ballplayers' small town cheers. The town mayor is known only for his local service station. From the eyes of the nation, my small town hides herself better than the deer in her woods. What's here today will be here tomorrow. Stories seldom change. The *Free Press* announces flea markets and farm shows to its non-paying public. Like rockers on the porch, New Freedom waits for nothing in particular. She merely waits.

5   Her people wait with her. Friday nights mean high school football or long walks down short country roads. The unobstructed Sun draws regular audiences to her daily curtain call. The neighborhood pizza shop fights no onslaught of customers. People in New

Freedom usually bed down by 10:00. Unlike Baltimore, New Freedom sleeps heartily every night. Rush hour here refers to two cars on the same one-lane bridge. New Freedom is far from flashy. She is not nationally known. She desires little more than fresh country air and children playing in her open fields. From the anxiety of the city, I voyage to the calm, flowing peace of New Freedom, Pennsylvania. From the excitement of the lights, I escape to the warmth of the departing Sun.

6   Twenty-seven miles, one half of an hour, and an entire world lie between Baltimore and New Freedom. The merciless clock adds headlines to former and dust to the latter. The city differs from the hometown in appearance, personality, and lifestyle. One bathes in the light of the nation while the other hides in the shadow. My trips from Baltimore to New Freedom illustrate the difference between city and rural life. I voyage not from town to town, not from city to country, but from life to life. Twenty-seven miles is longer than it sounds.

▶ QUESTIONS   1. What is Eppler's main idea? Where is it located? How does it control the piece?

2. How does Eppler organize this piece? What makes this organization effective?

3. What are the major differences between Baltimore and New Freedom? What details does Eppler provide to illustrate these differences?

4. What makes the details in this piece effective? Do these details exceed your expectations? (Consider how many people might contrast life in a small town and a large city.)

1. McPhee contrasts two items that most of us would believe are too similar to be contrasted: Florida and California oranges. In a similar method, choose two items that are closely related and analyze their differences. Finally, compose a paragraph that will describe those differences. Identify both an audience and a purpose for your paragraph.

2. Some studies seem to suggest that males and females not only talk differently but also think differently: Men are oriented toward social norms whereas women are oriented toward personal norms. Other studies suggest that men and women have different ethical systems: men judge actions based on their social consequences; women judge based on the action's effects on an individual. Even if these conclusions are valid, how important do you think those differences are? Discuss in a paragraph which you think are more important—the similarities between males and females or the differences.

3. Twain presents two real-life images—a river at sunset and a blushing girl—and shows how both can be interpreted in dramatically different ways, depending on the viewer's perspective. Consider another real-life situation and write a paragraph in which you contrast its possible interpretations. (You might want to discuss the construction of a shopping mall: some view it as a provider of jobs and a booster of real estate values; others see it as the symbol of materialism and the cause of congestion and pollution.)

▼ WRITING TIP

Be sure to check your paragraphs for confusing words by reading each sentence carefully. For more information on confusing words, see Part II, Chapter 13.

▼ Coherence Checklist

1. Have you used pronouns to avoid needlessly repeating the same words?

   _____

2. Have you used synonyms to reinforce important concepts?

   _____

3. If the piece is long enough, did you repeat key structures to emphasize primary ideas?

   _____

4. If you repeated key terms or phrases, what was your purpose in doing so?

   _____

5. Have you varied the structure of your sentences?

   _____

6. Did you coordinate ideas of equal value in compound sentences?

   _____

7. Did you subordinate ideas of lesser value in complex sentences?

   _____

8. Have you used transitional words and phrases between sentences and between ideas?

   _____

9. Are the transitions appropriate? Do they represent the types of relationships you want to stress?

   _____

10. Could a reader easily follow the ideas presented in your paragraph?

    _____

▼ Comparison/Contrast Checklist

1. Does your paragraph offer readers an analysis of subtle, rather than obvious, points of comparison or contrast between the two items?

   _____

   _____

   _____

   _____

   _____

2. Did you organize your comparison/contrast effectively, presenting information about each item in the same sequence?

   _____

   _____

   _____

   _____

   _____

7

Diction

OBJECTIVES

1. To use appropriate diction for achieving a specific purpose.

2. To avoid slang, jargon, regional expressions, clichés, and dead metaphors.

3. To be aware of a word's connotations and denotations.

4. To use context to define a word.

5. To recognize and create tone.

6. To explore composing through cause/effect.

PREVIEW

Diction means the words you choose to interest your audience. Tone is the aural quality of your writing; it influences your audience and enhances the transmission of your message. Context is the prose surrounding a word.

Diction means word choice, the words you choose to convey your message. Depending on your choice of words, your message can be formal or informal, general or specific; moreover, your level of language adds precision to your sentences and helps to create tone. So you must be aware of the multiple meanings and suggestions of words as you decide which words to utilize.

Specific Words

One of the first aspects of diction to consider is the specificity of a word: how general or particular a word is. Whether a word is general (broad and all-inclusive) or specific (narrow and detailed) depends on the context in which it appears. For example, the word *mammal* is general if one then lists specific types of mammals; however, the same word can be specific if it appears under the heading *animals*, since it names a particular category of animals.

Frequently, beginning writers do not consider whether their words are specific or general. This failure to consider a word's level of specificity leads to imprecise and general sentences. Consider this example:

The man walked down the street.

Each of the major components of the sentence—the words *man, walked,* and *street*—is very general; these words are so vague, in fact, that a reader cannot easily visualize the person, his actions, or the street. Contrast the sentence above with this revision:

The man, almost seven feet tall, raced down the crowded city street.

This sentence, with its adjectives and descriptive verb, creates a sharper visual impression for the reader. The reader knows more about the person, his actions, and his location. Hence, the sentence is more vivid and precise because the words chosen are more specific.

As a writer, you should use specific words to help your reader precisely comprehend your message. On the other hand, if your goal is to confuse your audience deliberately and to avoid being tied to a particular opinion, then you *should* use general and abstract words. (Politicians and bureaucrats are noted for such vague diction.) By remembering your purpose, you can choose the appropriate level of specificity.

▼ EXERCISE 1

Revise the following sentences to make them more specific because you want your audience to understand your message. You can improve your diction by adding nouns, descriptive verbs, adjectives, adverbs, or prepositional phrases.

▶ Example: It was very hot today.

▶ Revision: The temperature climbed into the high 90s, and no breeze rustled the tree leaves today.

1. Terry likes the beach in summer.

_____

2. *Ghost* was a great movie.

_____

3. The cat sat on the sofa.

_____

4. The basketball player made two points.

_____

5. The horse jumped the fence.

_____

6. The judge passed sentence on the defendant.

_____

7. The car was in poor condition.

_____

8. It was a peaceful small town.

_____

9. The concert was quite good.

_____

10. The football game was exciting.

_____

Slang, Jargon, and Regional Expressions

Another aspect of diction is the use of slang, jargon, and regional expressions. These types of vocabularies have very specific uses and are comprehensible only by particular groups. If you choose to use slang, jargon, or regional expressions, you must keep your audience in mind; make sure your readers are members of the target group and will understand your word choices. Otherwise, you will fail to communicate with your reader.

SLANG

Each generation and group has its own slang, its own language that has meaning only for the group. This language is extremely informal and can often be understood only by members of that particular group. During the fifties, for example, the words *cool*, *cat*, *beat*, and *hip* were part of the slang used by teenagers, beatniks, and college students. In the sixties, hippies used the terms *groovy* and *freaked out*. For a brief period during the eighties, "Valley girl" slang was popular. Although this slang originated in Southern California, *awesome* and *barf* were used by teenagers around the country.

Within a particular group, slang is appropriate; it unifies the group, identifies its members, and serves as a "shorthand" or code vocabulary. However, slang is inappropriate when a writer wishes to address a larger audience that is *not* part of the particular group. By using slang here, the writer indicates a lack of concern for communicating ideas; therefore, the writer's message will not be understood by others.

JARGON

Like slang, jargon exists within groups. A particular vocabulary for a profession, business, or group, jargon may appear to be a rather formal vocabulary. For example, in a computer class, the terms *interface*, *modem*, and *access* have specific meanings and serve as a quick code for those who know the meanings. However, two problems occur when this specific language is used outside the particular group. First, people who use technical jargon in a discussion with those outside their field are inconsiderate and attempt to support their expertise through their use of this vocabulary and not through their ability to communicate ideas to others. Second, technical jargon loses its meaning when it is used outside the confines of a technical field; at best, it is inappropriate to say, "I accessed the information" without referring to a computer process. At worst, it is absurd to say, "The children interfaced with nature," when the children simply went outside to play.

REGIONAL EXPRESSIONS

Although regional expressions are used by larger groups of people than slang or jargon are, they also fall into the category of code words. One of the best features of the English language is its ability to be flexible. Within many geographical regions, certain names and terms have evolved over the years. As the expression *you all* typifies a Southerner, other phrases identify Americans from different sections of the country. The word *sub* can mean a submarine sandwich, stuffed with many types of cold cuts and cheeses; however, Philadelphians describe the sandwich as a *hoagy*. In New York, such a combination is called a *hero*, and in New Orleans, the sandwich is a *poor boy*.

When a writer wishes to stress regional differences, these expressions are appropriate. However, without a specific context and purpose, these words can create the same problems that slang and technical jargon do; since regional expressions are used only by a specific group, they fail to communicate ideas effectively to those outside the region.

▼ EXERCISE 2

The following sentences employ slang, jargon, or regional expressions. Revise the sentences so that they communicate ideas to a broader audience.

▶ Example: Please extinguish all forms of illumination as you exit the room.

▶ Revision: Please turn off the lights when you leave.

1. He's a bad dude.

_____

2. Jeremy considered his former friend an ex-home boy.

_____

3. She had to schlep all the way over to the elevated train.

_____

4. The flick was groovy.

_____

5. For sure, it's an awesome day.

_____

6. My cousins, both good old boys in Alabama, favor my sister's boys in Louisiana.

_____

7. That dirtbag stole the old woman's purse.

    _____

8. Her pad is boss.

    _____

9. His new state-of-the-art stereo interfaced with his television.

    _____

10. In light of the applicant's present socioeconomic stratum, the bank officer believed that an additional advance of fiscal relief was untenable.

    _____

Avoiding Clichés and Dead Metaphors

A third aspect of diction that you should be wary of is the use of clichés and dead metaphors. When you compare two concepts, the temptation to reach for the familiar can be strong, but you must resist it. Your goal as a writer is to communicate a *new* perspective to your reader; that is very hard to do if your wording is trite.

CLICHÉS

Clichés, expressions that have been used too often, contribute nothing to vivid writing. Comparisons such as *red as a rose*, *quiet as a mouse*, and *white as snow* have been so overused that they are no longer descriptive. Your readers should be able to visualize the action within a sentence; however, these phrases do not allow the readers to do that. They actually say very little, for the writer who resorts to them has not used imagination to create a new comparison, but has relied upon conventional, lifeless, overworked phrases instead.

DEAD METAPHORS

Dead metaphors are also overworked comparisons. (A metaphor is a comparison that does not use *like* or *as* to note the similarity between two items. For example, the clause *he is an oak* is a metaphor suggesting the person has the strong, stable qualities of an oak tree.) Many dead metaphors are used frequently: *Achilles' heel, swan song, flag waving, grandstanding,* and *explore every avenue* are heard daily. Like clichés, these metaphors have been heard so often that they really mean little, and rather than increase the vitality of writing, they actually reduce it.

Avoid dead metaphors and clichés in paragraphs. Using dead metaphors indicates that, while you wanted to make a comparison, you did not use your imagination to create a vivid one. These expressions interfere with the communication process by stifling your original thoughts and creating boredom in your reader.

▼ EXERCISE 3 | Identify the clichés and dead metaphors in the following sentences, and substitute original or vivid comparisons.

▶ Example: His money burned a hole in his pocket.

▶ Revision: He was a spendthrift; he spent his money as quickly as he earned it.

1. That coach is as stubborn as a Tennessee mule.

   _____

2. Sure as shooting, I'd be pleased as punch to do that for you.

   _____

3. She's as pretty as a picture.

   _____

4. At midnight, the house was as dark as a bottomless pit.

   _____

5. It's been a horrible day; it rained cats and dogs from morning until evening.

   _____

6. We'll ride the problem out.

   _____

7. As a negotiator, he's as tough as nails; as a person, he's a kitty cat.

   _____

8. Nothing perturbs Ms. Jones; she's a rock.

   _____

9. His Achilles' heel was his inability to reason under pressure.

   _____

10. He let his hair down and joined the party.

   _____

Connotations and Denotations

Denotation is a word's accepted meaning(s) in a dictionary; **connotation** is a word's *suggested* meaning. For instance, compare the terms *house* and *home*. Both words share the same definition in a dictionary, but a smart real-estate agent will sell a prospective buyer a *home*, not a *house*. The agent might have the buyer picture his furniture in the new dwelling by saying, "How lovely your antique cabinet will look in this corner," or the agent might remind the buyer of the benefits of the dwelling by adding, "Your family will enjoy many comfortable evenings around the fireplace." Consider the old cliché: It takes a family to make a house a home. Americans tend to believe that homes are more valuable than houses. From this example, it is evident that the term *house* has little emotional appeal to us, but the term *home* connotes security, safety, companionship, and love.

Most writers are consciously aware of a word's denotation when writing, but they may be less aware of its connotations. This is unfortunate because, by being aware of connotations and choosing words accordingly, authors create *tone*, the sound of their writing. In addition, they can generate specific responses from their readers, based on the different impressions conveyed by the chosen connotations.

Connotations are formed by two methods. First, connotations can be given to a word by a large group of people and spread by its use on television and radio. The word *appeasement*, for example, initially meant "to pacify or to soothe." However, in 1938, after British Prime Minister Neville Chamberlain said that he had *appeased* Hitler by not opposing Germany's military occupation of Czechoslovakia, the word *appeasement* acquired a negative connotation. Today, the word suggests an obsequious compromise in which moral principles are sacrificed for a temporary peace.

Advertisers also help create our general connotations. The word *natural*, for instance, has been applied not only to food grown without chemicals, but also to shampoos made from detergents and to ice cream made with chemical additives. Consider, too, the phrase *state-of-the-art*. The phrase itself is jargon and means little; it suggests, however, the most technologically advanced design. Many products today claim to be "state-of-the-art," and advertisers use our belief that what is new is better to sell cameras, cars, stereos, and computers.

Second, connotations can be personal, developed by individual experiences. Although the word *school* denotes an educational institution, the education one receives, or the members of an educational institution, its connotations can vary greatly. The word *school* may evoke one person's memories of the first day of school as a six-year-old child, or it may elicit another's memories of a particularly pleasant or frustrating academic year. The word may also remind one of a specific instructor or class. These personal connotations, however, are more difficult to convey to a general audience unless the writer recounts the experiences that helped to create the connotation.

▼ EXERCISE 4

Discuss some of the connotations, both general and personal, the following sets of words have. Explain when these words could be appropriately used.

1. teacher, instructor, professor, educator, lecturer, schoolmaster, pedagogue, mentor, coach

2. fat, hefty, corpulent, plump, stout, portly, obese

3. preppy, punk, jock, head, hippie

4. aristocracy, gentry, bourgeoisie, proletariat

5. love, adoration, respect, affection, sentiment, fondness, infatuation

6. friend, pal, chum, acquaintance, confidante, comrade, buddy, ally, companion

7. car, automobile, van, wagon, wheels, sports car, vehicle, jalopy, convertible

8. lawyer, barrister, prosecutor, defense attorney, counselor, advocate

9. talk, gab, converse, chatter, gossip, lecture, speak

10. hoax, trick, deception, lie, fraud, canard

SUGGESTED MEANINGS

By carefully choosing a word for its connotation, you can imply values that you might not want to state directly. You can also project an impression of the subject to your reader that will cause your reader to react in a predictable way. While seemingly being objective, you can control your reader's responses through diction and, perhaps, indulge your personal biases. Examine these three words for their connotations:

> politician
>
> statesman
>
> diplomat

All three words have the same meaning, but each conveys a different impression. Many people in public life hunger to be called statesmen; they will probably even gladly accept being referred to as diplomats. Few, however, would describe their occupations as politicians. Therefore, if you refer to someone as a statesman, you create an aura of wisdom, power, and efficacy around the person; on the other hand, if a public servant is called a politician, you may imply that the person is pragmatic and corrupt. By simply choosing a word for its connotation, you can project specific images. Note the different connotations in the italicized words below:

1. The pilot was surprised to see his *crony* at the boat show.

2. The pilot was surprised to see his *friend* at the boat show.

3. The pilot was surprised to see his *acquaintance* at the boat show.

4. The pilot was surprised to see his *buddy* at the boat show.

Each of the above sentences has a different tone or sound because of the wording. Although the meaning of the sentence remains the same, the reader's responses to the given information will differ because of the impressions created by the author's choice of words.

▼ EXERCISE 5

Read the following sets of paragraphs. Indicate a few specific words, along with their denotations and connotations, that contribute to each paragraph's tone. Describe the tone of each paragraph, and indicate its probable audience.

1.   A politician has many cronies. He is willing to deal with them in a variety of settings: bars, convention halls, offices, and perhaps even back rooms. He is able to help them, and usually they are able to aid him; it is a mutually satisfying relationship. Each one recognizes the limits of the relationship and knows not to go beyond them. Most of the time, the public is unaware of all the goings-on.

Word	Denotation	Connotation
_____	_____	_____
_____	_____	_____
_____	_____	_____
_____	_____	_____
_____	_____	_____

Tone: _____

Probable Audience: _____

2.   A diplomat marvels at his many acquaintances. He enjoys their company in a wide range of circumstances: at receptions, parties, concerts, business meetings, and conferences. He prides himself on his ability to manipulate them tactfully, and they return the favor; both sides benefit from the relationship. Each party adheres to the proprieties and understands the bounds of their unspoken arrangement. Usually, the general public remains blissfully ignorant of all the undercurrents.

Word	Denotation	Connotation
_____	_____	_____
_____	_____	_____
_____	_____	_____
_____	_____	_____
_____	_____	_____

Tone: _____

Probable Audience: _____

WORDS IN CONTEXT

When you read and analyze material in order to synthesize its ideas with your own knowledge and to use them in your own writing, you may read words that are unfamiliar. One way to deal with this problem would be to keep on reading and forget about the new word, but that rejection would probably interfere with your comprehending the material. Another way to deal with an unfamiliar word is to make it known: learn the meaning by looking the word up in the dictionary. That method, too, presents problems: you lose time, lose your train of thought, and must decide on the most appropriate given meaning. The practical way to define a new term *while you read* is to use its context to help you make an educated guess about its meaning, to help you approximate the dictionary definition.

The **context** of a word is the environment in which it is found—the writing in which the word is embedded. You can use context clues to determine a general meaning of an unfamiliar word. The context helps you define a word by providing a description, summary, explanation or example, a synonym or antonym; sometimes it even provides a definition by means of the punctuation used. Although the context will not always enable you to define a word, you should be aware of it as a possibility and be willing to try it. In this way, you can develop your vocabulary and incorporate your new knowledge into your writing. Furthermore, as a writer, you can help your readers to understand unfamiliar words by providing them with ample context clues.

Context: Punctuation

Certain elements of punctuation sometimes provide clues to the meaning of a word; they let the reader know that a definition is being provided. Analyze these sentences:

> Hanukkah (an eight-day Jewish holiday) is celebrated by exchanging gifts.

> The debate was enlivened by the participants' witty repartee: clever exchanges of comments and banter.

> Some political commentators have been harassed, continually annoyed, while lecturing on college campuses.

> Agoraphobia—fear of open spaces—prevents some people from even leaving their houses.

Define these words:

Hanukkah _____

repartee _____

harassed _____

agoraphobia _____

In each of the preceding sentences, punctuation clues alerted you to a forthcoming definition. In your writing, if you have one concept that is central to your argument, be sure to define it if there is any possibility that your reader will misunderstand or misconstrue your point. To do this, use punctuation clues: commas, parentheses, dashes, or colons. Your choice of a particular punctuation mark will depend on how much you want to emphasize the definition. Dashes and colons clearly separate the word's meaning from the rest of the sentence, so they tend to highlight and emphasize it. Commas help the word's meaning blend into the sentence, while parentheses indicate that extra information (e.g., the definition of a word) is included for those who need it.

Context: Synonyms and Antonyms

Synonyms are words that have the same meaning; antonyms are words that have opposite meanings. Sometimes the meaning of an unfamiliar word can be determined from a synonym or antonym the author provides in the context of the sentence. Synonyms include one concept in a larger group, and antonyms exclude a concept from a larger group. Here are some examples:

The mother tried to assuage the toddler's anger by comforting and soothing him.

The community strongly opposes any changes in the zoning laws; their aversion is based on a desire to maintain the historical character of the village.

To paraphrase Marc Antony, have we come to extol the mayor or condemn him?

Instead of abstaining from high-calorie foods, you have been gorging on them.

Using the context of the sentences, define these words:

assuage _____

aversion_____

extol_____

gorging _____

Context: Explanation or Example

Frequently, an author will signal that an explanation or example of an unfamiliar concept is being provided by using a transition like *for instance* or by using the abbreviations *i.e.* (that is) or *e.g.* (for example). Look at these examples:

Because humans are bipedal—i.e., walk on two feet—their hands are free to use tools.

The plot centered on several morbid events—e.g., the death of an infant, the suicide of a parent, and the kidnapping and murder of an heiress.

Not only civilization but nature, too, supports parasites; for example, mistletoe derives nourishment from its host and kills the tree in the process.

The instructor is overly concerned with picayune facts; that is, he asks detailed questions about the color of a character's eyes, the style of the milkmaid's dress, and the exact location of the manor's kitchen.

Try to define these words:

bipedal_____

morbid _____

parasites _____

picayune _____

Remember that examples provide only *some* information about an unfamiliar word. They do not include the whole group or the complete con-cept, as demonstrated in the following sentence:

> On the first warm day in spring, the forest resounded with the sounds of its denizens—i.e., the gobbles of turkeys, the chatter of squirrels, and the growls of bears.

Denizens mean inhabitants, but, obviously, there are more animals in a forest than just turkeys, bears, and squirrels. The examples provide you with enough infor-mation to define *denizen*, but they do not give you a complete picture of the forest environment.

Context: Description

Occasionally, in order to define a word for a reader, an author will describe, or present a picture of, the concept. Study these examples:

> If a figure has eight angles and eight sides, it is probably an octagon.

> Because the child reads two-and-a-half years below his grade level, he is classified as remedial.

> If he is less than one year behind his fellow student, he is considered developmental.

> Some fraternity parties become bacchanalia, filled with carousing drunkards, noisy revelers, and riotous activity.

Try to define these words:

octagon _____

remedial _____

developmental _____

bacchanalia _____

Context: Summary

Another way to define an unfamiliar word is to summarize it. This means providing familiar information first and then stating the unfamiliar concept. Here are some examples:

> By working from dawn to midnight, seven days a week, Oscar acquired a reputation as a workaholic.

Because he donated untold sums of money to build libraries, orphanages, and even Carnegie Hall, Andrew Carnegie is remembered as a philanthropist, rather than a robber baron.

Unfortunately for Jay Gould, he invested his ill-gotten gains in additional business enterprises and high living; therefore, his reputation has not been revised like Carnegie's. Jay Gould is still considered the premier robber baron.

Try to define these words:

workaholic _____

philanthropist_____

robber baron_____

Context: Definition

The easiest way for you to learn the meaning of a word is for the author to define it. Authors use this method most frequently in textbooks when the reader *must* comprehend a word. Analyze these examples:

Bilingual means being literate in two languages.

A protist is a one-celled creature that is not clearly a plant or an animal; it has some of the characteristics of both king-doms.

Generally, literacy means being able to write and compre-hend on the fourth-grade level.

Few people know that a married man is also a benedict.

Define these words:

bilingual _____

protist _____

literacy _____

benedict _____

▼ EXERCISE 6

Using context clues, define each of the italicized words; then consult a dictionary to check your answers.

1. A CEO's *amanuensis* differs from other executives' secretaries in terms of status, glory, and longer working hours.

2. *Phobias* (irrational fears) afflict millions of Americans each year.

_____

3. *Paraplegics*, persons paralyzed in their lower bodies, are still human beings with functioning brains and minds; they deserve attention.

_____

4. Unlike the *carnivore*, the herbivore eats plants, not meat.

_____

5. The *ego* is the self; the individual is aware of himself or herself.

_____

6. *Neonatology*—i.e., the study of human newborns—is a relatively restricted field.

_____

7. Although their appearances are markedly different, *mammals* (e.g., whales, dogs, and humans) are remarkably similar anatomically.

_____

8. No one questions the motives behind giving overt financial aid because the aid is obvious to anyone who cares to examine the records; *covert* aid, on the other hand, is always being questioned.

_____

9. *Autarchy*, unlimited sovereignty, is not a popular form of government these days.

_____

10. Because he thinks of the concerns of others before his own, because he willingly sacrifices his goals to help others, Mr. Baumgartern is *altruistic*.

_____

Recognizing and Creating Tone

Tone, the aural quality of prose, the sound of language, was mentioned earlier in this chapter. The tonal aspect of writing depends upon diction; diction and tone are inextricably linked. Tone can take many forms. Usually, it is discussed by citing opposites: formal or informal tone, ironic or sentimental tone, objective or subjective tone, and humorous or antagonistic tone.

In speech, tone is easily recognized by the loudness, the pitch, and the inflection of a voice, and by facial expressions and body gestures. In your writing, your purpose and your intended audience control your choice of a particular tone, which you convey by using specific words and details. If you are discussing a serious topic, such as capital punishment, the need for unilateral disarmament, or civil rights, with a general audience, then your tone must be equally serious. It would be inappropriate to include jokes or colloquial language in such a discussion. In the same manner, you would create an inappropriate tone if you chose to use polysyllabic words in a description of a camping trip. In this case, the formality of the language would conflict with the recreation of a camping trip.

All writing uses a specific tone. If, for example, you want to convince a faculty committee to include a new course in the curriculum, then your tone must be objective to present the benefits of the course, formal to communicate with those who anticipate a well-articulated proposal, and, finally, persuasive to convince those who may be ambivalent about the proposition.

Even writing that purports to be totally objective often has an identifiable tone created by the author's choice of details and words. Consider the example of an objective newspaper story. Assigned to report on the problems of unemployment, a journalist will certainly check current statistics and interview those people who administer programs for the unemployed and who are responsible to the state and federal governments for the allocation of funds. The journalist will also interview people who are unemployed. Although the writer will remain as objective as possible, he or she will select certain details that give the piece a specific tone. Contrast two possible introductions that could begin such a column. One introduction might begin by quoting statistics over the past year. The other might detail the daily routine of a person who has long been unemployed. Certainly, these introductions, in their approaches to the subject, create different tones. The first seeks to be authoritative in its use of statistics; the second focuses on the people who comprise the statistics and encourages the reader to react emotionally to the piece. Both introductions are acceptable; both describe the situation objectively. However, a reader will respond differently to each of the articles because the tones differ.

▼ EXERCISE 7

Read the following pairs of paragraphs. Then, within each pair, identify and contrast each paragraph's tone and indicate which words and connotations contribute to it. Finally, indicate the paragraph's intended audience.

1. a.   The portly executive assumed his most regal stance in an attempt to intimidate the insubordinate clerk. Then the awesome personage glanced disdainfully at the sniveling nonentity. Lastly, without even a whisper of sound, he turned on his heels and strode into the inner office, leaving the petitioner in a state of fear and wonder.

Tone: _____

Word	Denotation	Connotation
_____	_____	_____
_____	_____	_____
_____	_____	_____

_____ _____ _____

_____ _____ _____

Audience: _____

b.　　The fat banker stood up, hoping to look a bit taller and perhaps overwhelm the rebellious clerk. Then he glared at his cringing subordinate. Finally, very quietly, he turned and walked out of the room, leaving a fear-filled and wondering person behind.

Tone: _____

Word	Denotation	Connotation
_____	_____	_____
_____	_____	_____
_____	_____	_____
_____	_____	_____
_____	_____	_____

Audience: _____

2. a.　　Today the bottom fell out of the stock market. The Dow Jones plummeted an unbelievable forty points and caused investors to scurry for their lives and their pocketbooks. The traders desperately tried to stonewall the shocking story in an attempt to belittle the events. But Mr. John Q. Public was not fooled; he cashed in his stock certificates and looked for the gold bugs.

Tone: _____

Word	Denotation	Connotation
_____	_____	_____
_____	_____	_____
_____	_____	_____
_____	_____	_____
_____	_____	_____

Audience: _____

b.　　Stock prices declined today; the Dow Jones Industrial Average fell by forty points, probably due to a combination of factors: institutional profit-taking and shaky investor confidence. Traders noted that today's decline represented less than 5 percent of the market's value, a development not worth much media attention. However, the general public seemed apprehensive about falling stock prices. The number of shares traded increased by 25 percent, and the purchase of gold futures rose by 18 percent.

Tone: _____

Word	Denotation	Connotation
_____	_____	_____
_____	_____	_____
_____	_____	_____
_____	_____	_____
_____	_____	_____

Audience: _____

Look again at paragraphs 1a and 1b. Basically, three actions take place:

1. A man stands up.

2. He looks at another person.

3. The first man leaves the room.

By supplying adjectives and adverbs to describe the people and their actions, and by selecting those modifiers carefully, the author not only created tone, he also suggested who was the better person. Which character does his tone seem to favor: the portly executive or the insubordinate clerk? the fat banker or the rebellious clerk? The author controlled his reader's response by choosing his words carefully. That should be your goal when you write: to choose your words with care in order to express your ideas clearly and help your reader to understand them and react to them.

▼ EXERCISE 8

Look again at paragraphs 2a and 2b in Exercise 7.

1. Which paragraph is more fact filled and objective? _____

2. Which paragraph is obviously subjective and conveys the author's opinion? ___

_____

3. List the words in the subjective paragraph that are "opinion" words: _____

_____

4. What is the purpose of paragraph 2a? Why did the author write it?_____

_____

_____

5. What is the purpose of paragraph 2b? What do you think the author is trying

to accomplish? _____

_____

_____

You have already compared the tone of each paragraph. Note that the choice of words is dictated by the author's purpose and audience and that word choice clearly influences tone.

Consider the following selection, which describes a local boxing event. What details and words suggest a specific tone?

On this Saturday night, there are no reporters packing press row—no national television coverage, no Don King or Bob Arum, no cigar smoke curling about the hot lights above the ring. In fact, it proves somewhat difficult to find the arena: an antiseptic place called Novak Field House at Prince George's Community College outside Washington, D.C. Rather than the bright lights of a marquee, a fan encounters a hand-lettered poster, tacked onto a campus sign, pointing the way. Ninety minutes before fight time, the parking lot is nearly empty. Inside, workmen are still erecting the ring, and the Maryland State Boxing Commission's office proves to be a physical-education classroom.

A visitor is struck by the competence and calm with which the Commission staff handles the myriad forms and the inevitable problems. Seconds are licensed, as one of the officials remarks to no one in particular, "Can you believe this? A professional fighter forgot his shoes." Most of the young fighters come from nearby: Hyattsville, Laurel, Washington, Philadelphia. A number are eager but awkward; at least one is making his professional debut. The punches tend to be wide and the footwork somewhat sloppy. But the 400 fans, a family crowd containing a number of young children, seem generally pleased, especially with a rousing lightweight bout that generates sustained applause. Three bouts go the distance; three end in technical knockouts. The five ring officials, all widely experienced, alternate as judges and referee. They step in quickly to protect the fighters. One reluctant warrior is dispatched to the showers in the first round.

Generally sympathetic, the writer's tone also proves ironic at times. Consider the details he uses. The fight is held in a local college gym, not in Las Vegas or Atlantic City. The gym itself is "antiseptic." With only a few minutes left before the scheduled bout, the ring is being assembled—this is not a major fight center. The boxers, although not described specifically, are identified as "young," "eager," and "awkward." They are not high-ranking professional fighters: one fighter has forgotten his shoes; their footwork is "sloppy"; and one leaves quickly after the first round. A "family" crowd watches the bouts; "young children" are present. Certainly, a fight such as this would not draw large crowds or press coverage; these are inexperienced fighters who are learning their trade as experienced referees "protect" the fighters from injury. Contrast this description of a local fight with the coverage a national title fight would receive. The writer stresses the difference between a local fight and a national championship by describing the place, the fans, the skill of the fighters, and the officials. These details and words create the author's tone.

▼ EXERCISE 9

Construct a writing situation for the following topics. Identify an audience, purpose, and an appropriate tone for a paragraph. (Remember that each topic could be addressed to several audiences; be specific about identifying your readers.)

1. a discussion of the homeless population

2. a discussion about requiring sex-education classes in high schools

3. a description of a meal

4. a description of an athletic event

5. a discussion of health care for the elderly

▼ EXERCISE 10

Rewrite the selection about the local boxing event. This time, imagine that you are the public relations manager for one of the contenders. Your intended audience is the sports editor for the *Washington Post*. Your purpose is to generate favorable publicity for your boxer.

▼ EXERCISE 11

Complete one of the following exercises, and explain your choice of tone for each of the audiences.

1. Write three brief paragraphs that describe your classroom, one to each of the following audiences:

   • the school administrators who want to know how to improve the educational setting

- a friend who has never visited the campus

- a brochure to be distributed to high-school seniors to encourage them to enroll at your school

2. Write three brief paragraphs that describe the campus student center, one for each of the following audiences:

- students who commute to campus daily

- a teacher who is interested in student activities

- your parents, who will visit the campus soon

3. Write three brief paragraphs that describe a car, one from each of the following points of view:

- as a consumer

- as a salesperson

- as an insurance agent

▼ Writing Strategy: CAUSE/EFFECT

As inquisitive beings, we constantly ask, "Why did that happen?" and "What are the consequences?" Without such inquiry into the causes and the effects of actions, we would not be able to learn to analyze situations to determine an appropriate course of action; instead, we would be forced to repeat the same mistake time and time again. Therefore, we would not be able to synthesize and utilize our experiences as a foundation for knowledge about the world. Consider, for example, the effects of an economic recession. Nearly everyone in a country suffers when prices rise uncontrollably as the value of currency declines. Certainly, if we wish to avoid recession, we must investigate its causes and take steps to ensure that these causes are not repeated. While this example proves the need to analyze national problems, consider a more commonplace analysis: each time someone asks why we enjoyed a particular movie, play, novel, or television show, we respond by giving our reasons—the causes—for our satisfaction.

As a writing strategy, cause/effect requires a logical analysis of an action or problem. Causes and effects can be divided into two categories: immediate and ultimate. Immediate causes and effects are those we think of first. For example, in response to the question, "Why did you not study for an announced test," a student might respond that she decided to see a movie instead on the night she should have studied. However, this analysis is incomplete since it asks only for a superficial response. We must look to the ultimate causes (as far as one can reasonably trace them) and the ultimate results (as far as we can follow or predict them). The student who failed to study for a test might finally admit that she is not interested in the course, that she is confident of her abilities in that subject, or that a personal concern was more important at that time than an academic responsibility. Any one of these answers might be true; they also indicate that other, ultimate reasons determined her choice to see a movie rather than to study for a test.

Your purpose for writing determines the structure of a cause/effect paragraph. If you address only the causes or only the effects, then the paragraph will be more effective because you will have the necessary space to describe and explain thoroughly the causes or effects. You can choose to order your ideas in one of two ways: chronological order or order of importance. Your purpose in writing the paragraph will help you decide which one is more effective.

The Arrest of Rosa Parks
MARTIN LUTHER KING, JR.

During 1955 and 1956, Martin Luther King, Jr. helped to organize the black community of Montgomery, Alabama, in a boycott against the city's segregated buses. The event described below was the catalyst for the boycott, one of many in the 1950s and 1960s. Through King's leadership, these peaceful, nonviolent protests changed the course of America's political, social, economic, and cultural life.

On December 1, 1955, an attractive Negro seamstress, Mrs. Rosa Parks, boarded the Cleveland Avenue Bus in downtown Montgomery. She was returning home after her regular day's work in the Montgomery Fair—a leading department store. Tired from long hours on her feet, Mrs. Parks sat down in the first seat behind the section reserved for whites. Not long after she took her seat, the bus operator ordered her, along with three other Negro passengers, to move back in order to accommodate boarding white passengers. By this time every seat in the bus was taken. This meant that if Mrs. Parks followed the driver's command she would have to stand while a white male passenger, who had just boarded the bus, would sit. The other three Negro passengers immediately complied with the driver's request. But Mrs. Parks quietly refused. The result was her arrest.

▶ QUESTIONS

1. What does the fact that Rosa Parks was a seamstress tell you about those who defend their civil rights?

2. Why did Rosa Parks refuse to move to the back of the bus? What was the effect?

3. Was Mrs. Parks's action a heroic one?

4. What is the tone of this passage?

Severing the Human Connection
H. BRUCE MILLER

H. Bruce Miller considers some of the reasons why we now must pay first in this example of gas stations.

The pay-before-you-pump gas station (those in the trade call it a "pre-pay") is a response to a real problem in these days of expensive gas and cut-rate ethics: people who fill their tanks and then tear out of the station without paying. Those in the business call them "drive-offs." The head of one area gasoline dealers' association says drive-offs cost some dealers $500 to $600 a month. With a profit margin of only about a nickel a gallon, a dealer has to sell a lot of gallons to make up that kind of loss. The police aren't much help. Even if the attendant manages to get a license plate number and description of the car, the cops have better things to do than tracking down a guy who stole $15 worth of gas. So the dealers adopt the pre-pay system.

▶ QUESTIONS
1. List the immediate and ultimate causes presented in this paragraph.

2. Why won't the police help the gas station owners?

3. What solution did the retail gas sellers finally opt for?

4. Jargon is used twice in the paragraph. Point out the jargon words and define them.

Primitive War
MARVIN HARRIS

Marvin Harris is a well-known cultural anthropologist; his specialty is examining the history of cultures to determine the reasons for their taboos, restrictions, and laws.

1   In most primitive societies, warfare is an effective means of population control because intense, recurring intergroup combat places a premium upon rearing male rather than female infants. The more numerous the adult males, the stronger the military force which a group dependent upon hand weapons can put into the field and the more likely it is to hold onto its territory against the pressure exerted by its neighbors. According to a demographic survey of over 600 primitive populations carried out by William T. Divale of the American Museum of Natural History, there is an extraordinarily consistent imbalance of boys over girls in the junior

and infant age ranks (up to about 15 years old). The average ratio of boys to girls is 150:100, but some groups even have twice as many boys as girls. The Tsembaga ratio of boys to girls falls close to the average of 150:100. When we turn to the adult ranks, however, the average ratio between men and women in Divale's study falls closer to unity, suggesting a higher death rate for mature males than mature females.

2   Combat casualties are the most likely reason for the higher death rate among adult males. Among the Maring, male battle casualties outnumber female casualties by as much as 10 to 1. But what accounts for the reverse situation in the junior and infant age categories?

3   Divale's answer is that many primitive groups follow a practice of overt female infanticide. Female children are suffocated or simply left unattended in the bush. But more often infanticide is covert, and people usually deny that they practice it—just as the Hindu farmers deny that they kill their cows. Like the unbalanced sex ratio among cattle in India, the discrepancy between human female and male infant mortality rates usually results from a neglectful pattern of infant care, rather than from any direct assault on the female baby's life. Even a slight difference in a mother's responsiveness to her children's cries for food or protection might cumulatively account for the entire imbalance in the human sex ratios.

4   Only an extremely powerful set of cultural forces can explain the practice of female infanticide and the preferential treatment given to male infants. In strictly biological terms, females are more valuable than males. Most males are reproductively redundant, since one man can suffice to impregnate hundreds of females. Only females can give birth to the young and only females can nurse them (in societies that lack baby bottles and formula substitutes for mother's milk). If there is going to be any kind of sex discrimination against infants, one would predict that the males would be the victims. But it is the other way around. This paradox gets harder to understand if we admit that women are physically and mentally capable of performing all the basic tasks of production and subsistence quite independently of any help from males. Women can do every job that men can do, although perhaps with some loss of efficiency where brute strength is required. They can hunt with bows and arrows, fish, set traps, and cut down trees if taught to do so or permitted to learn. They can and do carry heavy burdens, and they can and do work in gardens and fields throughout the world. Among cut-and-burn horticulturists like the Maring, women are the main food producers. Even among hunting groups like the Bushmen, female labor provides over two-thirds of the group's nutritional needs. As for the inconveniences associated with menstruation and pregnancy, modern leaders of women's liberation are quite correct when they point out that these "problems" can easily be eliminated in most jobs and production activities by minor changes in work schedules. The alleged biological basis for a sexual division of labor is a lot of nonsense. As long as all the females in a group are not found in the same stage of pregnancy at the same time, the economic functions considered to be the natural male prerogative—like hunting or herding—could be managed very nicely by women alone.

5   The one human activity, other than sex itself, for which male specialization is indispensable is armed conflict involving hand weapons. On the average, men are taller, heavier, and more muscular than women. Men

can throw a longer spear, bend a stronger bow, and use a bigger club. Men can also run faster—toward an enemy in attack and away from one in defeat. To insist along with some women's liberation leaders that women too can be trained to fight with hand weapons does not alter the picture. If any primitive group ever trained women rather than men as its military specialists, it made a big mistake. Such a group surely committed suicide because not a single authentic case is known from any quarter of the globe.

6   Warfare inverts the relative value of the contribution made by males and females to a group's prospects for survival. By placing a premium upon maximizing the number of combat-ready adult males, warfare obliges primitive societies to limit their nurturance of females. It is this, and not combat per se, that makes warfare an effective means of controlling population growth.

▶ QUESTIONS

1. What is female infanticide? Why is female infanticide practiced? What are the effects of female infanticide?

2. Why are males "reproductively redundant"?

3. According to Marvin Harris, there is only one activity in which women cannot be as proficient as men. What is that activity? Why does he believe this?

▶ # A Place to Come Home To

RYAN BROMWELL

In this student essay, Ryan Bromwell discusses the effects of his childhood home upon his life.

1   When the going gets tough, the tough go home. During my youth, my little house on Wentworth Avenue provided a safe bunker to retreat to when the world's crossfire heated up. Much more than a house, it was home. Through all my honest endeavors and childish escapades, my parents remained calm and understanding as they nurtured a curious young boy through adolescence to become a worldly young man. The conniving neighborhood kids, however, dedicated themselves

to corrupting any virtue of innocence still left undeveloped by my parents. My neighbors, always the voice of honesty and wisdom, encouraged me to mature and develop into a successful young man. My home on Wentworth Avenue was like a tiny home base in a giant game of tag. Over the years, my parents, my friends, and my neighbors have offered the safety and encouragement a grow-ing boy needs along the way to young adult-hood.

2   From the beginning of my life, my parents have given me unconditional love and support in everything which I have tried. Whether I wanted to play Little League baseball or travel halfway around the world, my parents gave their blessing and support. I can still remember the day at age eleven when I hit my first homerun in a Harford Park Little League baseball game. The way my parents cheered and carried on, I think that they were more excited than I was. A few years later on the day when I resolutely announced that I wished to travel to Europe, they were less excited and a little apprehensive, yet they allowed me to go on one condition: I had to pay for the trip. Though at first I abhorred these little conditions which my parents attached to many things, they taught me to be responsible and self-reliant. Now that I am a young man, I understand and appreci-ate all the values and lessons which my parents have tried to instill within me. As a young boy,

however, I desired only to forget my responsibilities and to run wild and free.

3   Freedom reigned when I joined my neighborhood friends to play freeze tag, cowboys and Indians, or my personal favorite: bike races. Sometimes we would even collect crab apples, hide in my treehouse, and wait for the bigger kids down the street to attack. When the big kids never ambushed, we usually pelted the next-door neigbor's dog with the apples. Echoing from underneath the porch steps next-door, her pitiful whimpers protested our reckless misdeeds. Looking back, I realize how harmless these childhood games were. Now that we are big kids, my friends and I play more dangerous games like driving, dating, and drinking. Life seems so different from the simple days when, at the coaxing of a big kid, I innocently asked my mother what birds and bees had to do with one another. Today most of my neighborhood friends have moved away. I have made new friends. Together we face the crossfire of complex decisions and contemporary issues affecting us all. The days have vanished when crab apples meant the difference between virtue and vice.

4   If I could avoid vice, my seemingly omniscient neighbors saw to it that I did. My neighborhood included mostly elderly people who offered a young boy of eleven a multitude of opportunities. Sometimes they would ask me to mail postcards

for them or rake their leaves. Eagerly, I jumped at these small tasks in hopes of receiving stamps for my collection or a tin full of freshly baked cookies as a reward. I could see them smiling at me from their windows as I knocked door-to-door selling wrapping paper or candy bars to support my school or soccer team. Everyone always bought something no matter how often I appeared on the doorstep. Now that I am older, I earnestly repay the generosity which these kindly people showed me. As a volunteer in the Social Service Program, I minister to the aging and infirm at my community nursing home. Just as my neighbors watched out for me as I matured from childhood to young adulthood, so now I keep an eye out for them as they grow older and older. Even as I grow older, I shall always practice these virtues of trust and generosity which these elderly neighbors have shown me.

5   As I have grown from boyhood to young adulthood, my parents, friends, and neighbors have given me a lifetime of memories and values which can withstand any raging crossfire. Overlooking the fact that all their dogs were once spotted with crab-apple bruises, my neighbors never cease to share their wisdom and generosity with me. Intent on destroying any glimmer of innocence within me, my friends succeed only in bolstering my common sense and community awareness. Providing love and support, my par-

ents once again stand beside me and urge me onward as I prepare to attend college and enter into the real world. The future holds a number of challenges in store for me. Soon I must leave the safety of my tiny home base and travel into the midst of the great wide world. However, I shall never forget the little house on Wentworth Avenue where I grew up, and the people who made it home.

▶ QUESTIONS

1. What is Bromwell's main idea? Where is it located? How does it control this piece?

2. In the second paragraph, Bromwell states that "my parents have given me unconditional love and support in everything which I have tried." What specifics does he offer to illustrate this statement?

3. In each paragraph that develops the main idea, Bromwell explains how certain people—his parents, friends, and neighbors—influenced him as a child and as an adult. Look carefully at paragraphs 2–4. How have these people influenced him? What caused this influence?

4. In paragraphs 2–4, list the causes and effects of Bromwell's values as a young adult.

5. Analyze Bromwell's diction and tone. What makes them effective or not effective?

▼ PARAGRAPH
ASSIGNMENTS

1. Sometimes, seemingly good solutions to problems—such as pre-paid gas or deinstitutionalization of the mentally ill—have unintended ill effects. Think of a social problem and some suggested solutions. Consider whether those solutions would solve the problem or whether their effects would generate even greater problems.

2. Most major events in our lives (graduation, first car, first job, death of a family member) are remembered as isolated incidents; they have no before and after. Yet, of course, these events do have causes and effects. Write about an important occurrence in your life and analyze its causes and results.

3. Each of us likes to believe that at some time we have behaved heroically. Describe such a time in your own life and discuss the effects of your action. Identify an audience and purpose for the paper.

4. Sometimes people's motives and actions are misunderstood by others. These misunderstandings lead to friction and tension between friends, coworkers, or loved ones. Describe a time when your motives or actions were misunderstood, and discuss the effects this misunderstanding had on your relationship with that person. Address your comments to the person involved, and define a purpose for the paper.

▼ WRITING TIPS

Consider your words carefully. The first word that occurs to you may not be the best choice to communicate your precise meaning. Do not settle for just any general word; don't "make do." Make your word choice a partner in the communication process; let your diction help you to get your message to your reader.

Check your writing for agreement between verbs and their subjects. If there are some subjects, such as indefinite pronouns or collective nouns, whose number you are unsure of, check Part II, Chapter 7 for the correct form.

▼ Cause/Effect Checklist

1. Does your paragraph begin with causes or effects?

   _____

   _____

2. Do the causes and effects go beyond the obvious ones? Did you include ultimate causes and effects as far as is reasonably possible?

   _____

   _____

   _____

3. In what order have you presented the causes and effects?

   _____

   _____

   _____

   _____

4. Is that order effective in supporting your topic sentence? Why or why not?

   _____

   _____

   _____

5. Are the causes and effects verifiable by historical fact, statistics, or logic?

   _____

   _____

   _____

   _____

▼ Diction Checklist

1. Are your key concepts represented by carefully chosen words?

   _____

   _____

2. Can you replace any general words with more specific ones, or
   add descriptive words to make an image more precise?

   _____

   _____

   _____

3. Have you eliminated slang, jargon, regional expressions, clichés,
   and dead metaphors from your paragraph?

   _____

   _____

   _____

4. Have you provided context clues to help your reader understand
   terms that might be unfamiliar?

   _____

   _____

   _____

5. Does your paragraph achieve the tone you intended?

   _____

   _____

   _____

8

Style

▶ **OBJECTIVES**

1. To develop a style suitable to your audience, purpose, and message.

2. To create a suitable style by effectively using voice, verbs, subordination, parallel constructions, and sentence variety, and by avoiding wordiness.

3. To explore composing through definition.

▶ **PREVIEW**

Style is your individual way of communicating your message. Voice is the specific verb form used to indicate the relationship between a verb and its subject. Sentence variety comes from using different types of sentences, including periodic and loose sentences, as well as varied sentence beginnings.

As a final writing strategy, you should revise your work for an effective style. By performing this final revision, you can reduce wordiness, use active-voice and descriptive verbs, use subordination effectively, develop parallel constructions, and vary sentence structure.

Avoiding Wordiness

You can easily revise by eliminating unnecessary words. Consider this example of a wordy sentence:

> The school that is located in the valley has increased its enrollment with so many students to the point that the school is overcrowded and filled with students. (*Total number of words* = 28)

Now, consider this revision of the same sentence:

> Because the school in the valley has enrolled so many students, classes are overcrowded. (*Total number of words* = 14)

The revised sentence is more effective because it is not too wordy. Here are the major revisions made in the sentence:

1. The relative clause *that is located in the valley* is wordy since the prepositional phrase *in the valley* tells where the school is located. Therefore, the words *that is located* can be eliminated.

2. The verb phrase *has increased its enrollment* can easily be reduced to *has enrolled*.

3. The phrase *to the point that* actually establishes a cause/effect relationship; therefore, the word *because* can be substituted for the longer phrase, with no loss of meaning.

4. The phrase *filled with students* is synonymous with the word
    overcrowded. Hence, the phrase can be eliminated.

These revisions cut the length of the sentence in half without altering its meaning.

STEPS TO ELIMINATE WORDINESS

Use the following process to eliminate wordiness in your sentences:

1. Identify the main idea in the sentence.

2. Locate and remove any repetitive elements.

3. Consider one-word synonyms to replace longer phrases.

▼ EXERCISE 1

Revise the following sentences to eliminate wordiness. Be prepared to explain your revisions.

1. During the time of the year in the fall, Cheryl made a decision and
    determined that she should enlist in and join the army.

    _____

2. The gas occupies a space of four cubic feet.

    _____

3. The frozen precipitation, the snow, fell quickly and rapidly at 3 p.m. in the
    afternoon.

    _____

4. At that point in time, Thomas decided to move to the state of Oregon.

    _____

5. The student, a pupil of Ms. James, nervously and anxiously paced the floor
    and walked back and forth down the corridor as he awaited the decision of
    the principal about his conduct.

    _____

6. The parade, held in honor of St. Patrick's Day, attracted a large crowd with
    many people dressed in green clothes.

    _____

7. The vehicle, a four-wheel-drive Jeep, climbed the steep and narrow and
    winding road on the mountain easily and effortlessly.

    _____

8. The gymnast performed and executed several difficult tumbling maneuvers and routines.

_____

9. The writer of newspaper articles reported on the latest and most current developments of the stock exchange on Wall Street in New York City, New York.

_____

10. After he had appeared in several television programs and stories, the actor performed and starred in a movie.

_____

Using Active Voice

Transitive verbs, those that can take a direct object, have either active or passive voice. An active-voice verb carries the action from the subject to the direct object. Look at the following example:

> Gerald wrote his term paper.

The subject of the sentence, *Gerald*, performs the action of the verb *wrote*; the direct object *paper* receives the action of the verb. (The direct object answers the question, "What was written?") In this sentence, each element of the sentence performs its traditional role: the subject acts; the verb names the action; and the direct object receives the action of the verb. However, the focus of the sentence shifts when the verb is in passive voice:

> The term paper was written by Gerald.

In this sentence, the subject *paper* does not act as a subject traditionally does; instead of performing the action of the verb, this subject receives the action of the verb. In effect, the subject *paper* acts as a direct object would. The person who actually performed the action of writing is Gerald; however, the noun *Gerald* is the object of the preposition *by*. The importance of the actor has been reduced in the sentence. In fact, the actor could be eliminated entirely:

> The term paper was written.

In this version, there is no indication of who wrote the paper. The writer simply acknowledges that the paper has been completed.

In general, writers prefer active voice for several reasons.

1. With active-voice constructions, the subject of the sentence does what it is supposed to do: it performs the action of the verb.

2. Active voice directly states who or what performed an action.

3. Active voice names the actor who must assume responsibility for the action. In a passive-voice construction, the actor is

often hidden in a prepositional phrase and, therefore, takes no direct responsibility for the action.

4.   Sentences with active-voice verbs are usually more concise.

However, you can use the passive voice effectively in the following two cases:

1.   When the identity of the actor is not known.

▶ Example: Before we tried to enter the gym, the door *had been locked.*

In this sentence, the identity of the person who locked the door is not as important as the fact that the door was locked.

2.   When, for whatever reason, the writer does not want to identify the actor. Usually, in this case, the writer wants to focus on the result of the action, not the actor.

▶ Example: The computer program *was completed* on time.

In this sentence, the completion of the program is more important than the people who designed it.

The chart below will help you identify active and passive verb constructions. The verb "to write" is presented in each tense.

TENSE	ACTIVE VOICE	PASSIVE VOICE
Present	*write* or *writes*	*am, is* or *are written*
Past	*wrote*	*was* or *were written*
Future	*will write*	*will be written*
Present Perfect	*has* or *have written*	*has* or *have been written*
Past Perfect	*had written*	*had been written*
Future Perfect	*will have written*	*will have been written*
Present Progressive	*am, is,* or *are writing*	*am, is,* or *are being written*
Past Progressive	*was* or *were writing*	*was* or *were being written*
Future Progressive	*will be writing*	*will be being written*
Present Perfect Progressive	*has* or *have been writing*	*has* or *have been being written*
Past Perfect Progressive	*had been writing*	*had been being written*
Future Perfect Progressive	*will have been writing*	*will have been being written*

NOTE:
The form of helping verbs, those verbs preceding the main verb and indicating the verb tense, in some cases is determined by the number and person of the subject. For example, note in the present progressive how subjects take different helping verbs: I *am* knowing, he or she *is* knowing, and they *are* knowing.

▼ EXERCISE 2

In the following sentences, change the ineffective and indirect passive voice to more effective and direct active voice. Supply actors when necessary.

▶ Example: The car was driven furiously by a reckless octogenarian.

▶ Revision: A reckless octogenarian drove the car furiously.

1. The novel was written by a well-known historian.

_____

2. The television program was cancelled after five weeks because of its poor ratings.

_____

3. The windows were washed last week during our spring housecleaning.

_____

4. The church doors were opened by the priest as the newly married couple walked up the aisle.

_____

5. The information was gathered by Harriet, not by Jason.

_____

6. The table was refinished by an expert artisan.

_____

7. The police were summoned to the scene of the crime by an anonymous caller.

_____

8. The elderly man was mugged by four adolescents.

_____

9. The forest was destroyed so that a shopping mall could be built.

_____

10. The bond bill, insuring funds for a new park, was passed by the county voters.

Using Descriptive Verbs

Verbs, the most important element in a sentence, label the action that the subject performs. Why is it important to your style for you to use descriptive verbs? Descriptive verbs offer the reader a visual image. In fact, if you choose your words with care, you can present a specific image to the reader and avoid any confusion about your meaning.

▶ Example: The child *walked* down the street.

The child *strolled* down the street.

The child *scooted* down the street.

The child *ambled* down the street.

The child *trotted* down the street.

Although *walked* is an action verb and it does present a visual image, the alternate verbs are obviously much more vivid and accurate. There are several degrees of activity levels between *ambled* and *trotted*. Each descriptive verb presents a specific image to your readers that helps them understand your meaning.

In contrast, linking verbs, such as *to be*, *seem*, or *appear*, do *not* create images for readers. Instead, these verbs offer equations or only approximations of actions: for example, he *is* an engineer, or she *seems* happy. Therefore, these linking verbs are not as vivid as verbs that describe actions. Since these linking verbs are not very expressive, try to use descriptive verbs whenever possible in your writing. Such use will make your writing style much more effective.

Analyze the following paragraph. Pay particular attention to the verbs in this description of the Brooklyn Dodgers written by sportswriter Roger Kahn long after the baseball team left Brooklyn for Los Angeles. In this passage, Kahn depicts the changes created by the passing of nearly twenty years.

> The team grew old. The Dodgers deserted Brooklyn. Wreckers swarmed into Ebbets Field and leveled the stands. Soil that had felt the spikes of Robinson and Reese was washed from the faces of mewling children. The New York *Herald Tribune* writhed, changed its face and collapsed. I covered a team that no longer exists in a demolished ball park for a newspaper that is dead.
>
> (from Roger Kahn, *The Boys of Summer*)

With its four one-syllable words, the first sentence signals the passage of time. The years, like the words, move along quickly, and the verb *grew* marks the change from young baseball players to more mature men. In the second sentence, another brief construction not only tells what happened but also offers the writer's judgment, clearly a negative one, of the Dodgers' flight to Los Angeles in

1958. In the third sentence, Kahn turns from the Dodgers to the field where they performed. The verbs in this sentence, *swarmed* and *leveled*, tell the reader not only what happened but also the author's response to the change. Both verbs have negative connotations, and *swarmed*, a metaphor, powerfully compares the workers to insects engaged in mindless destruction. Had Kahn chosen less vivid verbs—for example, "construction workers entered Ebbets Field and took apart the stands"—the sentence would have been much weaker. Sentence four strikingly juxtaposes past and present. The ground upon which numerous World Series were played now supports an apartment project. To emphasize such desecration, Kahn personifies *soil*. Previously, it had *felt* the spikes of Pee Wee Reese and Jackie Robinson, the first black major-league player, as they turned double plays. Now, it is washed from the faces of young children as they cry and crawl where skilled athletes once strutted. Having dealt with the team and its stadium, Kahn moves in sentence five to the newspaper for which he covered the Dodgers in the early 1950s. To detail the demise of the New York *Herald Tribune*, Kahn uses three potent verbs—*writhed, changed,* and *collapsed*—with the first two personifying the newspaper to make its death more graphic. The final sentence, which serves as the paragraph's topic sentence and conclusion, records Kahn's sense of loss for the *team that no longer exists*, for the *demolished ball park*, and for the *newspaper that is dead*. Appropriately, the sentence ends with a sense of finality, as *dead* intensifies the theme of change that runs throughout the paragraph. Through his use of descriptive verbs and appropriate participles, Kahn carefully orchestrates his idea that nothing good can last, that the boys of summer must inevitably become the men of winter.

▼ EXERCISE 3

Replace the italicized weak verbs with strong, descriptive verbs. Revise the sentence as necessary.

1. The jogger *ran* down the street.

   _____

2. The football team *is* on the field.

   _____

3. The soprano *sang* the National Anthem well.

   _____

4. The bird *flew* from tree to tree.

   _____

5. The wolf *moved* toward the lamb.

   _____

6. St. Louis *is* on the Mississippi River.

   _____

7. The skaters *are* on the ice.

   _____

8. The play *is* an exciting one.

   _____

9. The child *is* at the playground.

   _____

10. The car's engine *sounds* strange.

    _____

Using Effective Subordination

Complex sentences contain one independent clause and one or more dependent clauses. Both types of clauses contain subjects and verbs. An independent clause expresses a complete thought and can stand alone as a sentence whereas a dependent clause cannot stand alone as a complete sentence. Dependent clauses usually begin with subordinate conjunctions (for example, *although, because, while, after, before,* and *as*), which introduce the clause, or relative pronouns (*who, which,* and *that*), which act often as the subjects in the dependent clause. Consider the following example of a complex sentence:

> Although the new television program received numerous awards, network executives cancelled the show because it failed to attract a large audience.

The independent clause *network executives cancelled the show* contains the most important information in the sentence. The dependent clause *although the new television program received numerous awards* presents a contrast, for the program was dropped from the schedule *even though* it was recognized as an outstanding program. The second dependent clause, *because it failed to attract a large audience,* provides the reason for the cancellation.

By effectively subordinating the two less important ideas, the author made the presentation of information more interesting. Because the writing flows easily and the ideas join effortlessly, the reader is not bored. Consider these sentences, which offer the same information but without distinguishing relative importance.

> The new television program received numerous awards. Network executives cancelled the show. The show failed to attract a large audience.

Remember that since it can stand alone as a sentence, the independent clause should contain the most important piece of information in the sentence. The dependent clauses should contain only additional information, since these clauses are not capable of acting as complete sentences.

▼ EXERCISE 4   Read the following paragraph carefully and answer the questions that follow it.

College students appreciate their spring break for many reasons. First, there is the spring break, which is a well-deserved vacation for some students, who have worked diligently throughout the semester. Those students who spend their vacation by relaxing at one of their favorite beach resorts are lucky. Second, spring break is a time in which students who work part-time during the academic year can work more hours during the break to earn additional money to pay for their college expenses. Also, many seniors, who can use the time to apply for jobs and go on interviews, will be graduating in May or June. This extra time gives them an advantage over those students who do not apply for jobs until the summer. Finally, those students who use this time to complete assignments and readings and to prepare for upcoming final examinations often procrastinate during the first part of the semester. College students choose to spend their spring breaks in several ways since the break is a welcome week away from academic pressures and schedules.

1. What is the topic sentence of the paragraph?

_____

2. What is the controlling idea in the topic sentence?

_____

3. What items of information support this controlling idea?

_____

4. How many supporting ideas are located in dependent clauses? How many supporting ideas are located in independent clauses?

_____

5. Is there a problem with the focus of the sentences? If so, why?

_____

6. Revise the paragraph so that supporting ideas are located in independent clauses.

_____

_____

_____

_____

_____

_____

_____

Using Parallel Constructions

Within a sentence, elements in a series should be parallel; this means that all of the similar items must take the same grammatical form. They can all be nouns, verbs, verbals, prepositional phrases, or dependent clauses. Consider the following example:

> Hiking, jogging, and to swim are his favorite activities.

The subjects of the sentence—*hiking, jogging,* and *to swim*—are not parallel in grammatical form. The words *hiking* and *jogging* are gerunds (verbals ending in *ing* that act as nouns); however, the word *to swim* is an infinitive (a verbal using *to* plus the base form of the verb that acts as a noun, adjective, or adverb). Consider this revision:

> Hiking, jogging, and swimming are his favorite activities.

In the revision, the subjects are now all gerunds, and the series is parallel. Here are some useful types of parallel constructions.

1. **Nouns** (A noun is a person, place, or thing.)

   ▶ Example: Ms. O'Connor excels as an *author, teacher,* and *administrator.*

2. **Verbs** (A verb describes action or existence. For instance, the verbs *run, act,* and *swim* describe actions. The verbs *be, seem, become,* and the verbs of the senses—*feel, taste, smell, look, sound*—describe existence.)

   ▶ Example: Jeremy *jokes, laughs,* and *teases* easily.

3. **Participles** (Present participles are formed by adding *ing* to the base form of a verb. Participles act as adjectives.)

   ▶ Example: *Joining* the health club and *exercising* every day, Hank soon acquired additional strength and confidence.

4. **Gerunds** (Gerunds are formed by adding *ing* to the base form of a verb. Gerunds act as nouns.)

   ▶ Example: *Winning* the championship and *demonstrating* sportsmanship were important to the volleyball players.

5. **Infinitives** (Infinitives are formed by adding the word *to* to the base form of the verb. Infinitives act as nouns, adjectives, and adverbs.)

   ▶ Example: Allie plans *to complete* her master's degree, *to obtain* an executive position, and *to scale* Pike's Peak within the next four years.

6. **Prepositional phrases** (Prepositional phrases are formed by a preposition—for example, *by, to, from, outside, behind,* and *through*—and a noun or pronoun, the object of the preposition.)

▶ Example: *From every town, from every city,* and *from every farm* came volunteers for the armed forces.

7. **Dependent clauses** (Dependent clauses have a subject and a verb but cannot stand alone as a complete sentence. Dependent clauses are introduced by *subordinate conjunctions* or *relative pronouns.* The words *although, before, when, while,* and *because* are subordinate conjunctions; the words *who, which,* and *that* are relative pronouns.)

▶ Example: Sally is a woman *who accepts a challenge, who works diligently,* and *who accomplishes her goals.*

▼ EXERCISE 5

The following sentences do not have parallel constructions. Analyze the sentences and revise them so that items in a series are parallel.

1. After he had purchased a sleeping bag, backpack, and hiking shoes, Gawain was prepared to camp and hiking in the mountains.

_____

_____

2. Approaching the fence, jumping it cleanly, and to land gracefully, the rider received a round of applause from the spectators.

_____

_____

3. My grandmother enjoys cooking, to read, and singing.

_____

_____

4. The old cathedral with its stained-glass windows, high arches, and spires that towered was impressive.

_____

_____

5. For the audition, she planned to sing a favorite aria but preparing it poorly.

_____

_____

Varying Sentences

TYPES OF SENTENCES

Four types of sentences add variety to paragraphs: simple, compound, complex, and compound-complex. Each of these types is identified by clausal structure, either independent or dependent. Both types of clauses require subjects and verbs. Independent clauses can stand alone as complete sentences; however, dependent clauses cannot act as complete sentences. Consider the following examples of independent and dependent clauses.

▶ Independent clause: The whale swam slowly down the channel to the sea.

▶ Dependent clause: Before we began the test.

The dependent clause leaves the reader wanting to know what happened before the test started, yet the writer has not included the information. Dependent clauses usually begin with subordinate conjunctions (*although, because, since, even though, until,* and *after*) or relative pronouns (*who, which,* and *that*), which often act as subjects for the dependent clauses.

Here are the four types of sentences listed according to their clausal structure.

1. A **simple sentence** contains **one independent clause.**

   The whale is a mammal.

2. A **compound sentence** contains **two or more independent clauses.** These clauses are joined in one of three ways:

   • with a comma and a coordinate conjunction (*for, and, nor, but, or, yet,* and *so*)

   • with a semicolon (;)

   • with a semicolon (;) and an adverbial conjunction (*therefore, however, moreover,* and *nevertheless*) followed by a comma

   The school bus arrived an hour late, for one of its tires was flat and had to be repaired.

3. A **complex sentence** contains **one independent clause and one or more dependent clauses.**

   After the track meet was over, we enjoyed a pizza at a local restaurant.

4. A **compound-complex sentence** contains **two or more independent clauses and one or more dependent clauses.**

   Because they hope to win a fortune, many people place a dollar bet on the lottery each week; however, few win the jackpot because the odds are simply against them.

   Paragraphs using only one type of sentence become stale, repetitive, and predictable. Imagine, for example, a paragraph containing only simple sentences.

Because there are few transitions and combinations of ideas, readers are forced to provide their own transitions and interest in the paragraph. A different type of problem exists with a paragraph filled with compound-complex sentences. Since these sentences can be long and involved, readers must be constantly alert to the intricacies of the prose. Both extremes, from the elementary simple sentence to the complicated compound-complex sentence, indicate the writer's unwillingness to adapt to an audience and failure to consider the most effective structure for the message. Therefore, a considerate writer varies sentence structure according to the audience's needs and according to the message.

▼ EXERCISE 6

Combine the simple sentences in the paragraph below to form different sentence types. Consider your purpose for each sentence and construct an effective sentence for the message. Identify the types of sentences you use.

> The towns along the California coast have provided settings for many novels. John Steinbeck described Monterey in several of his novels. These novels ranged from *Cannery Row.* *Cannery Row* chronicles the adventures of the poor and a biologist in the town. Another of his novels to use the town of Monterey as its setting was *Tortilla Flat.* A little bit south of Monterey is the coastal town of Big Sur. Jack Kerouac used this town as the setting in his novel *Big Sur.* Big Sur is a small community, situated on high cliffs overlooking the Pacific. Raymond Chandler portrayed life in Los Angeles and its suburbs. He wrote detective novels. One of these novels was *Farewell, My Lovely.* Another novel was *The Big Sleep.* Other novelists also described Los Angeles and Hollywood. Nathanael West was one of these. He explored the falsity of Hollywood movies. He did this in his novel *The Day of The Locust.* Those novels all use the California coastal towns as their settings.

USING PERIODIC AND LOOSE SENTENCES

In addition to varying sentences by their clausal structure, you can vary the focus of sentences by using periodic and loose sentences. In a **periodic sentence,** the subject, verb, and direct object come at the end of the sentence. In this final position, the major elements of the sentence receive more attention and provide a climax for the sentence. The sentence may begin with prepositional phrases, participial phrases, adverbs, adjectives, or dependent clauses. Consider the following example of a periodic sentence:

> In the early spring morning, the first gentle day after the heavy snows and bitter winds of winter, a solitary robin appeared.

The last part of the sentence, *a solitary robin appeared*, provides a dramatic contrast to the description of a harsh winter. With the traditional spring bird as its subject, the independent clause also reinforces the first mention of the spring morning. Consider now the same sentence with its elements rearranged:

> A solitary robin appeared in the early spring morning, the first gentle day after the heavy snows and bitter winds of winter.

The sentence now begins with the subject and verb, but these parts of speech are no longer the focus of the sentence. Instead, the reader's attention is drawn to the description of winter. The opposite of a periodic sentence, this revision is called a **loose sentence.** With its subject and verb in an initial position, a loose sentence adds more information as it moves toward a conclusion. The loose sentence focuses on the accumulation of phrases or clauses rather than the central message contained in the subject and verb. Both types of sentences are effective, but they create different focuses for the reader.

▼ EXERCISE 7

Identify the following sentences as periodic or loose. Revise the periodic sentences to create loose sentences. Revise the loose sentences to create periodic sentences.

1. The mass of men serve the state thus, not as men mainly, but as machines, with their bodies.

   (from H. D. Thoreau, "Civil Disobedience")

   Sentence type:_____

   Revision: _____

   _____

   _____

2. Brooklyn had been a heterogeneous, dominantly middle-class community, with remarkable schools, good libraries and not only major league baseball, but extensive concert series, second-run movie houses, expensive neighborhoods and a lovely rolling stretch of acreage called Prospect Park.

   (from Roger Kahn, The Boys of Summer)

   Sentence type:_____

   Revision: _____

   _____

   _____

3. By comparison with meaner looking places with a gas station, barbecue shack, general store, junkyard, empty lots and spilled gasoline, a redneck redolence of

dried ketchup and hamburger napkins splayed around thin-shanked, dusty trees, Plains felt peaceful and prosperous.

(from Norman Mailer, *"Plains, Ga."*)

Sentence type:_____

Revision: _____

_____

_____

4. In June she married Tom Buchanan of Chicago, with more pomp and circumstance than Louisville ever knew before.

(from F. Scott Fitzgerald, *The Great Gatsby*)

Sentence type:_____

Revision: _____

_____

_____

5. Rather than love, than money, than fame, give me truth.

(from H. D. Thoreau, *Walden*)

Sentence type:_____

Revision: _____

_____

_____

SENTENCE BEGINNINGS

If every sentence in a paragraph were a simple sentence, then the paragraph would be repetitive and juvenile. The same problem occurs if all sentences within a paragraph have the same basic structure of subject-verb-object. Because the English language lends itself so well to this traditional order, though, a beginning writer usually relies on this pattern. However, you can easily vary your sentences by altering the traditional order. Here are several types of beginnings that will keep your sentences interesting.

1. **A prepositional phrase:**

   Through the woods was a lovely old mansion.

   (In this sentence, the normal word order is reversed. The verb comes before the subject in this inverted sentence.)

2. **An infinitive phrase:**

    To achieve her goal, Ellen must practice her skating routine every day.

3. **A participial phrase:**

    Dancing around the ballroom, Fred and Ginger attracted everyone's attention.

4. **The direct object:**

    The *book* I gave to him.

5. **A dependent clause:**

    Even though the first day of spring had passed, the trees were bare of buds.

6. **An adverb:**

    Happily, James walked down the aisle to receive his diploma.

7. **An adjective:**

    Ecstatic, the young man laughed with his friends.

8. **A coordinate conjunction** (this method is usually considered to be informal usage):

    Jack approached the mountain curve cautiously. *For* he knew of the dangerous bend in the road and the drop to the canyon below.

9. **An absolute construction:**

    Book in hand, Katie returned to the classroom.

    (These absolute constructions are usually elliptical. In the sentence above, the phrase *book in hand* could actually mean *with her book in her hand*, a prepositional phrase, or *carrying her book in her hand*, a participial phrase.)

▼ EXERCISE 8

Use at least five kinds of sentence beginnings, adding original information as necessary, to give the sentences below more interest. Identify the beginnings you use.

1. Tom handed Jill the tennis racquet.

    _____

    Type of beginning: _____

2.   The captain, energetic and courageous, boarded the alien vessel.

_____

Type of beginning: _____

3.   The swimmer was exhausted when he reached shore.

_____

Type of beginning: _____

4.   The children played joyfully at the beach.

_____

Type of beginning: _____

5.   The bear climbed the tree clumsily but steadily.

_____

Type of beginning: _____

6.   The desk had been stripped of its finish; now, it was ready for a coat of paint.

_____

Type of beginning: _____

7.   The instructor, with his briefcase filled with papers, faced several days of constant grading.

_____

Type of beginning: _____

8.   The baseball team, replete with ten rookies, hoped for a better season than it had last year.

_____

Type of beginning: _____

9.   The city zoo first opened its doors on May 1, 1908.

_____

Type of beginning: _____

10. The movie won an Academy Award for its visual effects.

Type of beginning: _____

▼ EXERCISE 9

Revise a recent paper of your own for style. Edit sentences carefully to avoid wordiness. Try to use active-voice and descriptive verbs, effective subordination, and parallel constructions. Be sure to vary sentence structure and beginnings. Identify the stylistic revisions you make, and share your paper with another student. Do others find your revisions effective?

▼ WRITING STRATEGY: Definition

A definition sets limits or boundaries for a word. Three types of definitions prove useful to writers: dictionary, logical, and extended definitions.

A **dictionary definition** describes a word's most common, accepted meaning(s), held by a vast number of people. Some dictionaries, particularly the *Oxford English Dictionary*, also chronicle the changes in a word's meaning over several centuries and indicate who first used the word. For example, according to the *Oxford English Dictionary*, the word *thrid* is an archaic spelling of the word *thread*; used in the eighteenth and nineteenth centuries, the word meant "to wind between."

A **logical**, or **formal, definition** requires that the term being defined be assigned to a larger *genus*, or class, and then be limited by its specific characteristics. Consider the following logical definition: *A diplomat is a person who demonstrates courtesy, tact, and civility.* In this logical definition, the term being defined, *diplomat*, is assigned to a larger *genus*, the group of *people*, and limited by the specific characteristics of *courtesy, tact,* and *civility*.

Although these two types of definitions are helpful, they do not thoroughly explain many abstract terms. Consider, for example, the concepts *friendship, love,* and *faith*. Although a dictionary defines each term, these definitions are incomplete because the terms are often used outside the boundaries of a strict dictionary definition. To see this, consider the uses of the word *love* in the following examples.

Julie loves Tom; they plan to marry this June.

There is a popular television advertisement for New York State that declares, "I love New York."

Bumper stickers read, "I love my cat" or "I love my dog."

The word *love* is used differently in each sentence. Julie may feel a romantic love for Tom, but the person who declares, "I love New York" (or a particular type of ice cream, or a particular car) is indicating enjoyment of or appreciation for an item, not romantic love. Likewise, pet owners tend to feel deep affection and concern for their animals, but their love is not the kind of emotion that the dictionary defined. Instead, an extended definition would best describe this emotion.

Extended definitions provide specific examples that make abstract concepts more concrete. For example, an extended definition of the word *love*, developed at length in an essay, could describe the different types of love, each with its own characteristics and illustrations. Extended definitions can be developed in several ways.

1. Classification can explain a term. Consider the difficulty you would face if you tried to define *comedy* in only a sentence or two. At best, the definition might indicate that comedy is humorous or funny. Certainly, though, this definition would be inadequate since many types of humor exist. Also, you would have created another problem: you must now define *humorous* or *funny*. However, if you classified different types of comedy (for example, slapstick, satire, and puns), then you could list specific examples of each type. These classifications and examples would give the reader a more concrete explanation of *comedy* than would a single sentence.

2. Illustration by example can also define abstract terms. An altruist is known for his or her good deeds; hence, in an extended definition of *altruism*, examples of good deeds could provide a specific definition of the term.

3. Comparison and contrast can define terms that are close in meaning. Consider, for example, the problems of defining the terms *socialism* and *communism*. Since many people confuse the terms, an extended definition that enumerates similarities and differences would clarify the definitions of each political system.

These three methods of extended definitions do not represent all the methods of development. However, they will guide you as you begin to explore definitions.

▶ The American Dream

BETTY ANNE YOUNGLOVE

The pursuit of the "American Dream" has enticed many people to leave their homes and set out for the United States. Now, many people are decrying the loss—or death—of that dream. Betty Anne Younglove here discusses that dream.

1   First, let us get this dream business—and business it now seems to be—straight. The word *dream* is not a synonym for *reality* or *promise*. It is closer to *hope* or *possibility* or even *vision*. The original American dream had only a little to do with material possessions and a lot to do with

choices, beginnings and opportunity. Many of the original American dreamers wanted a new beginning, a place to choose what they wanted and a place to work for it. They did not see it as a guarantee of success but an opportunity to try.

2   The dream represented possibilities: Get your own land and clear it and work it; if nature cooperates, the work might pay off in material blessings. Or the dream represented the idea that any citizen with the minimum qualifications of age and years of citizenship could run for President even if he were born in a humble log cabin. He had no guarantee he would win, of course, no more than the man clearing his land was guaranteed a good crop.

▶ QUESTIONS   1. What method does the author use to define the American dream?

2. What is her definition of the "original" American dream?

3. What does Younglove mean by the phrase "and business it now seems to be"?

▶ On Being a Cripple
Nancy Mairs

Nancy Mairs has multiple schlerosis, a degenerative disease of the nervous system. Because her MS did not manifest itself until middle age, she is able to discuss the "abled-disabled" question from both sides of the problem.

1   First, the matter of semantics. I am a cripple. I choose this word to name me. I choose from among several possibilities, the most common of which are "handicapped" and "disabled." I made the choice a number of years ago, without thinking, unaware of my motives for doing so. Even now, I'm not sure what those motives are, but I recognize that they are complex and not entirely flattering. People—crippled or not—wince at the word "cripple," as they do not at "handicapped" or "disabled." Perhaps I want them to wince. I want them to see me as a tough customer, one to whom the fates/gods/viruses have not been kind, but who can face the brutal truth of her existence squarely. As a cripple, I swagger.

2   But, to be fair to myself, a certain amount of honesty underlies my choice. "Cripple" seems to me a clean word, straightforward and precise. It has an honorable history, having made its first appearance in the Lindisfarne Gospel in the tenth century. As a lover of words, I like the accuracy with which it describes my condition: I have lost the full use of my limbs. "Disabled," by contrast, suggests any incapacity, physical or mental. And I certainly don't like "handicapped," which implies that I have deliberately been put at a disadvantage, by whom I can't imagine (my God is not a Handicapper General), in order to equalize chances in

the great race of life. These words seem to me to be moving away from my condition, to be widening the gap between word and reality. Most remote is the recently coined euphemism "differently abled," which partakes of the same semantic hopefulness that transformed countries from "undeveloped" to "underdeveloped," then to "less developed," and finally to "developing" nations. People have continued to starve in those countries during the shift. Some realities do not obey the dictates of language.

▶ QUESTIONS

1. What is "semantics"?

2. Why does the author want to be considered a "tough customer"?

3. Mairs states that some words used to describe her condition and that of others like her are too removed from reality. Such words "widen . . . the gap between word and reality." On the line below, write each of the words generally used as synonyms for "cripple," beginning with the word that is closest to reality and ending with the word that is farthest removed from the reality of her condition.

_____

Most   Least
real   real

Backtracking
JACOB BOWERS

The author frequently writes about hunting and outdoor life.

1   Some people go hunting; others are hunters. The difference has nothing to do with skill or refined ethics or game taken. One is not generally superior to the other. The difference may be written in the molecular dots and dashes of genetic code; it may have to do with bending character in the tender years of childhood. Whatever the case, the result is the same.

2   An outfitter friend of mine had a client with time and money enough to put a lot of heads on the walls of his spacious trophy room. One day, the client called my friend and said he meant to sell his trophies. He had gotten himself a new wife who disapproved of hunting.

3   It was a long while before I came around to understanding that man. My first reaction was glib. Get another wife. Then I wondered how a man marries a woman without knowing she is going to grind him for hunting and, if he does know her inclination, why bother with her at all?

4   Fact is, my thinking was all wrong. I expect that man did what was right for him. I hope he simply cared more for the woman than he did for

hunting. I hope he was just the sort of man who goes hunting. Because he and his new wife have hard times coming if he is a hunter.

5   Except for those hampered by ill health or advanced age, people who "used to hunt" invariably turn out to be people who went hunting. They will tell you how they quit when they went away to college or moved to the city. They make quitting sound casual, like changing shirts. They make it seem reasonable, as if reason counted for anything. To a hunter, these explanations sound more than slightly strange. As in, "Yes, I used to breathe a lot, but it really is too much trouble when you live in Chicago." For the hunter, you see, does not go as a matter of convenience. He goes because he must. And even if you sentence him to pavement for an indeterminate period, he remains a hunter. He will cease to be a hunter when he ceases being.

6   At the end of his life, my father was sick for a long time. We both knew he was never going to get better. And two weeks before he died, we talked about a new gun he wanted, the shooting he would do with it. He was a hunter.

7   Ask a man who goes hunting what he is and he will probably give you his occupation—fry cook, podiatrist, astronomer. Like as not, he thinks of himself as being that job. The hunter will ordinarily make the same kind of response. He is lying. He will state his occupation to satisfy social convention, but he knows full well that the thing he does for money is not what he is.

8   As an aside, the term "sportsman" is one I have never liked much as a synonym for "hunter." It makes me think of polo players, racing yachts, and men who lack purpose. It also makes me think of winning, losing, and competition, which are fine in athletics and business but are sorry reasons for hunting.

9   By the same token, "sportsmanship" seems a rather feeble word for the behavior required of hunters. A bad sport is disagreeable. A bad hunter is corrupt.

10   Sportsmanship is about manners, politeness, and being gracious to an opponent. This world could use more kindness and consideration. They are excellent qualities, but insufficient to guide a person through the complexities of a hunting life.

11   The animal hunted is not an opponent. It is an abiding mystery that, while the hunter may claim the life of the quarry, the animal taken in fair chase is never defeated or vanquished. Furthermore, hunting is decidedly not a game. Hunters are not players. Sports are essentially contrived and theatrical. Hunting is natural and real. Doubters might compare the relative significance of entertainment and death.

12   There is no certain way to predict whether a person will be a hunter, one who goes hunting, or one with utterly no desire to hunt. A partner of mine, whose family traditions are deeply rooted in hunting, has a son who was introduced properly, encouraged, and given every opportunity to become a hunter. He is a fine young man in all respects, but you could not make him show up in deer camp with a club. Another man of my acquaintance was born to a family of aristocratic, city-dwelling intellectuals. He never spent a day in the field until he was grown and had a family of his own. Despite the odds, he is a hunter to the bone. Pushing a youngster in either direction is useless.

13   I knew parts of this years ago. Yet the whole came clear only within the last month, as I read a promotional flier for an outdoor magazine. The flier contained a single sentence, reportedly spoken by Sitting Bull, which is about as strong and straight as words can be: "When there are no more buffalo, we will hunt mice, for we are hunters and want our freedom."

14   A non-hunter might get tangled in the plight of the buffalo and the injustices visited on the Sioux; the hunter will not. This is not a statement of sorrow and regret. Instead, it is an eloquently simple observation on the nature of hunters and hunting as natural. It also contains the absolute justification for hunting when basic survival is no longer at issue.

15   The modern hunter routinely leaves the comforts of home, travels great distances, spends considerable amounts of money, and endures physical hardship. These things are done with no assurance of success. Indeed, the hunter often knows in advance that the odds are heavily against him.

16   Hunters have not been reduced to hunting mice precisely because they saw that wildlife required assistance almost a century ago. Hunters have a perfectly legitimate claim to the animals they pursue, a claim far more compelling than the perverted foolishness of the "animal-rights" movement. Until such time as the laws of Nature are changed to mandate free housing and medical care for the beasts of the field, hunter and hunted will continue to be bound by mutual need.

17   Hunting is more than recreation, more than a wildlife management tool, more than a remnant of an ancient occupation. Some are hunters and want their freedom.

▶ QUESTIONS   1. What is the significance of the title?

2. How does Bowers define "hunters"? How does he define "going hunting"? Explain how he defines both terms.

3. Explain Sitting Bull's statement, "for we are hunters and want our freedom." What is the relationship between hunters and freedom?

▶ **War Games**

RAY STOLLE

In this paragraph, Ray Stolle explains war games, now popular with many groups.

The term "war game" can not only be defined

as the science of military theory or the art of practicing military maneuvers, but war games also attempt to simulate realistically historical or fictional conflicts in a more or less conventional game format. The games played by war-gaming enthusiasts can typically be identified by their scope, method, and scale. First of all, the scope of a game is the subject matter which it covers. War games are, obviously, about war or conflict. However, the particular subject or historical focus of conflict that any given game might cover could be virtually anything. A war game could be about battling clans of Neanderthals against Homo-Erecti, or it could be about giant, hyper-intelligent, cosmic protoplasms engaging in deadly mental duels. As long as the scope of play involves killing, wounding, or otherwise subduing one's opponent, the game may be classified as a war game. Next, the method by which a war game is played is a description of its rules and components. Most war games are played like conventional games on a game board with playing pieces; however, many are not played in this way. Some are played with miniatures, cards, or sometimes just blank notebook paper. Regardless, their rules distinguish them as war games, not their components. As mentioned, the rules deal with conflict and will usually attempt to present a realistic simulation of the subject covered. Rules can be simple, but in order to simulate realism, the rules of most war games try to cover in detail as many aspects as possible of the conflict involved. Rules covering morale, combat resolution, supply, movement, victory conditions, and a host of other factors to be considered offer a comprehensive and complex simulation of the conflict in question. Lastly, the scale of a game is the when, where, and over how much time the game takes place, or in other words, how "big" the game is. War games can deal with individual encounters, battles, and campaigns as well as entire wars, eras, and civilizations. Depending on the subject matter, the game board(s) can represent anything from a small arena to whole galaxies. Subsequently, playing pieces will denote individual warriors, squads, corps, divisions, or even whole fleets or army groups. Depending on the scenario covered, the time scale of each game turn will reflect the space and period over which the game is to be played. Turns in a game about gladiatorial combat will be in seconds or minutes while turns in a game about the conquests of the Mongol hordes will be years or decades. Thus, any game that can be identified by its scope of conflict and its method of attempting to present a realistic simulation of the conflict through its rules in a defined scale of unit, area, and duration, can be called a war game.

▶ QUESTIONS

1. What definition does Stolle give of "war games"? What methods does he use to define the term? What is his topic sentence? Where is it located?

2. How is the paper developed? How do the primary support sentences support the topic sentence?

3. Define the following words: *simulate, subduing, morale,* and *hordes.*

▼ PARAGRAPH
ASSIGNMENTS

1. The definition of "the American dream" has changed over the past two centuries. Originally it meant a guarantee of the "pursuit of happiness." Today it seems to mean a promise of happiness. What does the American dream mean to you? What elements are vital to its fulfillment?

2. Nancy Mairs obviously believes that words are important. She feels that the most accurate word must be used, even if that word is tactless and hurtful. However, since the English language offers so many euphemisms for distasteful subjects (such as death, suicide, and obesity), it would seem that society generally disagrees with her. What is your opinion? Do you think it is more important to be accurate and realistic or to be tactful and discrete? Illustrate your response by defining a controversial term such as *abortion, euthanasia,* or *freedom of speech.*

3. Some people deride hunters, calling them barbaric and cruel. Others support hunters by saying they are merely supplying meat to their families by an alternate means and helping manage the wild herd populations as a "natural" predator. Jacob Bowers, too, supports hunters, but not for these reasons. He feels that hunters are responding to an innate need. What do you think of hunters and hunting?

▼ WRITING TIP

Be sure to check your paragraphs for pronoun reference. Read each sentence carefully and note whether each pronoun has a clearly stated antecedent. Then check for agreement in number and person between the pronoun and its antecedent. For more information on pronoun reference, see Part II, Chapter 8.

▼ Style Checklist

1. Are any of your sentences needlessly wordy? Remember: Don't try to "pad" your writing to meet a word count.

    _____

2. Do your sentences use active-voice verbs?

    _____

3. If you are using passive-voice verbs, why? Do you have a valid reason for using that construction?

    _____

4. Look over your sentences. Can you substitute an effective, specific descriptive verb for a weaker one?

    _____

5. Are any of your sentences complex? Check their subordinate clauses. Make sure the less important idea is in the dependent clause.

    _____

6. Do any of your sentences have items in a series? Check them for parallel construction.

    _____

7. Are there any compound sentences? Check to be sure they are correctly punctuated.

    _____

8. Would any sentence be more effective if it were a periodic sentence?

    _____

9. Would any sentence be more comprehensible if it were a loose sentence?

    _____

10. Have you varied the beginnings of your sentences?

    _____

▼ Definition Checklist

1. Does your paragraph use classification of types for an effective extended definition?

   _____

   _____

   _____

   _____

   _____

2. Can you use an illustration by example for your extended definition?

   _____

   _____

   _____

   _____

   _____

   _____

   _____

3. Can you use comparison and contrast to define terms that are close in meaning?

   _____

   _____

   _____

   _____

   _____

   _____

The Whole Essay

9

▶ **OBJECTIVES**

1. To use the writing process to develop a coherent, organized, and unified essay.

2. To develop an effective thesis statement.

3. To develop an appropriate introductory paragraph.

4. To write a clear summary.

5. To write a useful critique.

6. To make an informed evaluation.

▶ **PREVIEW**

A summary is a paragraph that delineates the key points of an essay. A critique examines the merits of an essay. An evaluation presents an informed judgment about the usefulness of an essay.

Longer and more thoroughly developed than the paragraph, the essay allows you to expand a description, narration, explanation, or argument. Consider, for example, a description of a favorite beach on a summer's day. In a single paragraph, you are forced to choose one very limited topic for development. You could, for instance, describe a particular group of people at the beach, the appearance of the beach within a certain restricted area, the activities available at the beach itself or at a surrounding area, or your own enjoyment of the day. In an essay, however, you have room to explore more ideas and include many observations. Specifically, you could describe three or four of the many types of people at the beach (from sun worshippers to tourists to residents of a beach town); you could narrate the day's events for a group of friends or discuss the problems of erosion and overdevelopment, which plague many beach towns, for a local environmental group. Hence, you can choose a broader topic and provide more information in an essay than in a paragraph.

Invention

Despite the differences in length and topic development, paragraphs and essays share the same composing process. In an essay, as in a paragraph, you must generate ideas and details, discover what you mean, identify your audience and purpose, organize your details, revise, edit, and, finally, proofread for correctness. (See "The Writing Process" in Chapter 1 of Part I.)

In the process of writing an essay, prewriting encourages your creativity, invention, and exploration of a topic. For example, before deciding upon a specific topic, many writers discuss potential topics with others, observe situations and places, play with ideas, and research topics. Through these activities, you can investigate many possibilities and discard those you choose not to develop.

Brainstorming, freewriting, and outlining will guide you in the selection of a topic. During a brainstorming session, call upon your memory of personal experiences and knowledge gained through reading to generate ideas. If no ideas come to mind quickly, then use the questions newspaper reporters ask: who, what, when, where, why and how. The answers to these questions may direct you to specific topics and audiences. (See "Prewriting" in Chapter 1 of Part I and "Identifying Audience and Purpose" in Chapter 2 of Part I.)

▼ EXERCISE 1

In a brainstorming session, generate at least five possible essay topics for each category below. Include potential audiences and purposes for each topic.

1. Television news programs
2. Television comedies
3. Science-fiction movies
4. Computers
5. Divorce
6. Family structures
7. Current movies
8. Musicians
9. Sports
10. College life

To test your knowledge of a specific essay topic, use freewriting. This method has a number of advantages. First, you can quickly determine whether you need to research a topic in order to develop it fully. Second, freewriting can eliminate any anxiety you might have about putting pen to paper; after a freewriting session, you know that you have something valuable to say about a topic. Finally, you can use freewriting at any point in the composing process. If you believe you have reached a dead end, then freewriting will help you generate additional ideas for your essay quickly.

Whatever prewriting form you use, outlining can assist you in both generating ideas and testing them. If you need to see how ideas relate, then diagrams or grids can help you identify major ideas quickly and determine which ones need further support. Also, after you have used brainstorming or freewriting, an outline allows you to test your ideas as you organize them. Finally, you can use outlines at any point in the composing process when you need to check the unity of paragraphs.

▼ EXERCISE 2

Choose two of the specific topics you generated for Exercise 1. Freewrite for fifteen to twenty minutes. When you have finished, compare your freewriting to that of other students. Which of your ideas can be incorporated into an essay? Which ideas need more development?

Thesis Statements

In a paragraph, the topic sentence states the writer's opinion, predicts what the writer will discuss in the paragraph, and controls the development of the paragraph. In an essay, the **thesis statement** functions in the same manner. Usually located in the first paragraph, the thesis statement is the main idea in the essay. Like the topic sentence, the thesis statement defines, predicts, and controls the essay.

First, the thesis must identify the writer's position; therefore, it must contain the writer's opinion. Consider this example:

> At Casebook College, 60 percent of the freshmen indicate that they plan to major in business administration.

This thesis is not adequate because it presents only factual information. Consider the following revision:

> At Casebook College, 60 percent of the freshmen indicate that they plan to major in business administration because the program provides a solid background in theory, allows the students to operate a campus business for experience, and places students during their senior year in internships with businesses.

In the revised version, the writer retains the factual information and adds reasons, either identified from personal experience or from studies conducted, why the program is popular. By incorporating the reasons for the program's popularity, the writer also indicates that he or she will discuss these reasons in the essay's supporting paragraphs.

Second, a thesis statement, like a topic sentence, has a subject and a controlling idea. Consider these examples:

> *Subject*
> Before graduation, *every college student* should
> *Controlling idea*
> *be required to take at least one computer course.*

> While commuting to college has many advantages,
> *Subject*   *Controlling idea*
> *living on campus* offers *valuable benefits* to students.

In the first example, the writer announces his or her position in an argument. In the second example, the writer obviously favors living on campus and is prepared to provide reasons for this position. In addition, the writer could easily compare the advantages of commuting to the advantages of living on campus. Notice that the writers avoid vague adjectives, such as *good, bad,* or *fantastic,* in their controlling ideas.

Finally, thesis statements control the development of the essay. Consider the following example:

> *Subject*
> Popular with many Americans, the *Rambo movies* extol
> *Controlling ideas*
> *rugged individualism, patriotism, and private justice.*

In this thesis statement, the writer identifies the essay's development and the controlling ideas. Readers can expect each controlling idea to be thoroughly defined and explained in an individual supporting paragraph of the essay. Hence, this thesis statement automatically directs the content and organization of the paper.

▼ EXERCISE 3

Analyze each thesis statement below. If the thesis statement is adequate (if it defines, predicts, and controls), then place a check (√) beside it; circle the subject and underline the controlling idea. If the thesis is inadequate for any reason, then revise the sentence.

_____ 1. Child abuse can have a devastating effect on an entire family.

_____ 2. Crime is a great problem in many urban areas.

_____ 3. Twenty percent of all faculty members at State College are women.

_____ 4. After the long decades of decay in urban areas, many cities are being revitalized by new tourist attractions, development of historic districts, and new cultural opportunities.

_____ 5. Mountain climbing is an excellent hobby.

_____ 6. Only 40 percent of all college students graduate in four years.

_____ 7. American slang changes constantly.

_____ 8. Because of peer pressure, academic demands, and new social situations, high school can often be a bewildering experience for teenagers.

_____ 9. Each fast-food restaurant attracts its own clientele.

_____ 10. Americans are known for their optimism.

▼ EXERCISE 4

For the general topics below, create at least two thesis statements for each topic. Identify an audience for each statement. *Or* return to Exercise 2 and create two thesis statements from each of your freewriting sessions.

1. Concerts

2. Movie videos

3. Amusement parks

4. Health clubs

5. A controversial topic (such as a local problem or major public concern)

Introductions

The beginning paragraph of an essay, the introduction, must perform three functions:

1. contain the thesis statement (the main idea and purpose)

2. suggest an audience to establish the writer's tone and opinion

3. attract the reader's attention and make the reader interested in the subject and its presentation.

The thesis statement can be placed at any point within the first paragraph. Its placement, however, is determined by your purpose. As the first sentence, the thesis immediately announces your opinion and subject; the rest of your introduction may list ideas and explanations that you will develop in the body paragraphs of the essay. If the thesis is in the middle of the introduction, then you catch your audience's interest, state your thesis, and discuss how it will be supported. If the thesis is the last sentence, then you attract the reader's attention, provide necessary explanation of a problem, and then identify your position.

The introduction should also establish the tone of the essay and identify its intended audience. Through your choice of words, you create one of many possible tones for the essay. For example, if you choose to use colloquial language, then you suggest that the essay is for your peers. A more formal level of language suggests the seriousness of the topic and an audience that must be informed of the topic's seriousness. To illustrate this formal tone, consider the seriousness with which you would persuade high-school students to avoid drugs and alcohol. Or consider the presentation of a proposal for a university-run day-care center that you might make to the president of the university. On the other hand, if the essay is to be a humorous account of a blind date, then you might establish your tone by incorporating some jokes, and you will identify the audience by the types of details you indicate you will develop in the essay. (See "Recognizing and Creating Tone" in Chapter 7 of Part I.)

Finally, your introduction must attract your reader's attention. Any number of methods will accomplish this goal; listed below are four of the many different types of introductions.

"FOCUS-DOWN" INTRODUCTIONS

You can "focus down" from general to specific. This technique begins with a general, broad statement. Each successive sentence is narrower in scope than the preceding one. The thesis, the most precise statement in the paragraph, is last. Consider, for example, the problem of presenting in a history paper a thesis that requires background information before the writer can state the thesis. Specifically, a thesis presenting the causes of American involvement in World War I requires that background information be stated first. Hence, the thesis would be placed at the *end* of the introductory paragraph. Consider the following introductory paragraph.

> The average American participates in sports for many reasons: to exercise, to relieve tension, to get out of the house, or simply to have fun. Yet the seriousness with which many Americans play makes one wonder if sports do not cause more tension than they relieve. Is it how you play the game? Or is it whether you win or lose? My experiences in an adult softball league suggest that winning, not sportsmanship or fun, is what counts.

In this student paragraph, the writer moves from the general subject of Americans and sports in the first sentence to the more specific discussion of the seriousness with which Americans play. Finally, the writer uses his experience in a specific sport to pinpoint his topic, the importance of winning.

COMMONPLACE STATEMENTS

You can begin with a commonplace statement. For example, even the title of Thomas Wolfe's novel *You Can't Go Home Again* could be used as an introduction to a paper describing a college student's first visit back to her home town after a few months at college. Analyze the following introductory paragraph from a long article on Ebbetts Field, the old home of the Brooklyn Dodgers.

> It was too small. The public urinals were fetid troughs. Its architecture suggested a mail-order tool shed, and every August the grass began to die. The work crews had to spray the outfield with green paint. There weren't enough seats and the parking was impossible and worst of all it had been designed in days when a baseball possessed the resiliency of a rolled sock. Later the ball would leap from bats, and pitchers working there developed sore arms, Jello-O hearts, shell shock. Ebbets Field, 1913–1957. RIP.
>
> (from Roger Kahn, *"In the Catbird Seat"*)

Kahn begins with a commonplace remark, "It was too small." In *Sports Illustrated*, this remark appeared after the title and pictures of Ebbets Field. Hence, the readers knew the reference of the pronoun *it*. Without these guides, however, the reader can still understand the reference; the last two sentences (actually fragments) reveal the stadium's name. In addition, the last two sentences, arranged as an inscription on a tombstone, announce Kahn's thesis and subject: he will describe the history of the once-famous ballpark from its early days through its demolition.

QUOTATIONS AND STATISTICS

You can begin with a pertinent quotation or statistic. (Quotations can easily be found in any number of dictionaries of quotations in the library. Statistics can be found in the *Statistical Abstracts of the United States*, located in the reference room of most libraries.) Analyze the following introductory paragraph. Is the opening quotation effective?

> "Let us be thankful for the fools," said Samuel Clemens. "But for them the rest of us could not succeed." These "fools" think school is like taking a long walk under the pounding sun of a muggy summer day: it is quite unpleasant, but it is the only way for one to get where he or she is going. Serious students, on the other hand, know that school is more like climbing up a ski slope: all the hard work pays off when one gets to the top and can "swoosh" down the rest of the way. One's attitude toward school takes root early but becomes most evident in high school. This

attitude can later be seen in the student's reasons for going to college. Furthermore, a student's outlook on education may even reflect his or her outlook on life. Many students simply do not care about learning, while others actually see the importance of an education.

This introductory paragraph links the quotation about "fools" to a type of student who simply does not care about his or her education. The paragraph then compares two types of students: those who are unconcerned about their education and those who appreciate it.

Consider this paragraph, which begins with a statistic:

> After years of inflation and high unemployment, the current unemployment figure of 7.3% seems to be relatively low. While this single-digit figure is small, it represents approximately 30 million Americans who live below the poverty level because there is no work for them. Until this figure can be reduced by an increase in American production and jobs, the federal government should be responsible for fulfilling the needs of the unemployed.

This introductory paragraph contrasts the seemingly low unemployment rate with the vast numbers of Americans who are affected by unemployment. The writer then argues for governmental support for the unemployed.

ANECDOTAL INTRODUCTIONS

You can begin dramatically by repeating a conversation or by telling a story. This method has many variations, each with the same intent: to make your reader aware of realistic situations and to encourage your reader to respond to the situations. Consider, for example, the effect of describing the living conditions of the poor in ghettos as the introduction to an essay on the plight of the poor. Certainly your reader would be more sympathetic to the essay and its arguments if you make the statistics of poverty come alive by describing people who live under those conditions. Analyze the following lead paragraph of a newspaper article that discusses the crisis of illiteracy.

> One afternoon two years ago, the telephone rang in my English Department office. Barely had I said hello when the voice of an unidentified caller barked: "Do you know about Chaucer and all them writers who wrote around him?" Before I had a chance to reply, the voice barked again: "Did he write different than we write now?" This phone call was startling. Was it the glaring lack of manners? Was it the absence of correct English? Was it the caller's bewilderment about the history of his native tongue? Or was the most disturbing factor the laziness—that lack of intellectual curiosity—that kept the caller from going to the nearby library and seeing quite easily that Chaucer did, indeed, "write different than we write now"? Illiteracy is a

pressing problem—a problem so urgent that it threatens to rend the fabric of American culture.

(from Vincent Fitzpatrick, "Why Something Must Be Done About Illiteracy")

This paragraph could easily have begun with statistics demonstrating the problem of illiteracy; however, the dramatic lead, with an unidentified caller demanding information, proves to be more effective. Although many people may not have studied Chaucer, most would head to the library to find the answer to the caller's question. In addition, the caller's question, filled with errors, does point to the insidious nature of illiteracy: the caller wants someone else to tell him the answer rather than researching the question himself.

▼ EXERCISE 5

Analyze the following introductions, written by students. Identify the type of introduction each writer used. Also, identify the thesis statement in each paragraph. If an introduction does not adequately attract the reader's interest, lacks a thesis statement, or fails to suggest an audience and purpose, then revise the paragraph.

1. As I planned my vacation to Jamaica, travel agencies and brochures provided what I thought to be a complete picture of the island paradise. I found, however, that this perfect picture excluded many hard realities of life in Jamaica. There were parts of the island which were as beautiful as I had expected, but there was an abundance of problems such as poverty and crime which contrasted sharply with my preconceived visions of the island.

2. More often than not, people assume that any kind of professional dance is all the same. This is not true. Two distinct types of dance are classical ballet and modern dance. The dictionary defines *ballet* as "dancing in which conventional poses and steps are combined with light flowing figures (such as leaps and turns)." To illustrate one of their differences, modern dance is not even defined in the dictionary. Modern dance is only about twenty years old and was pioneered by Martha Graham. The main differences between ballet and modern dance are the way that the body's turn out is used and the different footwear worn. Both types of dance are expressive, but each in its own style.

3. To a newcomer, the barrio was a farming ghetto with people just above the poverty line. In this farming suburb of Manila, all wore haggard faces and blistered hands. Day in and day out, they slaved over their crops to produce minimal income. Poverty was evident in their faces, their homes, and their lives. But in this pathetic condition, the barrio produced hard-working people bent on improving their situation. One of these rare individuals who displayed insurmountable supplies of hope, determination, and perseverance was my uncle.

4. Of all the home computers on the market, the Excel 600X and the Discovery 128 are two of the most competitive. Many people do not investigate the advantages and disadvantages of both and, thus, buy the more advertised of the two—the Discovery. Only through careful comparison of the two would one find that the Excel is the better buy for the money.

5.   A town like hundreds of other G.I. towns across America, Leesville, Louisiana, blossomed with the influx of military pay vouchers and raced headlong from insignificance to prosperity. Seemingly overnight, whole blocks of bars, pawn shops, and liquor stores appeared, eager to give the soldiers a place to spend their money. Typical of these places was the Golden Nugget.

▼ EXERCISE 6

Return to Exercise 4, in which you developed thesis statements for five topics. Choose two of these thesis statements and create a different type of introductory paragraph for each.

Supporting Details

Contained in the middle paragraphs, the body of the essay supports the thesis statement by supplying illustrations, examples, definitions, points of comparison and contrast, separate causes or effects, or points in an argument. These body paragraphs develop the thesis in much the same way that primary and secondary supports develop the topic sentence in a paragraph. The chart below demonstrates the similarities between paragraphs and essays.

PARAGRAPH	ESSAY
1. The *topic sentence* defines the writer's opinion, predicts the discussion, and controls the paragraph.	1. The *thesis statement* defines the writer's opinion, predicts the discussion, and controls the essay.
2. The *primary support sentences* develop the controlling idea in the topic sentence.	2. The *body paragraphs* develop the controlling idea in the thesis statement. Each body paragraph has a topic sentence that directly supports the thesis statement.
3. The *secondary support sentences* provide additional information, such as examples, descriptions, or explanations, about the primary support sentences.	3. Individual body paragraphs have primary and secondary supports that provide additional information about the topic sentence of the body paragraph.
4. The *concluding sentence* restates the topic sentence and primary supports, or provides a logical conclusion.	4. The *conclusion* summarizes the thesis statement and the topic sentences of the body paragraphs or provides a logical conclusion and suggestions.

    An essay's thesis statement is supported by body paragraphs that explain, narrate, describe, or argue points of the thesis. Consider this thesis statement:

> While commuting to college has many advantages, living on campus offers valuable benefits to students.

Each body paragraph of this essay would develop one benefit of living on campus. Of course, each body paragraph needs its own topic sentence and supporting details.

After generating a thesis statement, try brainstorming for specific supporting ideas. This method will give you many ideas for body paragraphs and probably will provide some details. Consider this example.

▶ Thesis: While commuting to college has many advantages, living on campus offers valuable benefits to students.

▶ Brainstorming   chance to live on one's own for first time
    Ideas:
            able to participate in campus activities easily

            closer to library and school's facilities

            able to make friends with others in dorm

            able to participate in social activities in dorms

            set schedule for oneself

            responsible for own actions

            do not have to waste time commuting

            can join campus clubs

            can seek help from friends

            learn valuable interpersonal skills of dealing with others

▶ Organizing Ideas: Paragraph 1. Living on campus allows the student to take advantage of many campus facilities to develop academic skills.

    A. The library offers not only resources but also a quiet place to study, something students may not have at home.

    B. Students can use the campus computers at any time.

    C. By living on campus, students can more readily meet with professors and instructors.

D. Students can use labs and workshops in the evenings.

Paragraph 2. Living on campus allows students to participate in campus activities more fully.

A. Since they live on campus, students have more access to nighttime cultural events, such as concerts and lectures.

B. Students can join clubs and participate more directly in the organization of the campus.

C. Students can enjoy activities in the dorms, such as intramural sports and social gatherings.

Paragraph 3. Finally, living on campus allows students to become more mature since they are responsible for their actions.

A. Students must learn to budget their time carefully since no one will remind them of their responsibilities.

B. Students must learn to budget their money carefully.

C. Students must learn to perform domestic chores for themselves.

D. While living in the dorms, students must learn how to deal with others.

As you can see, a brainstorming session can yield topics that can be developed into separate paragraphs and also details for those paragraphs. This method can save time as well; you not only generate ideas quickly, but you can also determine an organization for those ideas. In addition, you can quickly judge whether or not your supports are unified. As the sentences in a paragraph must be unified, so too must the paragraphs in an essay be unified. Each paragraph and its sentences must develop the thesis statement. Finally, for those who have difficulty devising a thesis, brainstorming for details about a topic might identify particular ideas that can be used for the thesis. (See Chapter 4 in Part I.)

You have explored various writing strategies for organizing details in paragraphs. These same strategies apply to essays as well. During the first few drafts of an essay, you should remain open to new ideas and details that you might discover. Also, you should take the time in the first few drafts to explore what you want to say and how you can say it more effectively. As you have seen, any number of writing strategies can provide a structure for details; however, your audience and purpose should guide you in developing an appropriate structure and selecting the most convincing details for your essay.

Analyzing Essays

Analyzing an essay requires that you consider its contents, structure, and purpose. During this process, keep your personal reading goals in mind: you are reading the essay to analyze, synthesize, and utilize the information it provides. Three steps will enable you to read an essay effectively. "Effectively" is the key word in this process; you don't just want to let your eyes roam the page. Instead, because you want to comprehend the essay, you must summarize, critique, and evaluate it.

SUMMARIZING

Summarizing is a frequently used technique. When you tell a friend a condensed version of a movie's plot, when you provide the highlights of a basketball game, and when you review a lecture class, you are summarizing. You should also use summaries to help you study; rather than rereading an entire chapter before an exam, you should read the chapter's summary. Instead of hastily skimming all of your supplementary readings, you should read the summary you wrote for each article. Likewise, businesses rely on summaries; executives demand brief reports about business transactions, conferences, and important events. They do not want blow-by-blow descriptions; they want summaries.

Summarizing is thus essential to both the reading and the writing process. Being able to compose an accurate summary indicates that you, the reader, were able to analyze the written material, to comprehend its key points, and to take the first step towards synthesizing and utilizing new information.

A summary is a shortened version of an original article, book, event, etc. A summary reviews a thesis and key supporting ideas. A summary should include the major arguments and/or reasons given by the author to support his or her point of view and perspective of the situation. In effect, the summary provides an outline of the given material in paragraph form.

Developing a summary involves several steps. First, you cannot expect to write an accurate summary without comprehending the material; therefore, you must read and analyze the material carefully. Next, skim the essay. (Remember that when you skim you are trying to determine the author's thesis and essential support. See "Skimming" in *To the Student*.) After reading and skimming, you should thoroughly understand the topic. Third, you can begin to assess the relative importance of all the material you have just assimilated; decide what is most important, what is least important, and what are really just details and examples. Outlining will probably aid you at this point because it will enable you to visualize the relationships between ideas, to weigh the relative importance of each concept, and to organize the important ones. Finally, write the summary in one paragraph. Be sure to use complete sentences in your paragraph and to paraphrase the author. (In other words, use your own words; don't quote.)

EXERCISE 7

Look ahead and read the essay "On Friendship" in Exercise 9, and write an accurate summary of it. Remember that your audience will use your summary to decide whether the article is worth reading.

CRITIQUING

Remember the definition of an essay: this short composition discusses one topic, presents a personal perspective on the topic and does not, therefore, attempt to discuss that topic in exhaustive detail. Although essay writers present a personal perspective, their goal is to convince, persuade, or suggest to readers that their personal viewpoints are *not* subjective; they want their audience to concur that their opinions are the logically correct ones, founded on reliable evidence.

As a reader, you must determine whether the authors have achieved their goals. By critiquing an author's material, you can determine the validity of his or her perspective. Then, if the opinion is valid, you can synthesize the newly learned information or perspective with your own knowledge and perspectives, arrive at a new body of information, and develop new insights into the topic.

When you critique an essay, you judge the merits of its arguments and determine its strengths and weaknesses. To judge fairly, you must read and analyze carefully; here, your summary will help you. In the summary, you noted the author's thesis and reasons. Now, when critiquing, continue the analytical process. Look at the facts, statistics, examples, and so on provided by the author. Do they really explain each topic sentence, provide more details about the topic, and support the author's viewpoint?

The following questions may help you to critique new material:

1. What is the author's thesis?

   State the topic.

   State the author's viewpoint.

2. List the reasons given to support the author's opinion.

3. What details does the author provide to explain each reason?

   Are the details relevant to the thesis?

   Are the details factual and easily verifiable?

   Are the details based on subjective or objective experience?

   What are the sources of these details?

4. Does the author make a strong case to support his or her belief?

   Does the author provide enough evidence to convince a skeptic that the personal opinion is logical and valid?

   If you answer "yes" to the last question, then you can synthesize the essay's information because you have decided that it is worthwhile to incorporate that information into your store of knowledge.

 **EXERCISE 8**   Critique the essay "On Friendship" in Exercise 9. Use the questions above to decide whether the authors have presented a strong argument for their point of view.

EVALUATING

The last step in processing an essay is evaluating it. You must decide whether or not to utilize the essay's information. If the evaluation is favorable, then you will act upon the information and incorporate it into your writing. However, if the evaluation is unfavorable, then you will not utilize the given material because you don't want your ideas to be inadequate or unacceptable.

When evaluating an essay, you must remember that it is not an exhaustive examination of a topic. After all, an essay is not a book. Because of its comparatively short length, an essay omits much information. The decision to include or exclude material is made by the author, based on his or her purpose, intended audience, and desired length of the essay. In some cases, the author may decide to exclude some important material because it may undermine or contradict his or her thesis.

When you evaluate, you decide whether the author has presented a thorough analysis of the topic, whether he or she has fairly presented both sides of the issue, and whether the evidence justifies the author's conclusion.

How do you evaluate an essay? You must familiarize yourself with additional evidence and opposing views. In that way, you can judge for yourself whether an author is completely honest in presenting this viewpoint or whether he or she omitted material that is potentially devastating. To complete this step, you must be well informed or, at the very least, familiar with your library and with research techniques.

The following questions may help you to evaluate an essay.

1. What would be the most likely opposing thesis?

   State it.

2. How would opponents of the author's opinion support their viewpoint?

   What reasons would they give for their opposition?

3. Does the author refer to his or her opponents' views?

   Does the author try to refute their ideas?

   Is this refutation successful?

4. What facts, statistics, or details contradict the author's viewpoint?

   What facts, statistics, or details weaken his or her case?

5. Are there acknowledged experts on the topic whose opinions differ from the author's?

   Who are they?

   Are their conclusions valid?

   Do they support their views with facts, studies, and other data?

▼ EXERCISE 9

Brainstorm the topic in the following essay, "On Friendship," to develop an opposing perspective. If you need additional evidence, research the topic. Then decide whether the authors' viewpoint is valid. Finally, write an essay on the topic that incorporates all the information you have gathered and synthesized.

▶ On Friendship
MARGARET MEAD AND RHONDA METRAUX

1   Few Americans stay put for a lifetime. We move from town to city to suburb, from high school to college in a different state, from a job in one region to a better job elsewhere, from the home where we raise our children to the home where we plan to live in retirement. With each move we are forever making new friends, who become part of our new life at that time.

2   For many of us the summer is a special time for forming new friendships. Today millions of Americans vacation abroad, and they go not only to see new sights but also—in those places where they do not feel too strange—with the hope of meeting new people. No one really expects a vacation trip to produce a close friend. But surely the beginning of a friendship is possible? Surely in every country people value friendship?

3   They do. The difficulty when strangers from two countries meet is not a lack of appreciation of friendship, but different expectations about what constitutes friendship and how it comes into being. In those European countries that Americans are most likely to visit, friendship is quite sharply distinguished from other, more casual relations, and is differently related to family life. For a Frenchman, a German or an Englishman friendship is usually more particularized and carries a heavier burden of commitment.

4   But as we use the word, "friend" can be applied to a wide range of relationships—to someone one has known for a few weeks in a new place, to a close business associate, to a childhood playmate, to a man or woman, to a trusted confidant. There are real differences among these relations for Americans—a friendship may be superficial, casual, situational or deep and enduring. But to a European, who sees only our surface behavior, the differences are not clear.

5   As they see it, people known and accepted temporarily, casually, flow in and out of Americans' homes with little ceremony and often with little personal commitment. They may be parents of the children's friends, house guests of neighbors, members of a committee, business associates from another town or even another country. Coming as a guest into an American home, the European visitor finds no visible landmarks. The atmosphere is relaxed. Most people, old and young, are called by first names.

6   Who, then, is a friend?

7   Even simple translation from one language to another is difficult. "You see," a Frenchman explains, "if I were to say to you in France, 'This is my good friend,' that person would not be as close to me as someone about whom I said only, 'This is my friend.' Anyone about whom I have to say *more* is really less."

8   In France, as in many European countries, friends generally are of the same sex, and friendship is seen as basically a relationship between men. Frenchwomen laugh at the idea that "women can't be friends," but they also admit sometimes that for women "it's a different thing." And many French people doubt the possibility of a friendship between a man and a woman. There is also the kind of relationship within a group—men and women who have worked together for a long time, who may be very close, sharing great loyalty and warmth of feeling. They may call one another *copains*—a word that in English becomes "friends" but has more the feeling of "pals" or "buddies." In French eyes this is not friendship, although two members of such a group may well be friends.

9   For the French, friendship is a one-to-one relationship that demands a keen awareness of the other person's intellect, temperament and particular interests. A friend is someone who draws out your own best qualities, with whom you sparkle and become more of whatever the friendship draws upon. Your political philosophy assumes more depth, appreciation of a play becomes sharper, taste in food or wine is accentuated, enjoyment of a sport is intensified.

10   And French friendships are compartmentalized. A man may play chess with a friend for thirty years without knowing his political opinions, or he may talk politics with him for as long a time without knowing about his personal life. Different friends fill different niches in each person's life. These friendships are not made part of family life. A friend is not expected to spend evenings being nice to children or courteous to a deaf grandmother. These duties, also serious and enjoined, are primarily for relatives. Men who are friends may meet in a café. Intellectual friends may meet in larger groups for evenings of conversation. Working people may meet at the little *bistro* where they drink and talk, far from the family. Marriage does not affect such friendships; wives do not have to be taken into account.

11   In the past in France, friendships of this kind seldom were open to any but intellectual women. Since most women's lives centered on their homes, their warmest relations with other women often went back to their girlhood. The special relationship of friendship is based on what the French value most—on the mind, on compatibility of outlook, on vivid awareness of some chosen area of life.

12   Friendship heightens the sense of each person's individuality. Other relationships commanding as great loyalty and devotion have a different meaning. In World War II the first resistance groups formed in Paris were built on the foundation of *les copains*. But significantly, as time went on these little groups, whose lives rested in one another's hands, called themselves "families." Where each had a total responsibility for all, it was kinship ties that provided the model. And even today such ties, crossing every line of class and personal interest, remain binding on the survivors of these small, secret bands.

13   In Germany, in contrast with France, friendship is much more articulately a matter of feeling. Adolescents, boys and girls, form deeply sentimental attachments, walk and talk together—not so much to polish their wits as to share their hopes and fears and dreams, to form a common front against the world of school and family and to join in a kind of mutual discovery of each other's and their own inner life. Within the

family, the closest relationship over a lifetime is between brothers and sisters. Outside the family, men and women find in their closest friends of the same sex the devotion of a sister, the loyalty of a brother. Appropriately, in Germany friends usually are brought into the family. Children call their father's and their mother's friends "uncle" and "aunt." Between French friends, who have chosen each other for the congeniality of their point of view, lively disagreement and sharpness of argument are the breath of life. But for Germans, whose friendships are based on mutuality of feeling, deep disagreement on any subject that matters to both is regarded as a tragedy. Like ties of kinship, ties of friendship are meant to be irrevocably binding. Young Germans who come to the United States have great difficulty in establishing such friendships with Americans. We view friendship more tentatively, subject to changes in intensity as people move, change their jobs, marry, or discover new interests.

14   English friendships follow still a different pattern. Their basis is shared activity. Activities at different stages of life may be of very different kinds—discovering a common interest in school, serving together in the armed forces, taking part in a foreign mission, staying in the same country house during a crisis. In the midst of the activity, whatever it may be, people fall into step—sometimes two men or two women, sometimes two couples, sometimes three people—and find that they walk or play a game or tell stories or serve on a tiresome and exacting committee with the same easy anticipation of what each will do day by day or in some critical situation. Americans who have made English friends comment that, even years later, "you can take up just where you left off." Meeting after a long interval, friends are like a couple who begin to dance again when the orchestra strikes up after a pause. English friendships are formed outside the family circle, but they are not, as in Germany, contrapuntal to the family nor are they, as in France, separated from the family. And a break in an English friendship comes not necessarily as a result of some irreconcilable difference of viewpoint or feeling but instead as a result of misjudgment, where one friend seriously misjudges how the other will think or feel or act, so that suddenly they are out of step.

15   What, then, is friendship? Looking at these different styles, including our own, each of which is related to a whole way of life, are there common elements? There is the recognition that friendship, in contrast with kinship, invokes freedom of choice. A friend is someone who chooses and is chosen. Related to this is the sense each friend gives the other of being a special individual, on whatever grounds this recognition is based. And between friends there is inevitably a kind of equality of give-and-take. These similarities make the bridge between societies possible, and the American's characteristic openness to different styles of relationship makes it possible for him to find new friends abroad with whom he feels at home.

The same methods you use to analyze a professional writer's essay can be applied to a student's writing as well. Within the composing process, an analysis of an essay will enable you to identify areas that need to be revised and to evaluate the essay's effectiveness in the areas of audience, purpose, organization, and supporting details.

▼ EXERCISE 10   Read and analyze the following student essay. Consider the writer's thesis and the supporting body paragraphs. Be prepared to answer the questions that follow the essay.

1   I grew up in the Garden of Eden. This land of milk and honey provided me with the essentials of boyhood: a park with baseball diamonds, friends for companionship, and a haunted house. As I grew older, my garden died. A specific combination of intangibles separated my neighborhood of Mayfield from the other neighborhoods in the city. The school down the block, St. Francis of Assisi School, educated me. The kids who went there taught me. The dreams I believed in still live there in Mayfield. Only when I left did I realize what I was leaving behind. As a boy in Mayfield, I learned through my school, my friends, my dreams, and my departure.

2   In many ways, Mayfield differed from other neighborhoods. In a section of the city near Lake Roland, Mayfield resembles any other neighborhood. Maybe Mayfield was special because I lived there. Walking down the street, one felt as if he were reading *Our Town*. Each family owned a house with a small yard and sidewalk. The Protestant church, St. Matthew's Church, sat at the corner of Mayfield and Norman Avenues. A few streets over, the Catholic church and school held masses and classes. The Irish and Italian families dwelt among the German and English families. My family stood alone as the only Asian family in Mayfield. Everyone knew everyone else through the church, the PTA, or through gossip.

3   St. Francis of Assisi School initiated me into the life of Catholic education. Sister Grace Christie introduced my pure mind to the realm of *A, B, C's* and 1, 2, 3's. She did not scare me as some of the other nuns did: "Oh, another Lee! I can't wait until I have you in my class!" Sister Edwards would screech while pinching my left cheek. The youngest child in the family often deals with these uncomfortable occasions. The first year of my formal education amused me. But by the second grade, Mrs. Young informed me that I was no longer a child. I was a student. Eager at first, I soon was overwhelmed by spelling tests and two-digit addition. I wanted to go home.

4   When I got home from school, I often spent my free time playing with the many kids in Mayfield. Usually the youngest, I envied and imitated the big kids. I thought the big kids in fifth grade could do anything. Wanting to be accepted, I would practice doing the things that big kids did. Dave, a kid my age, and I rode our bikes without using our hands, pretended to patrol Kinley Avenue as the cops did, and even spoke those bad words the big kids used. Sometimes the kids would elect someone to steal apples from the yard of the haunted house. I promised myself that when I finally got big I would never make the little kids do what I had to do. The big kids would teach me important stuff that Sister Grace did not know like how to play baseball or where babies come from. Competing with the other

kids, I often wondered about being big.

5   At Mayfield, I dreamed the usual boyhood dreams that still exist in other kids. As a child who never experienced the world outside Mayfield, I assumed that since I made the pee-wee league baseball team as a seven-year-old, I would play in the American League. Not only would I make the professional baseball team, but I would go to the moon and visit Mars. Maybe I could save the president and win the Olympics. More practical dreams came to me later as my parents felt my destiny to follow a medical route. The other kids in the neighborhood dreamed themselves to be firemen, movie stars, nurses, teachers, and scientists. Dreams change, and some die as kids grow older.

6   When I moved from Mayfield on September 7, 1977, I could not pack everything I wanted to take. So many items, some good and some bad, remained. I wanted to take my friends. Mom and Dad swore that they would buy me a new two-wheeler when they decided to leave the old one behind. I wondered if we would ever come home. Although still too young to understand, I knew that I could follow my dreams elsewhere. So I left most everything behind, but I packed away my hope which remained after such a trauma.

7   Looking back, I wonder what happened to my hopes. Growing up in the Garden of Eden, I possessed everything. Somehow I let it slip away. The friends I had still exist. My education still frustrates me. I still

dream like a child. But I am one of the big kids. In

my quest for fulfilling my hopes, I perverted my

intentions. My curiosity forced me to grow up

too fast.

▶ QUESTIONS   1. What type of introduction does the writer use? Does it capture the audience's attention? What is the writer's thesis? How will the writer develop the thesis? Has the writer developed a specific tone?

2. Examine each body paragraph carefully. Note the topic sentences for each one. Do they support the thesis?

3. Write an outline for each body paragraph. Identify the specific supports for each topic sentence. Are any sentences unnecessary or unclear? List the primary and secondary supports in each body paragraph. What transitional words or expressions connect the paragraphs?

4. What type of conclusion does the writer use? Does the writer remind the reader of the introductory paragraph?

▼ EXERCISE 11

In Exercise 6, you developed introductions and thesis statements. Choose one of those introductions now, and brainstorm for ideas for supporting body paragraphs. Organize your list of details, and write at least two body paragraphs for your thesis. Compare your paragraphs with those of other students. Are your paragraphs unified?

▼ EXERCISE 12

Choose one of the topics below, and write an essay.

1. Describe an aspect of your childhood.

2. Describe your high school by focusing on teachers, students, activities, and buildings.

3. Describe your favorite place.

After you have completed your essay, ask your classmates to analyze it with you. What process did you use to create the essay? Why did you choose this process?

Revising

Many beginning writers simply stop after the first draft of an essay; they do not go on to evaluate their essay's unity or organization. While the essay may be somewhat organized, these writers do not make the commitment to revise the essay and provide transitions and effective details. However, through revision, you can make *your* essays more effective and discover more about the topic. Revision requires many stages. First, you must consider the essay's topic and organization. Second, you must analyze your details carefully. Did you include the best examples, descriptions, or arguments? Are these details specific? Third, you should determine whether your paragraphs are effective. Would any paragraph be better placed elsewhere in the essay? Does each paragraph have a topic sentence and supporting details? Fourth, you must provide transitions for the reader. Are your transitions appropriate?

Since it is almost impossible to perform all of these checks at once, you can revise in stages so that each area of the essay is analyzed carefully and not prematurely pronounced "adequate." Answers to the following questions will guide you in the revision process.

I. *Thesis*

  A. Is there a thesis?

  B. Is the thesis accurate?

  C. How does the thesis define your opinion, predict the discussion, and control the essay?

  D. How could the thesis be worded more clearly?

  E. If there is no stated thesis, then what seems to be the main idea in the essay?

II. *Organization*

  A. How effective is the final organization of the essay? If, for instance, you are narrating an event, then is the narration in chronological order?

  B. Would your paragraphs be better arranged in another manner?

III. *Body Paragraphs*

  A. Does each body paragraph in the paper have a topic sentence?

  B. How does each topic sentence refer to or support the thesis?

  C. How do these body paragraphs present the best ideas possible to support the thesis? Or can you now think of other examples that might be more effective and interesting?

  D. Did you include specific details?

  E. How do the sentences in each paragraph support the topic sentence?

  F. Are these paragraphs unified?

IV. *Introduction*

  A. How does the introduction develop the reader's interest?

  B. Does the introduction supply enough information about the background of the topic?

  C. Is the introduction too short?

  D. Would another type of introduction be more effective?

V. *Transitions*

  A. What are the transitions between paragraphs?

  B. What makes the transitions between the sentences within paragraphs effective?

C. Can the reader easily follow the ideas presented in the essay?

In addition to the questions above, there are other revision strategies that can help you determine and improve the effectiveness of your paper. For instance, you can produce three or four drafts of a paper, each with a different goal, before the paper is complete. Second, you can outline your paper to isolate problems in the development of ideas. After all, if you cannot outline your own paper, then certainly your audience too will have difficulty following your ideas. Third, you can gloss the paper to identify problems with unity and development. (See "Revision Strategies" in Chapter 5, Part I.)

▼ EXERCISE 13

Use the revision questions from the previous page to analyze the following student essay. Where should the student revise the essay? Make specific suggestions about the types of revision the student should make. Compare your comments to those of other students. Finally, revise the essay yourself.

1   There are many memorable places that captivate one's mind from time to time. One of the most memorable places to me is a secluded place located in my elementary school's yard. When I was in elementary school, my friends and I used to meet every day after school to decide our plans for that afternoon; our meetings took place at a beautiful, small bridge next to the school yard.

2   The bridge, which is a footbridge, spans a man-made creek. It unites the neighborhood, in which most of the students live, with the school. The bridge is made of concrete and seems as if it has been standing for many years. It extends approximately thirty-five feet long and hangs ten feet above the water. Two green, solid-metal railings guard each side of the bridge. Both railings are constructed with three parallel bars running the length of the bridge. These guardrails are designed to prevent small

children from falling into the creek.

3   At the foot of the neighborhood side of the bridge there is a small pathway. This pathway leads from one of the neighborhood streets to the bridge. It is made of scattered gravel and loose dirt. Trees shelter the street, and the swaying branches produce a very serene atmosphere. A few of the branches hang very low, so adults find it difficult to pass through; however children can easily run under the branches.

4   Once on the bridge, the view captures the winding creek. The water in the creek is shallow, and fallen leaves float downstream. Along the creek, trees are suspended over the water and throw shadows on the small bridge. The trees and bridge complement each other in forming a beautiful, relaxing scene.

5   At the school yard end of the bridge stands an enormous oak tree, which seems as if it has been standing longer than any of its neighbors. It looks as if kids have been playing on and around it for years. The beaten path, around the oak tree, clearly shows this. The oak tree has etchings of long-forgotten school-yard crushes.

6   The bridge is a beautiful sight and structure. The surroundings overwhelm the viewer, and the place is calm. But to me the bridge is a meeting place, a place where I spent many hours with my young friends. This bridge is a sentimental landmark to me. It brings back memories which have been misplaced, but not forgotten.

▼ EXERCISE 14   Look carefully at the essay you wrote in Exercise 12. With the assistance of other students, decide what revisions would make the essay more effective. List them, and then revise the essay. Use the revision checklist as a guide.

Editing

While editing a paper, you must focus upon the individual sentences in each paragraph. At this stage, you work to ensure that the sentences themselves are effective, concise, and correct. This act of "polishing" the essay gives you another chance to evaluate your essay.

Since there are many points to consider, editing, like revision, can best be accomplished in stages. You should edit each paragraph separately and read it aloud. Often the act of reading aloud will alert you to potential problems. If, for example, sentences sound unclear when they are read aloud, then you need to edit them. The list below can guide you in editing your papers.

I. *Clarity*

    A. Do all of your sentences mean what they say? Or are they ambiguous?

    B. Have you used the correct words to communicate your meaning?

II. *Coherence* (See Chapter 6 in Part I.)

    A. Did you use pronouns to achieve coherence? Are any pronouns ambiguous in their reference?

    B. Did you use synonyms? Are they accurate?

    C. Did you use limited repetition to achieve coherence?

    D. Did you use sentence combining to achieve coherence?

III. *Diction* (See Chapter 7 in Part I.)

    A. Did you use specific words?

    B. Did you avoid slang, jargon, and regional expressions?

    C. Did you use clichés? Can you think of another way to express your meaning?

    D. Did you create a specific, identifiable tone through word choice? Is this tone appropriate for the intended audience?

IV. *Style* (See Chapter 8 in Part I.)

    A. Are sentences wordy?

    B. Did you use active voice and descriptive verbs?

    C. Did you subordinate ideas effectively?

    D. Did you vary your sentence structure?

V. *Correctness*

    A. Are there any fragments, run-ons, or comma splices? (See Chapters 4, 5, and 6 in Part II.)

    B. Do subjects and verbs agree in number? (See Chapter 7 in Part II.)

    C. Are there any unnecessary shifts in verb tense? (See Chapters 1 and 2 in Part II.)

D. Are there any unnecessary shifts in point of view?

E. Are your pronouns correct in case, number, and gender? (See Chapter 8 in Part II.)

F. Did you check marks of punctuation? Are commas, semicolons, colons, and other marks of punctuation used correctly? (See Chapters 9, 10, 11, 12, and 13 in Part II.)

G. Are words spelled correctly? (See any good dictionary.)

 **EXERCISE 15**

Use the guidelines above to edit the following essay for sentence problems. Make your corrections here.

1   When I look back on my life to see which stage of developement has influenced my attitudes the most, I see that my childhood had a major impact. The values and interests I picked up during this period have stayed with me throughout my life. My love of sports and athletic competition stem from my childhood experiences. Specifically, my family and childhood environment have caused, to a great degree, the intense competition and sometimes unsportsmanlike conduct that I exhibited when I play sports.

2   The intensity with which I play sports has been evident since early childhood. As a young boy, I often played different sports with my father, and I can well remember our on-going rivalry in basketball. As I grew taller and more skilled, I was able to beat him almost every time, however, there were games in which the "old man" would get lucky and beat me. I never took defeat lightly, and I usually stomped off the court in anger after a loss. Maybe that fact that I seldom lost made defeat harder to swallow.

3   Whereas my fierce competition in playing

against my dad almost reached the point of being unsportsmanlike. It certainly reached this point when I competed with my younger brother. Since we lived in a small community, my brother and me usually played games, such as football, baseball, soccer, and basketball one-on-one rather than with other boys. When we played I always won, which is not surprising considering that I was three years older than him and several inches taller. Still, despite my obvious advantages, I never gave him an inch and prided myself on the fact that he had never beaten me in any of the sports we played. When he did come close to winning, I would usually go into a rage and preceded to double my efforts to defeat him. Sometimes I even resorted to cheating to keep from losing. I did whatever it took to win, and after doing so, I would jump and holler in celebration as if I had just won the World Series or the Super Bowl.

4   When I played sports outside of my family, I usually controlled my intensity, but much of the same behavior was displayed. I always played to win; even if I am just playing in an intramural games, and sometimes I become quite depressed when I lost. Losing also led me to do some very childish acts, such as slamming down balls and bats, yelling unmentionables, and stomping off the playing field in anger. These actions mirrored the behavior I exhibited playing against my father and brother, but now my conduct was being witnessed outside of my family.

5   The causes of this behavior are threefold, and all three are linked to my childhood experiences. Foremost is the competition within my family, especially with my brother. My behavior was worst when I played against him, because of my need to dominate him since I was older. I never had to accept defeat playing against my brother because I never lost. My love of sports and the great importance I placed on them also led to the intensity I exhibited. I was introduced to sports at a young age and participated in them throughout my childhood. The importance I placed on sports is linked with an underlying cause; my need to be a sports superstar. While I had done well on the teams I played on, I had never been a superstar. However, when I played against my brother I was able to dominate him and, in effect, become the star I never was. Even when I played against my peers, I always strive to be the best.

6   The seriousness with which I play sports has led to unfortunate results. This attitude has cause unnecessary tension and immature behavior that has, in turn, caused embarrassment. I have not set a good example for my brother and as a result, he has displayed similar actions at times. If I had played sports just for fun and not take them so seriously, then I would surely have enjoyed playing much more.

▼ EXERCISE 16

Return to the essay you revised in Exercise 14 and edit it now for sentence-level problems. Ask others to assist you, and compare your ideas with theirs.

Proofreading

After revising and editing an essay, you must copy or type it neatly for submission. Since you may be rushed at this point, you may overlook typing errors (such as transposed letters in words), omitted words, and stray marks of punctuation. Therefore, always proofread the final copy of the paper for such errors. You can easily make minor corrections in pen and insert missing words neatly. (Most instructors will accept final papers with some corrections on them.) Use the following guidelines for proofreading the final copy.

1. Is each word spelled correctly? (Too often when writers proofread quickly, they see what they anticipate they will see, and they will miss simple spelling or typing errors. To break this pattern of anticipation, read the paper backwards. In this manner, you can focus on each word in isolation and easily check its spelling.)

2. Are words omitted? Or are words repeated? (Again, writers anticipate what they meant to say and misread what is actually on the paper. Read each sentence aloud slowly and carefully. Listen closely to the words. Are there any errors?)

3. Are there stray marks of punctuation? (Isolate each sentence by placing pieces of paper around it; read the sentence carefully.)

▼ EXERCISE 17

Read the following two paragraphs of a student essay. Proofread this final copy carefully. Make any necessary corrections here.

> The running craze has reached enormous
> proportions in recent years. One can not help but
> notic the increase in the number of runners; the
> streets and sidewalks ahve been invaded by these
> fitness freak. Anumber of them are serious competi-
> tiors, entering any number of the countless races
> held held every week end. Of these racers, no two
> follow exactly the same training regiment; still all
> routines are based on either high-milage running or
> speed-oriented workouts, or a combination of the two.
> Each method has its benefits and drawbacks.
>
> Both training methods can be use to prepare
> for middle-distance and long-distance racing. Distance

traiining consists running at least a couple of miles
at a steady and is used to develope stamina. Speed-
oriented workouts, on the other hand, involve
running short distances of under one mile at a fast
pace. This training is used to build spped and to
simulate the final mile of a race in terms of pace and
intensity.

▼ EXERCISE 18

Make a final copy of your edited paper from Exercise 16 for submission to your instructor. Use the proofreading guidelines to check the copy carefully.

Writing Assignments

1. Tell about a time when your world seemed to have turned upside down. Consider the larger social implications of this event. What can others gain from your narration? Write the article for an appropriate magazine and identify the magazine's audience.

2. For a newspaper, cover a local event of some importance (such as a demonstration, a town meeting, a natural disaster, or a political rally), or narrate an activity (such as a day at the race track, a rock concert, or a sports event). Identify your audience and purpose.

3. Describe a person in his or her environment. Be specific about the qualities and characteristics of the person that are evident in this environment. Consider, for example, how you might describe a businessperson in the office, a lawyer investigating a case, or a homeless person on the street. Identify an audience and purpose for your piece.

4. Describe for a local city council the condition of a section of town that should be rehabilitated. Your purpose will be to demonstrate to the city council members that the project is worthwhile.

5. Before financial speculators commit themselves to a project, they demand market research to prove the profitability of the investment. Therefore, classify shoppers at a local mall to show your financial backers that another, more upscale mall is needed.

6. For a foreign-exchange student who has just arrived at your school, classify the American student. What specific types of

students does the exchange student need to understand in order to adapt to American culture?

7. Arrange interviews with several people of the same age, for example, young adults, middle-aged adults, or older adults. In the interviews, ask each person what he or she perceives to be the advantages and disadvantages of not only his or her own age but also other ages. In an essay for a sociology class, present your findings. Illustrate the age group by providing examples from your interviews.

8. Others often hold great expectations for us. Describe a time you surprised someone by surpassing his or her expectations of you. Direct the paper to the person you surprised and create a purpose for the paper.

9. Choose a task you know how to perform well. In a directional process analysis, guide a novice through the process so that he or she can complete the task by reading your instructions. Also, provide a reason for him or her to wish to learn this task.

10. Describe in an informational process analysis the method by which you compose an essay. Be as specific about your writing process as possible, and identify the type of writing you do most frequently. Your audience should be the members of your composition class; remember that your explanation may assist others in the writing process.

11. Interview a member of another generation to learn that person's views about the changes in American life during his or her lifetime, about the problems he or she identifies today in American society, and about his or her attitudes on traditions and values in American life. Compare or contrast your own views with this person's. Imagine you will present this paper to the members of an introductory sociology class. (Before the interview, create specific questions that will guide the person in the discussion of his or her values.)

12. As a travel agent or travel writer, compare or contrast two vacation spots or two regions of the country for publication in a local newspaper. To prepare for this assignment, read the travel section of a local paper or national magazine.

13. Most major events in our lives (graduation, first car, first job, death of a family member) are remembered as isolated incidents; they have no before and after. Yet, of course, these events do have causes and effects. Write about an important occurrence in your life and analyze its causes and effects.

14. Students attend college, rather than getting a full-time job or enrolling in a trade school, because they expect that the

college experience and a college degree will ultimately benefit them. This may be a misperception. Write an essay about the results—both good and bad—of attending college as if you were presenting college as one of several possible options to a group of high-school seniors.

15. Many words we use frequently have different meanings for others. Choose one of the following terms and define it in an essay for a specific audience: *educated, gifted, brave, adventurous,* or *humorous.*

16. Part of the American dream is to become successful. Examine several major magazines carefully and determine how each one portrays success. In an essay, define *success* for a group of foreign businesspeople who will be working in the United States.

17. There are many injustices in today's world. Limit your essay to a discussion of one injustice and your proposed course of action to remedy the injustice. Direct your piece to an appropriate audience.

18. America is a society of laws, yet many of those laws are considered misguided, unenforceable, and/or poorly administered. Discuss a law you think should be changed and explain your views to your local state legislator.

19. Nearly every town in America has homeless people on its streets. For your local city council, argue that the city or state is or is not responsible for the needs of the destitute.

20. Identify a campus problem that needs to be addressed. In an essay to the appropriate administrator, present your arguments concerning this issue.

The following writing assignments are based upon the photographs that appeared in Part I.

1. Using the picture on page 23 as your guide, describe your most memorable day at a beach or lake. Focus on the sensory images created by the sun, sand, and water.

2. Examine the photograph of the crowd on page 1 carefully. What do you notice about the composition of the photo? In a short piece for your school paper, describe this group of young people.

3. In the photograph on page 95, the players are blocking a lacrosse shot. Consider the techniques or skills that certain sports require. Choose one sport and explain these skills to a beginning player.

4. On page 63, consider the risks that the climber is taking as she moves slowly up the rock face of the mountain. Create an analogy of her risks to the ones you might take when you compose. What points of the processes are similar? Include a discussion of the rewards of taking such risks in your piece.

5. The photograph on page 95 focuses on two players reaching for a ball. Examine their facial expressions. For a piece in the sports section of your campus newspaper, describe the players' efforts and discuss the apparent indifference of the spectators.

6. In the photograph on page 129, two gymnasts seem to be practicing a routine. For a group of parents of high school students, explain the importance of the school's athletic program.

7. Consider the photograph on page 173. Although soccer usually requires a number of players to coordinate a strategy, what are the individual player's responsibilities? In an essay, enumerate the player's responsibilities to himself and to the team.

8. Compare or contrast the two styles of jumping that are demonstrated in the photograph on page 199. Provide this analysis for a sports magazine devoted to track and field events.

9. In many sports, once a player has control of the ball, he or she can choose from among a wide range of strategies. Likewise, once a person earns a college degree, a variety of career possibilities develop. Explain the need for a college education as a prerequisite to a specific career to a group of high-school students.

10. The photograph on page 269 juxtaposes a diver and the American flag. What is the connection between sports and patriotism? Examine the role of the Olympics as a political and athletic event.

11. Describe the picture of the windsurfer (page 23) to someone who has no experience with the sport. What can you infer about the windsurfer's characteristics and personality? What details in the picture support these inferences?

12. After examining the pictures on pages 173 and 237, consider the personality type suggested by each picture. Is there a relationship between a sport and personal characteristics? Address your essay to a group of parents whose children are signing up for after-school sports.

13. The picture of the diver (page 269) has a flag as its background. Consider the basic elements of patriotism. Must one

of these elements be self-denial, either by athletes or soldiers? Present your definition of *patriotism* to a group of new American citizens.

14. Although lacrosse and gymnastics seem to be very different sports, they both emphasize speed, agility, and self-discipline. Think of two other apparently different activities or hobbies and write about their hidden similarities.

15. What types of people would be most likely to be windsurfers (page 23) or rock climbers (page 63)? Compare or contrast the attitudes and characteristics of these two athletes.

Grammar Review

PART II

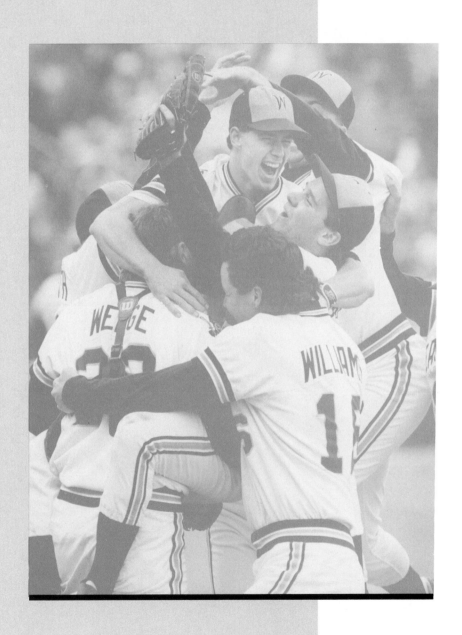

Introduction

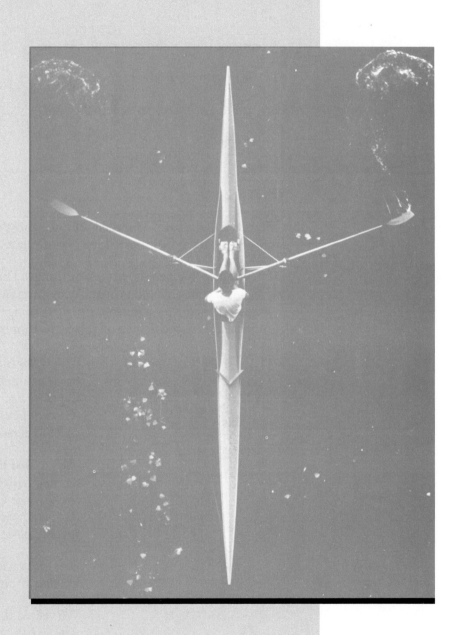

▶ **OBJECTIVES**

1. To review the parts of speech.

2. To introduce identification of subjects and verbs.

3. To introduce four basic sentence formats.

▶ **KEY CONCEPT**

A sentence must fulfill two requirements:

1. It must have a subject and a verb.

2. It must express a complete thought.

Parts of Speech

There are eight parts of speech. Because most of these terms will be used throughout the book, it is helpful if you can recognize them.

1. **Nouns** name people, places, or things. There are two kinds of nouns: common and proper. A common noun provides a general name for a person, place, or thing; a proper noun identifies a specific person, place, or thing and is capitalized.

▶ Examples: The *doctor* operates daily. (*Doctor* is a common noun naming a person.)
Captain Lewis whistled softly.
(*Captain Lewis* is a proper noun naming a specific person.)

We crossed the *valley*. (*Valley* is a common noun naming a place.)
We saw the *Grand Canyon*.
(*Grand Canyon* is a proper noun naming a specific place.)

The *boat* raced away. (*Boat* is a common noun naming a thing.)

We visited the *Queen Elizabeth II*.
(*Queen Elizabeth II* is a proper noun naming a specific thing.)

A noun can also be abstract or concrete. Abstract nouns name intangible ideas, ideals, or qualities. Concrete nouns name tangible people, places, or things. Concrete nouns can be perceived through at least one of the five senses: touch, taste, smell, sight, or sound.

▶ Examples: The terms *love, honor,* and *patriotism* are difficult to define precisely.
(*Love, honor,* and *patriotism* are abstract nouns.)

The *animals* at the *zoo* pleased the *tourists.*
(*Animals, zoo,* and *tourists* are concrete nouns.)

2. **Verbs** are words that describe action or existence.

▶ Examples: Each afternoon, the children *run, skip,* and *jump* during recess.
(*Run, skip,* and *jump* are verbs that show action.)

Ellen *seems* very happy. She *is* a certified public accountant.
(*Seems,* the present tense of the verb *seem,* and *is,* the present tense of the verb *be,* are verbs that show existence.)

In addition to describing action or existence, some forms of specific verbs can be used as *helping verbs;* these helping verbs aid the reader in determining the correct time and conditions of an action. (These helping verbs are always used with another *main verb* that shows action or describes existence.) The chart below lists a number of helping verbs that can be used to determine the time and condition of the verb *to go.*

▶ Examples:

is going, are going	will go
was going, were going	has gone, have gone
will be going	had gone
has been going, have been going	will have gone
had been going	shall go
will have been going	did go
should have gone	may go
can go	could go
could have gone	might go
might have gone	would have gone

Although the basic action in each of the above examples is the same (*to go*), the time (present, past, and future) and the conditions (obligation, possibility, ability, emphasis, and permission) of the action change in each example.

Below is a list of the most common helping verbs:

can	is/are/am	may	shall
could	was/were	might	should
do	has/have	must	used to
does	had	ought to	will
did			would

3. **Pronouns** are words that take the place of nouns.

> ▶ Examples: The pronoun *he* can take the place of the nouns *Bill*, *Jack*, or *man* (or any other noun that is masculine and singular).
> The pronoun *they* can take the place of a number of people.

The many types of pronouns are listed below:

- Personal Pronouns
  Subjective or Nominative case: I, you, he, she, it, we, they
  Objective case: me, you, him, her, it, us, them
  Possessive case: my, mine, your, yours, his, her, hers, its, our, ours, their, theirs

- Indefinite Pronouns
  all, anyone, anything, anybody, each, everybody, everyone, everything, no one, nobody, nothing, several, some, some-one, somebody

- Relative Pronouns
  who, whom, whose, which, that, whoever, whomever, whichever

- Demonstrative Pronouns
  this, that, those, these

- Intensive/Reflexive Pronouns
  myself, yourself, himself, herself, itself, ourselves, your-selves, themselves

- Interrogative Pronouns
  who, which, whom, whose, what

4. **Adjectives** describe nouns. They tell what color, shape, size, amount, mood, or temperature a noun is.

> ▶ Examples: Our trip to the beach was marred by the *cold, gray* day.
> (The words *cold* and *gray* describe the day in terms of temperature and color.)
>
> The *large, octagonal*, brightly *colored* rug was a gift.
> (The words *large, octagonal*, and *colored* describe the rug in terms of its size, shape, and color.)

NOTE: The words *a*, *an*, and *the* are adjectives; these three words are called *articles*.

5. **Adverbs** modify verbs, adjectives, or other adverbs. They tell when, where, how, and to what degree.

▶ Examples: The cat jumped *gracefully*. (*Gracefully* tells how the cat jumped.)

We have been *here before*. (*Here* tells where, and *before* tells when.)

She thanked him *very graciously* for the flowers. (*Very* tells to what degree she thanked him; *graciously* describes how she thanked him.)

6. **Conjunctions** join words or groups of words. There are three major types of conjunctions.
    Coordinate conjunctions join words, word phrases, or sentences of equal value.

▶ Examples: Ann *and* Hilda (*And* joins the names of two people.)

The girls tried to open the window, *but* it was painted shut.
(*But* joins two sentences.)

There are seven coordinate conjunctions: *for, and, nor, but, or, yet,* and *so*.
    Subordinate conjunctions join a dependent clause (a group of words with a subject and a verb that does not make a complete thought) and an independent clause (a group of words with a subject and a verb that does form a complete thought).

▶ Examples: *After* the flood waters had receded, the towns-people began to remove the debris left behind.
(*After*, a subordinate conjunction, joins the dependent clause to the independent clause, "the townspeople began to remove the debris left behind.")

The dog acted *as if* he had never seen a cat before.
(*As if*, a subordinate conjunction, joins the dependent clause to the independent clause, "The dog acted.")

Below is a list of frequently used subordinate conjunctions:

after	since	whenever
although	so that	when
as (as if)	unless	where
because	until	whether
even though	wherever	while
if		

Conjunctive adverbs (or *adverbial conjunctions*) are used with a semicolon to join two or more independent clauses to form one compound sentence.

▶ Examples: The house was overpriced; *moreover,* the couple did not need so many rooms.
(*Moreover* joins two independent clauses.)

The couple planned a small wedding; *however,* their parents invited over two hundred friends.
(*However* joins two independent clauses.)

Below is a partial list of conjunctive adverbs:

consequently	however	otherwise
furthermore	moreover	therefore
hence	nevertheless	thus

7. **Prepositions** are used to show the relationship between a noun or a pronoun and another word in a sentence.

▶ Examples: The island *across* the bay is owned *by* the city.
(*Across* is a preposition. It helps describe which island, and it connects *bay* and *island* to describe the location. *By* is also a preposition; it describes who owns the island.)

The thief ran *behind* the house *on* the corner.
(*Behind* is a preposition; it describes the location of the hiding place of the thief. *On* is a preposition; it identifies the location of the house.)

Here is a sample list of prepositions:

about	during	through
after	due to	to
around	inside	under
behind	outside	with
below	since	

8. **Interjections** are words that are used to express strong emotions, such as anger, joy, sorrow, or surprise. Often an exclamation point comes after the interjection.

▶ Examples: *Wow!* She won five million dollars in the weekly state lottery.
(*Wow* expresses happiness and surprise.)

Whew! It sure is hot today.
(*Whew* expresses discomfort.)

Practice

Write the part of speech of each italicized word in the following sentences above the word.

1. *In* the past four years, college *tuition has risen* three times faster than the rate of inflation.

2. *Boy!* That's a *gorgeous* Maserati.

3. Alice *and* Arlene *must serve* detention for a week.

4. The air conditioner *seems* to be malfunctioning.

5. Each *society* photographer seeks to catch his subject in a *revealing* and *memorable* pose.

6. The dancers swayed *slowly* and *gracefully; however,* they did not win a prize.

7. *Although she* had walked on the moon *and* flown to Jupiter, she decided to retire from the space program.

8. *Oh my gosh!* The *kerosene* heater *has* exploded.

9. *Everyone should* complete one year of service *to* the community.

10. *Warden James* just paroled "The Shark," a *vicious mass* murderer.

11. The children *danced* and *sang before* the program ended.

12. A car *with* a blue hood and *purple* wheels has been found abandoned *by* the railroad tracks.

13. *Shyness* and introspection are the *characteristics of* an introvert.

14. *We* can go to the movies, *or* we can go *to* the beach.

15. *You* lost *my* book; *that* wasn't *very* nice.

16. *Jerome failed his* comprehensive examination, *for* he had not completed the required course work.

17. *On* our vacation this *summer,* we saw Naples *by* the sea, *Andorra near* the Pyrenees, and Oslo *at* the tip *of* a fjord.

18. Even though a thesaurus is helpful, I find a dictionary more *useful* and *informative.*

19. The kindergarten students laughed *gleefully as* they *quickly* raced *through* the tunnel.

20. "I *have been rejected* for a promotion once *too* often!" he shouted.

Check the answer key.

Subjects and Verbs

Subjects and verbs provide the core portion of a sentence, because they tell who performed an action and what the action was. **Subjects** must be nouns or pronouns. **Verbs** show action or existence. The easiest test for locating the subject and verb in a sentence is to ask these questions:

1. What is the action? or What word shows existence? The answer is the *verb*.

2. Who or what is performing the action? The answer is the *subject*.

Locate the subject and verb in the following sentence.

> ▶ Example: Barry sang.
>
>   1. What is the action? *sang* (the verb)
>
>   2. Who is performing the action? *Barry* (the subject)

Sentence Formats

There are four basic sentence formats in American English. You should be able to recognize each of these, because they are used frequently. These formats give information about the construction of sentences.

1. Format 1 is **Subject/Verb.**

    > ▶ Example: Teresa laughed.
    >
    >   The subject is *Teresa.*
    > The verb is *laughed.*

2. Format 2 is **Subject/Verb/Direct Object.**

    > ▶ Example: The lawyer won the case.
    >
    >   The subject is *lawyer.*
    > The verb is *won.*
    > The direct object, which receives the action of the verb, is *case.*

3. Format 3 has two forms:

    A. **Subject/Linking Verb/Predicate Adjective**

    > ▶ Example: Grammar seems difficult.
    >
    >   The subject is *grammar.*
    > The linking verb, which shows existence, is *seems.*

The predicate adjective, which modifies the subject, is *difficult*.

B. Subject/Linking Verb/Predicate Nominative

▶ Example: Writing is an exercise in thought.

The subject is *writing*.
The linking verb is *is*.
The predicate nominative, which renames the subject, is *exercise*.

4. Format 4 is **Subject/Verb/Indirect Object/Direct Object.**

▶ Example: She handed him a plate.

The subject is *she*.
The verb is *handed*.
The direct object is *plate*.
The indirect object, which tells to whom the plate was handed, is *him*.

NOTE: See Chapter 3 in Part II for further explanation of subjects, verbs, and sentence formats.

1

Verbs I: The Present, Past, and Future Tenses

▶ **OBJECTIVES**

1. To recognize and use the basic verb tenses—past, present, and future.

2. To form correctly regular and irregular verbs in past, present, and future tenses.

3. To use a consistent and appropriate verb tense when writing.

▶ **KEY CONCEPT**

To communicate accurately and effectively, a writer must know and use the correct present, past, and future tenses of the appropriate verb.

Action Verbs and Linking Verbs

Verbs are divided into two categories:

1. **Action verbs** are words that show movement. For example, *to run*, *to dance*, and *to cry* are action verbs.

2. **Linking verbs** are verbs that do not show action. Instead, they convey existence, being, becoming, and, sometimes, one of the five senses (touch, taste, smell, hearing, or sight). For example, the verbs *to be*, *to seem*, and *to become* are linking verbs. Linking verbs connect, or make equal, the subject and the word after the linking verb.

NOTE: The basic verb form is the word *to* plus the basic verb—*to be*, *to run*. This form is called the **infinitive.** All verb forms are made from the infinitive.

▶ ## PRACTICE 1

Identify the following verbs as action verbs or linking verbs.

1. to jump _____	6. to become _____
2. to be _____	7. to sing _____
3. to drive _____	8. to work _____
4. to dance _____	9. to draw _____
5. to seem _____	10. to read _____

Check the answer key.

Conjugating Verbs

In order to use the various forms of a verb correctly, you must learn to **conjugate** the verb—that is, produce its different forms from the basic form, the infinitive.

You can determine the verb forms by using the following pronouns as subjects (a pronoun takes the place of a noun—a person, place, or thing):

First Person:	*I* is singular (you are talking about your own actions)
	we is plural (you are talking about your actions and the actions of one or more other people; for example, if you wanted to substitute a pronoun for "Joe and I," you would use the pronoun *we*)
Second Person:	*you* is singular (you are talking directly to another person)
	you is plural (you are talking directly to two or more people)
Third Person:	*he, she, it* are singular (you are talking about one other person or thing)
	they is plural (you are talking about two or more people or things)

Pronouns must agree in number (the number of people, places, or things) and in gender (masculine, feminine, or neuter) with the nouns they replace.

PRACTICE 2

Substitute pronouns for the nouns listed below.

▶ Example: Joe and I _we)_

1. Tom _____   6. the house _____

2. Mrs. Jones _____   7. Sam, Tim, and Helen _____

3. a horse _____   8. the buildings _____

4. the test _____   9. the firefighters _____

5. a rose _____   10. Mr. Duff and I _____

Check the answer key.

When you conjugate a verb, use the following chart:

Singular	Plural
I _____	we _____
you_____	you_____
he, she, it_____	they _____

The Present Tense

All verb tenses indicate time. The present tense has four functions:

1.   It describes what is taking place now.

> ▶ Example: The soccer player *kicks* the ball.

2.   It shows an habitual action, one that is often repeated.

> ▶ Example: Each weekday morning, the children *go* to school.

3.   It identifies an action that will take place in the near future.

> ▶ Example: The play *starts* in ten minutes.

4.   As the historical present, it is used primarily in the analysis of a literary text. In discussing *Hamlet*, for example, a writer should not say, "Hamlet procrastinated because he doubted his father's ghost," or "Hamlet said, 'To be, or not to be. . . .'" Rather the student should write, "Hamlet *procrastinates*," or "Hamlet *says*." The historical present is used for two reasons: the text as a living entity endures beyond the date of composition, and, for the reader encountering the text, the action actually does exist in the present.

> ▶ Example: In *The Adventures of Huckleberry Finn*, Mark Twain *creates* many memorable characters.

The present tense is formed from the infinitive of the verb. **Regular verbs** follow a set pattern in the present tense. **Irregular verbs** do not follow this pattern; you must learn those verbs individually. Fortunately, most verbs are regular ones.

For example, the verb *to talk* is a regular verb. Say the word aloud and use the pronoun chart for conjugation. Your conjugation of the verb *to talk* in the present tense should be:

I talk	we talk
you talk	you talk
he, she, it talks	they talk

Because this is a regular verb, what conclusion can you draw about the conjugation of regular verbs in the present tense? Consider where the verb changes. Which pronoun form takes a different ending? Your answer should be third-person singular (the *he, she,* or *it* form). How does that form change? It adds an *s* to the end of the verb.

You have now developed a rule for conjugating regular verbs in the present tense. The basic form of the verb does not change from the infinitive except for the third-person singular. Add *s* or *es* to the third-person singular to form this conjugation.

▶ ## PRACTICE 3

Conjugate the following verbs in present tense.

1. to walk: I_____   we _____

   you _____   you _____

   he, she, it _____   they_____

2. to read: I_____   we _____

   you _____   you _____

   he, she, it _____   they_____

3. to dance: I_____   we _____

   you _____   you _____

   he, she, it _____   they_____

4. to hide: I_____   we _____

   you _____   you _____

   he, she, it _____   they_____

5. to call: I_____   we _____

   you _____   you _____

   he, she, it _____   they_____

Check the answer key.

Irregular verbs do not follow this pattern for the present tense. You must simply memorize the forms. Sometimes, if you simply say the verb and its conjugation aloud, you may recognize the forms. Two familiar irregular verbs are *to be* and *to have*. Learn the conjugations of these verbs.

to be

I am _____   we are _____

you are _____   you are _____

he, she, it is _____   they are _____

to have

I have _____   we have _____

you have _____   you have _____

he, she, it has _____   they have _____

▶

PRACTICE 4

Fill in the blanks with the appropriate present-tense form of the verb.
Use the verbs provided for the sentences.

▶ Example: I ____**go**____ to school each weekday.
                     (to go)

1. He _____ to his girlfriend every day.
        (to talk)

2. Doris _____ four miles each day.
          (to run)

3. You _____ one library book, but he
        (to have)

    _____ the one you need.
        (to have)

4. It _____ a very hot August day.
       (to be)

5. The Allegheny Mountains _____ a lovely sight in
                            (to be)

    the fall.

6. Ted and I _____ a joint checking account.
            (to have)

7. Many thousands of people _____ the state of
                            (to visit)

    Kentucky.

8. She _____ very well; her sketches
        (to draw)

    _____ now on display at the local museum.
        (to be)

9. On family trips, my father _____ .
                             (to drive)

10. Many luxuries _____ now necessities. The
                 (to be)

    telephone _____ one example.
             (to be)

Check the answer key.

The Past Tense

The *past tense* of verbs describes an action that took place in the past and that was
completed before the present time. Look at the following sentence:

▶ Example: Bill Rodgers *won* the New York City Marathon
                     in 1980.

                     The verb *won* is in the past tense. The action
                     took place in 1980, so it was in the past.

                     Also, the action was completed before the
                     current year.

Look at the following conjugations of the verbs *to walk* and *to revolve* in the past
tense:

to walk

I walked	we walked
you walked	you walked
he, she, it walked	they walked

to revolve

I revolved	we revolved
you revolved	you revolved
he, she, it revolved	they revolved

Because these are regular verbs, what conclusion can you draw about how regular verbs are formed in the past tense? Both verbs add what endings? *d* or *ed*?

You have now developed a rule for forming the past tense of regular verbs: add *d* or *ed* to the basic form of the verb.

▶ PRACTICE 5

Form the past tense of the following regular verbs:

1. to dance: I_____   we _____

   you _____   you_____

   he, she, it _____   they _____

2. to pour: I_____   we _____

   you _____   you_____

   he, she, it _____   they _____

3. to mark: I_____   we _____

   you _____   you_____

   he, she, it _____   they _____

4. to paint: I_____   we _____

   you _____   you_____

   he, she, it _____   they _____

5. to call: I_____   we _____

   you _____   you_____

   he, she, it _____   they _____

Check the answer key.

Irregular verbs in the past tense are formed in a number of ways:

1. By changing the vowels in the basic verb form: for example, *to know* becomes *knew* in the past tense.

2. By changing the vowels and adding a *t:* for example, *to teach* becomes *taught* in the past tense.

3. By changing a *d* to a *t:* for example, *to build* becomes *built* in the past tense.

4. By changing the entire form: for example, the verbs *to be, to have,* and *to do* follow no set pattern.

NOTE: If you are uncertain about the formation of a verb in the past tense, check a dictionary. Look at the following entry for the verb *to draw* from *Webster's Ninth Collegiate Dictionary.**

¹**draw**\ˊdrȯ*vb* **drew**\ˊdrü\; . . .

The second form of the verb is the past tense. Therefore, to conjugate the verb *to draw* in the past tense, one would write the following:

I drew	we drew
you drew	you drew
he, she, it drew	they drew

The following chart identifies many frequently used irregular verbs in their infinitives, past tenses, and present and past participles. (Present participles are used to form the progressive tenses. Past participles are used to form the perfect tenses. In the progressive and perfect tenses, present and past participles require helping verbs, such as *is, am, are, has, have,* or *had,* to identify the time periods. See Chapter 2 in Part II for information on the progressive and perfect tenses.)

INFINITIVE	PAST	PRESENT PARTICIPLE	PAST PARTICIPLE
1. to be	was or were	being	been
2. to become	became	becoming	become
3. to begin	began	beginning	begun
4. to bite	bit	biting	bitten
5. to blow	blew	blowing	blown
6. to break	broke	breaking	broken
7. to bring	brought	bringing	brought
8. to build	built	building	built
9. to burst	burst	bursting	burst
10. to buy	bought	buying	bought
11. to catch	caught	catching	caught
12. to choose	chose	choosing	chosen
13. to come	came	coming	come
14. to deal	dealt	dealing	dealt

By permission. From *Webster's Ninth Collegiate Dictionary,* © 1991 by Merriam-Webster, Inc., publisher of the Merriam-Webster ® Dictionaries.

INFINITIVE	PAST	PRESENT PARTICIPLE	PAST PARTICIPLE
15. to dive	dove (dived)	diving	dived
16. to do	did	doing	done
17. to draw	drew	drawing	drawn
18. to drink	drank	drinking	drunk
19. to drive	drove	driving	driven
20. to fall	fell	falling	fallen
21. to feel	felt	feeling	felt
22. to fly	flew	flying	flown
23. to forget	forgot	forgetting	forgotten
24. to freeze	froze	freezing	frozen
25. to go	went	going	gone
26. to grow	grew	growing	grown
27. to have	had	having	had
28. to hit	hit	hitting	hit
29. to hold	held	holding	held
30. to know	knew	knowing	known
31. to lay (place)	laid	laying	laid
32. to lead	led	leading	led
33. to lie (recline)	lay	lying	lain
34. to make	made	making	made
35. to read	read	reading	read
36. to ride	rode	riding	ridden
37. to ring	rang	ringing	rung
38. to rise	rose	rising	risen
39. to run	ran	running	run
40. to see	saw	seeing	seen
41. to shake	shook	shaking	shaken
42. to shrink	shrank (shrunk)	shrinking	shrunk (shrunken)
43. to sing	sang	singing	sung
44. to sink	sank	sinking	sunk
45. to sit	sat	sitting	sat
46. to speak	spoke	speaking	spoken
47. to spring	sprang	springing	sprung
48. to sting	stung	stinging	stung
49. to stride	strode	striding	strode
50. to strike	struck	striking	struck
51. to swim	swam	swimming	swum
52. to take	took	taking	taken
53. to teach	taught	teaching	taught
54. to tear	tore	tearing	torn
55. to tell	told	telling	told
56. to throw	threw	throwing	thrown
57. to wake	woke	waking	waken
58. to wear	wore	wearing	worn
59. to weave	wove	weaving	woven
60. to write	wrote	writing	written

PRACTICE 6

Fill in the blanks with the correct form of the past-tense verb. Use the verbs provided.

▶ Example: The dog ___*ran*___ down the street.
(to run)

1. Julie _____ the same song over and over for an hour.
   (to sing)

2. Faulkner _____ many of his stories about a mythical
   (to wrote)
   county in Mississippi.

3. Sherri _____ home early because she
   (to go)
   _____ ill.
   (to feel)

4. The spring of 1987 _____ many unusual weather
   (to bring)
   patterns; many states _____ excessive rainfall and
   (to experience)
   floods.

5. We _____ the book *Animal Farm* by George Orwell.
   (to read)

6. Pope John Paul II _____ many countries in 1983; he
   (to visit)
   _____ to Poland and countries in Central America.
   (to go)

7. India _____ part of the British Empire until 1947.
   (to be)

8. The American Revolution _____ a new country into
   (to bring)
   existence.

9. During World War I and World War II, many Americans
   _____ in the armed services.
   (to enlist)

10. Unemployment _____ 10 percent in 1982; it
    (to reach)
    subsequently _____ to 6 percent in 1987.
    (to drop)

Check the answer key.

The Future Tense

The *future tense* indicates actions that will take place in the future. The time could be within the next few minutes: I *will begin* dinner in five minutes. Or it could be in thousands of years: In the year 3000, the world *will be* very different from what we know today.

Look at the following conjugations of the verbs *to write* (a regular verb) and *to be* (an irregular verb):

to write

I shall/will write	we shall/will write
you will write	you will write
he, she, it will write	they will write

to be

I shall/will be	we shall/will be
you will be	you will be
he, she, it will be	they will be

What pattern is followed? The word *will* is combined with the infinitive base of the verb. Thus, the rule for forming the future tense for both regular and irregular verbs is to add the word *will* to the infinitive base of the verb.

When the future tense is used to form a question, the helping verb *will* precedes the subject of the sentence and the infinitive base of the verb follows.

▶ Example: *Will* you *meet* us for dinner tonight at the new French restaurant?

NOTE: In first-person singular and plural forms of the future tense, the word *shall* is used (for example, I *shall go* home). However, in current American English, many people prefer to use *will* in place of *shall*. When you use *will* and the *infinitive base* in first-person singular and plural forms in the future tense, you indicate a great conviction (for example, I *will go* home). This form of the future shows that you are determined to go and that you have made a definite choice.

▶ ## PRACTICE 7

Supply the future-tense forms of the verbs in the following sentences. Use the verbs provided.

▶ Example: Harry __will come__ to dinner on
                                    (to come)

Thursday.

1. I _____ my homework tonight.
      (to complete)

2. Jason _____ Mary to the Senior Dance.
              (to ask)

3. _____ you _____ home tonight?
      (to be)

4. A serious runner _____ over fifty miles a week.
                        (to run)

5. Before we move to Seattle, we _____ our house in
                                        (to sell)

   Los Angeles.

6. _____ they _____ their father at the
      (to meet)

   airport?

7. Each presidential candidate _____ across the country
(to travel)

to gain the voters' support.

8. The new industry _____ the town in a number of ways.
(to benefit)

9. College _____ a testing ground for many students.
(to be)

10. With determination and effort, students _____
(to succeed)

academically in college.

Check the answer key.

Consistency of Verb Tenses

Since verbs indicate the time an action occurred, you should make certain that all verbs in a sentence use the appropriate tense. For example, if you are describing an event from your childhood, then you should use only the past tense. You would confuse your reader if you included future or present actions in the paragraph. Examine the following sentences with inconsistent verbs tenses and their revisions.

▶ Example: When she *was* fifteen years old, Barbara *trains* horses.

▶ Revision: When she *was* fifteen years old, Barbara *trained* horses.

▶ Example: As soon as the train *arrived*, we *board* it quickly.

▶ Revision: As soon as the train *arrived*, we *boarded* it quickly.

▶ PRACTICE 8

Read the following paragraph carefully. Check all italicized verbs for consistent tense. Change any verb that is not consistent.

(1) My first cooking experience *was* a memorable one. (2) I *decide* to bake some chicken; not knowing what to do, I *will fumble* my way through all the steps of a recipe. (3) The end result *is* a cooked piece of rawhide; the chicken *was* so tough that it *begun* to solidify while it *cooks*. (4) Not knowing where I *went* astray, I *will scrape* the contents of my plate into the garbage can and *proceeded* to go out to dinner. (5) When I *return*

home, the dirty pots, pans, and dishes *wait* to be cleaned; I *will toss* them into the sink where they *sat* for nearly a week. (6) In addition, this cooking experience *created* an aversion to doing the dishes. (7) In my house, I *will do* the dishes when I *ran* out of plates, or I can no longer find the sink. (8) In either case, I eventually *did* the dishes. (9) However, I *am* too lazy to scrub them, and into the dishwasher they *went* untouched. (10) After the dishwasher *completes* its cycle, I *will put* the clean dishes away; the dirty ones *remained* in the dishwasher for another wash. (11) Fortunately, I *will learn* to correct my cooking errors and cleaning habits.

Check the answer key.

Verbs II: The Perfect Tenses and the Progressive Forms

2

▷ **OBJECTIVES**

1. To recognize and use the three perfect tenses correctly.

2. To recognize and use the six progressive verb forms correctly.

3. To use a consistent and appropriate verb tense when writing.

▷ **KEY CONCEPT**

To communicate clearly and effectively, a writer must be able to choose the correct perfect tense or progressive form.

The Perfect Tenses

You have learned the three basic tenses that tell when an action took place—the past, the present, and the future. In addition, there are periods of time that other verb tenses cover. The *perfect tenses* help to describe these other times.

You now know two major forms of the verb: the infinitive and the past tense. Now, in order to conjugate the perfect tense verbs, you must use and recognize the **past participle** as the third major verb form. Consider the following examples of the verb *to see:*

1. Mike *saw* the bus. (*Saw* is the past tense of the verb *to see;* at a definite time in the past, Mike did see a particular bus.)

2. Mike *has seen* the bus. (*Seen* is the past participle of the verb *to see,* and *has* is a helping verb—it helps determine the time period; in this sentence, Mike did see a bus at some point before the present, but the tense does not indicate a particular or definite time in the past.)

Past participles are formed from the infinitive of the verb. For regular verbs, the past tense and the past participle will be the same form.

▶ Example: to dance (infinitive)
danced (past tense)
danced (past participle)

NOTE: The past and the past participle of regular verbs like *to dance* are formed by adding *d* or *ed* to the infinitive.

Irregular verbs, of course, form past participles differently. The past participles may be formed in a variety of ways:

1. Add *n* or *en* to the infinitive; for example, *known* is the past participle of *to know.*

2. Change the vowels in the verb form; for example, *begun* is the past participle of *to begin.*

3. Change the vowels and add *n* or *en;* for example, *frozen* is the past participle of *to freeze.*

4. Change the vowels and add a *t*; for example, *felt* is the past participle of the verb *to feel*.

5. Change a *d* to a *t*; for example, *sent* is the past participle of *to send*.

For all cases of irregular verbs with which you are unfamiliar, check a good dictionary. The dictionary will provide the correct form of the past participle.

▶ PRACTICE 1

Complete the chart below by forming the past and the past participle of the given verbs.

	Infinitive	Past	Past Participle
▶ Example:	to swim	*swam*	*swum*

Infinitive	Past	Past Participle
1. to dive	_____	_____
2. to sing	_____	_____
3. to write	_____	_____
4. to fly	_____	_____
5. to drink	_____	_____
6. to steal	_____	_____
7. to teach	_____	_____
8. to learn	_____	_____
9. to give	_____	_____
10. to receive	_____	_____

Check the answer key.

THE PRESENT PERFECT TENSE

The present perfect tense indicates one of two conditions:

1. At an undetermined time in the past, an action took place.

▶ Example: He *has gone* to his grandmother's many times. Can you give a specific time when he went?

2. An action took place in the past and is continuing in the present.

> ▶ Example: He *has attended* this school for two years. He obviously started in the past, and he is presently a student.

The **present perfect tense** is formed by using *has* or *have* (the present tense of the verb *to have*) and the past participle of the verb. Your use of *has* or *have* is determined by the noun. If it is third-person singular, use *has*. If it is plural or first- or second-person singular, then use *have*. Consider the following conjugation of the verb *to walk* in the present perfect tense:

I have walked	we have walked
you have walked	you have walked
he, she, it has walked	they have walked

▼ EXERCISE 1

Write the rule for forming the present perfect tense:

_____

_____

Have your instructor or tutor check your work.

▶ PRACTICE 2

Fill in the blanks with the correct form of the present perfect tense of the verb. Use only the verbs given.

> ▶ Example: He <u>has strolled</u> down this street many times.
> (to stroll)

1. I _____ a good school year.
   (to have)

2. Terry _____ to Europe several times.
   (to be)

3. In presidential campaigns, foreign policy _____ a
   (to be)

   major issue between the two candidates.

4. They _____ us many times.
   (to visit)

5. He _____ a fine young man.
   (to become)

6. Women _____ many of the rights they fought for
   (to receive)

   during the 1960s and 1970s.

7. Stella _____ the dress she wanted.
   (to buy)

8. He _____ in several marathons.
   (to race)

9. Mary and I _____ the movie *Psycho* four times.
   (to see)

10. Students _____ for the fall semester at the college.
    (to enroll)

Check the answer key.

THE PAST PERFECT TENSE

The past perfect tense describes a time in the past that occurred before another past action.

▶ Example: Bob *had passed* his examination before he received his license.
               By the time he received his license (an action that took place in the past), he had already passed the exam (an action that took place *before* he got the license).

Examine this sentence and explain the time sequence:

▶ Example: After he *had run* ten miles, he *fainted*.
               Which past action occurred first? *had run*
               Which past action occurred last? *fainted*

The rule for forming the past perfect tense is a simple one: use *had* and the *past participle*. Here is the conjugation of the verb *to drive* in the past perfect tense:

I had driven   we had driven
you had driven   you had driven
he, she, it had driven   they had driven

PRACTICE 3

Fill in the blanks with the correct form of the past perfect tense of the verb. Use the verbs given.

1. If he _____ home, we would have visited him.
   (to be)

2. When the teacher _____ the lesson, the class
   (to finish)

   applauded.

3. After the bank teller _____ the transaction, the
   (to complete)

   robbers left.

4. The lawyer _____ his star witness before the
   (to call)

   defendant confessed.

5. Before the bomb could have exploded, the police officers

   _____ it.
   (to defuse)

6. Before the referee blew his whistle, he _____ the foul.
   (to determine)

7. After the star basketball player _____ his foul shot,
   (to make)

   the crowd in the gym exploded.

8. After the college students _____ their tour of
   (to complete)

   London, they boarded a train to Scotland.

9. The student _____ his topic before he began to write
   (to choose)

   his essay.

10. After we _____ the heavy chest upstairs, we decided
    (to move)

    that it was too large for the small room.

Check the answer key.

THE FUTURE PERFECT TENSE

The future perfect tense tells about a future event that will have been completed before another event. Look at the following sentence:

▶ Example: I *will have worked* for three months by the time I start school this fall.

Both actions will take place in the future. Which action will be completed first? *will have worked.* This action must be in the future perfect tense.

The rule for forming the future perfect tense is simple: add *will have* or *shall have* to the *past participle of the verb.* Here is the verb *to go* in the future perfect tense:

I will have gone   we will have gone

you will have gone   you will have gone

he, she, it will have gone   they will have gone

NOTE: See "The Future Tense" in Chapter 1, Part II, for a discussion of *shall* and *will.*

PRACTICE 4

Fill in the blanks with the correct form of the future perfect tense of the verb. Use only the verbs given.

1. The satellite _____ in orbit for five years before its
   (to be)
   power source is depleted.

2. The archaeologists _____ for seven years at the dig
   (to work)
   before they uncover the first layer of the forgotten city.

3. By the end of the week, Kerri _____ her project.
   (to finish)

4. When he completes graduate school, he _____ in
   (to be)
   school continuously for twenty years.

5. By the year 2000, Disneyworld _____ over three
   (to welcome)
   billion visitors.

6. Professor Abbot _____ for thirty years by the end of
   (to teach)
   this semester.

7. Sheila _____ the novel *Crime and Punishment* by
   (to read)
   Friday.

8. By July, the North Carolina Outer Banks _____ their
   (to celebrate)
   four hundredth anniversary.

9. By March, the architects _____ their proposals for the
   (to submit)
   new city hall.

10. When he wins his 300th game, the pitcher _____
    (to throw)
    about 10,000 baseballs.

Check the answer key.

The Progressive Forms

The progressive forms of verbs indicate an action that is, was, or will be in
progress. The progressive form requires a present participle as the base of the
form. The present participle is formed by adding *ing* to the infinitive base. For
example, *jumping* is the present participle of *to jump.*

▼ EXERCISE 2

Form the present participle of the following verbs.

1. to hop_____

2. to sleep_____

3. to become _____

4. to honk _____

5. to work_____

Have your instructor or tutor check your work.

The progressive forms exist in the present, past, and future. The forms are constructed by adding the appropriate form of the verb *to be* to the present participle.

Look at the following conjugations of the verb *to show:*

- **Present Progressive** (The action is taking place now.)

I am showing	we are showing
you are showing	you are showing
he, she, it is showing	they are showing

NOTE: Use the *present* tense of the verb *to be* to form the present progressive.

- **Past Progressive** (The action was taking place in the past.)

I was showing	we were showing
you were showing	you were showing
he, she, it was showing	they were showing

NOTE: Use the *past* tense of the verb *to be* to form the past progressive.

- **Future Progressive** (The action will be taking place in the future.)

I will be showing	we will be showing
you will be showing	you will be showing
he, she, it will be showing	they will be showing

NOTE: Use the *future* tense of the verb *to be* to form the future progressive.

The three perfect tenses—the past perfect, the present perfect, and the future perfect—also have progressive forms. These perfect progressive forms follow the rules of the perfect tense (in telling when an action occurred) and the progressive (an action in progress).

Here are the conjugations of the verb *to practice* in the perfect progressive forms. These are also constructed by adding the appropriate form of the verb *to be* (to indicate the time) to the present participle:

- **Present Perfect Progressive** (The action began in the past and continues to the present; this form stresses the continuing action.)

I have been practicing	we have been practicing
you have been practicing	you have been practicing
he, she, it has been practicing	they have been practicing

▶ Example: The band *has been practicing* for five weeks for the state contest.

- **Past Perfect Progressive** (The action in progress was completed in the past before another event.)

I had been practicing	we had been practicing
you had been practicing	you had been practicing
he, she, it had been practicing	they had been practicing

▶ Example: I *had been practicing* my violin when Mother told me to stop.

- **Future Perfect Progressive** (The action will continue into the future and be completed before another future action.)

I will have been practicing	we will have been practicing
you will have been practicing	you will have been practicing
he, she, it will have been practicing	they will have been practicing

▶ Example: We *will have been practicing* our songs for three weeks before the contest begins.

PRACTICE 5

Complete the progressive forms of the verbs indicated below.

1. The present progressive of *to ask*   I _____

2. The past perfect progressive of *to do*   They _____

3. The future progressive of *to sing*   We _____

4. The present perfect progressive of *to hit*   He _____

5. The future perfect progressive of *to deal*   You _____

6. The past progressive of *to swim*   They _____

Check the answer key.

PRACTICE 6

Fill in the blanks with the correct progressive forms of the verbs indicated. Pay particular attention to the time sequence; the time will tell you which tense to use.

1. We _____ for four hours when the fireworks begin.

(to dance)

2. He _____ his work now.

(to complete)

3. She _____ the dog when the phone rang.
   (to bathe)

4. The lawyer _____ on this case for two years.
   (to work)

5. Jean _____ to her grandmother's house since she was
   (to go)

   five.

6. The guests _____ soon.
   (to leave)

7. Last year, she _____ on her law degree; this year, she
   (to work)

   _____ law.
   (to practice)

8. The toaster _____ not _____ properly;
   (to work)

   I _____ my toast every morning for the past week.
   (to burn)

9. Last year, Harold _____ for a city council post; this
   (to run)

   year, he _____ a concession stand at the stadium.
   (to operate)

10. The college football team _____ its rivals next week.
    (to play)

Check the answer key.

Helping Verbs

As you have seen in the perfect tenses and progressive forms, some verbs have a dual function. When acting alone, they describe action or existence; when acting as part of a verb phrase, they help the reader correctly determine the time frame, conditions, and tone (in some tenses) of an action. When they act as **helping verbs,** these verbs will precede the main verb.

	HELPING VERBS (CONDITION)		
MEANING	VERB	TENSE	EXAMPLE
able to	can	present	I can pay
	could	past	I could pay, I could have paid
permitted to	may	present	I may pay
	might	past	I might pay, I might have paid
expected to	shall	present	I shall pay
	should	past	I should pay, I should have paid
willing to	will	present	I will pay
	would	past	I would pay, I would have paid

HELPING VERBS (TIME AND TONE)

HELPING VERB	TENSE	EXAMPLE
has, have	present perfect	I have swum He has swum
had	past perfect	He had swum
shall, will	future perfect	I shall have sum He will have swum
am, is, are	present progressive	I am swimming He is swimming They are swimming
was, were	past progressive	I was swimming They were swimming
will be	future progressive	He will be swimming
has been, have been	present perfect progressive	He has been swimming They have been swimming
had been	past perfect progressive	He had been swimming
will have been	future perfect progressive	He will have been swimming
do, does	present emphatic	I do swim He does swim
did	past emphatic	He did swim

PRACTICE 7

Fill in the blank with the verb and tense that are requested in the parentheses.

1. My mother told me that I _____ with my cousin at least once tonight. (conditional past tense of *to dance*)

2. This professor _____ at the college for over thirty years. (present perfect progressive of *to teach*)

3. The candidate _____ to correct the misstatements in his résumé. (present emphatic of *to plan*)

4. The infant _____ across the floor to retrieve his favorite toy. (past perfect of *to crawl*)

5. Her counselor indicated that she _____ able to take physics if she wanted to, but she opted for a calculus course instead. (past tense of *to be*)

6. The patient _____ well after surgery, but then his condition deteriorated. (past perfect progressive of *to do*)

7. Even though the patient died, let us remember that he _____ for over one hundred days with an artificial liver. (past emphatic of *to live*)

8. By the time he qualifies for the Olympic team, Charles _____ for more than ten years. (future perfect progressive of *to compete*)

9. If the party _____ me, I would have been proud to serve in the office. (past perfect of *to nominate*)

10. She _____ the committee's draft report. (present perfect of *to accept*)

Check the answer key.

Consistency of Verb Tenses

Verb tenses should be consistent in most cases. Because verb tenses show time, it is important that they express exactly what time you wish to describe. For example, if you are writing about an event that occurred in the past, use the past tense. Imagine how confused your reader would be if he read a sentence like this:

▶ Example: Tomorrow, the pilot *flew* the plane.

When is the action taking place? The verb *flew* is the past tense form of *to fly*, yet the time is *tomorrow*.

With this confusion corrected, the sentence would read:

▶ Example: Tomorrow, the pilot *will fly* the plane.

When you write a paragraph or an essay, make sure that the verb forms you use are in the same tense, or time period.

▶ ## PRACTICE 8

Make the verb tenses of the underlined verbs consistent. Use the first verb in the sentence as your guide. If it is present tense, make the second verb present tense also. If it is past tense, make the second verb past tense also.

▶ Example: When I <u>ran</u> home, I ~~find~~ *found* the front door open.

1. Before he <u>called</u> Alice to ask her for a date, he <u>takes</u> a deep breath.

2. As the band <u>marched</u> onto the football field, the football players <u>are</u> still on the gridiron.

3. College <u>offers</u> many activities to students, yet many students <u>failed</u> to take advantage of the extracurricular activities.

4. The mechanic <u>tested</u> the car's engine, only to find that it is not <u>working</u>.

5. Dreiser's novel *An American Tragedy* <u>was written</u> in 1925; the same year, Fitzgerald's novel *The Great Gatsby* <u>is published</u>.

6. The typewriter <u>will become</u> obsolete one day because the word processor <u>replaced</u> it.

7. When the football player <u>caught</u> the ball, he <u>turns</u> to look at his coach.

8. After the photographer <u>took</u> the picture, he <u>will develop</u> the film.

9. Before the Olympic Games <u>begin</u>, many thousands of athletes <u>arrived</u> in Seoul.

10. The train trip across Canada <u>took</u> so many days that we <u>will miss</u> our appointment in Seattle, Washington.

Check the answer key.

PRACTICE 9

Read the following paragraph carefully. Check the italicized verbs for consistent tense. Change any verb that is not consistent.

(1) "If I had been able to study, I *will have passed* the test," exclaims a distraught teenager. (2) "But I *do* not *have* a sufficient amount of time." (3) All parents *have heard* this excuse at one time or another. (4) Helping teenagers become mature, responsible adults *was* a difficult job. (5) Unfortunately, some parents do not succeed, but that is not because

they *had* not *tried*. (6) They diligently read books and articles on the topic; they faithfully *attended* parenting classes, and they regularly set aside "quality time" for family discussions. (7) But all their efforts *have been* in vain. (8) Some people *managed* to cross the threshold into so-called adulthood even though they are still self-indulgent, egocentric, and petty.

Check the answer key.

3

Subjects, Verbs, and Prepositional Phrases

OBJECTIVES

1. To identify subjects, verbs, and prepositional phrases.

2. To recognize and write sentence patterns.

3. To identify and write the major types of sentences.

KEY CONCEPT

A complete sentence requires a subject and a verb; it also must express a complete thought.

Subjects

A sentence must have a subject. A **subject** is a *noun* (a person, place, or thing) or a *pronoun* (a word that takes the place of a noun).

TYPES OF NOUNS

A **proper noun** names a specific person, place, or thing. It is always capitalized.

▶ Examples: *Mr. Smith, Professor Thomas, New York City, Ford*

A **common noun** names an object, place, or person. It does *not* name a *specific* object, place, or person.

▶ Examples: *dog, animal, tree*

A **concrete noun** names anything you can perceive through one of the five senses—touch, taste, smell, hearing, or sight.

▶ Examples: *chair, room, ball, wind, music, paint*

An **abstract noun** names an emotion, quality, or idea. You cannot perceive this noun through one of the five senses.

▶ Examples: *love, hate, anger, philosophy*

A **collective noun** names a group of individuals.

▶ Examples: *army, jury, team, committee*

TYPES OF PRONOUNS

A **pronoun** takes the place of a noun.

▶ Examples: Meredith went to the movies; she saw the Bogart movie *The African Queen.*
In this sentence, *she* is a pronoun that takes the place of the proper noun *Meredith.*

Each of the following pronouns could be used as the subject of a sentence:

▶ Personal
pronouns:

I, you, she, he, it, we, you, they

▶ Indefinite
pronouns:

*everyone, everybody, somebody, someone, each,
nobody, no one, none, anybody, anyone, some, all,
several*

PRACTICE 1

a. List five proper nouns:

1. _____

2. _____

3. _____

4. _____

5. _____

b. List five common nouns:

1. _____

2. _____

3. _____

4. _____

5. _____

c. List five concrete nouns:

1. _____

2. _____

3. _____

4. _____

5. _____

d. List five abstract nouns:

1. _____

2. _____

3. _____

4. _____

5. _____

e. List five collective nouns:

1. _____

2. _____

3. _____

4. _____

5. _____

f. List five pronouns:

1. _____

2. _____

3. _____

4. _____

5. _____

Have your instructor or tutor check your work.

Verbs

A sentence also must contain a **verb.** There are two types of verbs:

1. **Action** verbs are words that show movement. For example, *to sing, to joke, to run,* and *to walk* are action verbs.

2. **Linking** verbs are verbs that do not show action. Instead, they convey existence, being, becoming, and sometimes, one of the five senses. For example, the verbs *to be, to seem, to appear,* and *to become* are linking verbs. Linking verbs connect, or make equal, the subject and the word after the linking verb.

▶ PRACTICE 2

a. List five action verbs:

1. _____

2. _____

3. _____

4. _____

5. _____

b. List three linking verbs:

1. _____

2. _____

3. _____

Have your instructor or tutor check your work.

Identifying Subjects and Verbs

The easiest way to identify the subject and verb in a sentence is to ask these questions:

- What is the action? or What word links two or more other words? the *verb*

- Who or what is performing the action? the *subject*

▶ Examples:

1. Barbara sang.

   What is the action? *sang* (verb)
   Who sang? *Barbara* (subject)

2. Robert leaped.

   What is the action? *leaped* (verb)
   Who leaped? *Robert* (subject)

PRACTICE 3

Identify the subjects and verbs in the sentences below.

1. Terry laughs.

    verb _____

    subject _____

2. Children play.

    verb _____

    subject _____

3. The bullet hit the target.

    verb _____

    subject _____

4. I swam.

    verb _____

    subject _____

5. The doctor fainted.

    verb _____

    subject _____

Check the answer key.

SIMPLE AND COMPOUND SUBJECTS AND VERBS

The sentences you have worked with up to this point have contained only one subject and one verb. A single subject is referred to as a **simple subject;** a single verb is referred to as a **simple verb.**

▶ Example: The police officer quickly drew her pistol.

Subject—*police officer* (one actor—simple subject)
Verb—*drew* (one action—simple verb)

However, a sentence may also contain a **compound subject:** two or more stated nouns or pronouns perform the same action.

▶ Examples: Charles and the boys have gone to the movies.
What is the action? *have gone* (one action—simple verb)
Who has gone? *Charles* and *the boys* (two stated actors—compound subject)

He and I decided to backpack through South America.
What is the action? *decided* (one action—simple verb)
Who decided? *He* and *I* (two stated actors—compound subject)

A sentence may also contain a **compound verb:** the subject performs two or more actions.

▶ Examples: Trendy people frequently drink, dance, and party through the night.

What is (are) the action(s)? *Drink, dance,* and *party* (three actions—compound verb)
Who drinks, dances, and parties? *Trendy people* (one stated group—simple subject)

NOTE: In the last sentence, the fact that the subject *people* is a plural noun is not significant. Only *one* performer of the action—people—is given; therefore, there is only one subject and it is a simple subject.

In addition to sentences with simple subjects and verbs, there are three other possible combinations of simple and compound subjects and verbs.

Compound Subject/Simple Verb. In this case, two or more subjects perform one action.

▶ Example: George and Frank went to Mexico.

What is the action? *went*
Who went? *George* and *Frank*

In this sentence, both *George* and *Frank* are performing the same action. The compound subject is *George* and *Frank.*

Simple Subject/Compound Verb. The simple subject of the sentence performs two or more actions. Answer the questions in this example:

▶ Example: The audience booed and hissed the performer.

What two actions are performed?_____

What is the subject? _____

In this sentence, the *audience* performed two actions—booed and hissed. The compound verb is *booed* and *hissed.*

Compound Subject/Compound Verb. This means that two or more subjects perform two or more actions. Answer the questions in this example:

▶ Example: Curly, Larry, and Moe danced and ate all night.

What actions are performed? _____

Who performed them? _____

In this sentence, *Curly, Larry,* and *Moe*—the compound subject—*danced* and *ate*—the compound verb.

PRACTICE 4

Find the subjects and verbs in the following sentences.

1. Fords and Chevrolets are two makes of American cars.

   verb ——————————   subject ——————————

2. The cat hissed and scratched.

   verb ——————————   subject ——————————

3. Caleb and Rachel read and siudy.

   verb ——————————   subject ——————————

4. Angela became a doctor.

   verb ——————————   subject ——————————

5. Carl and Martha took a vacation last spring.

   verb ——————————   subject ——————————

6. Tina seemed sad.

   verb ——————————   subject ——————————

7. Ice cream and cake are his favorite foods.

   verb ——————————   subject ——————————

8. Puerto Rico and St. Thomas are beautiful vacation spots.

   verb ——————————   subject ——————————

9. Nita appears happy.

   verb ——————————   subject ——————————

10. The dolphin leaped and swam.

    verb ——————————   subject ——————————

Check the answer key.

EXCEPTIONS

The words *there, here,* and *where* can never be the subject of a sentence, so you must look for another word—a noun or a pronoun—as the subject of the sentence.

▶ Example: There is my car.

                  What is the verb? *is*
                  What is the subject? *car*

PRACTICE 5

Find the subjects and verbs in each of the following sentences.

1. There are my best friends.

   verb _____   subject _____

2. Here is the manuscript for the new television series.

   verb _____   subject _____

3. Where are Harry's ball and bat?

   verb _____   subject _____

4. Here is the answer to your question.

   verb _____   subject _____

5. Here come Linda's boyfriend and another girl.

   verb _____   subject _____

Check the answer key.

HELPING VERBS

In the previous examples and practice exercises, you might have noticed that most of the verbs have consisted of only one word. Because most of the sentences used the present tense (present time), only one word was needed for the verb. However, because verbs tell us about time, it is sometimes necessary for a verb to have more than one word in order to convey a particular time. The **main verb** (major action) may be accompanied by **helping verbs** that help describe the time of the action.

Look at the following sentences. All of them contain a form of the verb *to ask*. Notice the helping verbs.

I ask.	I am asking.
I asked.	I was asking.
I will ask.	I will be asking.
I have asked.	I have been asking.
I had asked.	I had been asking.
I will have asked.	I will have been asking.

Practice 6

Find the subjects and the verbs in the following sentences. Be sure to include any helping verbs.

1. Tom will have left school by 4 o'clock.

   verb _____   subject _____

2. The senator will have been in office four years this spring.

   verb _____   subject _____

3. The car had been demolished in the wreck.

   verb _____   subject _____

4. The animals at the zoo will be released into a natural-habitat park.

   verb _____   subject _____

5. The disc jockey was playing records by Willie Nelson and Hank Williams, Jr.

   verb _____   subject _____

Check the answer key.

NOTE: Do not include negatives (such as the word *no*) in the verb.

▶ Example: Helen is not going to the dance.

The subject is *Helen.*
The verb is *is going.*

Prepositional Phrases

A sentence may have many phrases and additional words. One type of phrase that can seem confusing and make a sentence seem more complex is a prepositional phrase. A prepositional phrase consists of a **preposition** (for example, *of, for, to, in, out, around, through*) and a noun or pronoun (called the **object of the preposition**); it may also contain adjectives and/or adverbs.

Prepositions are easily recognized. Prepositional phrases provide additional information to the reader of the sentence. Usually, prepositions express the time of the action or other relationships. The prepositions on the following page introduce information in the categories of time, place, and other.

TIME	PLACE		OTHER	
after	above	inside	about	in order of
before	across	into	against	like
during	among	near	at	of
until	around	out	because of	off
	behind	outside	by	on
	below	over	due to	onto
	beneath	through	except	past
	beside	to	for	such as
	between	under	from	with
	beyond	up		
	by	within		
	in	without		

The following are examples of prepositional phrases:

> under the forbidding mountain   behind the door
> into the green room   since May
> after the game   with her

NOTE: To help determine if a word is a preposition, use this test: a preposition expresses any relationship that makes sense with regard to a house.

▶ Example:

> *into* the house
> *around* the house
> *to* the house
> *outside* the house
>
> *Into, around, to,* and *outside* are prepositions.
>
> This test will help you locate prepositions that describe place; it will not help locate those that express time.

A number of prepositional phrases in a sentence may make it difficult to find the subject and the verb. Remember that the *noun* or *pronoun* in a prepositional phrase is *the object of the preposition;* this word can never be the subject of the sentence!

To find the subject and verb in a sentence, simply eliminate the prepositional phrases in the sentence.

▶ Example:

> The Board of Trustees of the college is meeting now in the conference room of the Administration Building.

Cross out the prepositional phrases (as well as any other adjectives and adverbs) in the above sentence, and find the subject and the verb. Your sentence should now look like this:

~~The~~ Board ~~of Trustees of the college~~ is meeting ~~now in the conference room of the Administration Building~~.

What is the verb? *is meeting*
What is the subject? *Board*

PRACTICE 7

Cross out any prepositional phrases in the following sentences. Then, underline the subject and verb in each sentence and label them.

▶ Example: ~~In the center~~ ~~of the room~~ <u>stood</u> <u>Jim</u>. *(verb subject)*

1. The cat ran under the porch.

2. Broncho Davis was a famous football player for twenty years.

3. The greyhound with the matted coat and an evil look in his eyes frightened the schoolchildren.

4. The drive to Orlando is a pleasant one.

5. Bing Crosby and Bob Hope were a successful team for more than fifteen years.

Check the answer key.

Sentence Formats

SENTENCE FORMAT 1: SUBJECT AND VERB

An example of a Format 1 sentence is:

Birds sing.

The abbreviation for Sentence Format 1 is S-V. Consider the abbreviation and explain it by using terms you have already encountered. (*S* stands for _____ . *V* stands for _____ .)
   The Subject. What words other than *birds* can be substituted into the sentence? Remember, construct a sentence that will have meaning.

_____ sing.

_____ sing.

_____ sing.

_____ sing.

_____ sing.

_____ sing.

What types of words are *birds* and the ones you substituted? Words that can be substituted for each other belong to the same format. The words you supplied have the same relationship with *sing* as the word *birds* has with *sing*. They are all the same type of words—nouns or pronouns.

If you used *he, she, we, I, it, they,* or *you* for the subject, then you used **pronouns,** not nouns. Pronouns take the place of nouns, so they can also be used as the subject of a sentence.

▼ EXERCISE 1

Fill in the blanks with words that follow Sentence Format 1.

1. _____ squawk.

2. _____ yell.

3. _____ meow.

4. _____ dance.

5. _____ jump.

6. _____ sink.

7. _____ swim.

8. _____ leap.

Have your instructor or tutor check your work.

The Verb. The noun or pronoun—the subject—is only part of Sentence Format 1; the second portion of the format is the **verb.** In the example sentence, *Birds sing,* what words can be substituted for *sing*? These are **action verbs** because they name an action.

Birds _____ . Birds _____ . Birds _____ .

A word that can be substituted for *sing* is a verb.

▼ EXERCISE 2

Fill in the blanks with verbs to complete the sentences.

1. Dogs _____ .   5. Windows _____ .

2. Monkeys _____ .   6. Joggers _____ .

3. Cars _____ .   7. Airplanes _____ .

4. Houses _____ .   8. Radios _____ .

Next, using Sentence Format 1 (S-V), write your own sentences.

1. _____
2. _____
3. _____
4. _____
5. _____

Have your instructor or tutor check your work.

▼ EXERCISE 3

Using Format 1, write five sentences with pronouns as the subjects.

1. _____
2. _____
3. _____
4. _____
5. _____

Have your instructor or tutor check your work.

SENTENCE FORMAT 2: THE DIRECT OBJECT

Sentence Format 2 builds upon Sentence Format 1 (S-V). It simply adds another word and relationship to the format.

▶ Example: Harry hit the baseball.

Consider carefully the relationships among the words. You should recognize that *Harry* is the subject and *hit* is the verb. However, what relationship does *baseball* have to *hit? Baseball* is the **direct object** of the verb. Nouns and pronouns can act as direct objects. The direct object receives the action of the verb. When you ask, "What was hit?" and locate an answer, then you have found the direct object.

The abbreviation for Sentence Format 2 is S-V-DO.

▼ EXERCISE 4

Fill in the blanks with one word that will complete the sentence. Identify the word you used. Is it a subject (S), a verb (V), or direct object (DO)?

____ 1. _____ threw a ball.

____ 2. Tom _____ his lunch.

____ 3. I dropped my _____ .

____ 4. Grandmother _____ her knitting.

____ 5. _____ read the book.

____ 6. Dad drove the _____ .

____ 7. My little brother _____ the dog.

____ 8. The bus hit the _____ .

____ 9. He bought the _____ .

____ 10. The cat _____ its kittens.

Have your instructor or tutor check your work.

▶ PRACTICE 8

Label each of the following sentences Format 1 or Format 2. Write the format abbreviation for each sentence in the blank to the right. Also, identify subjects, verb, and direct objects.

	S V	**Format**
▶ Example:	I ran.	I S-V

Format

1. Tom forgot.   _____

2. The band won the contest.   _____

3. Helen read a book.   _____

4. I swam.   _____

5. The dog crossed the road.   _____

6. The arrow struck a tree.   _____

7. The baseball team lost.   _____

8. The child broke the vase.   _____

Check the answer key.

▼ **EXERCISE 5**

In Practice 8, three sentences followed Format 1. Add a word or words to those three sentences to make them Format 2 sentences.

1. _____

2. _____

3. _____

Have your instructor or tutor check your work.

▶ **PRACTICE 9**

Label each sentence either Format 1 or Format 2, and write its abbreviation. Identify the subjects, verbs, and direct objects.

▶ Example:

              S   V   **DO**

The runner won the New York City Marathon.

Format

2 S-V-DO

	Format
1. The police caught the thief.	_____
2. Our television broke.	_____
3. The horse won the Triple Crown.	_____
4. The children jumped the fence.	_____
5. Mary cried.	_____
6. The moon rose over the field.	_____
7. The fullback caught the football.	_____
8. The rooster crowed at dawn.	_____
9. The airplane left the runway.	_____
10. The scuba diver speared a barracuda.	_____
11. His shoelaces broke.	_____
12. The president of the corporation fired his assistant.	_____
13. The speaker declined the invitation.	_____

14. The chair fell.

Format
_____

15. Children like ice cream.

_____

Check the answer key.

▼ EXERCISE 6

Write five sentences of your own that follow Format 2.

1. _____

2. _____

3. _____

4. _____

5. _____

Have your instructor or tutor check your work.

SENTENCE FORMAT 3: THE INDIRECT OBJECT

Identify and label the following sentence:

Hector threw the ball.

You should be familiar with this format; it is Sentence Format 2. Now, label the next sentence:

Hector threw me the ball.

In the sentence above, *Hector* is the subject, *threw* is the verb, and *ball* is the direct object. But the sentence has an additional word—*me. Me* is a pronoun; it tells to whom the ball was thrown. A pronoun or a noun with this relationship to the verb is called an *indirect object.* You could construct the sentence in this manner: Hector threw the ball to me. Notice that *me* is now the object of the preposition *to.* You can place *to* or *for* in front of the indirect object.

To test for indirect objects in a sentence, follow these two steps:

1. Rewrite the sentence to follow Format 2 (S-V-DO).

2. Add *to* or *for* plus the word in question to the end of the sentence.

▶ Example: May gave me the book.

In order to decide if *me* is the indirect object, follow the two steps of the test:

Step 1.   Rewrite the sentence to follow Format 2:

May gave the book. (S-V-DO)

Step 2.   Add *to* or *for* plus the word in question to the end of the sentence:

May gave the book to me.

Because *me* can be placed into a prepositional phrase, *me* is the indirect object. *Me*, finally, holds the book.

▶ Examples: Harold sent Tracy the roses.

Apply the two-step test:

_____

Dad paid Vicki her allowance.

Apply the two-step test:

_____

Do the sentences make sense? If they do, you have found the indirect objects.

The abbreviation for Sentence Format 3 is S-V-IO-DO.

PRACTICE 10

Label all subjects, verbs, indirect objects, and direct objects.

▶ Example: $\overset{S}{\text{I}}\ \overset{V}{\text{gave}}\ \overset{IO}{\text{Jim}}\ \text{the}\ \overset{DO}{\text{award}}$ for academic excellence.

1. Tim awarded Henry the prize.

2. The boy bought the girl a flower.

3. The nervous young man handed his girlfriend a diamond ring.

4. My English teacher gave me a high mark on my test.

5. Tim fed the dog his dinner.

6. The bird built his mate a nest.

7. I gave my friend an umbrella.

8. She brought Jim a soda.

9. The kidnappers gave the child a candy bar.

10. Sharon bought her father a wool sweater.

Check the answer key.

▼ EXERCISE 7   Write ten sentences of your own that follow Format 3.

1. _____

2. _____

3. _____

4. _____

5. _____

6. _____

7. _____

8. _____

9. _____

10. _____

Have your instructor or tutor check your work.

SENTENCE FORMAT 4: THE PREDICATE ADJECTIVE AND THE PREDICATE NOMINATIVE

The fourth sentence format introduces two new elements. Look at these examples.

▶ Examples: Harry is tall.
                Harry is a freshman.

Notice that a new type of verb is included: a **linking verb.** Any form of the verb *to be* is a linking verb, as are the verbs *seem, feel, appear,* and *become.* Linking verbs (LV) connect the word that follows them to the subject in a special relationship. It almost seems as if the linking verb equates both sides.

The Predicate Adjective. Consider these Format 4 sentences:

▶ Examples: Cathy is cute.
                The sky appears cloudy.
                Horses are strong.
                The runners became tired.

In these sentences, the words connected to the subjects by the linking verbs are **adjectives;** they describe or characterize the nouns that are the subjects. You could write *cute Cathy, cloudy sky, strong horses,* or *tired runners.* These adjectives in Sentence Format 4 are called *predicate adjectives,* because they describe the subject.

NOTE: If you took only the subjects and verbs of the sentences, then you would not have complete sentences: *Cathy is, The sky appears, Horses* *are*, and *The runners became*. The predicate adjective is needed to describe the subject and to complete the sentence.

The format for the sentence *Harry is tall* is: S-LV-PA

▶ PRACTICE 11

In the following sentences, underline the linking verbs. Write the predicate adjective and the subject together and identify the format.

	PA-S	LV	Format
▶ Example: The weather is bad.	*bad weather*	*is*	S-LV-PA
	PA-S	LV	Format
1. The weightlifter is powerful.	_____	_____	_____
2. Tom appears sad.	_____	_____	_____
3. Mary looks happy.	_____	_____	_____
4. The dinner tasted good.	_____	_____	_____
5. Earl Bruce was cooperative.	_____	_____	_____
6. The cat sounds angry.	_____	_____	_____
7. He seems tired.	_____	_____	_____
8. The onion smells sour.	_____	_____	_____
9. The road becomes rough.	_____	_____	_____
10. The apple was red and delicious.	_____	_____	_____

Check the answer key.

▼ EXERCISE 8

Complete the following sentences by adding predicate adjectives.

1. He becomes _____ .

2. The mouse was _____ .

3. The movie seemed _____ .

4. The sky turned _____ .

5. Sam is _____ .

6. Baseball seems _____ .

7. The book appeared _____ .

8. The oranges are _____ .

9. The cake tasted _____ .

10. The dessert was _____ .

Have your instructor or tutor check your work.

▶ ## PRACTICE 12

You will find both Format 2 and Format 4 sentences in the following exercise. Identify each format. Underline the linking verb twice and write the predicate adjective in the blanks and label them. Underline action verbs once and write the direct objects in the blanks and label them DO.

NOTE: Linking verbs never take direct objects.

Format

▶ Examples: 1. He suddenly <u>became</u> weak.   weak - PA 4

2. Tom <u>bounced</u> a ball.   ball - DO 2

Format

1. The cowboy branded the calf.   _____

2. His car looks expensive.   _____

3. I enjoy comic books.   _____

4. The arrow struck a rock.   _____

5. His shoes are dirty.   _____

6. The girls were pretty.   _____

7. Gerry's Restaurant serves good food.   _____

8. The Gulf of Mexico has quite blue water.   _____

9. The teacher looks interested.   _____

10. The audience seemed uneasy.   _____

Check the answer key.

▼ ## EXERCISE 9

Write five sentences of your own that follow the format S-LV-PA.

1. _____

2. _____

3. _____

4. _____

5. _____

Have your instructor or tutor check your work.

> *The Predicate Nominative.* The second example sentence for Format 4 was:

Harry is a freshman.

The format is basically the same as S-LV-PA. *Harry* is the subject, and *is* is the linking verb. However, *freshman* is a noun, not a predicate adjective. A noun following a linking verb is called a **predicate nominative.** The predicate nominative might define the subject, identify it, or rename it. In other words, the predicate nominative, a noun, is equal to the subject, a noun. For example, in the example sentence, *Harry* and *freshman* are equivalent. The abbreviation for this second type of Format 4 sentence is: S-LV-PN

        S   LV   PN
Harry is a freshman.

PRACTICE 13

Identify the predicate nominatives in the following sentences. Write the predicate nominative and the subject on the lines to the right of the sentence. Use an equal sign to indicate their equality. Also, label the subjects and linking verbs.

> Example:

        S LV   **PN**   PN = S
Tom is the team captain. <u>captain – Tom</u>

1. The senator is the chairman of a

   major committee.   _____

2. Annapolis is the state capital of Maryland. _____

3. The mahogany desk is an antique. _____

4. Shawn became an astronaut. _____

5. Because of his ability as a blocker, John

   is a complete football player. _____

6. With her ability as a writer of feature

   stories, Jane is a considerable force in

   Houston journalism. _____

7. Television is one of the primary news

media today. _____

8. She is a good actress. _____

9. The girl with the red hair is my cousin. _____

10. An alligator on a shirt is a symbol of preppies. _____

Check the answer key.

▼ EXERCISE 10

Complete the following sentences by adding predicate nominatives.

1. Novels are _____ .

2. My car is _____ .

3. The captain was _____ .

4. Besides being test pilots, astronauts must also be _____ .

5. The pretty little girl became _____ .

6. Besides being students, many college students are also _____ .

7. The cowboy is also a _____ .

8. Jim is a _____ .

9. To Michelangelo, sculpture was _____ .

10. Multinational corporations are _____

Have your instructor or tutor check your work.

▼ EXERCISE 11

Write five sentences of your own that conform to the format S-LV-PN.

1. _____

2. _____

3. _____

4. _____

5. _____

Have your instructor or tutor check your work.

PRACTICE 14

Label each sentence by one of two formats: S-LV-PA or S-LV-PN. Label each part of the sentence.

▶ Example:

             S LV   PN

Harry is a good debater. S - LV - PN

1. She is an attractive girl in my opinion.   _____

2. His ideas about politics are ambiguous.   _____

3. Students always seem busy with their work.   _____

4. Doctors and lawyers are our highest-paid

    professionals.   _____

5. Most teachers are enthusiastic.   _____

6. Discos, once places for a popular

    entertainment, are now bowling alleys.   _____

7. Records and tapes are expensive.   _____

8. The latest dress craze is the mini-skirt.   _____

9. William Faulkner was one of the greatest

    American novelists.   _____

10. Silence and patience are virtues.   _____

Check the answer key.

▼ EXERCISE 12

The following questions will test your understanding of the four basic sentence formats.

1. What are linking verbs? Name some.

_____

2. Do linking verbs take direct objects?

_____

3. What is the relationship of a direct object to the verb?

_____

4. What is the relationship of a direct object to the subject?

_____

5. What is the relationship of a predicate nominative to the subject?

_____

6. What is the relationship of a predicate adjective to the subject?

_____

7. Give the abbreviation codes for the four sentence patterns.

_____

If you had trouble answering any of these questions, review the sections on Formats 1, 2, 3, and 4 before you continue.

PRACTICE 15

Identify each of the following sentences either Format 1, 2, 3, or 4. Label each part of the sentence.

	Abbreviation	Format
▶ Example: He is my basketball coach. S LV PN	**S - LV - PN**	**4**
	Abbreviation	Format

1. She is the star of our class play. _____ _____

2. The coach gave Tom his football

   equipment. _____ _____

3. The bread tastes stale. _____ _____

4. The dog caught the stick. _____ _____

5. The wealthy man gave the poor child

   a dollar. _____ _____

6. I walked into the room. _____ _____

7. The marathon runner became an

   Olympic hero. _____ _____

8. Women have joined many traditional

   men's clubs. _____ _____

9. Kim sang an aria from *Aida*. _____ _____

10. The horse tripped on the last jump. _____ _____

11. Jimmy Connors is a marvelous

    tennis player. _____ _____

12. The lawyer gave his client some

    advice. _____ _____

13. The student was sick yesterday. _____ _____

14. Maria invited Brad to the dance. _____ _____

15. The dog growled at the letter carrier. _____ _____

16. Freshly cut roses are an expensive gift. _____ _____

17. Bob caught a fish for dinner. _____ _____

18. Doctors seem quite intelligent. _____ _____

19. He gave me a present for my birthday. _____ _____

20. The television picture appears faded. _____ _____

Check the answer key.

Types of Sentences

There are four types of sentences, classified according to their purpose: declarative, interrogative, imperative, and exclamatory.

A **declarative** sentence makes a statement. You have been working primarily with declarative sentences. Notice that this type of sentence ends with a period.

▶ Example: The car will not start.
It is raining today.

An **interrogative** sentence asks a question. It ends with a question mark.

▶ Example: Will you go to the movies with me?
Subject: *you*
verb: *Will go*

NOTE: In a question, usually the helping verb comes before the subject and the main verb comes after it.

An **imperative** sentence expresses a command or a rhetorical question (you expect that the listener will comply with your request). It usually ends with a period, but an imperative sentence can also end with an exclamation mark for added emphasis.

▶ Examples: Help.
Help!

NOTE: This particular imperative sentence contains only one word. What is the verb in the sentence? *help*. But where is the subject? Consider this for a moment. Aren't you commanding or requesting that someone help you? Then, you are actually addressing someone else; it is as if you are saying, "*You* help." The subject of the sentence is called an **understood** *you*. It is written like this: (you)

▶ Example: Please pass the cake.
verb: *pass*
subject: (*you*)

An **exclamatory** sentence expresses surprise or shock. It ends with an exclamation mark.

▶ Example: The house is on fire!

PRACTICE 16

Classify each of the following sentences as one of the four types: declarative, imperative, interrogative, or exclamatory.

1. Watch out for that man. _____

2. Have you done your homework? _____

3. Time can be measured. _____

4. The car caught fire! _____

5. Tell me your name. _____

6. Exercise is good for you. _____

7. Do you like summer sports? _____

8. Help. _____

9. I got an A! _____

10. Horses are patient animals. _____

Check the answer key.

▼ EXERCISE 13

Now, write a sentence of your own as an example of each type.

1. Declarative: _____

2. Interrogative: _____

3. Imperative: _____

4. Exclamatory: _____

Have your instructor or tutor check your work.

4

OBJECTIVES

1. To recognize fragments, individually and in paragraphs.

2. To correct fragments.

3. To use the editing symbol for fragment (*Frag*) when proofreading.

KEY CONCEPT

A sentence is a group of words that expresses a complete thought. If a sentence is not complete, it is called a *fragment*. In other words, a fragment is an incomplete thought punctuated as if it were complete, as if it were a sentence. There are four sentence errors that can produce fragments.

Fragment Type 1: No Subject

Usually, in order to express a thought completely, a sentence must contain a subject and a verb. Sometimes, however, a sentence contains only a verb. This particular type of sentence, called an imperative sentence, is used to express commands: for example, "Stop!" The verb is *stop;* the subject is called an **understood *you*,** because the speaker is commanding someone else—you, the hearer—to stop.

When a group of words without a subject is *not* an imperative sentence, it is a fragment.

▶ Example: Were walking down the street in a great hurry.

Obviously, you don't write this type of sentence frequently, but it does happen. The mistake can be corrected by simply adding a subject.

▶ Correction: *The children* were walking down the street in a great hurry.

 **EXERCISE 1**

Follow the above example, and correct the following fragments.

1. Stopped on the side of the road.

_____

2. Hit the curb.

_____

3. Ran into the store.

_____

Have your instructor or tutor check your work.

Fragment Type 2: No Verb

A group of words written without a verb is a fragment.

> ▶ Example: The woman in the yellow-striped dress.

Again, this type of fragment isn't usually mistaken for a sentence, but it can happen. When it does, the simplest way to correct the error is to add a verb.

> ▶ Correction: The woman in the yellow-striped dress *is my teacher.*

NOTE: Often the reason for mistakenly punctuating this type of fragment as a sentence is that the group of words is used in apposition, as a further definition or limitation of another term.

> ▶ Example: That's my teacher. The woman in the yellow-striped dress.

If this is the basis for the mistake, then correct the fragment by attaching it to the sentence to which it is related.

> ▶ Correction: That's my teacher, the woman in the yellow-striped dress.

▼ EXERCISE 2

Follow the example above, and correct the following fragments.

1. The child in the clown costume.

_____

2. The tiger in the cage.

_____

3. The duck pond in the center of town.

_____

Have your instructor or tutor check your work.

Fragment Type 3: *-ing* Verb with No Helping Verb

A sentence containing an *-ing* verb without a helping verb (such as *is, are, was, were, have been, will be*) is a fragment.

> ▶ Example: Barry battling bravely against the encroaching ants.

This fragment can easily be corrected by adding an appropriate helping verb.

> ▶ Correction: Barry *was* battling bravely against the encroaching ants.

▼ EXERCISE 3

Follow the previous example, and correct the following fragments.

1. The wolves circling the injured doe.

_____

2. The helicopter hovering overhead.

_____

3. The plane landing on the runway.

_____

Have your instructor or tutor check your work.

Fragment Type 4: No Complete Thought

A dependent clause (a group of words that contains a subject and a verb but does *not* express a complete thought) punctuated as a sentence is a fragment.

> ▶ Example: That the children were very unhappy.

When editing very quickly, you might see a subject and verb in this dependent clause and incorrectly label it a sentence. But if you read the clause carefully, you can *hear* that it is not a complete thought. The fragment leaves the reader hanging in mid-air, asking who, when, or why.

NOTE: A dependent clause usually begins with a subordinate conjunction or a relative pronoun. (See Chapter 8 in Part I for a detailed explanation of dependent clauses.) The following words are some of the most common subordinate conjunctions and relative pronouns; you should be able to recognize most of them.

Subordinate Conjunctions

after	how	unless	wherever
although	if	until	whether
as (if)	since	what	while
because	so that	when	unless
before	than	where	until
even though	though	whereas	

Relative

that	wh...
what	whoever
whatever	whom
which	whomever
whichever	whose

(*Whichever, whoever,* and *whomever* are not often used.)

There are two ways to correct a dependent-clause fragment. Choose whichever method is more appropriate for your message.

1. Because it is the subordinate conjunction that transforms the independent clause (simple sentence) into a dependent clause, *get rid of the subordinate conjunction,* which will leave you with a simple sentence.

> ▶ Fragment: That the children were very unhappy.

> ▶ Correction: The children were very unhappy.

NOTE: This method does not always work with relative pronouns because they often serve as the subject of the dependent clause and thus cannot be dropped.

> ▶ Example: Which was difficult.
>
> If you omit the relative pronoun, you still would not have an independent clause:
>
> Was difficult.
>
> Instead, you would still have a fragment, because your group of words now does not have a subject. In such a case, use the second method to correct the fragment.

2. *Connect the dependent clause to an independent clause,* and create a complex sentence.

> ▶ Fragment: That the children were very unhappy.

> ▶ Correction: Anyone could see that the children were very unhappy.

> ▶ Fragment: Which was difficult.

> ▶ Correction: We had to take a make-up exam, which was difficult.

..s, and correct the following fragments.

.iileage.

_____

.est.

_____

.the scene of the accident.

_____

.ctor or tutor check your work.

..CTICE 1

...ecide whether each group of words below is a sentence or a fragment. If che sentence is correct, write *C* in the blank. If the group of words is a fragment, write *Frag* in the blank. Correct all fragments.

1. Man's best friend a dog.   _____

2. The summer which is a pleasant season.   _____

3. Mr. Jones is my English teacher.   _____

4. Which is a difficult subject.   _____

5. Many people vacation in Maine because the state

   offers outdoor activities and historical sites.   _____

6. Taking tests can be a grueling experience.   _____

7. The boy in the scuba outfit.   _____

8. The Roseland Ballroom a good place to dance.   _____

9. Many people buy designer jeans because they fit better.   _____

10. Harold swimming the English Channel.   _____

Check the answer key.

Comma Splices

5

OBJECTIVES

1. To recognize comma splices in individual sentences and in paragraphs.

2. To correct comma splices.

3. To use the editing symbol for comma splices (*CS*) when proofreading.

KEY CONCEPT

A *comma splice* occurs when two independent clauses (in compound and compound-complex sentences) are spliced (joined) by a comma and punctuated as a single sentence. Using only a comma to join two or more complete thoughts is incorrect.

▶ Example: The teacher was not smiling, he was frowning.

In this example, there are two complete sentences: *The teacher was not smiling*, and *he was frowning*.

Identifying the Problem

Comma splices occur only in compound or compound-complex sentences; these are the sentence types that have at least two independent clauses. To identify comma splices, look at the break between the two independent clauses. If the two independent clauses are joined by only a comma at this break, then the entire sentence is a comma splice. You must then correct the comma splice.

PRACTICE 1

Read the following sentences. If a sentence is correctly punctuated, write *C* in the blank. If the group of words is actually a comma splice, write *CS* in the blank, and draw a vertical line separating the two independent clauses.

1. The exhibit of Andrew Wyeth's paintings was excellent, we

    particularly appreciated the "Helga" series.   _____

2. Many films have been made of the conditions in Germany

    during the 1930s, *Cabaret* is one of the best of these.   _____

3. Jason decided to see a movie, he should have completed

    his work first.   _____

4. The space shuttle program was devastated by the

    Challenger accident, no new shuttles were launched for

    eighteen months afterward.   _____

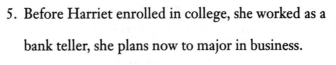

5. Before Harriet enrolled in college, she worked as a

bank teller, she plans now to major in business.   _____

Check the answer key.

Correcting the Problem

There are three acceptable ways to correct the comma splice.

1. *Make the two independent clauses into two separate, complete sentences.*

> ▶ Comma Splice: The teacher was not smiling, he was frowning.

> ▶ Correction: The teacher was not smiling. He was frowning.

▼ EXERCISE 1

Correct these comma splices by making two complete sentences.

1. George is an expert skier, he won three trophies.

_____

2. Morgan enjoys adventure movies, he saw *Robin Hood* ten times.

_____

Have your instructor or tutor check your work.

2. *Join the independent clauses with a comma and an appropriate coordinate conjunction.* The coordinate conjunction tells the reader that there is a relationship between the two independent clauses; furthermore, the conjunctions provide clues to the type of relationship. There are seven coordinate conjunctions: *for, and, but, so, yet, nor,* and *or.*

> ▶ Example: The teacher was not smiling, and he seemed very grumpy.

NOTE: Learn the type of relationship each coordinate conjunction stresses:

1. *For* shows cause.

2. *And* makes two independent clauses equal.

3. *Nor* shows negative choice.

4. *But* shows opposition.

5. *Or* shows choice.

6. *So* shows result.

7. *Yet* shows opposition.

▼ EXERCISE 2

Correct this comma splice by joining the two independent clauses with a comma and a coordinate conjunction.

The blizzard forced us to change our plans for a five-mile hike, we decided to stay home and build a fire.

_____

_____

Have your instructor or tutor check your work.

3. *Join the two independent clauses with a semicolon (;).*

▶ Example: The dean was not smiling; he seemed very grumpy.

NOTE: The semicolon tells the reader that a relationship exists between the two independent clauses; however, the semicolon does not identify the relationship. Although it is correct to use a semicolon to join two independent clauses, the clauses should be closely related. For example, the second independent clause can explain the first or provide an example of the first. This connection should be clear to your reader.

▶ Example: Many Civil War battlefields have been preserved by the Park Service; the Antietam battlefield is one of these.

In this example, the second independent clause provides a direct example of the first clause. The reader can easily understand the relationship between the two clauses.

▼ EXERCISE 3

Correct these comma splices by joining the two independent clauses with semicolons.

1. We did not buy the self-cleaning oven, the high cost of electricity to operate it would be beyond our budget.

_____

_____

2. Tammi's membership in the club was important to her, the club provided her with activities and social contacts.

_____

Have your instructor or tutor check your work.

NOTE: Often when you use a semicolon, you may want to include an **adverbial conjunction** (sometimes called a **conjunctive adverb**) to indicate what kind of relationship exists between the two independent clauses. There are four major adverbial conjunctions: *however, therefore, moreover,* and *nevertheless.* When you use one of these four adverbial conjunctions, you must place a semicolon before the adverbial conjunction and a comma after it.

▶ Example: It was raining constantly; nevertheless, we continued our climb up the mountain.

Here are the relationships that these adverbial conjunctions indicate:

1. *However* means "contradiction" or "opposition."

2. *Moreover* means "in addition to" and "also."

3. *Therefore* means "in conclusion."

4. *Nevertheless* means "in spite of."

The following list shows additional adverbial conjunctions:

also	indeed	rather
consequently	likewise	similarly
currently	next	then
finally	overall	thus
hence	primarily	

If you are unfamiliar with these adverbial conjunctions, check a dictionary for the relationships these conjunctions stress.

If you have only a comma in front of the adverbial conjunction in a sentence with two independent clauses, you still have a comma splice, so be careful to include a semicolon.

▶ Comma Splice: On the Fourth of July, all the banks were closed, moreover, all of the stores were closed.

▶ Correction: On the Fourth of July, all the banks were closed; moreover, all of the stores were closed.

Adverbial conjunctions can be used in a simple sentence, as well. If you use an adverbial conjunction in a simple sentence—one with only one independent clause—enclose it within commas.

▶ Examples: A dog is, moreover, man's best friend.

Therefore, you must work harder.

 **EXERCISE 4**

Correct these comma splices by joining the two independent clauses with semicolons and appropriate adverbial conjunctions.

1. Students must have free time during a school day, they must not spend all of their time in the student center.

_____

_____

2. Our opponents won the state championship three times in a row, we were confident of our abilities.

_____

_____

Have your instructor or tutor check your work.

▶ ## PRACTICE 2

In the blank at the right of each sentence, write *C* if the sentence is correct. Write *CS* if the sentence is a comma splice. Correct the comma splices.

1. April is a lovely month, but I like June best.   _____

2. Sally got a good promotion at her job, she also

   managed to take courses in the evening.   _____

3. The cost of living in Paris is very high, I heard

   that an apartment could cost as much as a

   thousand dollars a month.   _____

4. Last summer, Jerry spent most of his time at the beach,

   however, he never learned how to surf.   _____

5. One of the best jobs I ever had was as a lifeguard at

   Wildwood State Park, I could meet many new people.   _____

6. Photography is a good hobby; many people like

   to take pictures of people they know and places

   they have visited.   _____

7. Teachers prefer typed papers, yet many students don't

   own a typewriter.   _____

8. The parking facilities at this university are inadequate, each day I must drive around for at least thirty minutes before I find a space. _____

9. I prefer good restaurants, but I like fast-food places also. _____

10. Walt Whitman was a major American poet, he lived in Camden, New Jersey. _____

Check the answer key.

6

Run-Ons

▷ **OBJECTIVES**

1. To recognize run-ons, individually and in paragraphs.

2. To correct run-ons.

3. To use the editing symbol for run-ons *(RO)* correctly when proofreading.

▷ **KEY CONCEPT**

A run-on (sometimes called a **fused sentence** or a **run-together sentence**) contains two or more independent clauses that have been punctuated as one sentence; that is, no punctuation separates the two independent clauses.

▷ Example: The lawyer pleaded her client's case well she won the case.

In this example, there are two complete sentences: *The lawyer pleaded her client's case well,* and *she won the case.*

Identifying the Problem

Run-ons are found only in compound or compound-complex sentences; these are the sentences with two or more independent clauses. To identify run-ons, look at the break between the two sentences. If there is no punctuation at this point, then the sentence is a run-on.

▷ ## PRACTICE 1

Read the following sentences. If a sentence is correct, place *C* beside it. If the group of words is actually a run-on, place *RO* beside the sentence, and draw a vertical line separating the two independent clauses.

▷ Example: __RO__ I work at a factory during the night / I go to school during the day.

__C__ Drag racing is an exciting sport.

_____ 1. Harry is my best friend he will do anything for me.

_____ 2. Chemistry is a difficult subject.

_____ 3. America is a nation on the move many families move four times in a ten-year period.

_____ 4. Shelly is a good dancer she has been selected to appear with the New York Ballet Company.

5. The United Nations was formed from an

_____   older organization, the League of Nations.

Check the answer key.

Correcting the Problem

There are three ways to correct a run-on sentence.

1. *Break the run-on into two separate sentences with a period and a capital letter in each.*

▶ Run-on:	The dean smiled at the new freshmen they had survived their first week of classes.
▶ Correction:	The dean smiled at the new freshmen. They had survived their first week of classes.

▼ EXERCISE 1

Correct these run-ons by following the above example.

1. The students went to the dean's office they wanted to complain about a teacher.

_____

2. The accountant sighed as she left her office she had worked for fifteen consecutive hours.

_____

_____

3. Smoke detectors do not cost very much they have helped save many lives.

_____

_____

Have your instructor or tutor check your work.

2. *Connect the two independent clauses with a comma and the appropriate coordinate conjunction.* There are seven coordinate conjunctions: *for, and, nor, but, or, yet,* and *so.* Each coordinate conjunction tells the reader what kind of relationship exists between the two independent clauses.

Look at the following sentences and determine the relationship between the two independent clauses. Pay particular attention to the coordinate conjunctions.

a. Sue is going shopping, *and* her husband is going bowling.

b. Sue is going shopping, *but* her husband is going bowling.

c. Sue is going shopping, *so* her husband is going bowling.

d. Sue is going shopping, *for* her husband is going bowling.

In sentence a, the *and* tells the reader that neither one of the two independent clauses is more important than the other. In other words, the fact that *Sue is going shopping* is as important as the fact that *her husband is going bowling*.

In sentence b, the *but* shows opposition; it tells the reader that Sue and her husband are doing different things.

In sentence c, the *so* tells the reader that *her husband's going bowling* is the result of *Sue's going shopping*. You might imagine that her husband didn't want to go shopping, and he decided to go bowling while Sue was shopping.

In sentence d, the *for* tells the reader that *Sue is going shopping* because *her husband is going bowling*. In other words, Sue didn't want to go bowling, and she chose to go shopping instead.

NOTE: See Chapter 5 in Part II for a list of the relationships each coordinate conjunction stresses.

 ▼ EXERCISE 2

Following the example, correct these run-ons.

1. The snow thrilled us we wanted to go skiing.

_____

2. Doug gently unlocked the front door he did not want to awaken his parents at 4:00 A.M.

_____

_____

3. Nearly half of all car accidents involve a drunk driver many states have tightened their laws concerning driving under the influence of alcohol.

_____

_____

Have your instructor or tutor check your work.

NOTE: Using only a comma is not enough. You must use *both* the comma and the coordinate conjunction.

3. *Connect the two independent clauses with a semicolon (;)*. The semicolon implies to the reader that a relationship exists between the two sentences; however, it does not indicate the *type* of relationship. Use a semicolon when the two independent clauses are closely related. For instance, the second clause can provide an example or an explanation of the first one.

▶ Run-on: The giant black and white pandas are native to China in fact they are the national animals of China.

▶ Correction: The giant black and white pandas are native to China; in fact, they are the national animals of China.

▼ EXERCISE 3

Correct these run-ons by using a semicolon to separate the two independent clauses.

1. We could not buy the house it was priced at $150,000.

   _____

2. You must dress warmly in an Alaskan winter the average temperature is 0 degrees Fahrenheit.

   _____

   _____

3. In the 1800s, life in the American West was treacherous a pioneer might fall victim to natural disasters or wild animals.

   _____

   _____

Have your instructor or tutor check your work.

NOTE: Often when you use a semicolon, you may want to include an **adverbial conjunction** (sometimes called a **conjunctive adverb**) to indicate what kind of relationship exists between the two independent clauses. There are four major adverbial conjunctions: *however, moreover, therefore,* and *nevertheless.* When you use one of these four adverbial conjunctions, don't forget to use a semicolon before it and a comma after it.

▶ Example: We were supposed to be at school at 9:00 A.M.; however, our car wouldn't start.

Below is a list of other adverbial conjunctions. Each of these identifies a particular relationship between the two independent clauses. Check a dictionary to learn these relationships.

also	indeed	primarily
consequently	likewise	rather
currently	next	similarly
finally	overall	then
hence		thus

▶ PRACTICE 2

In the blank at the right of each sentence, write *C* if the sentence is correctly punctuated. Write *RO* if the sentence is a run-on. Correct the run-on sentences.

1. It was a cold, wet day; however, we still had our picnic

   at the beach.   _____

2. I plan to go to law school I hope that I am accepted.   _____

3. Mathematics is my hardest course English is my

   favorite course.   _____

4. Thelma will be a lawyer Thelma will be a doctor.   _____

5. Running is a good exercise; moreover, it relieves tension. _____

6. My uncle has a cabin in Maine, and he has a cottage

   at Cape Cod.   _____

7. The lake was crystal clear and warm the sky was a

   brilliant blue.   _____

8. Cumberland's basketball team won the semifinals

   now the team will compete in the state finals.   _____

9. College demands quite a lot from a student; however,

   it offers many rewards.   _____

10. Skiing is a difficult sport moreover it can be dangerous. _____

Check the answer key.

7

Subject-Verb Agreement

OBJECTIVES

1. To make subjects and verbs agree in number.

2. To correct problems in subject-verb agreement.

3. To use the editing symbol for subject-verb agreement *(S-V Agr)* correctly while proofreading.

KEY CONCEPT

Agreement of subjects and verbs means exactly what it says: in a sentence, the subject and verb must agree in **number.** If the subject is singular (one item), then the verb must also be singular. If the subject is plural (two or more items), then the verb must also be plural.

Singular and Plural Forms

Most singular subjects add an *s* or *es* to make a plural noun. For example, *dog* is singular, and *dogs* is plural.

PRACTICE 1

Label each of the following words either singular *(S)* or plural *(P).*

_____ 1. cat   _____ 6. miles

_____ 2. cats   _____ 7. ideas

_____ 3. he and I   _____ 8. his aunts

_____ 4. car   _____ 9. home

_____ 5. records   _____ 10. happiness

Check the answer key.

Most present-tense verbs that are singular end in *s* or *es;* most present-tense plural verbs do not end in *s.* For example, "She danc*es*" is singular, and "They danc*e*" is plural. Look at the following chart:

Number	Subjects	Verbs
Singular	—	*es* or *s*
Plural	*s* or *es*	—

The chart provides the basic rule for subject-verb agreement. By looking at the chart, you can easily see that, in general, *either* the subject or the verb, but not *both*, will end in *s* or *es.*

▶ Examples:

$$\overset{S}{}\quad\overset{V}{}$$

The <u>cat</u> <u>carries</u> her kittens.

Cat is singular.
Carries is singular.

$$\overset{s}{}\quad\overset{v}{}$$

The <u>cats</u> <u>carry</u> their kittens.

Cats is plural.

Carry is plural.

This chart provides a good test for subject-verb agreement. If both the subject and the verb end in *s* or *es*, check your work carefully. Usually, this combination means an error.

PRACTICE 2

Revise the following sentences to make the subjects and verbs plural. The subjects have been underlined once, and the verbs twice.

▶ Example: The <u>tree</u> <u>grow</u> straight.

    The trees grow straight.

1. The <u>boy</u> <u>laughs</u> at the clown.

   _____

2. The <u>mouse</u> <u>hides</u> in the pantry.

   _____

3. The <u>examination</u> <u>seems</u> difficult.

   _____

4. The <u>puppy</u> <u>nips</u> at my heels.

   _____

5. The <u>girl</u> <u>dives</u> into the water.

   _____

Check the answer key.

Verbs

There are some exceptions to the basic rule of singular and plural verb forms.

REGULAR VERBS

Regular verbs (most English verbs are regular) follow a pattern of conjunction in the present tense. Learn this pattern:

Singular	*Plural*
I (verb)	we (verb)
you (verb)	you (verb)
he, she, or it (verb + *es* or *s*)	they (verb)

▶ Example: The verb *to dance* is a regular verb, and it is conjugated in the present tense as follows:

to dance

I *dance*	we *dance*
you *dance*	you *dance*
he, she, it *dances*	they *dance*

Which form of the verb changes? *he*, *she*, or *it* (third-person singular) *dances*
How does the third-person singular form change? An *s* is added to the end of the verb.

IRREGULAR VERBS

Some English verbs that we use frequently are irregular; that is, these irregular verbs do not follow the pattern of conjugation of regular verbs. For example, the verbs *to be*, *to have*, and *to do* are irregular verbs. Learn the present-tense and past-tense forms of these verbs.

Present-tense form of *to be*:

I *am*	we *are*
you *are*	you *are*
he, she, or it *is*	they *are*

Past-tense form of *to be*:

I *was*	we *were*
you *were*	you *were*
he, she, or it *was*	they *were*

Present-tense form of *to have*:

I *have*	we *have*
you *have*	you *have*
he, she, or it *has*	they *have*

Past-tense form of *to have*:

I *had*	we *had*
you *had*	you *had*
he, she, or it *had*	they *had*

Present-tense form of *to do*:

I *do*	we *do*
you *do*	you *do*
he, she, or it *does*	they *do*

Past-tense form of *to do*:

I *did*	we *did*
you *did*	you *did*
he, she, or it *did*	they *did*

PRACTICE 3

In the following sentences, draw one line under the subject and two lines under the verb. In the blank space, write *S* if the subject is singular or *P* if the subject is plural. The first sentence is already done for you.

___**S**___ 1. The <u>cat</u> <u><u>carried</u></u> her kittens into the next room.

_____ 2. The child screamed for her mother.

_____ 3. Dolphins are supposedly the most intelligent marine

animals.

_____ 4. Hank Thompson always answers the office phone.

_____ 5. Gardens grow quickly with lots of rain and sunshine.

_____ 6. A student's grades depend upon his own efforts.

_____ 7. Tim works in an automobile factory.

_____ 8. Chrysler was able to recover from bankruptcy.

_____ 9. The dogs bark all night long.

_____ 10. They sat in the car.

_____ 11. Many millionaires own oil wells in Texas.

_____ 12. Headaches are often caused by stress.

_____ 13. The desk was in the middle of the room.

_____ 14. His favorite actor is Martin Sheen.

_____ 15. Hemingway's books make valuable reading.

_____ 16. An adolescent faces many problems.

_____ 17. The pewter bowl is on sale at the department store.

_____ 18. The reclining chair is very comfortable.

_____ 19. The bird's song was very pleasing.

_____ 20. The tennis player smashes the ball into the net.

Check the answer key.

Subjects

Always locate the subject first, because it determines whether the verb will be singular or plural. Also, remember that the noun in a prepositional phrase cannot be the subject of the sentence.

▶ Examples:

$$\overset{S}{\text{The } \underline{\text{Board}} \text{ of Directors } \underset{===}{\underline{\text{meets}}}^{V} \text{ on Thursdays.}}$$

Board is the subject of the sentence, and it controls the verb. *Directors* is the object of the preposition *of,* so it cannot be the subject.

SIMPLE SUBJECTS

Most subjects in sentences are usually one word. The most common type of subject is the simple subject (one noun or pronoun).

Pronouns. Pronouns take the place of nouns. For example, in the sentence "Mary went to the store because she needed a loaf of bread," *she* is a pronoun that takes the place of *Mary.* Here is a chart of the pronouns that are most commonly used as subjects:

Singular	*Plural*
I	we
you	you
he, she, it	they
this	these
that	those

▶ Examples:

$$\overset{S}{\text{Those } \underline{\text{doctors}}} \overset{V}{\underline{\text{believe}}} \text{ in the holistic theory of}$$
medicine. (simple subject—plural form)

$$\overset{S}{\underline{\text{She}}} \overset{V}{\underline{\text{has}}} \text{ agreed to render him an apology.}$$
(simple subject—singular form)

You should not have any problem making most simple subjects agree with their verbs.

▶ ## PRACTICE 4

In each sentence, change the plural subjects to singular ones; then, make any necessary changes in the verbs.

1. Students always feel tired after exams.

2. Dogs are usually considered man's best friend.

3. Children love to receive gifts.

4. The nations have amassed a budget surplus.

5. The plants need to be repotted.

Check the answer key.

Indefinite Pronouns. However, some simple subjects do cause problems. Below is a list of indefinite pronouns. All of them take a *singular* verb.

anybody	either	nobody
anyone	everybody	no one
anything	everyone	somebody
each	neither	someone

▶ Examples: Anybody is allowed into the school.

Each is responsible for his own gear.

Some indefinite pronouns (for example, *all, any, more, most, none, some*) can be either singular or plural, depending on the words that modify them. This situation usually occurs when the subject is a portion or percentage.

▶ Examples:

$$\underset{S}{\text{Most}} \text{ (of the swimmers) } \underset{V}{\text{refuse}} \text{ to enter the water. (plural)}$$

$$\underset{S}{\text{Most}} \text{ (of the summer) } \underset{V}{\text{is gone.}} \text{ (singular)}$$

$$\underset{S}{\text{Ten percent}} \text{ (of the money) } \underset{V}{\text{was recovered.}} \text{ (singular)}$$

$$\underset{S}{\text{Seventy percent}} \text{ (of all women) } \underset{V}{\text{want}} \text{ equality of the sexes. (plural)}$$

In these cases, in order to determine whether the subject is singular or plural, you must look at the modifier (usually a prepositional phrase):

- If the modifier is singular, then the subject is singular and takes a singular verb.

- If the modifier is plural, then the subject is plural and takes a plural verb.

▼ EXERCISE 1

Using the previous example sentences as models, change the subject in each of the sentences as indicated and make any necessary changes in the verb.

Change "of the semester" to "of my college years":

1. A quarter of the semester was spent studying Milton.

_____

_____

Change "of the child's day" to "of the class's time":

2. Ten percent of the child's day is devoted to art history.

_____

_____

Have your instructor or tutor check your work.

▶ PRACTICE 5

Identify the subject in each sentence and indicate whether it is singular *(S)* or plural *(P)*. Circle the verb that agrees with the subject.

▶ Example: ___**P**___ Many students (participates, (participate) in organized sports.

_____ 1. Each person (enjoy, enjoys) the rights established by the Constitution.

_____ 2. All of the cake (was, were) eaten last night.

_____ 3. Some of the boys (has, have) decided to go camping.

_____ 4. Each of the boys (play, plays) hockey.

_____ 5. Neither of the girls (wants, want) to work tonight.

_____ 6. All of the students (enjoys, enjoy) holidays.

_____ 7. Each teenager (wants, want) his own car.

_____ 8. The horses (gallops, gallop) along the fence.

_____ 9. Most adults (enjoys, enjoy) a vacation.

_____ 10. Half of the cherry pie (was, were) gone.

Check the answer key.

COLLECTIVE NOUNS

A collective noun is also a simple subject. Remember, a **collective noun** is one that refers to a group of individuals as a single unit, so it takes a *singular verb.* Here is a short list of collective nouns:

family	team	battalion	jury
crew	squad	company	union
herd	class	army	division
committee	crowd	quartet	mob

▶ Examples: The <u>class</u> <u>has</u> decided to go to Central Park for a picnic.

S   V

Congress has adjourned for the Fourth of July holiday.

▼ EXERCISE 2

Using the example sentences as models, make the suggested change in the subject in each of the following sentences and make any necessary changes in the verb.

Change "children" to "family":

1. The children are unhappy about forgoing a spring vacation this year.

_____

_____

Change "committee" to "executives":

2. The committee is undecided about the company's future plans.

_____

_____

Have your instructor or tutor check your work.

TITLES

The title of a written work, a movie or television show, an artistic creation, or a musical composition takes a *singular* verb.

▶ Examples:

                    S   V

           "Hansel and Gretel" is a well-loved children's tale.

                    S   V

           The Ring and the Book presents a tangled web of lies and half-truths.

▼ EXERCISE 3

Using the above sentences as models, make the suggested change in each of the following sentences.

Change "This" to "*All the King's Men*":

1. This is my favorite book.

_____

_____

Change "The Kiss" to "The Destructors":

2. "The Kiss" was not a very interesting short story.

_____

_____

Have your instructor or tutor check your work.

PLURAL-FORM SINGULAR-MEANING NOUNS

Some nouns are plural in form but singular in meaning; they take a *singular* verb. Here are some examples:

| aerobics | calisthenics | mathematics |
| aesthetics | economics | news |

▶ Example: The <u>news</u> <u>is</u> not good.   (s v)

Economics <u>was</u> not my best course.   (s v)

On the other hand, "jeans," "pants," and "trousers" always take a *plural* verb.

▶ Example: Designer <u>jeans</u> <u>are</u> the hottest clothing item right now.   (s v)

"Scissors" can be treated as singular or plural; base your choice on the sense of the sentence and its style. When in doubt about the number (singular or plural) of a word, consult your dictionary.

▼ EXERCISE 4

Make the suggested change in each of these sentences.

Change "history" to "physics":

1. Without a doubt, history is a boring subject.

_____

_____

Change "decor" to "aesthetics":

2. The decor of the room requires a restrained piece of statuary in the alcove.

_____

_____

Have your instructor or tutor check your work.

Nouns of Quantities. Nouns that refer to a quantity or to items that are considered a single unit take a *singular* verb.

▶ Examples:

                 S   *V*

Ten kilos is too much for one person to lift.

                  S   *V*

One thousand dollars was a lot to bet on the flip of a card.

▼ EXERCISE 5

Make the suggested change in each of these sentences.

Change "This" to "Two miles":

1. This is too far to walk.

_____

_____

Change "One gallon" to "Two gallons":

2. One gallon provides about an hour's worth of motorcycle riding.

_____

_____

Have your instructor or tutor check your work.

▶ PRACTICE 6

Identify the subject *(S)* in each sentence and indicate whether it is singular *(S)* or plural *(P)*. Circle the verb that agrees in number with the subject.

▶ Example:

    S   The flock of starlings (**seems**, seem) nervous.

_____ 1. This year, the gaggle of geese (has, have) stayed in this area for more than a month.

_____ 2. *The Crusaders* (is, are) a long-forgotten work by Margaret du Pleny.

_____ 3. Measles (is, are) no longer considered the scourge of humanity.

_____ 4. Trousers (has, have) made a fashion comeback.

_____ 5. One hundred pounds of potato salad (is, are) a lot to make each week.

Check the answer key.

Not all agreement problems are caused by simple subjects, however.

COMPOUND SUBJECTS

Whether a **compound subject** requires a singular or a plural verb depends on the sentence.

REMEMBER: A compound subject means that there is more than one subject in the sentence.

If the elements of the compound subject joined by *and* are still considered separate entities, they require a *plural* verb:

▶ Examples:

$\overset{S}{\underline{\text{Tom, Harry, Joe, and Hank}}}$ $\overset{V}{\underline{\underline{\text{are}}}}$ in the class-room now.

$\overset{S}{\underline{\text{Swimming and golf}}}$ $\overset{V}{\underline{\underline{\text{are}}}}$ my favorite sports.

However, if the nouns that are joined by *and* are considered one unit or refer to a single person, then a singular verb is required:

▶ Examples:

$\overset{S}{\underline{\text{Ham and eggs}}}$ $\overset{V}{\underline{\underline{\text{is}}}}$ my favorite breakfast.

$\overset{S}{\underline{\text{Meat and potatoes}}}$ $\overset{V}{\underline{\underline{\text{seems}}}}$ to be the only meal fit for this man.

My $\overset{S}{\underline{\text{friend and confidante}}}$, Lucille,

$\overset{V}{\underline{\underline{\text{has been stricken}}}}$ by pneumonia.

 **▼ EXERCISE 6**

Following the above examples, make the suggested change in each sentence and change the verb, if necessary.

Add "and one cat":

1. One dog is about all this apartment can hold.

_____

_____

Add "and Susan":

2. Sally is going to the movies tonight.

_____

_____

Have your instructor or tutor check your work.

If the compound subject is joined by *or, either . . . or,* or *neither . . . nor,* then the number of the subject that is closer to the verb determines the number of the verb.

▶ Examples:

          singular   *plural*   *v - pl.*

Either Sally or the boys are supposed to pick your father up at the station.

            plural   *singular*

Neither the teachers nor the administration

v-sing.

wants a strike this year.

▼ **EXERCISE 7**

Using the above sentences as models, make the suggested change in each sentence.

Change "Susan" to "the company":

1. Susan or Herman has to make a decision.

_____

_____

Change "newspapers" to *"Congressional Record"*:

2. Neither Congress nor the newspapers report results accurately.

_____

_____

Have your instructor or tutor check your work.

▶ ## PRACTICE 7

Underline the subject in each sentence. Decide whether the subject is singular *(S)* or plural *(P)*, and fill in the blank at the left. Circle the correct verb.

_____ 1. Jack and Eileen (wants, want) to get married.

_____ 2. Neither the foreman nor the union representatives (wants, want) to discipline the errant worker.

_____ 3. Harold or George (swims, swim) faster than you do.

_____ 4. My friend and Sue's husband (has, have) slipped into

alcoholism. (same person)

_____ 5. Quiche and hash just (doesn't, don't) seem to complement

each other.

Check the answer key.

The last two sources of confusion about subject-verb agreement stem from different types of sentences.

RELATIVE-PRONOUN CLAUSES

If you have a relative pronoun (*who*, *which*, or *that*) as the subject of the dependent clause in a complex sentence, then you must determine the noun to which it refers before you can decide whether the pronoun (and thus the verb) should be singular or plural.

▶ Examples:

    Her father, who is an Army major, is buying a
    new car. (*who* refers to *father*)

    Terry's book, which is on the table, costs ten
    dollars. (*which* refers to *book*)

▼ EXERCISE 8

Make the suggested change in each of the following sentences.

Make "brother" plural:

1. His brother, who is joining the Navy, likes the sea.

_____

_____

Make "friends" singular.

2. My friends, who are standing in the doorway, have just returned from a dance.

_____

_____

Have your instructor or tutor check your work.

NOTE: Be careful with relative pronouns in the construction "one of." Consider the following examples:

▶ Examples: He is *one* of the men who *receive* their pay on Friday.
The doctor is the only *one* of the staff members who *understands* the patient's condition.

In the first example, the relative pronoun *who* replaces the word *men;* hence, the verb must be plural. (In this sentence, the subject *he* is part of a group of men, all of whom receive their pay on Friday.) In the second example, the relative pronoun *who* substitutes for the word *one;* thus, the verb must be singular. (In this example, the doctor is identified as the "only one" who understands the problem.) If the construction *one of* is preceded by the word *only,* then the verb will be singular. However, if the construction *one of* does not have the word *only* preceding it, then you must analyze the sentence and its meaning to determine the noun or pronoun the relative pronoun replaces. Then, decide whether the verb should be singular or plural.

▶ ## PRACTICE 8

Underline the relative pronoun in each sentence; then, identify the noun to which the relative pronoun refers. Decide whether the subject is singular *(S)* or plural *(P),* and fill in the blank at the left. Circle the correct verb.

_____ 1. F. Scott Fitzgerald, who (was, were) a major literary figure in the 1920s, worked in Hollywood during the late 1930s.

_____ 2. Harris is one of the lawyers who (selects, select) their cases carefully.

_____ 3. This final calculus problem is the only one that (is, are) difficult.

_____ 4. The Stonehenge monument, which (is, are) in England, served as the site of many religious ceremonies.

_____ 5. Sam is the only one of her friends who (enjoys, enjoy) tennis.

Check the answer key.

INVERTED SENTENCES

In inverted sentences, which often begin with the adverbs *there, here,* or *where* or with prepositional phrases, the subject follows the verb. You must look for the subject after the verb before you can determine the number.

> Examples:
>
> $\overset{V}{\underline{\underline{\text{is}}}}$ $\overset{S}{\underline{\text{book}}}$
> There is the book.
>
> $\overset{V}{\underline{\underline{\text{are}}}}$ $\overset{S}{\underline{\text{children}}}$
> Here are the children.

▼ EXERCISE 9

Make the suggested change in each of the following sentences.

Make "outfits" singular:

1. There are the new outfits.

_____

_____

Change "dog" to "animals":

2. Here is the injured dog.

_____

_____

Have your instructor or tutor check your work.

► PRACTICE 9

Underline the subject of each sentence. Decide whether the subject is singular *(S)* or plural *(P)*, and fill in the blank at the left. Circle the correct verb.

_____ 1. There (is, are) too many people in this elevator.

_____ 2. At the end of the shady lane (stands, stand) the county courthouse and a church.

_____ 3. Here (is, are) your letters of recommendation.

_____ 4. For each of the applicants, there (was, were) long forms to complete.

_____ 5. Behind these locked doors (lies, lie) a fortune in gold bullion.

Check the answer key.

Pronoun Reference

8

<table>
<tr><td>

OBJECTIVES

</td><td>

1. To recognize pronoun-reference problems.

2. To correct pronoun-reference problems.

3. To proofread an essay for pronoun reference. The editing symbol for pronoun reference is *pro. ref.*

</td></tr>
</table>

KEY CONCEPT

A **pronoun** usually takes the place of a noun. The noun the pronoun replaces is called its **antecedent.** Usually, the antecedent is the closest noun.

                                         antecedent   *pronoun*

▶ Example: *Jill* was happy; in fact, *she* was ecstatic.

Personal Pronouns and Cases

The following chart lists personal pronouns; become familiar with them.

PERSONAL PRONOUNS

Nominative Case

Person	Singular	Plural
First	I	we
Second	you	you
Third	he	they
	she	
	it	

Objective Case

	Singular	Plural
First	me	us
Second	you	you
Third	him	them
	her	
	it	

Possessive Case

	Singular	Plural
First	my, mine	our, ours
Second	your, yours	your, yours
Third	his	their, theirs
	her, hers	
	its	

The **nominative** (or subjective) case is used when the pronoun is the subject of the sentence or when the pronoun is a predicate nominative.

                                         antecedent   *pronoun*

▶ Examples: The *girls* ate lunch in a Chinese restaurant; *they* enjoyed the meal greatly.

(In this sentence, the pronoun *they* is a subject.)

In last night's basketball game, *Ira* played very

antecedent

well. In fact, it was *he* who was chosen the most

pronoun

valuable player of the game.

(In this sentence, the pronoun *he* is a predicate nominative.)

The **objective** case is used when the pronoun is a direct object, an indirect object, or the object of a preposition.

▶ Examples: Jerry called *them* last night. (a direct object)
Time gives *us* grey hairs. (an indirect object)
Julie gave the textbook to *him*. (the object of a preposition)

To test for the objective case, place a *to* or *for* before the pronoun. If the sentence is clear, then you need to use the objective case.

▶ Example: The teacher gave *her* the test.
The teacher gave the test to *her*.

The **possessive** case indicates ownership.

▶ Example: The class gave *its* approval to the plan.
Mr. Mason made *his* famous chocolate cheese-cake.

▶ Practice 1

Provide the correct pronoun for each of the following nouns. Pay particular attention to the case of the pronoun.

	Nominative	*Objective*	*Possessive*
1. a dock	_____	_____	_____
2. dog	_____	_____	_____
3. Harry and Ellen	_____	_____	_____
4. James and I	_____	_____	_____
5. Sara	_____	_____	_____

Check the answer key.

Pronoun Agreement

NUMBER AGREEMENT

A pronoun must agree in number with its antecedent; that is, if a noun is singular, then the pronoun that replaces it must be singular. If a noun is plural, then the pronoun that replaces it must be plural.

▶ Example:

      antecedent   pronoun

The sophomore *women* decided that *they* would

      pronoun

return to *their* rooms.

GENDER AGREEMENT

Pronouns must agree with their antecedents in gender; that is, if the noun is masculine, then the pronoun must also be masculine. If the noun is feminine, then the pronoun must be feminine. If the noun is neuter (or has no determined gender), then the pronoun must be neuter.

▶ Example:

    antecedent pronoun

The little *boy* lost *his* toy. (singular, masculine)

    antecedent   pronoun

The elderly *woman* dropped *her* keys. (singular, feminine)

    antecedent   pronoun

The *chair* is missing one of *its* legs. (singular, neuter)

NOTE: Ships, planes, and countries are usually considered feminine.

PERSON AGREEMENT

Pronouns must also agree with their antecedents in person. You must be able to identify the speaker (first person), the person spoken to (second person), and the person spoken about (third person).

▶ Examples:

    antecedent   pronoun

I dropped *my* wallet. (first person, singular—the speaker)

    antecedent   pronoun

Your grandfather told only *you* to stay here. (second person, singular—the person spoken to)

    antecedent   pronoun

Harold believes *he* can win a gold medal in the Olympics. (third person, masculine, singular—the person spoken about)

PRACTICE 2

Use the pronoun chart to fill in the blanks with the correct pronoun.

1. Maria revealed that _____ had been married recently.

2. The actors decided that _____ did not like the script.

3. At student union meetings, only full-time students are allowed to express _____ opinions.

4. I realized that I would never get _____ dream car.

5. The baby waved _____ tin cup at each passerby.

Check the answer key.

PRACTICE 3

In each of the following sentences, circle the pronoun and its antecedent. Write the pronoun and its antecedent in the columns to the right.

▶ Example: We saw (Hook;) (it) was a marvelous film.

| it | Hook |
| *Pronoun* | *Antecedent* |

1. Maria gave her money to Hank.   _____   _____

2. Mr. Roberts, you must do your homework.   _____   _____

3. The teacher announced the test results to her class.   _____   _____

4. The radiologist completed his work.   _____   _____

5. The famous trial lawyer made her opening statement to the jury.   _____   _____

6. Steve and I decided that we had spent too much money on the new car.   _____   _____

7. The horse threw its rider.   _____   _____

8. Bring the books to me; then, take them to Mr. Stone.   _____   _____

9. The lamp, a gift from my grand-

mother, had been in her home

for years. _____ _____

10. The film industry caters to the

public's interests; recently it has

produced many science-

fiction movies. _____ _____

11. Give the pen to Rico; it needs to

be refilled. _____ _____

12. Bonnie and Jack, will you please

talk softly? _____ _____

13. The plants need to be watered;

I have not watered them for

three weeks. _____ _____

14. The mother rushed into the house

to see her child. _____ _____

15. The novel was read by many people;

it sold over six million copies. _____ _____

Check the answer key.

PRACTICE 4

The antecedents for the pronouns in the sentences appear in parentheses. Choose the pronoun that would most logically refer to the antecedent.

▶ Example: (Harriet) __She__ answered the phone.

1. Add some spices to the casserole; (the casserole) _____ is

bland.

2. (Paula) _____ takes violin lessons twice a week.

3. (Mary and I) _____ decided to take a vacation.

4. After John finished working, (John) _____ went straight home.

5. The musician played a song that (the musician) _____ had written.

6. The congresswoman gave (the congresswoman's) _____ support to the loyal mayoral candidate.

7. Mr. Willis, my chemistry instructor, told (Mr. Willis's) _____ students how to complete the experiment.

8. Martha bought a new suit. (The suit) _____ fits her well.

9. The principal and the faculty will drive (the principal's and the faculty's) _____ cars to the convention.

10. The reporter asked the president very tough questions. (The president) _____ refused to comment.

11. Please check the oil in the car. (The oil) _____ needs to be changed.

12. Whales have been hunted for many years, but now (whales) _____ have become an endangered species.

13. (Samantha and Janice) _____ plan to become vice presidents in the firm.

14. Take the meat out of the freezer. (The meat) _____ needs to thaw.

15. (The hockey players) _____ practice for five hours each day.

Check the answer key.

Special Problems

SPLIT SUBJECTS

Either . . . or and *neither . . . nor* often confuse writers. For sentences that contain *either . . . or* or *neither . . . nor*, the antecedent closer to the pronoun controls the number and gender of the pronoun.

► Example:

antecedent   pronoun
Neither *Tim* nor his *friends* have *their* own cars.

antecedent pronoun
Neither his *friends* nor *Tim* has *his* own car.

antecedent
Either *Major Banks* or the *captains* will issue

pronoun
their orders.

antecedent   pronoun
Either the *captains* or *Major Banks* will issue *his* orders.

PLURAL SUBJECTS

Subjects joined by *and* are usually plural, and they take a plural pronoun.

► Example:

antecedent   antecedent   pronoun
The *seniors* and the *juniors* will plan *their* party.

COLLECTIVE NOUNS

Collective nouns are words that stand for a group of members, but they are considered to be singular because the group acts as a unit. For example, the following words are collective nouns:

army	committee	trio
team	group	jury
pair	family	flock
class	herd	society

► Example:

antecedent   pronoun
The *army* is planning *its* practice maneuvers.

antecedent   pronoun
The Smith *family* is planning *its* vacation.

However, if the collective noun refers to a group as a number of individuals acting on their own, then it may be plural and require a plural pronoun.

► Example:

antecedent   pronoun
The *jury* are casting *their* ballots.

However, this plural form sometimes sounds awkward. It would be better to revise the sentence: *The members of the jury are casting their ballots.*

INDEFINITE PRONOUNS

The following words are *singular* indefinite pronouns:

anybody	anyone
each	every
everybody	everyone
no one	one
someone	somebody

These singular indefinite pronouns usually take masculine, singular pronouns.

antecedent   pronoun

▶ Example: Does *everyone* have *his* book?

You will notice that this traditional use of masculine, singular pronouns to replace indefinite pronouns excludes the women in the audience. The same problem can occur when you want to provide a pronoun for a noun that does not identify gender, such as *student, officer, doctor,* or *athlete.* Certainly, this usage is not always appropriate, as the following sentence demonstrates:

Each *student* must register *his* car before *he* parks on campus.

This sentence, similar to many in college catalogs, is appropriate only at an all-male institution. It is inappropriate for a catalog that addresses both men and women. To avoid sexist language, you can use a number of methods.

1. Use the correct form of the expression *he or she.*

    ▶ Example: Each student must register *his or her* car before *he or she* parks on campus.

    However, if you use this alternative in a lengthy passage, you will find that the constant repetition of *he or she* is awkward and can distract your readers.

2. Alternate masculine and feminine pronouns throughout a passage.

    ▶ Example: Each student must register *his* car before *he* parks on campus. To register a car, each student must present *her* current campus identification, the car's registration, and a check for twenty dollars to the bursar.

    At best, this usage is confusing to your readers.

3. Use only nouns, instead of pronouns, in a passage.

    ▶ Example: Each student must register the student's car before the student parks on campus.

    Certainly, this method will become repetitive for your readers.

4.   Use plural nouns or plural indefinite pronouns.

▶ Examples: Students must register *their* cars before *they* park on campus.
All students must register *their* cars before *they* park on campus.

This usage includes everyone, male and female, in the audience. In addition, it avoids confusion and repetition.

The following indefinite pronouns can be *singular* or *plural: all, any, some, many, most,* and *none*. The number of these pronouns is determined by the number of the noun in the prepositional phrase that follows the indefinite pronoun.

▶ Examples: *antecedent*
All of the police officers are required to report

pronoun
to *their* posts at once.

In this sentence, *all* is plural because the noun in the following prepositional phrase, *police officers*, is plural.

Some of the cake was left.
In this sentence, *some* is singular because the noun in the prepositional phrase, *cake*, is singular.

antecedent   *pronoun*
Some of the swimmers have completed *their* laps.

Since the word *some* is followed by the prepositional phrase *of the swimmers*, *some* is plural.

▼ EXERCISE 1

Fill in the correct pronoun in the following sentences. Circle the antecedent.

1. Every freshman must complete _____ housing request as soon as possible.

2. Some of the sophomore women called _____ parents the first week of classes.

3. Every man and woman in the armed forces serves _____ country proudly.

4. Half of the seniors plan to apply to graduate school before _____

complete this semester.

5. All of the cars on this lot need repair because _____ have been driven

over sixty thousand miles.

Have your instructor or tutor check your work.

SINGULAR PRONOUNS

A singular pronoun is used with nouns that appear to be plural but are actually
singular. For example, the nouns *news, physics, economics, mathematics,* and *genetics*
are all singular and require singular pronouns.

> ▶ Example:

antecedent   *pronoun*
Physics operates by *its* own principles.

MISTAKING THE ANTECEDENT

Sometimes prepositional phrases and relative pronouns (*who, which, that*) can
cause confusion if they come between the pronoun and its antecedent.

> ▶ Examples:

antecedent   prep phrase   pronoun
Each (of the dogs) buried *its* bone.

antecedent
Jean is just one of the senior *women* who have

pronoun
already received *their* awards.

AMBIGUOUS ANTECEDENTS

Be very careful not to confuse your reader by writing a sentence that has an
ambiguous pronoun reference.

> ▶ Example:

Jim told Pablo that *he* should go home.

Can you tell from this sentence who should go
home? No. Instead, use dialogue to resolve the
reference problem.

> ▶ Example:

Jim told Pablo, "I should go home." (Jim
should go home.)

Jim told Pablo, "You should go home." (Pablo
should go home.)

PRACTICE 5

Fill in the correct pronoun in each sentence. Write the antecedent on the line to the right of the sentences.

▶ Example: The jury is making __*its*__ final   *jury*
decision.

1. Most societies care for _____ older people and infants.   _____

2. The herd of cattle is approaching _____ favorite watering _____ hole.

3. Everybody must bring _____ books.   _____

4. Neither the coach nor her players are happy about   _____ _____ loss.

5. Some of the fathers are bringing _____ children.   _____

6. The company offered _____ employees a sizable raise.   _____

7. The class must learn _____ lesson.   _____

8. Neither of the two girls is capable of repairing _____ car.   _____

9. The board of trustees had _____ final meeting.   _____

10. She is one of the women who are making major strides in   _____ _____ fields.

11. The flock of birds sighted _____ nesting ground.   _____

12. Do all of the freshmen students have _____ registration   _____ cards?

13. The dean and his associates are discussing _____   _____ options.

14. The doctor and her staff plan to present _____ research   _____ findings on Monday.

15. The *New England Journal of Medicine* announced _____   _____ new board of directors.

Check the answer key.

9

Commas to Separate

OBJECTIVES

1. To recognize the need for commas in sentences and in paragraphs.

2. To use commas correctly.

3. To proofread a paper for comma mistakes, and to use correctly the editing symbol for comma mistakes (*P*).

KEY CONCEPT

Commas are used to separate six different parts or elements in a sentence:

1. Independent clauses joined by coordinate conjunctions

2. Items in a series

3. Coordinate adjectives

4. Long introductory elements

5. Dates and addresses

6. Any elements that might be misread or misunderstood if they were not separated by commas.

Independent Clauses

An independent clause is a group of words that contains a subject and a verb and can stand alone. In other words, it is a simple sentence and may be punctuated as such. However, you may want to join two independent clauses and write them as one compound sentence; in that case, you must use one of two methods:

1. *Join two independent clauses with a* **semicolon.**

> ▶ Examples:

The teachers elect their representatives. (independent clause)
The administration approves them. (independent clause)
The teachers elect their representatives; the administration approves them. (compound sentence)

The children decided to buy their parents a gift. (independent clause)
They raided their piggy banks. (independent clause)
The children decided to buy their parents a gift; they raided their piggy banks. (compound sentence)

2. *Join two independent clauses by adding a* **comma** *and a* **coordinate conjunction.**

▶ Examples: The teachers elect their representatives, but the administration approves them.
The children decided to buy their parents a gift, so they raided their piggy banks.

NOTE: The comma comes before the coordinate conjunction. There are only seven coordinate conjunctions: *and, but, for, so, or, yet,* and *nor.*

▼ EXERCISE 1

Join the following independent clauses to form a compound sentence by using a comma and a coordinate conjunction.

Independent clauses: Susan cooked an elaborate dinner.
John washed the dishes afterwards.

Compound sentence:

_____

Independent clauses: The manager reviewed the sales figures.
He was not happy with what he saw.

Compound sentence:

_____

Have your instructor or tutor check your work.

NOTE: Remember that the comma precedes the coordinate conjunction only when it is joining two independent clauses, but usually not when the conjunction is joining words, phrases, or dependent clauses.

▶ Examples: The boys decided to swim and fish. (joins prepositional words)

The girls are either at the beach or at the pool. (joins phrases)

A child must know that his parents love him and that they will care for him. (joins dependent clauses)

PRACTICE 1

If there is a comma error in a sentence, write *P* in the blank, and then correct the sentence by inserting a comma wherever necessary. If a sentence is correctly punctuated, write *C* in the blank.

1. The boys and girls could not decide whether to swim

    or fish.   _____

2. On Thursday the governing board will decide on next

    year's budget and this year's dues obligation.   _____

3. The children played in the schoolyard for the teachers

    were attending a faculty conference.   _____

4. The bride wanted to party for another hour but the groom

    was anxious to begin the honeymoon.   _____

5. The cake must bake for an hour and the cookies have to

    bake for forty minutes.   _____

Check the answer key.

Items in a Series

Commas are used to separate each item in a series from the preceding item.
Remember that a series is a group of three or more items having the same
function and form in the sentence.

▶ Examples: Sara, Mike, and Elton are good friends. (series
                   of words)

                   The dog likes to play in the living room, in the
                   playroom, and in the basement. (series of
                   phrases)

                   Mary Jean promised that she would be a good
                   girl, that she would not bite her brother, and
                   that she would not climb onto the television.
                   (series of clauses)

▼ EXERCISE 2   Add commas wherever necessary in the following sentences.

1. We bought apples peaches and bananas at the fruit store today.

2. The instructor looked through his briefcase through his desk and around the
   office for the lost grade book.

3. Despite the facts that she was only 5'2" tall that she weighed 180 pounds and
   that she had dyed her hair green Marcie believed she could get a job as a high-
   fashion model.

Have your instructor or tutor check your work.

PRACTICE 2

If there is a comma error in a sentence, write *P* in the blank and then correct the sentence by inserting a comma wherever necessary. If a sentence is correctly punctuated, write *C* in the blank.

1. People who want to buy a foreign car have a wide range of

   choices: Hondas Toyotas and Volkswagens.   _____

2. Milky Ways M&Ms and Mounds are my favorite candies.   _____

3. I bought a dress and a coat the other day.   _____

4. She buys gifts for Christmas Thanksgiving and Easter.   _____

5. I have to stop at the cleaner's buy some milk and pick up

   the twins at school.   _____

Check the answer key.

Coordinate Adjectives

Commas are used to separate coordinate adjectives. Coordinate adjectives are two or more adjectives that modify a noun or pronoun and that have equal value in modifying the noun or pronoun.

> ▶ Examples: happy, lively children
>   beautiful, sophisticated woman

To test whether two adjectives are coordinate, reverse the order of the adjectives and insert *and* between them. If the phrase still makes sense, then the adjectives *must* be separated by a comma.

> ▶ Examples: happy, lively children
>   lively and happy children
>
>   beautiful, sophisticated woman
>   sophisticated and beautiful woman
>
>   wholesome Italian food
>   Italian and wholesome food

NOTE: Obviously, the last phrase does not contain coordinate adjectives; therefore, it should not contain a comma. (*Wholesome* and *Italian* don't have equal value in describing food; *wholesome* describes *Italian food*.)

EXCEPTIONS: Adjectives that describe size, age, or color generally are not separated by a comma.

▶ Examples: big black Cadillac
                   little old lady

▼ EXERCISE 3

Follow the above examples, and insert a comma where necessary in the following sentences.

1. He acted the part of the charming convivial host.

2. That fancy expensive sports car has too many gadgets for my taste.

Have your instructor or tutor check your work.

▶ PRACTICE 3

Insert a comma wherever necessary in the following sentences. If a sentence is correctly punctuated, mark it *C.*

1. The little old woman seemed to shrink even more under her son's harsh impersonal gaze.

2. The yellow foreign roadster sped from the scene of the accident.

3. A dirty dingy file cabinet creates a bad impression in an executive's office.

4. The short blond-haired youngster was the prime troublemaker in the group.

5. The Irish setter with the long red hair seemed out of place among the poodles.

Check the answer key.

Long Introductory Elements

Long introductory elements must be separated from the rest of the sentence by a comma. The key words here are *long* and *introductory*. If the element is short, or if it is not at the beginning of the sentence, no comma is needed.

▶ Examples: On Tuesday we went to the movies. (short prepositional phrase)
                   On that fateful and fear-filled Tuesday, we went to the movies. (long prepositional phrase)

People feel guilty when they reject another's plea for help. (clause at end of sentence)
When they reject another's plea for help, people feel guilty. (introductory clause)

▼ EXERCISE 4

Correct these sentences by following the above examples.

1. Before going home the man decided to play one last game of pool.

2. After Susan decided to sue for divorce she moved out of the apartment.

Have your instructor or tutor check your work.

▷ PRACTICE 4

If there is a comma error in a sentence, write *P* in the blank, and then insert a comma wherever necessary. If a sentence is correctly punctuated, write *C* in the blank.

1. Having been introduced to the star once before Harry
   felt at ease in her presence.   _____

2. Tonight I want to go straight home.   _____

3. Before the group moved down the road each member
   checked his equipment.   _____

4. In the total darkness with only the ticking of the clock
   to guide him the burglar stumbled on the carpet.   _____

5. Because the tests are machine-graded it is unlikely that
   there would be an error.   _____

Check the answer key.

Dates and Addresses

Commas are used to separate individual items in a date or an address.

▷ Examples: Ty Cobb hit his last home run on September 11, 1927, at Wrigley Field.
The new Regency House is at 42 Marston Lane, Ridgefield, Ohio, a major metropolis.

NOTE: The commas before and after year are optional when only the month and year are given.

▶ Example: Most people believe the Great Depression began in October 1929 and ended with the advent of World War II.

▼ EXERCISE 5

Correct the following sentences by inserting commas where necessary.

1. My parents were married on August 14 1975 and divorced in May 1985.

2. Their first home was at 1225 Elm Street Florham Station Arizona.

Have your instructor or tutor check your work.

▶ PRACTICE 5

If there is a comma error in a sentence, write *P* in the blank and then correct the error. If a sentence is correctly punctuated, write *C* in the blank.

1. December 7 1941 is a date few people will ever forget.   _____

2. One famous address for Americans is 1600 Pennsylvania

   Avenue Washington D.C.   _____

3. The real-estate broker just mentioned that the house at

   27-01 32nd Avenue, Flushing, is for sale.   _____

4. Before you leave, let me remind you that the term project

   is due November 2, and not a day later.   _____

5. Even though you prefer the apartment at 227 Oak Crest

   Drive, it will not be available until July 1993.   _____

Check the answer key.

Elements That Might Be Misread or Misunderstood

The reason for a comma in this situation is obvious. Some sentences that are easily understood when you hear them can be misunderstood when you read them. In order to prevent this, separate any phrases that might cause confusion by inserting a comma.

▶ Example: Before eating the children washed their hands.

▶ Correction: Before eating, the children washed their hands.

The sentence should be punctuated with a comma; otherwise, your reader might assume that you eat children.

▶ Example: Although we were expecting only three fifty guests arrived.

▶ Correction: Although we were expecting only three, fifty guests arrived.

The above sentence needs a comma to prevent a misunderstanding about the number of guests.

▼ EXERCISE 6

Correct the following sentences by inserting a comma where necessary.

1. At eleven fifty Boy Scouts began the hike up Stone Face Mountain.

2. After mile twenty five more people dropped out of the race.

Have your instructor or tutor check your work.

▶ PRACTICE 6

If there is a comma error in a sentence, write *P* in the blank, and then correct the error. If a sentence is correctly punctuated, write *C* in the blank.

1. After jumping the dog raced toward the cat.   _____

2. Exactly at nine thirty men raced home.   _____

3. When old horses should be put out to pasture.   _____

4. Before Byron was thirty one masterpiece had been

published.   _____

5. Precisely at twelve o'clock four blasts were sounded

on the horn.   _____

Check the answer key.

Commas to Enclose

10

OBJECTIVES

1. To recognize poorly punctuated sentences, in isolation and in paragraphs.

2. To use commas to enclose or set off words, phrases, and clauses correctly.

3. To proofread a paper for comma errors and to use the editing symbol for a comma error *(P)*.

KEY CONCEPT

Commas are used to enclose or set off six major elements that interrupt sentences:

1. Direct address.

2. Speaker in a dialogue.

3. Appositives.

4. Out-of-place adjectives.

5. Nonrestrictive clauses and phrases.

6. Parenthetical expressions.

Interrupters are extra words or ideas added to the basic thought of a sentence. Because they are not necessary to the basic sentence, interrupters must be enclosed or set off by commas. Depending on its placement in the sentence, the interrupter will require either one or two commas to isolate it.

▶ Examples: If I'm not mistaken, his pay averages about $200 per week. (beginning of the sentence—one comma)

His pay, if I'm not mistaken, averages about $200 per week. (middle of the sentence—two commas)

His pay averages about $200 per week, if I'm not mistaken. (end of the sentence—one comma)

Commas in Direct Address

When the speaker in a sentence talks to another person and names that person, the process is called *direct address* because the speaker is addressing his audience directly.

▶ Example: I think, dear, you're wrong.

The speaker is talking to a person whom he calls "dear." Therefore, *dear* must be enclosed within commas. Because the interrupter is placed in the middle of the sentence, two commas are used to enclose it.

▶ Example: Your performance is poor, Nancy.

The speaker is talking to a particular person, and that person is named at the end of the sentence. Therefore, one comma is used to set off the noun in direct address, *Nancy*.

▶ Example: You poor little waif, you seem frozen.

The speaker is addressing a person whom he calls "you poor little waif." Because that direct-address interrupter is placed at the beginning of the sentence, one comma is used to isolate it.

▼ EXERCISE 1

Correct the following sentences by inserting the necessary commas.

1. The children don't trust any authority figure sir.
2. Let me assure you boss there's a reason for my tardiness.

Have your instructor or tutor check your work.

▶ PRACTICE 1

Correctly punctuate the following sentences.

1. Professor MacBride may I ask a question?

2. He really thinks Charles that he has grounds for a lawsuit.

3. Your Honor I object to the tone of his question.

4. Tomorrow you will go to the parade children.

5. Let's go to the game tonight Mary.

Check the answer key.

Commas in Dialogue

A dialogue is a conversation between two or more people. If the speaker (not the listener) in the conversation is identified, his name (or the noun or pronoun used to refer to the speaker) and the verb that refers to his speaking are enclosed within commas.

▶ Examples: Mary said, "I dislike concerts because the music is too loud."

"I dislike concerts because the music is too loud," said the girl.

"I dislike concerts," proclaimed the teenager, "because the music is too loud."

In each of these sentences, the speaker is identified. Therefore, in the first sentence the phrase "Mary said," which is at the beginning of the sentence, is set off by one comma. The phrase "said the girl" is at the end of the second sentence, so one comma is used. Finally, the phrase "proclaimed the teenager" is in the middle of the last sentence, so it is enclosed by two commas.

NOTE: Dialogue is usually punctuated by quotation marks. Therefore, if you see quotation marks, check to see whether the speaker is identified in the sentence. If so, enclose the speaker and the "speaking" verb within commas.

▼ EXERCISE 2

Correct the following sentences by inserting a comma where necessary.

"I'm as happy as a lark" yelled George.

She screamed "Don't you say another word."

Have your instructor or tutor check your work.

▷ PRACTICE 2

Correctly punctuate the following sentences.

1. "Teachers don't understand" screamed the disgusted student.

2. "Bugs" said the little girl quite primly "are dirty creatures."

3. Before he left home, six-year-old John stated very emphatically "I will not return."

4. "I am not at all interested" said Mother to the sales representative.

5. The proud owner of a prize-winning Persian unequivocally declared "Cats are much smarter than dogs."

Check the answer key.

Commas with Appositives

When a noun is immediately followed by a group of words that explains or renames it, the group of words is called an appositive and must be enclosed within commas.

▶ Example: Alexander Pope, the Neo-Classic poet, is famous for his monologues.

The Neo-Classic poet gives additional information about Pope; therefore, it is in apposition and is enclosed within commas. The appositive could be omitted, and the sentence would still make sense and provide enough information to be understood:

Alexander Pope is famous for his monologues.

▶ Example: The New York Jets, the underdogs, surprised everyone by winning the Super Bowl.

The underdogs is in apposition and is enclosed by commas. The appositive gives the reader additional information about the football team, but the phrase is not necessary for comprehending the sentence:

The New York Jets surprised everyone by winning the Super Bowl.

NOTE: When an appositive offers additional, *nonessential* information about the noun, it is enclosed in commas. However, some appositives are necessary to identify the noun. In this case, the appositive is not enclosed in commas. Consider the differences in meaning between these examples.

▶ Examples: The poet Dryden is famous for his satire.

My neighbor Mr. Taracks is the neighborhood busybody.

Neither of the above sentences could be rewritten without losing the sense of the sentence:

The poet is famous for his satire. *Which poet?*

My neighbor is the neighborhood busybody. *Which neighbor?*

The sense of the sentences has been lost. The information was necessary to identify the noun; therefore, no commas were used to enclose the information.

▼ EXERCISE 3

Using the example sentences as models, insert commas wherever necessary in the following sentences.

1. My only sister Sue is studying engineering.

2. *Childe Roland to the Dark Tower Came* an epic poem was written by Robert Browning.

3. Sally the class busybody loves to take charge of every project.

Have your instructor or tutor check your work.

▶ PRACTICE 3

In the blank to the right of each sentence, write *C* if the sentence is correctly punctuated or *P* if there is a comma error. Correct the comma errors.

1. My history teacher Professor Jones gives difficult tests. _____

2. Mrs. Smith Sally's neighbor likes to wear hot-pink shorts

   in the summer. _____

3. Old Lyin' George a famous panhandler died peacefully

   last night in a nursing home. _____

4. President Carter the nation's thirty-ninth chief executive

   refused to return to the peanut business. _____

5. My only brother Harry wants to join the Peace Corps. _____

Check the answer key.

Commas with Out-of-Place Adjectives

Because adjectives usually precede the nouns they modify, any deviation from that usual pattern catches the reader's attention and interrupts the flow of thought. When that happens, the out-of-place adjective(s) must be enclosed by commas.

▶ Examples:

The tall, slender girl attracted everyone's attention. (usual pattern)

The girl, tall and slender, attracted everyone's attention. (out-of-place)

The grand, imposing house required a large housekeeping staff. (usual pattern)

The house, grand and imposing, required a large housekeeping staff. (out-of-place)

▼ EXERCISE 4

Using the example sentences as models, correctly punctuate these sentences.

1. The woman witty and sophisticated charmed her hostile audience.
2. The toddler sturdy and daring was determined to climb out of the crib.

Have your instructor or tutor check your work.

▶ PRACTICE 4

In the blank to the right of each sentence, write *C* if the sentence is correctly punctuated or *P* if there is a comma error. Correct the comma errors.

1. My child bright and witty will be famous some day.   _____

2. The old man tired but undaunted faced his accusers.   _____

3. The fresh air of spring exhilarating and uplifting should

   be packaged and sold for use during the winter.   _____

4. The young boy senile before his time was a victim of

   a dreaded disease.   _____

5. The beautiful and happy baby laughed at the

   puppy's antics.   _____

Check the answer key.

Commas with Nonrestrictive Clauses and Phrases

A nonrestrictive clause or phrase gives extra information about the word it modifies, so it is not essential to the sentence and is enclosed by commas.

▶ Example: My brother, who has a weak knee, should not play football.

The basic thought of this sentence is that the speaker's brother should not play football. Because the speaker obviously knows his brother, he is able to offer the reason for that prohibition, but that reason is not essential to the sentence. Therefore, because the clause acts as an interrupter, stopping the flow of the sentence, it must be punctuated as one. Enclose it within commas. (If, however, the speaker has two brothers and only one has weak knees, the phrase would be "restrictive" and essential to identify which brother shouldn't play. In that case, do not set off the phrase with commas.)

▶ Example:
Steven Stomes, whose show you like, will host a party next week for disabled vets.

▼ EXERCISE 5

Using the example sentence as a model, correctly punctuate the following sentences.

1. Mary who is a great athlete is also an outstanding scholar.

2. King George III who lost the American colonies is not considered an outstanding monarch.

Have your instructor or tutor check your work.

NOTE: Remember, *non*restrictive clauses and phrases are enclosed within commas. Anything that is essential to the meaning of the sentence should be left as an integral part of the sentence and *not* enclosed.

▶ Example:
The man who is standing by the door is a security officer.

"Who is standing by the door" is essential for identifying the person; without this clause, the reader would have no means of identifying the security officer. Consequently, no commas are used in the sentence.

Now, note the effect commas can have on the meaning of a sentence.

▶ Example:
Journalists, who write well about crucial issues, are rewarded with a large audience.

The basic thought of the sentence is that journalists have large audiences; the nonrestrictive clause (which has been enclosed by commas) merely gives the reason for the large audiences. It provides extra information to the reader.

▶ Example:
Journalists who write well about crucial issues are rewarded with a large audience.

The meaning has changed. Now, it is *only* proficient journalists who reach large audiences. The clause is essential to the sentence because it identifies the journalists. Therefore, no commas are used.

PRACTICE 5

In the blank to the right of each sentence, write *C* if the sentence is correctly punctuated or *P* if there is a comma error. Correct the comma errors.

1. Parrots although notorious for their ability to mimic speech are really shy birds. _____

2. Puppies who at first always seem cute can turn a house upside-down. _____

3. Fashionable dress whose criteria change so often should not be used to judge another person's worth. _____

4. The parishioners who leave early disrupt the service. _____

5. The gentleman who is standing by the fireplace is a well-known composer. _____

Check the answer key.

Commas with Parenthetical Expressions

When a word or phrase is inserted into a sentence to explain or comment on that sentence, it is called a parenthetical expression. Because the word or phrase is not essential to the sentence (it is merely providing additional information), it is enclosed by commas.

▶ Example:

The dean, on the other hand, believes in vigorously recruiting students.

The basic thought of this sentence is the dean's desire to seek students actively. The phrase *on the other hand* serves as a *transition;* it helps to move the reader from one idea to another, in this case contrasting, idea. Because it acts as an interrupter in the middle of the sentence, it is enclosed by two commas.

▼ EXERCISE 6

Following the above examples, correctly punctuate these sentences.

1. In fact the author believes his works were plagiarized.

2. The original cowboy to tell the truth would not match today's idealized version of a cowpuncher.

Have your instructor or tutor check your work.

Following is a discussion of the two most common types of parenthetical expressions.

TRANSITIONAL EXPRESSIONS

In general, transitional expressions help give unity and coherence to an essay or paragraph. They influence the style of the writing, so they are enclosed by commas.

Below is a chart of some commonly used transitions and the type of relationship each one indicates.

TYPE OF RELATIONSHIP	TRANSITIONS
Cause and Effect	consequently, hence, therefore, thus
Chronology/Sequence	first, second, third, last, finally, later
Comparison/Contrast	similarly, however, nevertheless, on the other hand, in contrast, on the contrary
Example	for example, to illustrate, for instance
Importance/Repetition	as a matter of fact, generally speaking, in addition, in fact, on the whole, to say the least, to tell the truth, moreover
Summary/Conclusion	in brief, in short, to conclude, to summarize, therefore

Note that these expressions require the reader to pause while reading the sentence, so they are enclosed by commas.

On the other hand, some short parenthetical expressions of one or two words do *not* force the reader to pause; therefore, they would not be enclosed by commas. Here are some examples:

actually	at worst	perhaps
also	if any	then
at best	indeed	too
at least	of course	

▶ Examples: Then everyone decided to leave the dance hall.

Of course the inflation rate had also climbed to 20 percent by that time.

▼ EXERCISE 7

Correctly punctuate these sentences.

1. Perhaps the hospital expects too much from its volunteers.
2. Actually they have always expected too much.

Have your instructor or tutor check your work.

MILD INTERJECTIONS

Mild interjections are words such as *oh*, *wow*, and *ah*. They are usually placed at the beginning of a sentence to comment on it. Again, because they are not essential to the sentence and because they interrupt its thought, they are considered parenthetical elements and are enclosed by commas.

▶ Examples: Oh, I didn't know you were here.

Wow, that's some black eye!

▼ EXERCISE 8

Correctly punctuate these sentences.

1. Ah how I appreciate a fine cigar.
2. Oh that was an unexpected move.

Have your instructor or tutor check your work.

▶ PRACTICE 6

In the blank to the right of each sentence, write *C* if the sentence is correctly punctuated or *P* if there is a comma error. Correct the comma errors.

1. In fact she is quite a good cook.   _____

2. He is, I believe, determined to ascend the corporate

   ladder.   _____

3. Surprisingly Calhoun's Clogs won the

   steeplechase easily.   _____

4. To conclude productivity has improved, but not by
   as great a percentage as we had hoped.   _____

5. John Darlingston believe it or not is an accomplished
   pianist.   _____

Check the answer key.

11

Apostrophes

▶ **OBJECTIVES**

1. To recognize the need for apostrophes.

2. To use apostrophes correctly.

3. To proofread a paper for apostrophe errors. The editing symbol for apostrophes is *apos.*

▶ **KEY CONCEPT**

Apostrophes are used for three purposes:

1. To indicate possession.

2. To form contractions.

3. To form plurals of certain words.

Use of Apostrophes to Indicate Possession

An apostrophe is used to demonstrate possession. The apostrophe takes the place of omitted words of ownership. If you can reverse the order of the words and use *of* or *for,* then you need an apostrophe. For example, *child's book* becomes *the book of the child.*

▶ Examples: son's chores (the chores of the son)
sons' chores (the chores of more than one son)
Octavia's cake (the cake of Octavia)
Nelson's journey (the journey of Nelson)

NOTE: An apostrophe is *not* required for possessive pronouns. The pronouns *my, mine, your, yours, his, her, hers, its, our, ours, their,* and *theirs* do not need apostrophes to make them possessive.

▶ Examples: *His* car is not here. Shall we take *yours* or *mine?*
Each cat had *its* favorite spot in the house.

RULES FOR FORMING THE POSSESSIVE

1. *Add the apostrophe plus an* s *('s) to show possession in these cases:*

   a. A singular noun

   ▶ Examples: a cat's cry
   the astronaut's suit

   b. An indefinite pronoun

   ▶ Examples: someone's keys
   everyone's answers

c. Plural nouns that do not end in *s*

▶ Examples: children's coats
women's responsibilities
men's roles

d. Compound (more than one word) expressions used as a singular noun

▶ Examples: her father-in-law's chair
the chief-of-police's gun

e. Joint possession and separate possession

▶ Examples: Libby and Cindy's room (same room)
Libby's and Cindy's rooms (different rooms)

PRACTICE 1

Make the following items possessive.

1. the rules of the school_____

2. the idea of someone _____

3. the responses of some people_____

4. the regulations of the agency_____

5. the child whose parents are Thelma and Gene _____

6. the families of Mr. Grant and Mr. Stone _____

7. the quilt of my mother-in-law _____

8. the motives of the thief_____

9. the responses of the congregation_____

10. the insults of the crowd _____

Check the answer key.

2. *Add an apostrophe (') or an apostrophe plus an* s *('s) to* singular *words ending in* s.

a. Add the apostrophe plus the *s* to singular words of one syllable.

▶ Examples: my boss's schedule
the bus's tires

b. Add an apostrophe plus an *s* or an apostrophe only to singular words of two syllables. Your choice depends upon sound.

▶ Examples: Thomas's or Thomas' dog
discus' flight or discus's flight

c. Singular words of three or more syllables use only an apostrophe to make them possessive.

▶ Examples: Martinkus' book
                 Pythagoras' theory

▼ EXERCISE 1

Make the following proper nouns possessive.

1. the inhabitants of the Ozarks _____

2. the boat of Ross _____

   Have your instructor or tutor check your work.

3. *Add only an apostrophe (') to plural nouns ending in* s.

   ▶ Examples: goats' pasture
                    bridges' supports

▼ EXERCISE 2

Make the following words possessive.

1. the engines of the tractors_____

2. the caps of the swimmers_____

   Have your instructor or tutor check your work.

Use of Apostrophes to Form Contractions

Use apostrophes in place of some letters to form contracted words or numbers. Make sure that the apostrophe is in the same place as the omitted letters or numbers.

▶ Examples:

of the clock	o'clock
he did not	he didn't
she will	she'll
Kim will not	Kim won't
he is	he's
I am	I'm
they are	they're
1965	'65

   Usually, except for a contraction like *o'clock*, you should not use contractions in formal writing.

Use of Apostrophes to Form Plurals

Use apostrophes to form plurals of letters, numbers, abbreviations, and words referred to as words.

▶ Examples: Please distinguish between your *i*'s and your *t*'s.
Nathan's 7's often look like 9's.
The VIP's arrived at the gala opening of the new play.
You used too many *and*'s in your last paper.

▼ EXERCISE 3

Make the following words and letters plural.

1. the letters *t* and *b* _____

2. the abbreviations IBM PC (Personal Computer) and MP (Military Police)____

3. the numbers 17 and 1,000 _____

4. the words *make* and *sing*_____

Have your instructor or tutor check your work.

NOTE: In current usage, the plurals of this century's decades—the '20s, for example—are written without the apostrophe plus *s*. Instead, these decades appear with only the initial apostrophe to indicate that the first numbers are absent and the added *s* to indicate plural. The Sixties are now written numerically as the '60s.

▶ PRACTICE 2

Use an apostrophe to make the following sets of words possessive, contractions, or plurals.

1. the ball of the team _____

2. the work of a rabbi _____

3. the passengers of the bus _____

4. the passengers of the buses_____

5. the record of someone _____

6. the credit cards of Ms. Jones _____

7. the racquet of the tennis pro _____

8. the weather conditions of today_____

9. the motto of the Marines _____

10. the national anthem of America _____

11. the responsibilities of the commander-in-chief _____

12. the refrigerator of his grandparents _____

13. the restaurants of Jack and Tony (same restaurants) _____

14. the restaurants of Jack and Tony (different restaurants) _____

15. the special effects of the movie _____

16. the concern of the people_____

17. I will not_____

18. he cannot _____

19. they have _____

20. the plural of the word *several* _____

21. the plural of the word *yet* _____

22. the jungles of Brazil _____

23. the wares of the salespeople_____

24. the uniform of the soldier _____

25. the plural of the letter *z* _____

Check the answer key.

Capitals, End Punctuation, and Other Types of Punctuation

12

▷ **OBJECTIVES**

1. To recognize the need for capitals in sentences and in paragraphs.

2. To recognize the need for end punctuation in sentences.

3. To use capitals and end punctuation correctly.

4. To learn how to use other types of punctuation correctly.

5. To learn to proofread for punctuation errors and to correct them.

6. To learn to use the editing symbol *(P)* for punctuation errors.

▷ **KEY CONCEPT**

The rules for using capitals and end punctuation help the writer to communicate effectively with the reader. Writers also need to become familiar with a few other types of punctuation:

1. Colons (:) and semicolons (;).

2. Dashes (—) and hyphens (-).

Capitals

There are seven basic rules for using capitals. You are probably familiar with some of them:

1. *Capitalize the pronoun "I" wherever it appears in a sentence.*

   ▶ Example: I told her that I had only minutes to spare. She thought that I had lied to her.

▼ **EXERCISE 1**

Following the above example, circle the first letter of any word that should be capitalized.

She replied, "i believe that i will have finished by then. At least, i hope so."

   Have your instructor or tutor check your work.

2. *Capitalize any reference to God or any Supreme Being recognized by a religion. Also, capitalize any personal pronouns that refer to Him.*

   ▶ Examples: Some believe that God created His world in six days, as the Bible states.

                    Many primitive peoples believed in Mother Nature and Father Sun.

▼ **EXERCISE 2**

Following the above example, circle the first letter of any word that should be capitalized.

Some feminists believe that god is female, and so they refer to her works of creation.

    Have your instructor or tutor check your work.

NOTE: The word *God* is capitalized only when it refers to a specific, supreme being. If the word is used in a general sense, then it is *not* capitalized.

    ▶ Example: The Romans believed in many gods. They assigned to each god a specific area of responsibility; for example, Morpheus was the god of sleep, and Eros was the god of love.

▼ **EXERCISE 3**

Following the above example, capitalize any words that require it.

The Greeks, too, created a host of gods. In many cases, though, the Greek gods were more militant than the Roman ones.

    Have your instructor or tutor check your work.

3. *Capitalize the first word of a sentence including those that are quoted or enclosed in parentheses, and (usually) the first word of each line of poetry.*

    ▶ Examples: "The gray sea and the long black land;
And the yellow half-moon large and low;"
(Robert Browning)

        Every paramedic must complete a rigorous health course in order to be certified. It's a good regulation.

        She said, "Let's go to the restaurant now."

▼ **EXERCISE 4**

Following the above examples, circle the first letter of any word that should be capitalized.

1. psychologists have studied weather patterns for years. they think the patterns provide clues to man's behavior.

2. The instructor demanded, "whose spy are you?"

3. "busy, curious thirsty fly!

    drink with me, and drink as I:" (William Oldys)

    Have your instructor or tutor check your work.

NOTE: When part of a poem is set horizontally instead of vertically, then slashes divide the lines of poetry. (Usually, you would incorporate no more than three lines of poetry, or a single stanza if the poem is short, into a sentence. Set off and indent longer passages.)

▶ Example: One of William Blake's most famous poems, "The Tyger," begins dramatically: "Tyger! Tyger! burning bright / In the forests of the night, / What immortal hand or eye / Could frame thy fearful symmetry?"

You were probably already familiar with rules 1, 2, and 3 for capitalization. Now, review them in the following practice.

▶ PRACTICE 1

Capitalize any word that requires it by circling its first letter.

1. there is one major difference between monotheistic and polytheistic religions. The former recognize only one god, while the latter worship many gods.

2. "i insist upon seeing the manager," she said. "in fact, i demand it."

3. "ye gods!" he cried. "i can't stand it anymore."

4. according to one theory, sunny days invigorate people, and rainy days enervate them.

5. "he clasps the crag with crooked hands; / close to the sun in lonely lands, / ringed with the azure world, he stands." (Alfred Lord Tennyson)

Check the answer key.

The following rules for using capitals may be less familiar to you.

4. *Capitalize all the important words in the titles of books, magazines, newspapers, plays, poems, articles, and songs.*

▶ Examples: *Tender Is the Night* (novel)   *U.S.A. Today* (newspaper)
The New York Times (newspaper)   *Antony and Cleopatra* (play)
The Ring and the Book (poem)   *Ebony* (magazine)
Die Hard 2 (movie)   *The King and I* (play)

NOTE: Nouns, verbs, adjectives, and adverbs are usually considered important words, so they would be capitalized. Articles, prepositions, and conjunctions are usually considered unimportant, so they are not capitalized. However, if they are more than five letters long, or if they are the first or last word in the title, they *are* capitalized.

▶ Examples: "As Time Goes By"
In Search of History
Through the Looking-Glass

▼ **EXERCISE 5**

Following the above examples, circle the first letter of any word that should be capitalized in these titles.

1. *paper money*

2. *the mammoth hunters*

3. *the last crusader*

4. *how to succeed in business without really trying*

   Have your instructor or tutor check your work.

5. *Capitalize people's names, titles, and family names.*

▶ Examples: Aunt Teresa   Governor Edwards
Grandpa Smith   Reverend Milton
Captain La Rue   Lawrence Sandringham

NOTES: a. The title should be capitalized when it refers to a specific person, even if that person's name is not given.

▶ Examples: Thank you, Mr. President.
Right away, Senator.
I'll be glad to get it for you, Uncle.

b. The title should *not* be capitalized if it is preceded by a possessive pronoun (*my, our, their,* and so on).

▶ Examples:: My company's president had just filed for personal bankruptcy.
Our grandmother refuses to live in a nursing home.
Their senator ignored their requests for help.

▼ **EXERCISE 6**

Following the above examples, circle the first letter of any word that should be capitalized.

1. History will show that chairman mao changed his country's destiny.

2. The surgery will be performed by doctor cooley, the famous heart surgeon.

3. After we gave the gift to our grandfather, he thanked us all.

Have your instructor or tutor check your work.

6. *Capitalize all important words in the names of organizations, institutions, and brand names.*

▶ Examples: The Elks   Mid-Manhattan Hotel
The Chamber of   General Motors
   Commerce
National Association   Betty Crocker
   of Manufacturers
Parkland Memorial Hospital

▼ EXERCISE 7

Following the above examples, circle the first letter of any word that should be capitalized.

1. The moose club decided to hold its annual convention at walt whitman high school.

2. The unfortunate old woman was rushed to sloan-kettering memorial hospital.

3. I buy only ford trucks.

Have your instructor or tutor check your work.

Review rules 4, 5, and 6 before completing the following practice exercise.

▶ PRACTICE 2

Capitalize any words that require it.

1. On April 14, 1865, president Abraham Lincoln was shot while watching a play at ford's theater.

2. That was such a spectacle that even the *mountain eagle* ran a front-page story on it.

3. The local chapter of the american workers association wants to unionize the kitchen staff at tall oaks community hospital.

4. The one drawback is that our family doctor is not affiliated with any hospital.

5. I prefer wheaties to rice krispies.

Check the answer key.

The last rule encompasses the greatest amount of material.

7. *Capitalize proper nouns, their abbreviations, and adjectives derived from them.*

NOTE: A proper noun names a specific person, place, or thing; a common noun, on the other hand, is a general word for a person, place, or thing.

▶ Examples:

Common Noun	Proper Noun	Abbreviation	Adjective
country	France	Fr.	French
man	Karl Marx		Marxist
manufacturer	General Motors	G.M.	
region	South	So.	Southern
city	New York	N.Y.	New Yorker
day	Friday	Fri.	
people	Polynesia		Polynesian
document	the Constitution		Constitutional
decade	the Twenties		

NOTE: Designations of morning or afternoon time, *ante meridiem* and *post meridiem*, are abbreviated A.M. and P.M. Current usage, however, suggests that the abbreviations do not need to be capitalized.

▼ **EXERCISE 8**

Following the above examples, circle the first letter of any word that should be capitalized.

1. For my honeymoon, I'd like to go to acapulco, cape cod, or tahiti.

2. My girlfriend is a francophile. she eats french cheese, uses french perfume, wears french clothes, and plans to marry a frenchman.

3. Businesses generally agree that december and august are lost months; the former is too hectic for production work, the latter too hot.

   Have your instructor or tutor check your work.

NOTE: Do not capitalize the seasons of the year (winter, spring, summer, autumn) or the points of the compass (north, south, east, west) unless they appear as the first word in a sentence. Occasionally, poets will capitalize the seasons of the year as a personification of the season. In addition, make sure that you distinguish between the points of the compass and the regions of a country. Regions designated by location (the North, the South, the East, the West) are capitalized.

▶ Examples: Many senior citizens like to go south to Florida for the winter and then north to the Catskills for the summer.

Although Robert E. Lee had served in the U.S. Army during the Mexican War, he fought for the South in the Civil War.

> ## PRACTICE 3

After reviewing the rules for capitalization, capitalize any words that require it.

1. I think midwinter recess is a waste; however, spring vacation is great.

2. Many psychiatrists discount freud's theories, so they try to apply jungian principles to psychoanalysis.

3. Although we are taught that the middle ages was quickly followed by the renaissance, in reality there was quite an overlapping of the two eras.

4. napoleonic france and regency england were bitter enemies.

5. the declaration of independence led to the revolution.

6. even though she's a good teacher, i think it's ridiculous to have a person who doesn't believe in god teach a theology course.

7. Every spring, our grandparents travel east to missouri.

8. although he appears pompous, judge White actually is a decent fellow.

9. Before the child left for school, he kissed his mother.

10. Businesses are rejoicing because christmas sales have increased by 40 percent this year compared to last year.

Check the answer key.

End Punctuation

End punctuation has a very practical purpose; it lets the reader know where each thought ends. Without end punctuation, reading becomes a guessing game.

> Example: The day was bright and sunny, a relief after the weeks of rain however, the weather forecast was dismal it suggested that this was just a brief interlude before another storm what can be done to change the weather.

Obviously, reading that paragraph presents difficulties. It is much simpler to read with the appropriate end punctuation.

> Revision: The day was bright and sunny, a relief after the weeks of rain. However, the weather forecast was dismal. It suggested that this was just a brief interlude before another storm. What can be done to change the weather?

There are three marks of end punctuation, or end stops, as they are sometimes called:

- the period (.)

- the question mark (?)

- the exclamation point (!)

Each end stop performs a different task. The end stops replace the inflection, stress, and pitch of our voices, the clues we use in conversation to help our listener understand our thoughts.

▶ Examples: It's two down and ten to go. (merely a statement of fact)
It's two down and ten to go? (asking for information)
It's two down and ten to go! (an expression of strong emotion)

In each instance, the words are the same, but the intentions are changed by the end stops.

THE PERIOD (.)

The period ends statements, requests, or indirect questions.

▶ Examples: *Statements*
This year, classes will end ten days later than last year.
In fact, blue is a terrible color for her.

Requests
Please turn down the radio.
Kindly hold the elevator door for me.
Mow the lawn today.

Indirect Questions
Please tell me when the spring semester begins.
Let me know whether the item is in stock.
I wonder whether they're going to the show on Thursday.

NOTES: 1. A request does not anticipate a reply. It is assumed that the listener will comply with the request.

2. An indirect question is a tactful way of asking for information; it implies a request for information. It is not as straightforward as a direct question, and in conversation we would not raise the pitch of our voice at the end of the thought, as we do with a direct question.

▼ EXERCISE 9

Following the above examples, correctly end punctuate these sentences.

1. Although this may be hard to believe, soon there will be a glut of lawyers

2. Rather than learning a new trade, he preferred to retire

Have your instructor or tutor check your work.

THE QUESTION MARK (?)

The question mark ends sentences asking for information, that is, direct questions.

▶ Examples: What schedule did you choose?
                 When do you expect to graduate?

NOTE: Direct questions assume that the listener will make a response; the question is a blunt way of seeking information. Usually, a direct question begins with an interrogative pronoun like (*who, which, what*) or adverb (*when, where, why, how*), and its sentence order is inverted; in other words, the verb precedes the subject.

▼ EXERCISE 10

Following the above examples, correctly punctuate these sentences.

1. Do you think the conglomerate should make a bid for that company

2. Have her motives been determined

Have your instructor or tutor check your work.

THE EXCLAMATION POINT (!)

The exclamation point is used to indicate commands, strong emotions, surprise, or, in general, to emphasize thoughts.

▶ Examples: Stop! (command)
                 My son is wounded! (emotion)
                 Oh, my goodness! (surprise)
                 She won't do it! (emphasis)

NOTE: Exclamation points are rarely used in expository writing; they are more suited to dialogue and stories. Therefore, use them carefully and with forethought.

▼ EXERCISE 11

Following the above examples, correctly punctuate these thoughts.

1. What a horrible day

2. Watch out

Have your instructor or tutor check your work.

PRACTICE 4

Correctly punctuate the ends of the following sentences.

1. Since the beginning of time, we have tried to change our environment

2. Where is the seminar being held

3. Are you suggesting that a take-over may be pending

4. Go away

5. Have you found a solution to the problem

6. As you all remember, geometry requires you to memorize proofs

7. Interplanetary space travel is a possibility; one wonders if interstellar space travel can be far behind

8. Most new cars are quite expensive

9. Look out below

10. Some experts maintain that diamonds have lost one-third of their value is that so

Check the answer key.

Other Types of Punctuation

COLONS (:)

Colons inform the reader that the material following the colon is an explanation, illustration, or example of the material that preceded the colon.

▶ Examples: Please buy me some fruit: apples, peaches, pears, and bananas.

She has all the qualities necessary to be a captain: knowledge of navigation, ability to lead and command, and love of the sea.

The American Short Story: An Intriguing Analysis

NOTE: In the last example, the title and subtitle of a book are separated by a colon, because the subtitle provides additional information about the title.

▼ EXERCISE 12

Following the above examples, correctly punctuate these sentences.

1. The bargaining team suggested some novel demands paid paternity leave, on-site day care, and time off for excellent attendance.

2. To bake a great cake, do as he suggested 1) buy a box of cake mix, 2) read the directions carefully, 3) follow them, and 4) nap while the cake is baking.

Have your instructor or tutor check your work.

NOTE: Never use a colon to separate a verb from its object or its predicate nominative, or a preposition from its object.

▶ Examples:

Incorrect:	For her birthday the toddler wanted: a doll house, a doll carriage, and a wagon.
Correct:	For her birthday the toddler wanted a doll house, a doll carriage, and a wagon.
or:	For her birthday, the toddler wanted some expensive gifts: a doll house, a doll carriage, and a wagon.
Incorrect:	For the position of nursing supervisor, he had interviews with: the nursing staff, the nursing director, the chief of the medical staff, and the board of directors.
Correct:	For the position of nursing supervisor, he had interviews with the nursing staff, the nursing director, the chief of the medical staff, and the board of directors.
or:	For the position of nursing supervisor, he had interviews with the following: the nursing staff, the nursing director, the chief of the medical staff, and the board of directors.

▶ PRACTICE 5

Correctly punctuate the following sentences.

1. You must always remember one thing how to whistle.

2. *How to Succeed in Bankruptcy A Primer for the Overextended* has already sold over 500,000 copies.

3. The list of demands is never-ending a color television in the staff lounge, free parking spaces, birthdays and anniversaries off, six weeks of paid vacation, a low-cost lunch program, etc.

Check the answer key.

SEMICOLONS (;)

For a discussion of the use of the semicolon, see Part II, Chapters 5 and 6.

HYPHENS

Hyphens and dashes are frequently confused and misused.

- A **hyphen** (a one-space line) is used to separate elements within a *word*.

- A **dash** (a two-space line) is used to separate elements within a *sentence*.

The hyphen has several uses:

1. *To indicate that a word has been continued from one written line to the next.* When you are writing, it is not always possible to fit a whole word on the end of the typed line. In such a case, it is acceptable to break the word with a hyphen and to continue writing it on the next line.

> ▶ Examples: grada-   humani-   super-   in-   unim-
>   tion   tarian   fluous   active   peachable

In such a case, however, you must follow the rules for syllabication:

- Never divide a one-syllable word.

> ▶ Examples: three, night, clock

- Never leave a one-letter syllable alone on a line.

Incorrect	*Correct*
a-/lone	alone
i-/deal	ideal
i-/conoclast	icono-/clast

If in doubt about correct syllabication, check your dictionary.

2. *To form compound words.* A compound word is composed of two separate words that have been joined to form a new word.

> ▶ Examples: life-style   mother-in-law rock-ribbed

The process of forming compound words is not rigid. Frequently, the words are initially written as separate words; then, they are hyphenated, and, finally, common usage suggests that they be written as one word.

> ▶ Examples: steam ship   steam-ship   steamship
>   home sickness   home-sickness   homesickness

During the intermediate stage, the words should be hyphenated to form one word. If you are unsure whether a compound word is currently hyphenated, check your dictionary.

▼ **EXERCISE 13**

Following the previous examples, correctly punctuate these sentences.

1.   The vice principal issued his orders; the man at arms jumped.

2.   In Biblical times, each family prayed for a man child.

   Have your instructor or tutor check your work.

3.   *To join two words that become a* **compound modifier** *and function as a single adjective does to describe a noun.*

> ▶ Examples: gray-green eyes   wind-blown hair   water-logged motor

▼ **EXERCISE 14**

Following the above examples, correctly punctuate these sentences.

1. The jewel like colors of his evening clothes have made Charles a name to be reckoned with in the fashion world.

2. Bell bottom trousers made the transition from naval uniform to high fashion.

   Have your instructor or tutor check your work.

4.   *To join the prefixes self-, all-, ex-, and the suffix -elect to root words.*

> ▶ Examples: ex-spouse   self-control   all-important

5.   *To join the elements of an improvised compound word.*

> ▶ Examples: smarty-pants   fantasy-land   know-it-all

▼ **EXERCISE 15**

Following the above examples, correctly punctuate these sentences.

1. Many Japanese designers are breaking into the ready to wear market.

2. At home wear has captured a large percentage of the suburban, retail clothing market.

   Have your instructor or tutor check your work.

6. *To join the numerator and the denominator in written fractions, and to join the elements in compound numbers.*

▶ Examples: nine-tenths one-fifth twenty-eight

▼ **EXERCISE 16**

Following the previous examples, correctly punctuate these sentences.

1. Two thirds of the population owns one quarter of the VCR's.

2. Estimates suggest that seventy eight percent of Americans believe in the institution of marriage.

▼ **EXERCISE 17**

Remembering all the rules for using hyphens, correctly punctuate these words.

1. father in law   _____

2. well known   _____

3. four eighths   _____

4. commander in chief   _____

5. swept back   _____

6. governor elect   _____

Have your instructor or tutor check your work.

DASHES

The dash is used in three specific cases:

1. *To indicate a sudden break in thought.*

▶ Examples: He is the world's worst—no, I won't continue.

Maybe you're right—but I want to try this first.

2. *To emphasize a parenthetical element.* (Remember: a parenthetical element is an inserted expression that interrupts the thought of the sentence to explain or comment on it.)

▶ Examples: She was—I thought—a very good chief executive officer.

It is alleged that he knew—that he *must* have known—that his subordinates were breaking the law.

NOTE: It is also possible to separate parenthetical elements from the rest of the sentence by using commas or parentheses; dashes are sometimes preferred, because they add vigor and emphasis to the interruption.

3. *To set off an appositive or brief summary.*

▶ Examples: He has everything he needs—except money.

After a month of bone-chilling cold and mind-rattling wind, our destination was in sight—the tribesmen's camp.

▼ EXERCISE 18

Following the previous examples, correctly punctuate these sentences.

1. After the dance it was such a nice one I thought we could go to the club for drinks.

2. She has vision, competence, and the ability to inspire people everything a CEO should have.

Have your instructor or tutor check your work.

▶ PRACTICE 6

After reviewing the rules for using dashes and hyphens, correctly punctuate these sentences.

1. My brother the one who's the doctor is very soft hearted.

2. I wish I could tell you but I promised!

3. The well known opera star she drinks two thirds of the time has gained weight recently.

4. Thirty two thousand dollars! for a broken finger?

5. The heir apparent has little use for old fashioned conventions.

Check the answer key.

13

Confusing and Often Misused Words

▶ **OBJECTIVES**

1. To recognize words whose spelling and usage are frequently confused.

2. To use these words correctly.

3. To proofread a paper for errors in the use of these words and to use the editing symbol for a wrong word (*ww*) correctly.

▶ **KEY CONCEPT**

Some words are frequently misread and misused because the words are confused with similar-sounding and/or similar-looking words. Sometimes, the confusing words even have similar meanings, but are different parts of speech.

The following list defines each word and uses it correctly in a sentence. Study the list carefully.

1.	a	is used before a word that begins with a consonant sound. He owns *a* horse, *a* car, and *a* boat.
	an	is used before a word that begins with a vowel sound. In *an* hour, Sue will eat *an* egg for breakfast. (The *h* is silent in *hour*, so the first sound you hear is a vowel.)
	and	joins ideas, words, or phrases of equal worth. John *and* Mary went for a ride in a buggy. These words are frequently confused because of poor pronunciation.
2.	accept	means "to receive" or "to get." It is a *verb*. She *accepted* his token of appreciation.
	except	means "not included" or "excluded"; it is a *preposition*. Everyone went skiing *except* Bertha. These words are frequently confused because of poor pronunciation.
3.	advice	means "counsel" or "opinion"; it is a *noun*. Don't accept your mother-in-law's *advice*.
	advise	means "to offer an opinion" or "to offer counsel"; it is a *verb*. In-laws often try to *advise* newlyweds.
4.	affect	means "to influence"; it is a *verb*. Children can be deeply *affected* by the death of a pet.
	effect	as a *noun* means "result" or "consequence." There are many unfortunate *effects* of inflation. as a *verb* means "to cause" or "to bring about." The negotiators labored all night to *effect* a compromise between the opposing unions. Again, confusion results from poor pronunciation.

5.	all ready	means "everyone (or everything) is ready." The foreman told the judge, "We're *all ready* to give our verdict, sir."
	already	means "previously, before, or by a specific time"; it is an *adverb*. The paramedics were *already* at the scene of the accident.
6.	allot	means "to distribute, assign, or give"; it is a *verb*. The camp director *allotted* one bowl of rice and one cup of milk to each refugee.
	a lot	means "plenty of, much of." **NOTE:** It is *never* spelled as one word. He received *a lot* of money for his birthday.
7.	among	is used when discussing *at least three* ideas or concepts; it is a *preposition*. The budget is divided *among* many competing claimants.
	between	is used when discussing *two* concepts or ideas; it is a *preposition*. Let's decide *between* the movie and the party.
8.	borrow	means "to take something with the intention of returning it"; it is a *verb*. Right now, it is hard to *borrow* money for home improvements.
	lend	means "to allow someone to use something, on the condition that it is returned"; it is a *verb*. Many parents *lend* their children the down payment for their first house.
9.	bought	means "purchased"; it is the past tense of the verb *to buy*. They *bought* a new house.
	brought	means "taken from there to here"; it is the past tense of the verb *to bring*. They *brought* a quiche back from the party.
10.	break	means "to crack" or "to destroy"; it is a *verb*. Please be careful with that Ming vase; please do not *break* it.
	brake	as a *verb*, it means "to stop." To avoid hitting the child who had dashed into the street, the bus driver *braked* quickly.

as a *noun*, it means "the mechanical device for slowing the speed of a vehicle or machine."
Our *brakes* squeaked as we slowed for the stop sign.

11.	breath	is the *noun* form. Halitosis is a fancy word for bad *breath*.
	breathe	is the *verb* form. When she has an asthma attack, she can't *breathe*.
12.	bring	means "to cause to come here by carrying or leading"; it is a *verb*. "You may *bring* a friend with you," said the hostess, "provided he *brings* his own food."
	take	means "to grasp or get possession of" and "to carry from here to there"; it is a *verb*. Mothers always admonish their children "to *take* my hand when we cross the street."
13.	burst	means "to explode"; it is a *verb*. In early spring, the forsythia's yellow buds *burst* into bloom.
	bust	as a *verb*, it means "to destroy." (**NOTE:** The verb *bust* is actually slang; as such it rarely belongs in academic writing.) The fragile vase was *busted*.
		as a *noun*, it means "a sculpture of an individual's head and shoulders." A magnificent *bust* of Abraham Lincoln was placed in the Lincoln Monument yesterday.
14.	buy	means "to purchase"; it is a *verb*. She wants to *buy* a new dress for the party.
	by	means "next to, near, or according to"; it is a *preposition*. This article was written *by* a cub reporter.
15.	capital	means "chief, most important," or "money"; it is a *noun*. Business needs *capital* to create jobs. Tallahassee is the *capital* city of Florida.
	capitol	means "the building in which a *state* legislature meets"; it is a *noun*. The legislators burned the midnight oil at the *capitol* last night. When the word is *capitalized*, it refers to the building in Washington in which Congress meets. The president delivered his State of the Union address at the *Capitol* last night.

16.	choose	means "to make a choice"; it is the present-tense form of the verb *to choose*. She must *choose* a major.
	chose	has the same meaning, but is the past-tense form. She finally *chose* architectural engineering.
17.	cite	means "to quote from another source"; it is a *verb*. He *cited* passages from Thoreau's "Civil Disobedience" as his defense.
	site	means "a location for a building or activity"; it is a *noun*. They chose Carmel, California, for the *site* of their vacation home.
	sight	as a *verb*, it means "to get a glimpse of, to see, or to observe." As the weary sailors nearly abandoned hope, they *sighted* land.
		as a *noun*, it means "vision, the ability to see, or something worth seeing." We plan to see the *sights* of Paris this fall.
18.	complement	as a *verb*, it means "to complete or bring to perfection." A good wine *complements* the meal.
	compliment	as a *verb*, it means "to praise." She *complimented* him on his perspicacity.
		as a *noun*, it means "praise." Chefs love to receive a *compliment*.
19.	desert	as a *verb*, it means "to abandon." Soldiers are trained never to *desert* their unit.
		as a *noun*, it means "arid land." The *desert* is considered inhospitable to life.
	dessert	means "a sweet dish at the end of a meal"; it is a *noun*. I prefer ice cream for *dessert*.
20.	fewer	means "a smaller number of, not so many as"; it is an *adjective*. Because she became so cranky, she has *fewer* friends than she used to have.
	less	means "a smaller portion or quantity"; it is an *adjective*. Nowadays, I have *less* trouble meeting people than I used to have.
21.	hear	means "to listen"; it is a *verb*. She never *hears* her mother.

	here	means "a specific place nearby"; it is an *adverb*. Many people claim that George Washington slept *here* in this very bed.
22.	its	shows ownership. It is the *possessive* form, meaning "belonging to it." The boat lost *its* motor.
	it's	is a shortened form of "it is" or "it has." *It's* a nice day today. *It's* been a long time since I last saw you.
23.	lead	as a *verb*, it means "to direct, to guide." The concertmaster will *lead* the orchestra tonight. as a *noun*, it means "the heavy gray metal." There is a high *lead* content in this old paint; it must be removed.
	led	is the past-tense form of "to lead"; it is a *ve4b*. The hikers were *led* to safety by the park ranger.
24.	learn	means "to gain knowledge or understanding"; it is a *verb*. Each person must *learn* from his or her own mistakes.
	teach	means "to instruct, to assist in the learning process"; it is a *verb*. I can *teach* you how to tie your shoelaces, but you must practice it yourself.
25.	leave	means "to cause to remain behind, to go away from"; it is a *verb*. He must *leave* his teddy bear home when we *leave* for camp.
	let	means "to cause to, to allow to"; it is a *verb*. The stuck valve *let* the water pour through the broken water main.
26.	loose	means "not tight"; it is an *adjective*. Babies should wear *loose* clothing.
	lose	means "misplaced or lost"; it is a *verb*. Johnny frequently *loses* his money on his way to school.
27.	passed	means "went by"; it is the past-tense form of the verb *to pass*. The parade *passed* this way an hour ago.
	past	as a *noun*, it means "in former times." History teaches us about the *past*. as a *preposition*, it means to "go beyond." We drove *past* the haunted house.

as an *adjective*, it means "belonging to previous times."
The *past* decade brought many changes to America.

28.	precede	means "to come before"; it is a *verb*. The seniors will *precede* the juniors in the ceremony.
	proceed	means "to go on" and "to continue"; it is a *verb*. *Proceed* with your implausible story.
29.	principal	as an *adjective*, it means "chief, main, or most important." He is the union's *principal* negotiator. as a *noun*, it means "the head of a school." The *principal* sets school policy.
	principle	means "a fundamental truth or rule"; it is a *noun*. You must study geometric *principle* if you want to be an architect.
30.	quiet	as a *noun*, it means "peace and calm." Dad enjoys the quiet in the woods. as an *adjective*, it means "without noise." Libraries are *quiet* places.
	quite	is an *adverb* meaning "positively or really." She is *quite* an aristocrat.
31.	raise	means "to increase in height" and "to obtain"; it is a *verb*. Please *raise* the window; this room is stuffy.
	rise	means "to get up" and "to move upward"; it is a *verb*. The stock market's value is *rising*.
32.	right	as a *noun*, it means "privilege or claim." Our *rights* as American citizens are protected by the Constitution. as an *adjective*, it means "correct." Terrance gave the *right* answer to the calculus problem.
	rite	means "a ceremony, often religious"; it is a *noun*. There are few formal *rites* of passage for today's youth.
	write	means "to form letters on a surface, usually by means of a pen and paper"; it is a *verb*. Please *write* your address on your application.
33.	stationary	means "not moving"; it is an *adjective*. Mountains are usually *stationary* objects.
	stationery	means "writing paper"; it is a *noun*. Some correspondents try to get attention by using lilac *stationery*.

34.	suppose	means "to guess or assume"; it is a *verb*. I *suppose* he is coming to the wedding.
	supposed	implies an obligation; it means "should"; it is the past tense of the verb *suppose*. She was *supposed* to babysit for me tonight.
35.	than	is used when comparing two items; it is a *subordinate conjunction*. She is taller *than* her brother.
	then	refers to time; it is an *adverb*. *Then* the dog began chasing the cat.
36.	their	is the *possessive* form meaning "belonging to them." Those poor people lost *their* homes.
	there	is an *adverb* that refers to a place. I distinctly remember putting the keys right *there*.
	they're	is a *contraction*, a shortened form of "they are." *They're* going on a long vacation to New Zealand.
37.	thorough	means "complete"; it is an *adjective*. Hallie made a *thorough* search of the house for the missing car keys.
	through	means "to pass between or to move from one end to the other"; it is a *preposition*. On her way from New York to Florida, Janice will pass *through* seven states.
38.	to	means "toward or in the direction of"; it is a *preposition*. They are going *to* the movies.
	too	means "also" or "more than enough"; it is an *adverb*. I ate *too* much cake yesterday.
	two	refers to the number that is the sum of one plus one; it is an *adjective*. The child has *two* dollars to spend on a gift for his mother.
39.	weather	refers to the climate; it is a *noun*. The *weather* report for today is sunny.
	whether	indicates that one must make a decision; it is a *conjunction*. She doesn't know *whether* to go to law school or graduate school.
40.	who's	is a *contraction*, a shortened form of "who is." The police don't know *who's* the burglar.

	whose	is the *possessive* form meaning "belonging to whom." *Whose* hat is this?
41.	use	means "to make use of, or to employ"; it is a *verb*. Do you know how to *use* a dictionary?
	used	means "was accustomed to or was in the habit of"; it is the past tense of the verb *use*. I *used* to like pizza until I developed an allergy to cheese.
42.	your	is the *possessive* form meaning "belonging to you." Where is *your* warm-up suit?
	you're	is a *contraction*, a shortened form of "you are." *You're* a big bore!

PRACTICE

Underline the word that best fits the meaning of the sentence.

1. Because (its, it's) (a, an, and) beautiful day, I've decided to (accept, except) (your, you're) invitation.

2. (To, Two, Too) days before, he decided that (to, too, two) many people were involved.

3. George, Tom, (a, an, and) Harry were gravely (affected, effected) by (their, there, they're) first-grade teachers.

4. She (use, used) to go swimming every day.

5. (Hear, Here) are the books, and (their, there, they're) are the students.

6. If you climb four flights of stairs, (your, you're) likely to (loose, lose) (your, you're) (breath, breathe).

7. First, you must (choose, chose) (among, between) French, German, and Italian for (your, you're) language requirement.

8. You weren't (suppose, supposed) to do that!

9. Have you (passed, past) any course yet?

10. On his (advice, advise) she (bought, brought) some stock with all her available (capital, capitol).

11. (Who's, whose) to say that sunny (weather, whether) is the best?

12. Are you (quiet, quite) sure he meant to (complement, compliment) her on the (dessert, desert)?

13. I (adviced, advised) him to quit his job (quiet, quite) a long time ago.

14. (Weather, Whether) or not you (use, used) to eat strawberries is not important.

15. The (passed, past) few weeks have been (quiet, quite) hard on her.

16. The millionaire couldn't decide whether to (leave, let) his money to charity or to his wastrel nephew.

17. Light beer, which is really just a watered-down product, has (fewer, less) calories (than, then) regular beer.

18. Ever since she was a child, that girl has had (allot, a lot) of problems.

19. If the school goes to Washington, D.C., will the students visit the (capital, capitol, Capitol)?

20. Many people misunderstand (a, an, and) instructor's function: it is to (learn, teach). Only the student can (learn, teach).

PART II

Introduction

▶ **PRACTICE**

1. In—preposition
   tuition—noun
   has risen—verb
2. Boy!—interjection
   gorgeous—adjective
3. and—coordinate
   conjunction
   must serve—verb
4. seems—verb (linking)
5. society—adjective
   revealing—adjective
   memorable—adjective
6. slowly, gracefully—adverbs
   however—adverbial
   conjunction
7. although—subordinate
   conjunction
   she—personal pronoun,
   nominative case
   and—coordinate
   conjunction
8. Oh my gosh!—interjection
   kerosene—adjective
   has—helping verb
9. Everyone—indefinite

pronoun
should—helping verb
to—preposition
10. Warden James—proper
    noun
    vicious—adjective
    mass—adjective
11. danced, sang—verbs
    before—subordinate
    conjunction
12. with—preposition
    purple—adjective
    by—preposition
13. Shyness—noun
    characteristics—noun
    of—preposition
14. We—personal pronoun,
    nominative case
    or—coordinate
    conjunction
    to—preposition
15. You—personal pronoun,
    nominative case
    my—personal pronoun,
    possessive case

that—demonstrative
pronoun
very—adverb
16. Jerome—proper noun
    failed—verb
    his—personal pronoun,
    possessive case
    for—coordinate
    conjunction
17. On—preposition
    summer—noun
    by—preposition
    Andorra—proper noun
    near—preposition
    at—preposition
    of—preposition
18. useful—adjective
    informative—adjective
19. gleefully—adverb
    as—subordinate
    conjunction
    quickly—adverb
    through—preposition
20. have been rejected—verb
    too—adverb

Chapter 1

▶ PRACTICE 1

1. action	6. linking
2. linking	7. action
3. action	8. action
4. action	9. action
5. linking	10. action

▶ PRACTICE 2

1. he	6. it
2. she	7. they
3. it	8. they
4. it	9. they
5. it	10. we

▶ PRACTICE 3

1. I walk / we walk
   you walk / you walk
   he, she, it walks / they walk
2. I read / we read
   you read / you read
   he, she, it reads / they read
3. I dance / we dance
   you dance / you dance
   he, she, it dances / they dance
4. I hide / we hide
   you hide / you hide
   he, she, it hides / they hide
5. I call / we call
   you call / you call
   he, she, it calls / they call

▶ PRACTICE 4

1. talks	6. have
2. runs	7. visit
3. have, has	8. draws, are
4. is	9. drives
5. are	10. are, is

▶ PRACTICE 5

1. all forms take *danced*
2. all forms take *poured*
3. all forms take *marked*
4. all forms take *painted*
5. all forms take *called*

▶ PRACTICE 6

1. sang	6. visited, went
2. wrote	7. was
3. went, felt	8. brought
4. brought, experienced	9. enlisted
5. read	10. reached, dropped

▶ PRACTICE 7

1. will (shall) complete
2. will ask
3. Will (you) be
4. will run
5. will sell
6. Will (they) meet
7. will travel
8. will benefit
9. will be
10. will succeed

▶ PRACTICE 8

1. correct
2. decided, fumbled
3. was, correct, began, cooked
4. correct, scraped, correct
5. returned, waited, tossed
6. correct
7. do, run
8. do
9. correct, go
10. correct, put, remain
11. learned

Chapter 2

▶ PRACTICE 1

Infinitive	Past	Past Participle
1. to dive	dived (dove)	dived
2. to sing	sang	sung

	Infinitive	*Past*	*Past Participle*
3.	to write	wrote	written
4.	to fly	flew	flown
5.	to drink	drank	drunk
6.	to steal	stole	stolen
7.	to teach	taught	taught
8.	to learn	learned	learned
9.	to give	gave	given
10.	to receive	received	received

▶ PRACTICE 2

1. have had
2. has been
3. has been
4. have visited
5. has become
6. have received
7. has bought
8. has raced
9. have seen
10. have enrolled

▶ PRACTICE 3

1. had been
2. had finished
3. had completed
4. had called
5. had defused
6. had determined
7. had made
8. had completed
9. had chosen
10. had moved

▶ PRACTICE 4

1. will have been
2. will have worked
3. will have finished
4. will have been
5. will have welcomed
6. will have taught
7. will have read
8. will have celebrated
9. will have submitted
10. will have thrown

▶ PRACTICE 5

1. I am asking
2. They had been doing
3. We will be singing
4. He has been hitting
5. You will have been dealing
6. They were swimming

▶ PRACTICE 6

1. will have been dancing
2. is completing
3. was bathing
4. has been working
5. has been going
6. will be leaving
7. was working, is practicing
8. is working, have been burning
9. was running, is operating
10. will be playing

▶ PRACTICE 7

1. should have danced
2. has been teaching
3. does plan
4. had crawled
5. was
6. had been doing
7. did live
8. will have been competing
9. had nominated
10. has accepted

▶ PRACTICE 8

1. he *took*
2. players *were*
3. students *fail*
4. it *was working*
5. *The Great Gatsby was published*
6. word processor *will replace*
7. he *turned*
8. he *developed*
9. thousands of athletes *will have arrived*
10. we *missed*

▶ PRACTICE 9

1. would have passed
2. did have
3. correct
4. is
5. have tried
6. attend
7. are
8. manage

Chapter 3

▶ PRACTICE 3

Verb	Subject
1. laughs	Terry
2. play	children
3. hit	bullet
4. swam	I
5. fainted	doctor

▶ PRACTICE 4

Verb	Subject
1. are	Fords, Chevrolets
2. hissed, scratched	cat
3. read, study	Caleb, Rachel
4. became	Angela
5. took	Carl, Martha
6. seemed	Tina
7. are	Ice cream, cake
8. are	Puerto Rico, St. Thomas
9. appears	Nita
10. leaped, swam	dolphin

▶ PRACTICE 5

Verb	Subject
1. are	friends
2. is	manuscript
3. are	ball, bat
4. is	answer
5. come	boyfriend, girl

▶ PRACTICE 6

Verb	Subject
1. will have left	Tom
2. will have been	senator
3. had been demolished	car
4. will be released	animals
5. was playing	jockey

▶ PRACTICE 7

1. The *cat ran* ~~under the porch~~.
     (S: cat, V: ran)

2. *Bronco Davis was* a famous football player ~~for twenty years~~.
     (S, V)

3. The *greyhound* ~~with the matted coat and an evil look in his eyes~~ *frightened* the schoolchildren.
     (S, V)

4. The *drive* ~~to Orlando~~ *is* a pleasant one.
     (S, V)

5. *Bing Crosby* and *Bob Hope were* a successful team ~~for more than fifteen years~~.
     (S, S, V)

▶ PRACTICE 8

	Subject	Verb	Object		Format
1.	Tom	forgot		1	S-V
2.	band	won	contest	2	S-V-DO
3.	Helen	read	book	2	S-V-DO
4.	I	swam		1	S-V
5.	dog	crossed	road	2	S-V-DO
6.	arrow	struck	tree	2	S-V-DO
7.	team	lost		1	S-V
8.	child	broke	vase	2	S-V-DO

▶ PRACTICE 9

	Subject	Verb	Object		Format
1.	police	caught	thief	2	S-V-DO
2.	television	broke		1	S-V
3.	horse	won	Triple Crown	2	S-V-DO
4.	children	jumped	fence	2	S-V-DO
5.	Mary	cried		1	S-V
6.	moon	rose		1	S-V
7.	fullback	caught	football	2	S-V-DO
8.	rooster	crowed		1	S-V
9.	airplane	left	runway	2	S-V-DO
10.	diver	speared	barracuda	2	S-V-DO
11.	shoelaces	broke		1	S-V
12.	president	fired	assistant	2	S-V-DO
13.	speaker	declined	invitation	2	S-V-DO
14.	chair	fell		1	S-V
15.	Children	like	ice cream	2	S-V-DO

▶ PRACTICE 10

	Subject	Verb	IO	DO
1.	Tim	awarded	henry	prize
2.	boy	bought	girl	flower
3.	man	handed	girlfriend	ring
4.	teacher	gave	me	mark
5.	Tim	fed	dog	dinner
6.	bird	built	mate	nest
7.	I	gave	friend	umbrella
8.	She	brought	Jim	soda
9.	kidnappers	gave	child	bar
10.	Sharon	bought	father	sweater

▶ PRACTICE 11

	PA-S	LV	Format
1.	powerful weightlifter	is	S-LV-PA
2.	sad Tom	appears	S-LV-PA
3.	happy Mary	looks	S-LV-PA
4.	good dinner	tasted	S-LV-PA
5.	cooperative Earl Bruce	was	S-LV-PA
6.	angry cat	sounds	S-LV-PA
7.	tired He	seems	S-LV-PA
8.	sour onion	smells	S-LV-PA
9.	rough road	becomes	S-LV-PA
10.	red, delicious apple	was	S-LV-PA

▶ PRACTICE 12

	Verb	Format	
1.	branded	calf-DO	2
2.	looks	expensive-PA	4
3.	enjoy	books-DO	2
4.	struck	rock-DO	2
5.	are	dirty-PA	4
6.	were	pretty-PA	4
7.	serves	food-DO	2
8.	has	water-DO	2
9.	looks	interested-PA	4
10.	seemed	uneasy-PA	4

▶ PRACTICE 13

	Subject	Linking Verb	Predicate Nominative
1.	senator	is	chairman
2.	Annapolis	is	capital
3.	desk	is	antique
4.	Shawn	became	astronaut
5.	John	is	player
6.	Jane	is	force
7.	Television	is	one
8.	She	is	actress
9.	girl	is	cousin
10.	alligator	is	symbol

▶ PRACTICE 14

	Subject	LV	PA	PN	Format
1.	She	is		girl	S-LV-PN
2.	ideas	are	ambiguous		S-LV-PA
3.	Students	seem	busy		S-LV-PA
4.	Doctors, lawyers	are		professionals	S-LV-PN
5.	teachers	are	enthusiastic		S-LV-PA
6.	Discos	are		alleys	S-LV-PN
7.	Records, tapes	are	expensive		S-LV-PA
8.	craze	is		mini-skirt	S-LV-PN
9.	Faulkner	was		one	S-LV-PN
10.	Silence, patience	are		virtues	S-LV-PN

▶ PRACTICE 15

	Subject	Verb	IO	DO/PA or PN	Abbreviation	Format
1.	She	is		star-PN	S-LV-PN	4
2.	coach	gave	Tom	equipment-DO	S-V-IO-DO	3

Subject	Verb	IO	DO/PA or PN	Abbreviation	Format
3. bread	tastes		stale-PA	S-LV-PA	4
4. dog	caught		stick-DO	S-V-DO	2
5. man	gave	child	dollar-DO	S-V-IO-DO	3
6. I	walked			S-V	1
7. runner	became		hero-PN	S-LV-PN	4
8. Women	have joined		clubs-DO	S-V-DO	2
9. Kim	sang		aria-DO	S-V-DO	2
10. horse	tripped			S-V	1
11. Connors	is		player-PN	S-LV-PN	4
12. lawyer	gave	client	advice-DO	S-V-IO-DO	3
13. student	was		sick-PA	S-LV-PA	4
14. Maria	invited		Brad-DO	S-V-DO	2
15. dog	growled			S-V	1
16. roses	are		gift-PN	S-LV-PN	4
17. Bob	caught		fish-DO	S-V-DO	2
18. Doctors	seem		intelligent-PA	S-LV-PA	4
19. He	gave	me	present-DO	S-V-IO-DO	3
20. picture	appears		faded-PA	S-LV-PA	4

▶ PRACTICE 16

1. Imperative	6. Declarative
2. Interrogative	7. Interrogative
3. Declarative	8. Imperative
4. Exclamatory	9. Exclamatory
5. Imperative	10. Declarative

Chapter 4

▶ PRACTICE 1

1. Frag   3. C   5. C   7. Frag   9. C
2. Frag   4. Frag   6. C   8. Frag   10. Frag
Have your instructor or tutor check your corrections.

Chapter 5

▶ PRACTICE 1

1. CS   excellent/we
2. CS   1930s/*Cabaret*
3. CS   movie/he
4. CS   accident/no
5. CS   teller/she

▶ PRACTICE 2

1. C
2. CS   job; she *or* and, she
3. CS   high; I
4. CS   beach; however,
5. CS   Park, for
6. C
7. C
8. CS   inadequate; each
9. C
10. CS   poet; he
Have your instructor or tutor check your corrections.

Chapter 6

▶ PRACTICE 1

1. RO   friend/he
2. C
3. RO   move/many
4. RO   dancer/she
5. C
Have your instructor or tutor check your corrections.

▶ PRACTICE 2

1. C	6. C
2. RO	7. RO
3. RO	8. RO
4. RO	9. C
5. C	10. RO

Have your instructor or tutor check your corrections.

Chapter 7

▶ PRACTICE 1

1. S	6. P
2. P	7. P
3. P	8. P
4. S	9. S
5. P	10. S

▶ PRACTICE 2

1. The boys laugh at the clown.
2. The mice hide in the pantry.
3. The examinations seem difficult.
4. The puppies nip at my heels.
5. The girls dive into the water.

▶ PRACTICE 3

S or P	Subject	Verb
1. S	cat	carried
2. S	child	screamed
3. P	dolphins	are
4. S	Hank Thompson	answers
5. P	gardens	grow
6. P	grades	depend
7. S	Tim	works
8. S	Chrysler	was
9. P	dogs	bark
10. P	They	sat
11. P	millionaires	own
12. P	headaches	are caused
13. S	desk	was
14. S	actor	is
15. P	books	make
16. S	adolescent	faces
17. S	bowl	is

S or P	Subject	Verb
18. S	chair	is
19. S	song	was
20. S	player	smashes

▶ PRACTICE 4

1. The student always feels. . . .
2. A dog is usually considered. . . .
3. A child loves . . .
4. The nation has amassed . . .
5. The plant needs . . .

▶ PRACTICE 5

S or P	Subject	Verb
1. S	person	enjoys
2. S	All	was
3. P	Some	have
4. S	Each	plays
5. S	Neither	wants
6. P	All	enjoy
7. S	teenager	wants
8. P	horses	gallop
9. P	adults	enjoy
10. S	Half	was

▶ PRACTICE 6

S or P	Subject	Verb
1. S	gaggle	has
2. S	*The Crusaders*	is
3. S	measles	is
4. P	trousers	have
5. S	pounds	is

▶ PRACTICE 7

S or P	Subject	Verb
1. P	Jack and Eileen	want
2. P	union representatives	want
3. S	George	swims
4. S	husband	has
5. P	quiche, hash	don't

► PRACTICE 8

S or P	Subject	Verb
1. S	who (refers to Fitzgerald)	was
2. P	who (refers to lawyers)	select
3. S	that (refers to one)	is
4. S	which (refers to monument)	is
5. S	who (refers to only one)	enjoys

► PRACTICE 9

S or P	Subject	Verb
1. P	people	are
2. P	courthouse, church	stand
3. P	letters	are
4. P	forms	were
5. S	fortune	lies

Chapter 8

► PRACTICE 1

	Nominative	Objective	Possessive
1. dock	it	it	its
2. dog	it	it	its
3. Harry and Ellen	they	hem	their, theirs
4. James and I	we	us	our, ours
5. Sara	she	her	her, hers

► PRACTICE 2

1. she
2. they
3. their
4. my
5. her/his

► PRACTICE 3

Pronoun	Antecedent
1. her	Maria
2. you, your	Mr. Roberts
3. her	teacher
4. his	radiologist
5. her	lawyer
6. we	Steve and I
7. its	horse
8. them	books

Pronoun	Antecedent
9. her	grandmother
10. it	industry
11. it	pen
12. you	Bonnie and Jack
13. them	plants
14. her	mother
15. it	novel

► PRACTICE 4

1. it	6. her	11. It
2. She	7. his	12. they
3. We	8. it	13. They
4. he	9. their	14. It
5. he/she	10. He/She	15. They

► PRACTICE 5

Pronoun	Antecedent
1. their	societies
2. its	herd
3. his/her	Everybody
4. their	players
5. their	some
6. its	company
7. its	class
8. her	neither
9. its	board
10. their	women
11. its	flock
12. their	all
13. their	dean, associates
14. their	doctor, staff
15. its	*New England Journal of Medicine*

Chapter 9

► PRACTICE 1

1. C
2. C
3. P schoolyard, for
4. P hour, but
5. P hour, and

▶ PRACTICE 2

1. P   Datsuns, Toyotas, and
2. P   Ways, M&Ms, and
3. C
4. P   Christmas, Thanksgiving, and
5. P   cleaners, . . . milk, and

▶ PRACTICE 3

1. P   harsh,
2. C
3. P   dirty,
4. P   short,
5. C

▶ PRACTICE 4

1. P   before,
2. C
3. P   road,
4. P   him,
5. P   graded,

▶ PRACTICE 5

1. P   December 7, 1941,
2. P   Avenue, Washington, D.C.
3. C
4. C
5. P   July, 1993 or C

▶ PRACTICE 6

1. P   jumping,
2. P   nine,
3. P   old,
4. P   thirty,
5. C

Chapter 10

▶ PRACTICE 1

1. MacBride,
2. thinks, Charles,
3. Honor,
4. parade,
5. tonight,

▶ PRACTICE 2

1. understand,"
2. "Bugs," . . . primly, "are
3. emphatically,
4. interested,"
5. declared,

▶ PRACTICE 3

1. C
2. P   Smith, Sally's neighbor,
3. P   George, a famous panhandler,
4. P   Carter, . . . executive,
5. P   brother, Harry,

▶ PRACTICE 4

1. P   child, bright and witty,
2. P   man, . . . undaunted,
3. P   spring, . . . uplifting,
4. P   boy, . . . time,
5. C

▶ PRACTICE 5

1. P   Parrots, . . . speech,
2. P   Puppies, . . . cute,
3. P   dress, . . . often,
4. C
5. C

▶ PRACTICE 6

1. P   fact,
2. C
3. P   Surprisingly,
4. P   conclude,
5. P   Darlingston, . . . not,

Chapter 11

▶ PRACTICE 1

1. the school's rules
2. someone's idea
3. some people's responses

4. the agency's regulations
5. Thelma and Gene's child
6. Mr. Grant's and Mr. Stone's families
7. my mother-in-law's quilt
8. the thief's motives
9. the congregation's responses
10. the crowd's insults

▶ PRACTICE 2

1. the team's ball
2. the rabbi's work
3. the bus's passengers
4. the buses' passengers
5. someone's record
6. Ms. Jones's credit cards
7. the tennis pro's racquet
8. today's weather conditions
9. the Marines' motto
10. America's national anthem
11. the commander-in-chief's responsibilities
12. his grandparents' refrigerator
13. Jack and Tony's restaurants
14. Jack's and Tony's restaurants
15. the movie's special effects
16. the people's concern
17. I won't
18. he can't
19. they've
20. *several's*
21. *yet's*
22. Brazil's jungles
23. the salespeople's wares
24. the soldier's uniform
25. *z's*

Chapter 12

▶ PRACTICE 1

1. There
2. I, In, I
3. Ye, I
4. According
5. He, Close, Ringed

▶ PRACTICE 2

1. President, Ford's Theater
2. *Mountain Eagle*
3. American Workers Association, Tall Oaks Community Hospital
4. none
5. Wheaties, Rice Krispies

▶ PRACTICE 3

1. none
2. Freud's, Jungian
3. Middle Ages, Renaissance
4. Napoleonic France, Regency England
5. The Declaration of Independence, Revolution
6. Even, I, God
7. Missouri
8. Although, Judge
9. none
10. Christmas

▶ PRACTICE 4

1. .		6. .
2. ?		7. .
3. ?		8. .
4. ! *or* .		9. !
5. ?		10. value. so?

▶ PRACTICE 5

1. thing:
2. *Bankruptcy:*
3. never-ending:

▶ PRACTICE 6

1. brother—, doctor—, soft-hearted
2. you—
3. well-known, star—, two-thirds, time—
4. thirty-two, dollars!—
5. heir-apparent, old-fashioned

Chapter 13

▶ PRACTICE

1. it's, a, accept, your
2. Two, too
3. and, affected, their
4. used
5. Here, there
6. you're, lose, your, breath
7. choose, among, your
8. supposed
9. passed
10. advice, bought, capital
11. Who's, weather
12. quite, compliment, dessert
13. advised, quite
14. Whether, used
15. past, quite
16. leave
17. fewer, than
18. a lot
19. Capitol
20. an, teach, learn

▼ Acknowledgments

PHOTO CREDITS

p. 1: Frank Ward / © Amherst College; p. 23: © Christopher Brown / Stock Boston; p. 25: courtesy *Choctaw Community News*, Mississippi Band of Choctaw; p. 63: © Dean Abramson / Stock Boston; p. 95: Frank Ward / © Amherst College; p. 129: © Frank Ward; p. 173: Frank Ward / © Amherst College; p. 199: © John Blaustein / Woodfin Camp and Associates; p. 237: © Larry Kolvoord / Texas Stock; p. 269: © William Meyer / Tony Stone, Inc.; p. 299: © Kenneth Murray / Photo Researchers, Inc.; p. 335: © Barerra / Texas Stock; p. 337: © Mark Antman / The Image Works; p. 347: © Tim Davis / Photo Researchers, Inc.; p. 361: © Mike Valeri / FPG International, Inc.; p. 375: © James Carroll; p. 403: © Tom Cheek / Stock Boston; p. 409: © Tim Davis / Photo Researchers, Inc.; p. 417: © Anestis Diakopoulos / Stock Boston; p. 423: © Lehtikuva/Pentti Kushkinen / Woodfin Camp and Associates; p. 439: © Joe Epstein / Design Conceptions; p. 451: © Larry Kolvoord / Texas Stock; p. 461: © UPI / Bettmann Newsphotos; p. 473: © Jean-Claude Lejeune; p. 495: Frank Ward / © Amherst College.

TEXT CREDITS

Russell Baker, "Little Red Riding Hood Revisited" by Russell Baker, January 13, 1980. Copyright © 1980 by The New York Times Company. Reprinted by permission.

Jacob Bowers, "Backtracking" by Jacob Bowers. Reprinted courtesy Petersen's *Hunting* Magazine. Originally appeared in Petersen's *Hunting* Magazine, July 1991.

Peter Elbow, "Desperation Writing" from *Writing Without Teachers*, by Peter Elbow. Copyright © 1973, by Oxford University Press, Inc. Reprinted by permission.

Martin Gansberg, "38 Who Saw Murder Didn't Call Police," by Martin Gansberg, March 27, 1964. Copyright © 1964 by The New York Times Company. Reprinted by permission.

Holly Hall, "Fame in the Family" by Holly Hall from *Psychology Today* (April 1988). Reprinted with permission from Psychology Today Magazine. Copyright © 1988 (Sussex Publishers, Inc.).

Marvin Harris, from *Cows, Pigs, Wars and Witches* by Marvin Harris, Copyright © 1974 by Marvin Harris. Reprinted by permission of Random House, Inc.

S. I. Hiyakawa, "How Dictionaries Are Made" from *Language and Thought and Action*, fourth edition by S. I. Hiyakawa. Copyright 1978 by Harcourt Brace Jovanovich, Inc., reprinted by permission of the publisher.

Margaret Mead and Rhoda Metraux, "On Friendship" from *A Way of Seeing*, by Margaret Mead and Rhoda Metraux. Copyright © 1961, 1962, 1963, 1964, 1965,

1966, 1967, 1968, 1969, 1970 by Margaret Mead and Rhoda Metraux. By permission of William Morrow & Company, Inc.

H.L. Mencken, "The Boons of Civilization" from *A Mencken Chrestomathy* by H. L. Mencken. Copyright 1931 by Alfred A. Knopf, Inc. and renewed 1959 by August Mencken and the Mercantile Safe Deposit & Trust Co. Reprinted by permission of Alfred A. Knopf, Inc.

Elizabeth Stark, "Beyond Rivalry" by Elizabeth Stark from *Psychology Today* (April 1988). Reprinted with permission from Psychology Today Magazine. Copyright © 1988 (Sussex Publishers, Inc.).

John Steinbeck, from *The Grapes of Wrath* by John Steinbeck. Copyright 1939, renewed © 1967 by John Steinbeck. Used by permission of Viking Penguin, a division of Penguin Books USA, Inc.

Judith Viorst, "Friends, Good Friends — and Such Good Friends," Copyright © 1977 by Judith Viorst. Originally appeared in *Redbook*. Reprinted by permission of Lescher & Lescher, Ltd.

E. B. White, excerpt from "Here Is New York" from *Essays of E.B. White* by E.B. White. Copyright 1949 by E. B. White. Reprinted by permission of HarperCollins Publishers.

Instructor's Guide for
THE COMPLETE
PARAGRAPH WORKOUT BOOK

Instructor's Guide for
THE COMPLETE
PARAGRAPH WORKOUT BOOK

SECOND EDITION

CAROLYN H. FITZPATRICK

University of Maryland—Baltimore County

MARYBETH B. RUSCICA

St. Vincent's College of St. John's University

Instructor's Guide prepared by
CHERYL L. WARE

McNeese State University

D. C. Heath and Company
Lexington, Massachusetts   Toronto

Address editorial correspondence to:

D. C. Heath
125 Spring Street
Lexington, MA 02173

Published simultaneously in Canada.

Printed in the United States of America.

International Standard Book Number: 0-669-32799-9

10 9 8 7 6 5 4 3 2 1

Preface

As with the Instructor's Guide to the previous edition of *The Complete Paragraph Workout Book*, this Instructor's Guide is meant to complement the classroom text by offering additional information useful to the teacher as well as the students. The following features are included in the Instructor's Guide:

1. Teaching and The Writing Process: Methods of teaching composition have changed in the last twenty years or so. This section briefly discusses those changes.

2. Prewriting Techniques: This section provides a quick overview of prewriting techniques.

3. Peer Groups and Collaborative Learning: Many exercises in *The Complete Paragraph Workout Book* suggest that students work collaboratively in peer groups. This part of the Guide discusses the value of collaborative group work and the use of peer groups in the writing process.

4. Journals: Along with collaborative learning, journals are useful strategies in any class. This section of the Guide examines the different types and uses of journals.

5. Revision Worksheets: Basic guides for revising paragraphs and essays and for editing and proofreading are included to help students revise and edit their work in groups. These suggestions are based upon the guidelines outlined in specific chapters and may be expanded, as appropriate, for each class.

6. Sample Syllabi: This Instructor's Guide includes two sample syllabi, one for a regular semester of about 15 weeks and one for a quarter-term semester of 10 weeks.

7. Grading: This section briefly discusses grading techniques and methods.

8. Teaching Objectives: The beginning of each chapter includes an outline of the teaching objectives stated in the text.

9. Teaching Suggestions: The beginning of each chapter provides teaching suggestions for classroom instruction, with specific activities.

10. Additional Activities: In Part One, Chapters One through Nine contain recommended activities for reading and composing that may help students learn the key strategies presented in these chapters.

11. Answers for Exercises and Model Paragraphs and Essays: An answer key is included for exercises with objective answers. However, some exercises require students to generate their own answers; in these cases, an answer key is unnecessary. Reading levels based on the Fog Index are also provided for each model paragraph and essay.

12. Checklists for Writing and Rhetorical Strategies: Checklists for each writing and rhetorical strategy are included to guide students in their revisions.

13. A Bibliography for Writing Teachers: At the end of the Instructor's Guide, you will find a brief bibliography of works on writing, the writing process, and the teaching of writing. This bibliography is not meant to be exhaustive.

Cheryl L. Ware

Table of Contents

▼ Part I   Composing Paragraphs and Essays   19

▼ Part II   Grammar Review   89

Teaching and the Writing Process

In the last twenty years or so, a major shift has occurred in the way we think about and teach composition. Previous instruction focused almost exclusively on writing as product, and students were commonly given a single class period in which to choose a topic, write a rough draft, and complete a final draft. Only minor attention—no more than a passing mention at best—was given to how to achieve that product.

Current rhetorical theory emphasizes a focus on process rather than product, with much time and attention given to the various steps involved in achieving a final draft. The research in composition and rhetoric is substantial and growing.

Most important is the recognition that the writing process is recursive in nature, not neatly linear with clearly defined and separate stages.

The focus on process recognizes the following stages of writing:

1. Prewriting: any activity that generates information for writing. (See the section on prewriting.)

2. Writing: also called composing or drafting. There should be at least two versions, a rough and a final draft, but students are encouraged to write as many drafts as necessary.

3. Sharing: allowing someone else to read or listen to the piece; this can be part of peer group work or it could be for the entire class.

4. Revision: literally "re-vision"—seeing the piece again. A writer may rewrite a draft for unity, organization, development, and so forth.

5. Editing: proofreading and correcting grammar and mechanics.

6. Publishing: a finished piece is read aloud, turned in, placed in a class anthology, or otherwise made public.

Another element that has changed is the focus upon grammar. Research shows that grammar drills alone do not insure that students will write grammatically correct prose but merely that they will be able to recognize certain features; only grammar study in the context of students' own writing will be truly effective. Thus, grammar study should not be isolated from writing, but rather an integral part of it. Technical knowledge of grammar is not necessary for adequate writing but does provide part of a common language for discussing weaknesses and strengths in writing. For the more advanced writers, in fact, knowing technical details of grammar can be part of rhetorical choice.

Prewriting Techniques

Also known as invention or planning, prewriting is that part of the writing process devoted to generating ideas and to stimulating thought. After all, without ideas, writers have nothing to say. There are a variety of prewriting techniques— some more structured than others, some more particular than others. Different techniques will help different students. The following list briefly describes several of these techniques.

Freewriting: writing without stopping, often for set periods of time; writing without worrying about grammar. Freewriting allows the writer to jot down ideas and impressions in a stream of consciousness. It can be unfocused, without any kind of prompt, so that the student simply writes about whatever enters his or her mind, or it can be focused by a prompt such as music, pictures, and so on.

Brainstorming: listing ideas, usually related to a very general topic. There is no particular order here; ideas are simply jotted down as they come. Students can brainstorm individually, in small groups, or in large groups.

Clustering: also called mapping, and related to charting; a graphic presentation of ideas. A word or phrase acts as a stimulus for recording all of the associations that spring to mind in a short time period. The key word or phrase appears in a circle in the middle, and associated words appear in other circles; those words may themselves branch off into other ideas. The cluster resembles a wheel with spokes.

Charting: a graphic presentation of ideas. This technique uses a chart to categorize information—advantages, disadvantages; similarities, differences; sensory details.

Looping: Peter Elbow's method for discovering ideas; rather like freewriting; a way of narrowing a topic, of focusing an idea. In looping, the writer starts with a specific topic and writes without stopping for a set amount of time (usually 5–15 minutes). The writer stops, looks for a "hot spot" or focus, and then writes again, this time with the focus in mind. This can continue for several cycles of looping.

Cubing: thinking about one topic from six different directions or points of view. Students approach the topic from different methods of development: describing it, comparing it, analyzing it, applying it, associating it, arguing for or against it.

Questioning: the reporter's five W's—who, what, why, when, where.

Talking: noisy, but effective; brainstorming, discussing, interviewing, or conferencing. Talking means we hear other ideas, which often generates more thought.

Interviewing: self-explanatory.

Guided visualization: turn off the lights and have students close their eyes. In a low, soft, pleasing voice, instruct them to imagine a subject, paying careful attention to details. Take students on a mental walk, for example. After talking to them for a short time, turn on the lights, tell them to open their eyes, and have them write what they saw.

Journals: explained separately.

Peer Groups and Collaborative Learning

One of the most significant changes in teaching composition has been the shift to collaborative learning. The use of peer groups, already common in other disciplines and in many business settings, has many advantages for the composition teacher as well.

Throughout the exercises in *The Complete Paragraph Workout Book*, it is suggested that students form peer groups to analyze and respond to each other's writing. Such peer groups can also be used at any stage of the writing process, from prewriting to proofreading. Indeed, many times group work enhances individual learning.

Collaborative work means that students generate ideas together, serve as audiences and critics and editors, and, in fact, teach themselves as they teach others. Brainstorming as a group provides a dynamic setting for generating ideas; often, hearing someone else's idea sparks another's thoughts or suggests a different direction of thought. Working together on paragraph or essay drafts also demonstrates the concept of audience, as students become audiences for each other. Audiences can tell the writer whether or not ideas are clear, developed fully, and/or organized logically; audiences can immediately respond to content and development issues, to organization or structure problems, to awkward wording, and so forth, and the writer can revise that draft. Peer groups later in the writing process are beneficial also. Students can edit and proofread for grammar and mechanics. The checklists provided in the text will guide students in such peer work; additional guidesheets are included in this Instructor's Guide.

It is suggested that groups contain no more than four students; with more people, the group has too many papers to respond to and cannot function adequately. Sometimes pairs of students work well, also. Some instructors have students remain in the same groups all semester; others vary the groups from time to time.

You may want to consider the composition of the groups to balance stronger and weaker students and consider personalities as well. At times it may be necessary to intervene and restructure groups if personality conflicts arise.

Collaborative learning is useful in other ways, too. Working on exercises together makes an exercise more than "skill and drill" because students often discuss the answer and puzzle out how it was derived. Discussing readings in groups is also beneficial for the same reason. Learning becomes active with collaboration.

Some instructors hesitate to use peer groups, because they believe that they are giving up control of their classes and that they are left with little to do. In fact, an instructor remains quite active while students are working collaboratively. She or he needs to walk around, listen, respond to questions, and generally monitor the various groups. If a group is wandering, the instructor can help focus its work. Students will see their instructor actively engaged, not passively giving up the class. You need to be ready to give peer groups some time to work. Don't abandon peer groups if they don't work immediately.

Each student is finally responsible for his or her own work; peer groups only serve as another tool for learning.

Journals

The term *journal* is one we hear all the time, but coming up with a single definition is simply impossible. There are many types of journals which are equally useful for different purposes. In fact, there are probably as many variations as there are teachers who use them.

First of all, a journal is not a diary, nor is it a class notebook. However, the journal may combine features of both of these.

A journal provides a place for students to write freely, with a real audience other than themselves. It is not as private as a diary, but it may reflect personal opinions and experiences. (Peter Elbow and Jennifer Clarke maintain that the journal is writer-based rather than audience- or reader-based.)

A journal fosters the idea that writing is on-going, recursive, and reflective. Students do not have to worry about correct grammar or organized presentation. Their language may be colloquial. It is a place for ideas, not form. Since many students are really not used to writing frequently, the journal provides them an opportunity to practice without punishment.

Sometimes students may write on any topics they desire; sometimes they may be directed by the instructor to a topic. That topic might reflect assigned readings, or classwork, or writing assignments. Some instructors begin every class with a few minutes of journal writing; others give time less frequently.

Journals provide an opportunity for prewriting, where the writer reflects on what he or she has read or seen or discussed.

You may or may not want to collect the journals, but if you don't, students may not use them. Collecting them occasionally allows you to get some insight into individual students. Some instructors use journals as a kind of dialogue with students and actually respond in the journals to ideas. If you do pick up journals, it's not a good idea to actually mark them or grade the writing; that negates the idea that this is a place to practice writing without punishment. You might, however, give a participation check or grade for the journal.

Revision Worksheet: Paragraphs

Provide students with copies of this or a similar worksheet. They can use it to guide their own writing and to evaluate the rough drafts they read in peer groups.

FOR PARAGRAPHS:

1. What is the topic or subject of this piece?

2. Is there a topic sentence? Where is it?

3. Does the topic sentence limit the topic or make a statement about it? How does it do so?

4. Does the rest of the paragraph explain or develop that topic? How does each sentence develop it? Eliminate any that do not.

5. What are the primary support sentences? Are any more needed?

6. What are the secondary support sentences? Are any more needed?

7. Are the rest of the sentences in a logical order so that the ideas are easily followed? If any seem out of place, try rearranging them.

8. Are transitions needed between sentences?

9. Is there a concluding sentence?

ALTERNATE CHECKLIST FOR PARAGRAPHS

For each paper that you read in a group, answer the following questions for the writer. Return this information to the writer; then, discuss your responses with him or her.

1. What is the topic sentence of the paragraph? Where is it located?

2. List the supporting details the writer uses to develop the topic sentence. How does each support develop the topic sentence? If supports do not develop the topic sentence, then explain why they are not effective.

3. What is the writer's intended audience and purpose? How can you identify these from the paragraph?

4. How does the writer organize the paragraph? Why or why not is this organization effective?

5. In two or three sentences, describe your reaction to the paragraph. For example, were you amused, enraged, intrigued, or bored by it?

6. Place a check beside the grammatical and mechanical errors you found in the paragraph. Be prepared to explain why these are errors.

_____ fragments	_____ verb tense	_____ commas
_____ comma splices	_____ s-v agreement	_____ semi-colons and colons
_____ run-ons	_____ pro.-ref. agr.	
	_____ diction	_____ illogical sentences

Revision Worksheet: Essays

1. Is there a title? Does it act to attract interest or to state the topic?

2. Is there an introduction-body-conclusion structure?

3. Is there a stated thesis in the introduction?

4. Is the thesis limited? Does it have a controlling idea?

5. Where is the thesis located?

6. Does each body paragraph contain a topic sentence?

7. Does each topic sentence link clearly to the thesis?

8. Is each topic sentence limited?

9. Does each body paragraph develop its topic sentence?

10. Is there one clear focus in the paper? Are there any ideas which do not follow the thesis?

11. Are transitions needed anywhere?

12. Are the introduction and conclusion separate from the body of the paper?

13. Are there enough primary supports for the thesis?

14. Does each topic sentence or primary support have enough secondary support details? Are more needed?

ALTERNATE CHECKLIST FOR ESSAYS

For each paper that you read in a group, answer the following questions for the writer. Return this information to the writer; then discuss your responses with him or her.

1. What is the thesis of the essay? Where is it located?

2. What is the writer's intended audience and purpose? How can you identify these from the essay?

3. How does the writer organize the essay? Why or why not is this organization effective?

4. List the supporting details the writer uses to develop the thesis. How does each support develop the thesis? If supports do not develop the thesis, then explain why they are not effective.

5. In three or four sentences, describe your reaction to the essay. For example, were you angry, amused, curious, or bored by it?

Editing/Proofreading Worksheet

1. Does each sentence have a subject and a verb?

2. Are there any fragments?

3. Do subjects and verbs agree?

4. Are there any run-on sentences or comma splices?

5. Are the verb tenses correct? Are there any shifts in tense?

6. Are the verb forms correct?

7. Check the pronouns. Are they the correct case?

8. Do all pronouns agree in case, number, and gender with their antecedents?

9. Are there any dangling modifiers?

10. Is there a variety of sentence types and patterns?

11. Can any sentences be combined for more effective variety?

12. Are there any words that need defining?

13. Is the word choice appropriate and accurate?

14. Are all words spelled correctly?

15. Is there proper end punctuation for each sentence?

16. Check commas, apostrophes, semicolons, and so forth. Are they properly used?

NOTE: You may want to tailor this sheet to your students' particular needs.

Syllabus #1: For a Semester-Long Course

This is designed as a very general description of class assignments, rather than as a daily lesson plan. It will vary somewhat depending upon the students in each class section.

This syllabus assumes that the course requires students to work on paragraphs first and then in the final weeks of the semester to move to short multi-paragraph essays.

In general, avoid long stretches on any one chapter; rather, vary several topics in any class period. For example, you might start with writing and then move to grammar and then to group work. Varying pace and topic keeps the class moving; the students are less likely to lose interest and concentration.

How much you are able to cover in any one class period will vary depending upon two things: the length of the class period and the students themselves. A rigid daily class plan is nearly impossible to follow; flexibility is vital.

Ideally, grammar work should not be concentrated drill work. Research shows that grammar isolated from writing has little carry-over into writing; drill work leads to recognition but not to application. Consequently, move from grammar work in drill exercises to the students' own writing and have them apply the particular grammar lesson to their own work. For example, after studying sentence formats, students might use their own paragraphs to note different sentence formats and perhaps to rewrite those paragraphs to include more formats.

Finally, students should write often, daily if at all possible. Such writing can be journal writing, prewriting, drafting, and so on.

WEEK ONE

Day One: Diagnostic essay. Depending upon what the exit requirements are for your Developmental English class (a paragraph, a short essay), the nature of this diagnostic piece will vary. Give few instructions, other than the topic. Develop a topic that suggests some organization or structure. The purpose of this is to determine each student's writing level. You can use these diagnostic pieces to estimate your students' grammar problems, sentence problems, development problems, and so forth. This, in turn, helps you decide what topics to cover and to what degree to study them.

Day Two: Orientation to class. Class syllabus, policies, texts. Have students introduce themselves—perhaps interview each other and introduce another person. Set the class atmosphere.

WEEKS TWO–FOUR

Course should focus on sentence structure and grammar more intensively while students also write for practice but not for a grade; this will allow them to become comfortable with writing and to learn some basic elements of paragraph composition.

From Part One, cover "To the Student," Chapter One. Have students work through these exercises, write in journals, work in groups to discuss essays, prewrite, and revise.

From Part Two, concentrate on the following chapters, in the following suggested order:

> Introduction—Review, parts of speech, sentence formats
>
> Chapter One—Verbs (Complete Chapter Two if necessary. It is rather advanced for some levels of developmental students.)
>
> Chapter Three—Subjects, Verbs, and Prepositional Phrases
>
> Chapter Four—Fragments
>
> Also cover parts of Chapter Eight, on Active Voice and Descriptive Verbs
>
> Can cover part of Chapter Nine, on commas with independent clauses, items in a series, coordinate adjectives, and long introductory elements (as these sentence elements come up)

WEEKS FIVE–EIGHT

Course should focus on writing paragraphs for grades. Focus on revising and polishing work.

From Part One: Cover the following chapters in the order suggested:

> Chapter Two—Exploring Topics
>
> Chapter Three—Creating Topic Sentences
>
> Chapter Four—Organizing Details
>
> Cover part of Chapter Eight on wordiness and varying sentences

From Part Two, continue grammar in the following order:

> Chapter Five—Comma Splices
>
> Chapter Six—Run-ons
>
> Chapter Seven—Subject-Verb Agreement
>
> Chapter Eight—Pronoun Reference

WEEKS NINE–ELEVEN

From Part One:

> Chapter Five—Revising
>
> Chapter Six—Achieving Coherence
>
> Chapter Seven—Diction (You might consider covering some of this chapter earlier and returning to it periodically)
>
> Chapter Eight—Effective Style

From Part Two:

> Chapter Nine—Commas to Separate (though you should cover some parts of it earlier)
>
> Chapter Ten—Commas to Enclose

WEEKS TWELVE–FOURTEEN

Course should focus on multi-paragraph essay.

Concentrate on Part One, Chapter Nine—The Whole Essay.

Work out of Part Two as needed.

NOTE: You might consider using Part Two, Chapter Thirteen (Confusing and Misused Words) as a regular weekly item, assigning a certain number of sets of words per week. You can test students by listing the words in any order on the board and requiring students to use the words correctly in sentences; contextual use is the only way you'll know if students understand the differences between the words. You can give points for correct usage and for correct sentences, so you reinforce two elements simultaneously.

NOTE: If your course is not designed to include the short multi-paragraph essay, you have more time to extend the previous suggestions for weekly topics.

Syllabus #2: For a Quarter-Long Course

This is designed as a very general description of class assignments, rather than as a daily lesson plan. It will vary somewhat depending upon the students in each class section.

This syllabus assumes that the course requires students to concentrate on paragraph writing only.

In general, avoid long stretches on any one chapter; rather, vary several topics in any class period. For example, you might start with writing and then move to grammar and then to group work. Varying pace and topic keeps the class moving; the students are less likely to lose interest and concentration.

How much you are able to cover in any one class period will vary, depending upon two things: the length of the class period and the students themselves. A rigid daily class plan is nearly impossible to follow; flexibility is vital.

Ideally, grammar work should not be concentrated drill work. Research shows that grammar isolated from writing has little carry-over into writing; drill work leads to recognition but not to application. Consequently, move from grammar work in drill exercises to students' own writing and have them apply the particular grammar lesson to their own work. For example, after studying sentence formats, students might use their own paragraphs to note different sentence formats, and perhaps to rewrite those paragraphs to include more formats.

Finally, students should write often, daily if at all possible. Such writing can be journal writing, prewriting, drafting, and so on.

WEEK ONE

Day One: Diagnostic essay. Depending upon what the exit requirements are for your Developmental English class, the nature of this diagnostic piece will vary. Give few instructions, other than the topic. Develop a topic that suggests some organization or structure. The purpose of this is to determine each student's writing level. You can use these diagnostic pieces to estimate your students' grammar problems, sentence problems, development problems, and so on. This, in turn, helps you decide what topics to cover and to what degree to cover them.

Day Two: Orientation to class. Class syllabus, policies, texts. Have students introduce themselves—perhaps interview each other and introduce another person. Set the class atmosphere.

WEEKS TWO–FOUR

Course should focus on sentence structure and grammar more intensively while students also write for practice but not for a grade; this will allow them to become comfortable with writing and to learn some basic elements of paragraph composition.

From Part One, cover "To the Student," Chapter One. Have students work through these exercises, write in journals, work in groups to discuss essays, prewrite, and revise.

From Part Two, concentrate on the following chapters, in the following suggested order:

Introduction—review, parts of speech, sentence formats

Chapter One—Verbs (may do Chapter Two if necessary. It is rather advanced for some levels of developmental students.)

Chapter Three—Subjects, Verbs, and Prepositional Phrases

Chapter Four—Fragments

Also cover parts of Chapter Eight, on Active Voice and Descriptive Verbs

Can cover part of Chapter Nine, on commas with independent clauses, items in a series, coordinate adjectives, and long introductory elements (as these sentence elements come up)

WEEKS FIVE–SEVEN

Course should focus on writing paragraphs for grades. Focus on revising and polishing work.

From Part One cover the following chapters in the order suggested:

Chapter Two—Exploring Topics

Chapter Three—Creating Topic Sentences

Chapter Four—Organizing Details

Cover part of Chapter Eight on wordiness and varying sentences

From Part Two, continue grammar in the following order:

Chapter Five—Comma Splices

Chapter Six—Run-ons

Chapter Seven—Subject-Verb Agreement

Chapter Eight—Pronoun Reference

WEEKS EIGHT–TEN

From Part One:

Chapter Five—Revising

Chapter Six—Achieving Coherence

Chapter Seven—Diction (You might consider covering some of this chapter earlier and returning to it periodically)

Chapter Eight—Effective Style

From Part Two:

Chapter Nine—Commas to Separate (though you should cover some parts of it earlier)

Chapter Ten—Commas to Enclose

NOTE: You might consider using Part Two, Chapter Thirteen (Confusing and Misused Words) as a regular weekly item, assigning a certain number of sets of words per week. You can test students by listing the words in any order on the board and requiring students to use the words correctly in sentences; contextual use is the only way you'll know if students understand the differences between the words. You can give points for correct usage and for correct sentences, so you reinforce two elements simultaneously.

Grading

Probably the most worrisome element of teaching—for any teacher—is grading. Most students seem to think that a composition grade is highly subjective, and it is difficult to convince them otherwise.

You must consider whether your department has any grading guidelines for freshman composition; if so, use these as a measure of what your students need to produce in order to complete this course successfully. Knowing the exit requirements will help you determine what you're looking for in student papers. For example, will your students concentrate on paragraphs for the entire semester? Will they need to move on to short essays by the end of the semester? What does the freshman composition class require for a passing grade? Do students receive letter grades for this course? Or is it a pass/fail class? If there is a departmental description of A, B, C, D, and F level work, look at that as well. What do you expect an A paper to be? What about a B paper? Formulate your own description for each letter grade.

No matter the length or type of compositions, you will always look for certain elements: unity, coherence, and development (content and organization); and grammar and mechanics. How well a paper meets the standards for each of these will determine its grade.

You will also develop (if you haven't already) your own grading method. Will you deduct points? Will you use a sliding scale for major grammar and composition errors? Will you use a holistic grading method? Whatever method you decide upon, make that method clear to your students.

Some teachers of basic writing prefer not to grade written work early in the semester; they start to grade written work at midterm, so that the first half of the semester provides groundwork and practice, building confidence and ability in students who often lack both.

Marking papers in a useful way is another area of concern for most writing teachers. A paper filled with red marks and numbers is usually ignored; it often overwhelms students. Remarks that are useful take into consideration *why* students create the errors they do. Ideally, students have an opportunity to rewrite a paper after a teacher has read it and evaluated it: this is when intervention is still possible. This is also beneficial earlier in the course.

Peer evaluations, if taken seriously, can provide yet another tool for the basic writers who will use this text. Many teachers use portfolio assessment so that at the end of a semester, a student's entire portfolio of work is considered in the final determination of a grade. Some departments use group grading sessions to determine final grades for developmental classes.

There are many different methods and systems of grading, just as there are many grading philosophies.

To the Student
The Communication Process

Teaching Suggestions

The material in the text covers important points about the concepts of writer/speaker, reader/listener/audience, and purpose; the reading process itself; and an introductory analysis of written material. You can apply this material throughout the course, regardless of chapter focus.

Students seldom think about reading and writing being similar (if not interactive) communication processes which require thought and analysis. A discussion of listening skills and their importance, at this point, would also benefit students. Notetaking could be taught along with this chapter, especially as a corollary to reading texts and listening to lectures. When students are studying audience, you might briefly mention the need to consider what vocabulary are appropriate to a particular audience and when explanations of terms or information is necessary. To practice the reading process, you could use this text as a running example, previewing, skimming, and so forth, during the semester.

Additional Activities

Any activity which establishes and reinforces the concepts of sender/writer, audience/reader, and purpose would be useful. To be effective readers and writers, students need firm knowledge of these concepts.

1. Have students use their textbooks from other classes to talk about audience and purpose; they could also use these to practice the reading process.

2. Bring a collection of various popular magazines to class— *Newsweek, Time, Reader's Digest, Popular Mechanics, Seventeen, Vogue,* and so on. Students can work in groups. Give each group one or two magazines. Let each group discuss and analyze the audiences for gender, age group, education level,

and so on. Then have each group tell the rest of the class about its analysis.

3. Have each student select a topic of interest (sports, or fashion, for example) and then research discussions of that topic in local newspapers. Using news articles, editorials, letters to the editor, business articles, and so on, students should analyze the purposes and audiences for each piece and the interdependence of the two.

4. Bring a collection of popular magazines to class, deliberately choose those with a wide variety of audiences, or bring collections of advertisements. In groups, students can locate advertisements for one type of product (cigarettes, cars, liquor) and discuss how the ads differ. They should note how audience affects the ads.

5. Students can practice the reading process with almost any material you bring into class: short articles from newspapers or magazines are useful. Have them identify the source, consider biases, and identify subjects and main ideas.

Answer Key

1. Despite sibling rivalry, our relationship with our brothers and sisters is life-long, and it may outlast other intimate relationships.

2. High divorce rates and smaller families mean siblings may depend upon each other more; life crises may draw them together. Lingering rivalries may separate siblings, but seldom end the relationships. As siblings age, they often mellow, and closeness often increases; they may have more time for each other as family and career involve them less. As they age, too, they tend to idealize their pasts and, thus, reinforce sibling ties. Emotional support becomes more common, though other types of help are less common.

3. Sibling ties in later life gain strength and power, despite the rivalries many people associate with brothers and sisters.

▼ ## Composing Paragraphs and Essays

PART I

Chapter One
The Writing Process

 TEACHING OBJECTIVES

1. To develop a personal writing approach.

2. To understand the writing commitment.

3. To explore the entire writing process, from generating ideas to revising papers.

4. To generate ideas through prewriting.

Teaching Suggestions

This chapter discusses once more the communication process introduced in the previous section, "To the Student." Here, however, the focus is on the writer's role in the process, rather than the reader's. This chapter demonstrates the recursive nature of writing, and you can point out to students that teaching and learning are also recursive rather than linear. This continuity will allow you to reuse the material from "To the Student" for writing activity. Although the chapter does give an overview of the entire writing process, the focus narrows to highlight prewriting activities. The chapter also introduces narration as a writing strategy, and it includes four model essays to illustrate this writing strategy.

It is important for students to practice all the prewriting techniques, since we truly learn a new idea only by applying it. Also, students will find particular prewriting approaches more suitable than others.

A proven tool for any writer is the journal, which has many different forms and purposes. You might discuss the uses and types of journals with your students and encourage them to keep journals for this class. Journals can allow students to explore particular ideas or topics of personal interest; you can suggest topics at times. Students can write at home; you can use time in class occasionally or regularly for journal-writing. Journals need not be graded, and in fact the lack of a grade (other than for participation) allows the students to feel free and unencumbered in writing. Here they can write without "punishment."

Narration is an easy type of writing for students; they are telling about something that happened, in the order that it happened; it is not coincidental that our earliest literature was narrative.

Additional Activities

1. Use the topics that students researched in "To the Student." Students can brainstorm their topics. They might also try other prewriting techniques such as mapping or freewriting.

2. Students can use the advertisements from "To the Student" activities for prewriting techniques such as freewriting or mapping.

3. Have students try other prewriting activities with these or any other topics: cubing, in particular, can be most productive.

4. Play a piece of music for students and then let them freewrite for ten minutes about it.

5. Bring in a photograph or a painting and have students freewrite about it.

6. Pass an object, such as a pen, around the room and let students use cubing to prewrite about the object.

7. Bring in food (lollipops, for example, or chocolate kisses) and let students freewrite about the memories that the food evokes.

▼ Writing Strategy: NARRATION

Model Narrations

I. "AN EYE-WITNESS'S VIEW OF THE SAN FRANCISCO EARTHQUAKE" BY JACK LONDON (READING LEVEL: 6.3)

1. The sentence creates a sense of complete and total destruction, and using the present tense creates the impression that the destruction is current.

2. "Modern, imperial city" produces an image of a large urban sprawl of buildings that are crowded together over much land and that reach into the sky; the impression is positive.

"Doomed city" projects a different negative image, that suggests the destruction of that skyline, perhaps a flattening of it.

3. *Nabobs* are people of wealth and prominence.
   Lurid means glowing or glaring through a haze.
   Cunning means shrewd and crafty.
   Enumeration means a detailed list of items or a catalog.

4. Repetition is used to reinforce an idea or effect; here London reiterates the idea that all of these things are uncountable.

II. "THE CALLING" BY RUSSELL BAKER (READING LEVEL: 11.0)

1. Baker finally writes out of his own desire to recapture the warmth and humor of that evening meal. Because of his personal involvement in the writing, he successfully recreates what it was like to eat spaghetti for the first time. Because he thinks that this piece does not follow "the rules" and would earn a failing grade, he believes that he should write something else to satisfy the teacher and "the rules."

2. His description of Fleagle effectively presents a young student's vision of his English teacher. "Prim" evokes the stereotype of all English teachers.

3. The other students become part of the experience and laugh out of their enjoyment of Baker's—and their own—experience.

4. Baker's tone is matter-of-fact, reflecting on the significance of his experience but not exaggerating the event as a sixteen-year-old probably would have.

III. "38 WHO SAW MURDER DIDN'T CALL THE POLICE" BY MARTIN GANSBERG (READING LEVEL: 8.3)

1. People should help others and not ignore such situations.

2. Gansberg includes the most minute details, starting from a stark assertion that "For more than half an hour 38 respectable, law-abiding citizens in Queens watched a killer stalk and stab a woman in three separate attacks in Kew Gardens." He details the street, the victim's appearance and behavior, the assailant's actions, and the failure of any observer to respond. Gansberg does slant the piece, implying criticism of those who failed to act. His use of detail shows that the time elapsed would have allowed a response that might have saved Genovese's life.

3. "I didn't want to get involved"; "We thought it was a lover's quarrel"; "Frankly, we were afraid"; "I was tired [and] I went back to bed." None of the excuses appear valid.

4. Gansberg's tone is critical. He achieves this tone by piling up the details of the murder and then listing the various excuses people gave. In their excuses, no one indicates remorse or much emotion over either the murder or their own inaction. Word choice creates this impression: "sheepishly told," "knowingly if casually, said," "shrugged and replied."

5. This last sentence emphasizes that everyone had obviously watched Genovese's murder, from attack to ambulance, and "Then . . . the people came out." The sentence also suggests mild sarcasm.

IV. "THE ALL-AMERICAN JOB" BY JOE LIBERATORE (READING LEVEL: 5.6)

1. Not much: "It's called a job." He opens with this flat statement. The second sentence alerts you to this: "The most challenging aspect is trying to arrive on time."

2. The busiest time at his job is after the early church service lets out. "The food supply dwindles" and his customers complain that he can't work fast enough to meet the "'30 seconds or less' policy." He speeds up and sacrifices "quality, cleanliness, and value." The noise level rises. His manager threatens him and he becomes angry enough to slow down so much that "I begin to put forth no effort." One rush follows another and he is "trapped at the counter for three continuous hours of service."

3. There's nothing about this job that he seems to like. He feels bored, rushed, harassed, angry, and tired.

▼ Writing Process Checklist

1. What prewriting strategy did you use to generate ideas for this paragraph?

2. How did your audience and writing purpose influence the words you used?

3. How did you choose to organize your paragraph? Why?

4. How many drafts of this paragraph did you write? What was your revision purpose for each draft?

Chapter Two
Exploring Topics

▶ **TEACHING OBJECTIVES**

1. To identify paragraph topics.

2. To use details to discover paragraph topics.

3. To generate paragraph topics.

4. To narrow paragraph topics.

5. To explore composing through description.

Teaching Suggestions

This chapter contains a full discussion of topics, but it could be supplemented as suggested for previous material by using newspapers and popular general-interest magazines. You can collect articles on particular topics and analyze the way that each author's purpose and audience required him or her to present material; alternatively, you can have your students collect these articles. Students can work on these articles alone or in groups. There will be variety in topics, emphases, and even interpretations derived from identical facts. In fact, the variety will lead to fruitful discussions in class. Description is not necessarily the easiest strategy for students to try, so more attention is often needed with it than is needed for narration.

Additional Activities

1. Bring in food, as suggested previously. Now, though, have students describe the food: How does it taste, smell, appear, and so on?

2. Have students sit quietly with their eyes closed while you talk quietly to them. Using guided imagery, talk them through a scenario in which they physically travel to some favorite place. Tell them to pay attention to what they see and hear there. Take several minutes to do this; don't rush them through it. Then have them open their eyes and write whatever they saw and heard. When they're through, have them read their pieces. Ask them to note what details are there, and what details could be added. What details do they tend to include? Leave out?

3. Gather an assortment of common items such as a spoon, knife, rubber band, paper clip, coin, and so forth, and put them in a paper bag; don't include anything too complicated. In class, have all the students close their eyes while you have some of them grab an item from the bag. Without using the names of items or telling what an item does, have each student describe his or her item—size, shape, texture, and so on. What other properties does the item have (cool, flexible, rigid, and so on)? The rest of the class must guess what the items are. This exercise is useful at the beginning of a discussion on description because it focuses their attention on how often we leave out important details.

4. Have students sit quietly outside for ten minutes or so. Then have them write all the sensory details they can—what they heard, what they saw, what they felt (cold, heat, and so on).

5. Have students sit someplace like the student union and record what they observe there.

6. Bring in a painting and have students describe it objectively— not how it makes them feel. Compare their descriptions to decide what details are needed for a complete, objective description.

Answer Key

 **EXERCISE 1**

Answers will vary.

1. specific to general
    money

2. general to specific
    novel

3. general to specific
    bedroom
    my sister's bedroom

4. general to specific
    Caribbean cruise

5. specific to general
machine

6. general to specific
male Country-and-Western singers
Willie Nelson

▼ EXERCISE 2

1. *Specific Details:* functions vary, manufacturers transport goods, advertisers inform public, retailers sell products
Topic: functions of marketing people

2. *Specific Details:* American's materialism, robber barons, gangsters, democratic ideals, power of money
Topic: attitudes about and effects of money and power in America

3. *Specific Details:* trade with England, self-sufficiency, effects of Civil War
Topic: development of business production in America

4. *Specific Details:* hunts and fishes for hours without complaint, does odd jobs for neighbors, does everybody's business
Topic: Rip Van Winkle's dislike for his own required labor

5. *Specific Details:* dune sand is made of quartz, is small and rough, contains salt
Topic: characteristics of dune sand

▼ EXERCISE 4

1. 2 Dramatic television programs
3 *L.A. Law*
5 Weekly plots on *L.A. Law*
1 Television
4 Diversity of plots each week on *L.A. Law*

2. 5 Egyptians' contributions to geometry
3 Contributions of Egypt
1 Ancient civilizations
2 Egypt in the Pharoahs' times
4 Scientific contributions of Egyptians

3. 4 Revival of musicals in the 1980s
2 Broadway plays
1 Theater
3 Musicals on Broadway
5 Reasons for the revival of older Broadway musicals in the 1980s

4. 4 Effects of oil spills
1 Environment
2 Pollution in the environment
3 Effect of pollution
5 Effect of oil spills on aquatic life

5. 3   Mark Twain's stories
   1   American writers
   4   Humor in Mark Twain's stories
   2   Mark Twain
   5   Humor in Mark Twain's *Tom Sawyer*

▼ Writing Strategy: DESCRIPTION

Model Descriptions

I. "A BUILDING IN UPPER HARLEM" BY CLAUDE BROWN (READING LEVEL: 12.8)

1. The main impression is one of decay and deterioration.

2. Details: no hot water or electricity, rats, garbage piled up, missing stairs, no lightbulbs.

3. *Saving grace* means the single thing that rescues someone or something; *formidable* means inspiring awe or inducing fear.

4. Because this building does not offer a minimum level of shelter and protection.

II. "THE TURTLE" BY JOHN STEINBECK (READING LEVEL: 9.2)

1. The topic sentence begins "And over the grass at the roadside a land turtle crawled . . . "; it is the second sentence.

2. At first, he views the turtle from ground level. The scale changes, from this initial broad perspective to a narrower one, focusing on the individual turtle and his task. This change occurs in the second sentence.

3. Steinbeck's tone is objective, that of a reporter on the front. Certain words convey an eyewitness account: "stared straight ahead," "fierce, humorous eyes," "beaten trail," "level cement plain."

III. "THE BUFFALO STAMPEDE" BY ZANE GREY (READING LEVEL: 9.0)

1. Some details emphasize the sensation of sight: Gray describes what he sees as he "looked out upon the vast prairie"—telegraph poles, faces of men, the watch, the herd itself, the fire,

the lack of light, the smoke. Others describe touch: feet riveted to the ground, rocking on his feet, unstable ground, fingers all thumbs, earth solid again. Yet others indicate Gray's own physical and emotional responses: "shaking as one with the palsy," "My faculties, my blood, almost my heart itself, had stopped," "I almost fainted," "an automaton, reacting like a machine."

2. The herd is described first as "like the torrential flow of an ocean behind which there were unknown leagues of pushing waves." Next, it is a "rebounding black juggernaut with its myriad of shiny horns and fiery green eyes." It is a "rolling black sea."

3. The night setting enhances the quality of suspense in the piece. Since Gray has little light to see by, he cannot clearly or easily see what is happening and must rely upon other sensory details and upon his imagination.

4. *Riveted* means fastened or secured firmly, as with a rivet or bolt.
   A *juggernaut* is something that moves forward relentlessly and crushes onlookers beneath it.
   A *myriad* refers to a large number or great multitude.
   A *maelstrom* is any situation that resembles a whirlpool of great violence and power.
   A *canopy* is a covering above a person.

IV. "PARADISE CAN BE A CONCENTRATION CAMP" BY REGINA RAFFETY (READING LEVEL: 8.9)

1. Raffety's main idea is that, like most people, she had, as a child in Germany, a personal paradise where she could escape from the real world, but that as an adult she saw this paradise quite differently.

2. The number of details contributes to the sense of "overflowing." Also, the types of details suggest a difference in size: Raffety as adolescent, trees towering "miles" over her head and forming a tunnel over her favorite path. Words such as "majestic" and "bountiful" contribute to this sense of over-flowing abundance. She also indicates the many different types of trees. The size of cleared spaces ("a little larger than football fields") also suggests the contrast to her own size.

3. Raffety gained from the forest a sense of beauty; it also served as a place of fun and adventure.

4. As a child, Raffety viewed the forest as beautiful, majestic, and bountiful, but as an adult she felt differently, though not because the forest physically changed. Instead, a news article sent by a cousin when Raffety was in her late teens revealed

that the clearings had been the site of concentration camps and, thus, of many painful deaths. She now felt it an embarrassment "that I danced and played on people's graves as a child."

▼ Paragraph Topic Checklist

1. Have you narrowed the topic of your paragraph?

2. Is the paragraph directed to a specific audience?

3. Can you state your purpose for writing this paragraph?

4. What is the point of view of this paragraph?

5. Is the scale appropriate for the point of view?

▼ Description Checklist

1. Have you used specific details to create a visual image?

2. Have you used descriptive verbs which give a visual impression?

3. Does your paragraph have a topic sentence that supports the description?

4. What is the tone of your description?

5. Is there a dominant visual or emotional impression left by your paragraph? What is it?

Chapter Three
Creating Topic Sentences

▶ **TEACHING OBJECTIVES**

1. To identify controlling ideas in topic sentences.

2. To identify facts and opinions.

3. To generate topic sentences.

4. To discover topic sentences in paragraphs.

5. To place topic sentences according to their functions in paragraphs.

6. To explore composing through process analysis.

Teaching Suggestions

This chapter clearly discusses the two key aspects about topic sentences: the "controlling idea" and "facts and opinions." However, it is probably impossible to talk about topic sentences too much. Recognizing that a sentence is a limited, appropriate topic sentence rather than a statement of fact can be important for students. It means that their own writing will have focus and direction. It also means that as they read others' writing—in textbooks, newspaper and magazine articles and so on—they will be able to analyze and comprehend more effectively. Being able to differentiate between fact and opinion is a skill important for their daily lives as well as their class work. Their ability to recognize unfocused ideas that reach no unified conclusions or to recognize the presentation of opinion as fact (or the reverse) strengthens their analytical skills. They can see weaknesses in reasoning or presentations.

Once the initial discussions of topic sentences have taken place, you can periodically ask students to identify topic sentences, controlling ideas, supporting ideas, facts, and opinions using whatever reading material is at hand. Placement of topic sentences is also presented fully in the chapter. As students read model essays in later chapters, you can continue discussing the significance of topic sentence placement. For example, in model essays, ask students why topic sentences are placed where they are, and what effects different placements would create. Such discussions reinforce the notion that writers can control their writing, in part by choosing such placement for a particular effect.

Additional Activities

1. If students have previously been asked to generate a list of possible topics that they'd be interested in using, then use that list here. Students can work independently or in groups to generate various specific topic sentences for one topic.

2. Bring in a list of specific information—unemployment statistics, interest rates, housing starts, and so on—and then have students generate a suitable specific topic and topic sentence. Again, students can work singly or in groups.

3. Select two articles on the same topic, perhaps a straight news article and an editorial. Have students identify facts and opinions; examine the two for bias and supporting ideas.

4. Hand out sample paragraphs with missing topic sentences. Let students generate topic sentences and then decide on their best placement in the paragraphs. Have them discuss their choices, and then show the originals for comparison.

5. Hand out a list of numbered sentences that create a paragraph when shuffled into a different order. Have students decide on the proper sequence of the sentences, identifying the topic sentence. Compare these to the original and discuss.

6. Ask students to bring in samples of process analysis writing that fails to instruct the reader clearly.

7. At the beginning of class before you discuss process analysis, ask students to think of a place on campus and then to write directions for getting there from the classroom without using names of buildings or room numbers. Then have students exchange papers and try to follow each others' directions. Give them a time limit, though, so that they re-assemble in class in ten or fifteen minutes. When they return, ask them to evaluate the directions they tried to follow.

8. A variation on the exercise in #7 is to bring in a jar of peanut butter, a jar of jelly, a loaf of bread, and a knife. As students give you directions, try to make a peanut-butter-and-jelly sandwich. *Warning:* this can get messy, but students enjoy it and at the same time they see the problems created by unclear directions.

Answer Key

▼ EXERCISE 1

1. a great deal about Americans' images of themselves

2. time, patience, and determination

3. many problems for residents of large cities

4. knowledge of other cultures, languages, and customs

5. several rewards

6. instant wealth and fame

7. many far-reaching effects

8. five reasons for her popularity

9. expensive to buy, complex to operate, and enjoyable to use

10. a difficult task

▼ EXERCISE 2

The corrections will vary.

1. A: outstanding contributions

2. A: to describe many types of acquaintances

3. A: arduous process

4. A: promotes good muscle tone and cardiovascular fitness

5. I: interesting journey

6. I: part of our everyday speech

7. I: a fascinating piece of equipment

8. I: purchasing good cars

9. I: many changes to Americans

10. I: prefer multiple-choice tests

▼ EXERCISE 3

1. *Topic sentence:* The rocket engine has overcome these disadvantages.
   Topic: rocket engine
   Controlling idea: these disadvantages

Details: carries own oxygen supply, liquid fuel and liquid
oxygen mix, hot exhaust gases, moves by reaction

2. *Topic sentence:* His very person and appearance were such . . .
Topic: Sherlock Holmes' appearance
Controlling idea: strikes attention of any observer
Details: tall and lean; sharp, piercing eyes; hawk-like nose;
square, prominent chin; stained hands; delicacy of touch

▼ EXERCISE 4

1. c
2. b
3. d
4. b
5. b

▼ EXERCISE 5

1. opinion
2. fact
3. fact
4. fact
5. fact
6. opinion
7. fact
8. opinion
9. opinion
10. fact

▼ EXERCISE 6

1. limitation
2. fact
3. fact
4. fact
5. limitation
6. fact
7. limitation
8. fact
9. limitation
10. limitation

▼ EXERCISE 8

1. *Topic:* the word "run"
Significant details: personal locomotion, flaw in women's stockings, a bank with money problems, in baseball the difference between a win and a loss
Controlling idea: many and varied meanings
Students' topic sentences will vary.

2. *Topic:* some American presidents
   Significant details: Washington and troops, Jackson and the common folk, JFK and parades
   Controlling idea: times and attitudes have changed
   Students' topic sentences will vary.

▼ Writing Strategy: PROCESS ANALYSIS

Model Process Analyses

I. "LENSES" BY ANNIE DILLARD (READING LEVEL: 6.7)

1. Seeing through one eye with both eyes open, moving your hands wrong, moving the slide

2. Keeping both eyes open; looking with one eye; moving glass slides with hands to observe what's on the slide

3. *Purblind* means nearly or partly blind.
   Paradoxical maneuvers seem to contradict each other.
   Translucent objects allow enough light through to see distinct images through them.
   Someone who is *mesmerized* is hypnotized.

II. "HOW DICTIONARIES ARE MADE" BY S.I. HAYAKAWA (READING LEVEL: 12.5)

1. His thesis is the first sentence of paragraph five:
   "The writing of a dictionary, therefore, is not a task of setting up authoritative statements about the 'true meanings' of words, but a task of recording, to the best of one's ability, what various words have meant to authors in the distant or immediate past."

2. As Hayakawa explains in the last sentence of the first paragraph, "anyone who is willing to quarrel with the dictionary is regarded as either eccentric or mad." Americans, in particular, are prone to believe that whatever is in the dictionary is correct, permanent, and authoritative. These assumptions are incorrect, however.

3. Writers of dictionaries must use words within contexts to determine a word's meaning. This method suggests that language changes to accommodate new ideas and technology, that new words are added, and that meanings of words change.

Any language reflects current technology, thought, and culture. Thus, context is necessary to chart such changes.

III. "DESPERATION WRITING" BY PETER ELBOW (READING LEVEL: 8.1)

1. Many people panic because they fear they won't be able to write something when they need to.

2. First, admit the condition. Then write and keep writing until you've got enough material or until you're tired. Next, on small pieces of paper or 3x5 notecards, sum up the core thoughts, feelings, perceptions, or images. Write one sentence per card. Read through the cards several times, shifting them for different combinations until you can sort related cards into different piles. Now take each pile of cards, sort through them, and sum them up into one assertion, or further divide them into separate piles.

3. Elbow's tone is very matter-of-fact, assuming that anyone can follow this procedure. Words that set that tone include the following: job, playing solitaire, bringing energy to bear, drift, intuition, pile-making, growing, cooking.

4. A *hindrance* is an obstacle.
   A *metaphor* is a figure of speech in which two seemingly unlike items are compared.
   Comatose means unconscious or lethargic.
   Invariably means constantly or without changing.
   To *deploy* is to use something systematically.

IV. "WRITING A PAPER" BY TIM MAHER (READING LEVEL: 7.7)

1. Maher's topic sentence is the first sentence: "The process of writing a paper for me is long and many times frustrating."

2. He lists seven: choosing a topic, gathering information, organizing the information into an outline, drafting, revising, proofreading, and writing the final draft.

3. Maher gathers information by researching the subject in the library, reading over class material, or talking to the teachers.

▼ Topic Sentence Checklist

1. Does the topic sentence of your paragraph have a specific controlling idea?

2. Does the topic sentence state your opinion about the topic, or does it limit the topic?

3. Did you develop the topic sentence of the paragraph with details?

4. Have you placed the topic sentence in the best location to introduce, summarize, reinforce, or be a transition between the developing details of the paragraph?

▼ Process Analysis Checklist

1. Does your process analysis present directions or information?

2. What is the purpose of your process analysis? Who is the intended audience? What might the audience already know about this process? How will this information change your presentation?

3. How is the process analysis explained? What separate units of activity are in this procedure? How do these units organize the paper?

4. After reading the process analysis, can someone other than you now perform the task or explain the operation? Are all the necessary items and actions listed?

5. If you found any fragments, comma splices, or run-ons in your paper, how did you correct them? (See Part Two, Chapters 4–7.)

Chapter Four

Organizing Details

▶ **TEACHING OBJECTIVES**

1. To recognize unified paragraphs.

2. To identify and create primary support sentences.

3. To identify and create secondary support sentences.

4. To draw conclusions and make judgments.

5. To explore composing through classification.

Teaching Suggestions

This chapter focuses on some essential abilities, ones necessary for students both as writers and as readers. Focusing on the practical aspects of such abilities may make students see that writing is not an activity peculiar to English classes. It may also make them see that the skills involved in writing have much wider application. Organizing is essential; it means that someone can differentiate levels of meaning and relationships between ideas or items. The formal outlining that the chapter focuses upon may be a problem for some students, though, and these students may need more help in understanding it.

Recognizing unified paragraphs means distinguishing a main idea from supporting ideas. Distinguishing primary and secondary support sentences means that students can differentiate levels of specificity and meaning. Knowing the difference between facts and judgments allows them to see that judgments require evaluation and analysis from readers (or writers), not just haphazard emotional reactions. Drawing appropriate conclusions is a life skill, not just a writing skill. All of these abilities mean that students can read something—a textbook, a newspaper article, or an editorial—and sort through what they're reading, distinguishing valid arguments from invalid ones. Expand the discussion of judgment to include bias, distinguishing between bias and prejudice; discuss how these influence writing. Talk about the subtlety of bias and how difficult it may be to detect. Anytime that students can relate material in a class to something in "real life," they're more likely to understand it quickly and remember it longer. Classification is a writing strategy, but it is also a way of dealing with everyday life. We classify all sorts of things: places to eat, places to take dates, movies, teachers, employers, and so on.

     Link this chapter with previous chapters, too. Have students continue to look for topic sentences and discuss their placement; have them notice whether narration or description are used in development, and if so, how; have them consider the audience and purpose of pieces.

Additional Activities

1. Bring in an article. After students read it, have them identify its topic sentences, major points, and secondary support. Have them outline this article using any method of their own choosing.

2. Follow up #1, which requires individual work, by then using the same article and having the entire class help you outline it on the board.

3. Using the same article, have students brainstorm their own ideas on the topic in the article and then outline their ideas for a prospective essay.

4. Using an overhead projector, provide the students with a list of statements and/or separate items of information. Their task is to group similar items and then categorize the information by adding general and/or specific terms. In effect, they will be outlining.

5. Have students bring in articles or commentaries which demonstrate the uses of judgment or exhibit bias. Alternatively, you could select such material and provide it for them.

6. Bring an assortment of objects to class. Have students break into groups, classify a group of objects, and justify the classification to the rest of the class.

7. Have students classify students at your school, places to go on a date, types of entertainment, types of music, and so forth.

Answer Key

▼ EXERCISE 1

1. Topic sentence: #1
   Not supporting: #7

2. Topic sentence: #1
   Not supporting: #7 and #8

3. Topic sentence: #1
   Not supporting: #6, #10, #13

4. Topic sentence: #1
   Not supporting: #5, #7, #10

5. Topic sentence: #1
   Not supporting: #4, #5, #7, #10, #12

▼ EXERCISE 2

1. *While in high school, the lazy student (reflects his attitude by the way he studies, acts, and dresses.)* **#1** I know a student, for example, who does no homework at all; he foolishly wastes his free study periods in the cafeteria with others like himself. **#2** His actions also reflect his slothful attitudes. When walking between classes, he moves slowly and speaks with everyone; as a result, he is always late for his next class. After his last class, he jumps into his car and rushes out of the parking lot with the car radio blaring; his only desire is to leave school quickly. **#3** He cares neither about what he gets on his report card nor about his appearance during school hours. His shirt-tail always hangs out, and he has no problem wearing stripes with plaids. His hair is rarely combed, and his shoelaces are untied.

2. *Besides being destructive to one's health, smoking can also be (destructive to one's property.)* **#1** Over the years, smoking can result in property damage which will cost several thousands of dollars to replace. For example, the carelessly dropped hot ash or spark, as well as the burning cigarette left on the edge of an ash tray, can do considerable damage to both furnishings and clothing. Furniture may be marred by a burn, and clothing can be spotted with holes from ashes or sparks. **#2** Moreover, the destructive effect smoking has on property can inadvertently affect one's health and life. For instance, a smoldering mattress, the result of a careless smoker's unnoticed spark, can itself produce enough smoke to cause the death of the bed's occupant through smoke inhalation. A house fire, the result of a carelessly extinguished cigarette, can lead to serious burns or death of the occupants of the house. Also, a carelessly dropped cigarette can destroy an entire ecological system and its wildlife. If one thinks the effects of smoking on property are minimal, then think again.

3. *When I moved into my apartment, I had (to assume the household chores) my parents had previously done for me.* **#1** One of my first tasks was learning to push a vacuum cleaner. But about six weeks ago, the motor in my vacuum died. During this month and a half, the carpet went uncleaned. The carpet got so dirty that I was forced to make a decision: either borrow a vacuum

cleaner or allow the carpet to walk out the door on its own. So recently, I decided to pay my parents a visit and borrow their cleaner. I am sure I made the right decision; this fifteen-minute cleaning job made a noticeable difference in my carpet's appearance. **#2** I have also learned to clean the bathroom, mop the floor, and wash the windows. Although none of these chores are enjoyable, they are all done at regular intervals. For example, the bathroom fixtures are cleaned every two weeks, and the kitchen floor is mopped once a month. Finally, the windows are cleaned once every six months. Living on my own has taught me new responsibilities.

4. *The role-playing game Dungeons and Dragons has been blamed by some for causing (violent behavior, devil worship, and even suicides among its players.)* **#1** Critics claim that the game's violent nature—players imagine that they are medieval heroes who confront and destroy various monsters—encourages players to be more aggressive in real life. **#2** Opponents of the game also assert that the game, rather than being mere entertainment, is actually a form of mind control that alters the player's personality; they believe that the game's "occult" nature leads some players to devil worship. **#3** Moreover, critics claim that the game has led some players to commit suicide. Supposedly, the player becomes so involved with the game that he can no longer distinguish between fantasy and reality. According to the game's critics, a participant, believing that he or she will be brought back to life in the game, may kill himself or herself. However, such claims are poorly supported by facts.

5. *Other people support the position that Dungeons and Dragons is actually (beneficial to players.)* **#1** According to its advocates, the game encourages players to use their imagination and logic while they are finding solutions to problems they encounter during the course of the game. Proponents argue that this imaginative role-playing helps players to develop more mental flexibility and that the players, consequently, are more able to find solutions to real-life problems. **#2** Also, since the game relies upon a numerical rating system for combat, magic, characters, and other aspects, the players develop their mathematical skills and their abilities to work with and understand numbers. Hence, two distinct skills are developed by the game: inventive problem-solving and mathematical ability.

▼ EXERCISE 3

1. a. A
   b. B
   c. B
   d. A
   e. B

2. a. A
   b. B
   c. A
   d. A
   e. B

3. a. A
   b. A
   c. A
   d. B
   e. B
   f. A

4. a. B
   b. B
   c. A
   d. A
   e. B
   f. A
   g. B

5. a. A
   b. A
   c. B
   d. B
   e. B
   f. A

▼ EXERCISE 4

Indicated below are the primary supports which do not contribute to the development of the topic sentence. The corrections will vary.

1. PS 2
2. PS 4
3. PS 2
4. PS 3
5. PS 3

▼ EXERCISE 6

1. (CI: several informal rites)
   1. TS
   2. PS
   3. SS
   4. PS
   5. SS
   6. SS

      7. PS
      8. SS
      9. CS

2. (CI: degree of independence)
      1. TS
      2. PS
      3. SS
      4. SS
      5. SS
      6. SS
      7. PS
      8. SS
      9. SS
     10. SS
     11. SS
     12. SS
     13. CS

3. (CI: many other types of people)
      1. TS
      2. PS
      3. SS
      4. PS
      5. SS
      6. PS
      7. SS
      8. CS

4. (CI: not children's books at all)
      1. TS
      2. PS
      3. SS
      4. SS
      5. PS
      6. SS
      7. PS
      8. CS

5. (CI: too commercialized)
      1. TS
      2. PS
      3. SS
      4. SS
      5. SS
      6. PS
      7. SS
      8. SS
      9. SS
     10. CS

▼ EXERCISE 7

1. 1. 6 SS
    2. 10 SS
    3. 2 PS
    4. 4 PS
    5. 1 TS
    6. 5 SS
    7. 3 PS
    8. 7 SS
    9. 9 SS
    10. 11 PS
    11. 8 PS

2. 1. 4 SS
    2. 1 TS
    3. 2 PS
    4. 7 SS
    5. 8 SS
    6. 6 SS
    7. 9 SS
    8. 10 SS
    9. 3 PS
    10. 5 PS

3. 1. 1 TS
    2. 6 SS
    3. 4 SS
    4. 7 SS
    5. 2 PS
    6. 5 PS
    7. 3 SS

4. 1. 13 PS
    2. 9 PS
    3. 3 PS
    4. 6 SS
    5. 1 TS
    6. 10 SS
    7. 12 SS
    8. 11 SS
    9. 2 TS
    10. 5 SS
    11. 14 SS
    12. 8 SS
    13. 15 SS
    14. 4 SS
    15. 7 SS

5. 1. 3 SS
    2. 5 SS
    3. 2 PS

4. 1   TS
5. 7   SS
6. 4   PS
7. 6   PS
8. 8   PS

▼ EXERCISE 10

1. Concluding last sentence: This movie will not . . .

2. Concluding last sentence: The patient had a high fever . . .

3. Concluding last sentence: Americans must be awakened . . .

4. Concluding last sentence: People rarely buy . . .

5. Concluding last sentence: Many students have . . .

▼ EXERCISE 11

1. a. F
    b. J

2. a. F
    b. J

3. a. J
    b. F

4. a. J
    b. F

5. a. F
    b. J

▼ EXERCISE 12

1. a. F
    b. J

2. a. F
    b. J

3. a. J
    b. F

4. a. J
    b. F

5. a. F
    b. J

▼ Writing Strategy: CLASSIFICATION

Model Classifications

I. "THREE NEW YORKS" BY E.B. WHITE (READING LEVEL: 10.4)

1. Yes. The rest of the paragraph explains White's topic sentence clearly and simply.

2. White has three categories: the New York of native-born people, the New York of commuters, and the New York of those who settled from somewhere else.

3. White's tone is direct, informative, and positive.

II. "WHALES" BY RACHEL CARSON (READING LEVEL: COLLEGE)

1. Carson classifies whales by the food each type eats.

2. The sperm whale suffers most for its food. It must battle the squid in order to eat it, and its scars testify to such battles.

3. *Untenanted* means uninhabited.
   Writhing is twisting and turning.
   Temperate is moderate.
   Formidably means powerfully or impressively.

III. "FRIENDS, GOOD FRIENDS—AND SUCH GOOD FRIENDS" BY JUDITH VIORST (READING LEVEL: COLLEGE)

1. Viorst's thesis is located in paragraph three, sentence two: "for the friendships I have and the friendships I see are conducted at many levels of intensity, serve many different functions, meet different needs and range from those as all-the-way as the friendship of the soul sisters mentioned above to that of the most nonchalant and casual playmates."

2. Comments from other women demonstrate that Viorst is not alone in her classification of friendships; these comments strengthen and support Viorst's own statements.

3. Historical friends have known each other since childhood and are familiar with each other's families; historical friends preserve the past. Crossroads friends also share the past, but they share only a small portion of it.

4. Although she does combine some groups, Viorst's classification is effective. She does combine several groups under "men friends"; however, since she concentrates primarily on women

friends, the men do not need a separate classification system. She also combines "medium, and pretty good friends, and very good friends indeed" since these groups are distinguished by the amount of information one tells them.

IV. "STUDENTS AND THEIR SHOES" BY MOBEEN SAEED (READING LEVEL: 8.0)

1. Saeed's first sentence is her main idea: "The types of shoes individuals wear can provide insights into their personalities."

2. She supports her point of view by first dividing students into three groups based on their shoes: the sneaker-wearers, the casual-shoe wearers, and the dress-shoe wearers. She then describes how each group's footwear suggests what they wear, how they behave, what their interests are, and so on.

3. Her categories are not necessarily all-inclusive. What about ROTC/military students, for example?

▼ Classification Checklist

1. What is the basis for your classification?

2. Is the classification consistent?

3. Did you divide the topic into distinct categories? Do any categories overlap?

4. Does the classification include stereotypes? Can you omit these?

▼ Organization Checklist

1. Is each category in your classification listed in a primary support sentence?

2. What specific supports have you given for each category?

3. What type of concluding sentence did you use?

4. Did you try to draw any logical conclusions? If so, are they valid?

5. Did you make any judgments? If so, did you support them by the information given?

Chapter Five
Revising

1. To revise a paragraph effectively.

2. To edit a paragraph effectively.

3. To proofread a paragraph effectively.

4. To explore composing through illustration by example.

Teaching Suggestions

This chapter presents a full discussion of revision. The separate activities involved in revision often aren't clear and distinct to students. Consequently, they can use all the practice they can get. They may think that "real" writers get it all right the first time, and that they themselves are the only ones who rewrite anything. Some students may feel that revising a piece is recopying it; they need to see that "re-vision" involves editing and evaluating the content and organization of work, and that it involves proofreading for grammatical and mechanical errors.

Collaboration is particularly useful with revision, and peer groups can work quite effectively. Groups can work through paragraphs and essays several times. First, they can focus on larger, global issues such as unity and clear development; they can also comment on whether ideas are clear or not, on whether examples or details are appropriate and sufficient, on organization, on effective word choice, and on introductions and conclusions. They can read their work aloud for the other group members, who listen and then respond. Students can revise for content and organization and then bring the new piece back for comments. Only at the last draft should they proofread for problems in grammar and mechanics. To help them, you might write and duplicate brief, separate checklists for revising/editing and proofreading, so that students can use them easily in groups.

As before, link this writing strategy to previous ones, especially narration and description. Students may think that each writing strategy is used separately from the others, but you can show them how various modes of development are often combined within an essay that is structured by one particular mode.

Additional Activities

1. Provide students with an excerpt from the first draft of a famous work, perhaps Thomas Wolfe's *You Can't Go Home Again*. Ask the students to revise it. Then have them compare their revised draft with the final published piece.

2. Talk about revision in other contexts—textbook editions, for example (you could provide several editions of a textbook for them to examine)—or in other forms such as music or art.

3. For additional readings that use illustration by example, discuss "To Build A Fire" by Jack London, "The Road Not Taken" by Robert Frost, "Shakespeare's Sister" by Virginia Woolf, or "The Battle of the Ants" by Henry David Thoreau.

4. Students can use illustration by example to develop topics based on proverbs (such as "Honesty is the best policy"), showing whether or not that proverb is true.

Answer Key

▼ EXERCISE 1

1. Having lived my entire life in a house in the western part of Maryland, I adapted to the weather and the lifestyle of the residents. However, when I graduated from high school, I decided to spend my summer with friends working in Ocean City. For the first time, I was living on my own, which changed my lifestyle and responsibilities. I changed from a dependent person to an independent one at age eighteen. First, I went from going to school and working part-time in a small bakery in the mall to working as a full-time waitress at Lombardi's Italian Restaurant. I worked from five in the afternoon until two in the morning every day or from twelve in the afternoon until ten at night. In addition, I started to enjoy lying on the beach in the sun as much as I like skiing down a mountain. Freedom affected part of my lifestyle. First of all, I was able to come and go as I pleased since I did not have my parents around to watch over me. Because I did not have a curfew, I arrived at my apartment anywhere from one A.M. to seven A.M. Also, I was able to invite friends over any time I wanted. For example, if I had the night off, I could call up some people

to come over and have a party. Another freedom I enjoyed was the freedom to dress any way I wanted, without my parents, brothers, or sisters telling me to change. My living conditions, too, were affected by my move to the ocean. I went from a lonely two-bed, two-closet bedroom to a crowded two-bed, two-closet bedroom shared by three girls. Having no parents to pick up after me made me realize I would have to clean or it would not get done. Hence, I learned how to do laundry, clean the bathroom, and vacuum; however, these chores did not get done as often as I would have liked them to because of my working late, partying late, and being too tired. Besides learning how to clean, I also learned how to cook. A summer away from parents and pressures gave me a chance to see how I was going to handle moving away to college. I believe without a summer at the beach I would have had a hard time adjusting to college life.

2. San Diego, California and Rockville, Maryland are two cities separated by geography and culture. One difference is their variety of seasons. Summer and fall are the only two seasons San Diego really has. The summers last from early March to late November with the temperature fluctuating between 80 degrees and 101 degrees. The fall lasts from early December to late February with large amounts of rainfall. During this dreary season, the temperature does not fall below freezing. However, Rockville has four distinct seasons: spring, summer, winter, and fall. Spring, the most beautiful season of all, lasts from March to May. During the summer, which lasts from June to August, the humidity ranges from 70–80%. The fall lasts from August to late November, with pleasantly cool winds. Winter, the snow-filled season, is cold but gratifying. Another difference is the distance to travel for entertainment. In San Diego, the distance to and from entertainment is much less than than of Rockville. La Jolla Shores Beach is only twenty minutes away from downtown San Diego. McDonald's, the favorite hangout of high school students, is five minutes from Mt. Carmel High School; also, the widely-known San Diego Zoo is only a half hour away from that school. On the other hand, Rockville is three hours from Ocean City's beach. The regular high school hangout, McDonald's, is fifteen minutes from Magruder High School, and, at times, it seems like forever to get there. Furthermore, the National Zoo is an hour and a half away, a considerable distance to drive. Besides the seasons and distances, the attitudes of the people differ immensely. The people of San Diego possess a very "laid-back" attitude. They go about their daily lives in an unrushed manner. Work projects and punctuality are second priority to recreation and social activities. In contrast, the people of Rockville are much more hurried and tend to put work as their number one priority. Trivial incidents upset and aggravate Rockville inhabi-

tants, creating a very tense atmosphere. The seasons, distances, and attitudes are just some of the differences between the two cities which one should always keep in mind.

▼ EXERCISE 6

Competitiveness is very influential to students because it encourages the student and it improves the quality of the student's work. Most importantly, the competitive spirit encourages students to work. Through the years, humans have always tried to do better than their peers. Hunters compete with each other to see who shoots the greatest number of deer or who catches the most fish, so everyone has this natural instinct for competition with other individuals. This natural instinct is the whole idea for using competition in schools. Students are constantly trying to do better than each other, and teachers encourage this so that everyone tries to improve his or her standing in the class. As a result, students who work at their grades will improve. In addition, as a consequence of students' being challenged, quality becomes an important issue. To ensure a high grade, students want their work to be the best it can be. The student may spend hours and hours reading English papers to insure perfection. Furthermore, neatness is very important because it makes the instructor's job easier and, thus, gives the student an advantage over students who are sloppy writers. With this drive for perfection, a sense of pride in accomplishments occurs. Receiving a paper back with no mistakes from a teacher makes the student feel that the few extra hours of work paid off. In the long run, students are better off when they are challenged to succeed.

▼ Writing Strategy: ILLUSTRATION BY EXAMPLE

Model Paragraphs

I. "THE COMMUTER" BY E.B. WHITE (READING LEVEL: 12.2)

1. White suggests that they miss learning about the city itself, which he implies offers a rich and diverse culture.

2. His tone is one of puzzlement and sadness for all of the missed wonders that commuters deliberately overlook or ignore.

3. White's metaphor continues by referring to a home as a roost. Later, White also compares the commuter to a fisherman and to a wandering prairie dog.

4. *Gloaming* means dusk.
   Spewing is belching forth.
   Devious means indirect and hidden.
   Ramparts are protective barriers.

II. "SHARKS" BY PHILIPPE COUSTEAU (READING LEVEL: COLLEGE)

1. The topic sentence is in the middle and begins "It was in this climate of excessive vanity. . . . " This position enables the sentence to serve as a transition between the background information that precedes it and the supporting details for the controlling ideas that follow in the remainder of the paragraph.

2. Cousteau says that the diver becomes "an awkward and vulnerable creature" as soon as he enters the water, in contrast to the shark, and that it is intoxicating for the diver "to imagine himself stronger" than "a creature far better armed than he."

3. Initially, both divers were "frozen with terror" and clung to each other, but when the shark panics and leaves, they feel "an unjustified sensation of triumph" that, after several such encounters, led to their excitement, excessive confidence, and relaxed security measures.

4. Cousteau reveals his vulnerability, his suggestibility. Despite knowing the dangers of overconfidence, he was nevertheless lulled into a false sense of security.

III. "THE BOONS OF CIVILIZATION" BY H.L. MENCKEN (READING LEVEL: 9.9)

1. Mencken could live without telephones, radios, phonographs, movies, or automobiles. He dislikes them because they are noisy, distracting, jarring, and often uncomfortable; they prevent a peaceful, quiet life.

2. The thermostat, unlike the other inventions, enhances life because it eases labor and allows Mencken to spend his time more productively.

3. *Limned* means drawn.
   Vinous means caused by drinking wine.
   Usufruct is the right to enjoy the use, profits, and advantages of someone else's property without damaging it.
   Boons are useful and pleasant gifts.

4. He forgot it. Mencken implies that the inventor is less famous because, unlike the other inventors Mencken mentions, he did not invent anything involving speech or language.

IV. "DO SOMETHING DIFFERENT: GO BACK IN TIME" BY RAY STOLLE (READING LEVEL: 9.2)

1. Stolle's topic sentence is the first one: "Upon arriving at the entrance of the Maryland Renaissance Festival, one feels that

he is about to experience something different and exciting." It is a satisfactory topic sentence because it limits the topic and has a controlling idea that will guide development and structure.

2. This piece is developed through specific details, examples of the major points (the primary support statements) Stolle includes that illustrate "different and exciting." These primary support statements are the following: "The permanent location of the festival . . . "; "The interior of the Renaissance Festival . . . "; and "Maybe the most interesting aspect. . . . "

3. For each primary support statement, Stolle includes secondary support with detailed examples that illustrate. For example, the primary support statement about the interior being set up like an English town with shops, amusements, and food vendors is followed by examples of types of shops and amusements.

4. Stolle's tone is one of enjoyment. What he enjoys is that there are so many different and exciting things to see and do, and the sheer abundance of these things impresses him.

▼ Revision Checklist

1. List two revisions you made during the writing process. How did you determine what to revise? What changes did you make?

2. List any grammatical or punctuation problems you found during editing. How did you correct them?

3. List any typing errors you found during proofreading. How did you find them?

▼ Illustration Checklist

1. What is your topic sentence? Where is it located?

2. How do the major examples support the topic sentence?

3. How do specific details develop each example?

4. What is the structure of the paragraph? How are examples organized? What makes this organization effective?

Chapter Six

Achieving Coherence

1. To write a coherent paragraph by using pronouns, synonyms, limited repetition, sentence combining, and transitional words and expressions.

2. To explore composing through comparison and contrast.

Teaching Suggestions

This chapter fully explains coherence. However, some students may still be experiencing trouble writing a coherent paragraph. If the problem lies in jumbled ideas, then you need to review idea unity and idea order. These coherence problems are not solved by Chapter Six, which instead provides the mechanical tools for eliminating choppiness.

If students are having trouble with this second type of coherence, additional practice through controlled composition might be helpful. This technique is very effective with ESL students. Give students a paragraph and have them rewrite the paragraph, changing one element throughout ("John" to "Joan" or "the boys" to "the girls"). Such rewriting helps students to see the links between sentences and the impact that one change has on other sentences. It also helps them practice editing because it forces them to review the whole paragraph carefully. In addition, controlled composition teaches students to avoid unnecessary repetition by demonstrating its ineffectiveness. This type of exercise allows students to concentrate on coherence without worrying about content.

Again, you could link the comparison/contrast writing strategy to your students' everyday lives to show that these writing strategies often mirror the ways we process information. We constantly examine similarities and differences between things, usually to decide which is better or preferable. However, you need to stress that the two items under consideration must have something in common, or there would be no basis for a comparison.

Additional Activities

1. Have the class work as a group while you work at the board. Give them a topic most of them can relate to, such as "high school/college." (This may be boring, but it will serve for discussion.) Brainstorm the major points and details and organize them into an outline.

2. Have student write about things they're familiar with: two jobs they've held, two employers they've worked for, two teachers, two places they've lived, two dates, two places important to them, and so on.

3. Students could compare and contrast a childhood memory with their current vision of the same thing: a favorite childhood place, cartoons, how they view their parents, and so forth.

4. Bring in two recordings of the same piece of music; play both and have students brainstorm about the similarities and differences.

5. Bring in two photographs of the same person, at two different ages, and have students compare and contrast them.

NOTE: You might consider having students write two paragraphs on the same topic: one comparing (looking for similarities) and one contrasting (looking for differences). These paragraphs could be used later for a multi-paragraph essay, if the course includes essays as well as paragraphs.

Answer Key

▼ EXERCISE 1

1. he
2. her, they
3. he, he
4. he [or she]
5. his, they, he
6. his [or her]

7. it, its, it

8. its, he

9. its, its

10. they

▼ EXERCISE 2

These are some of the possibilities; others may also be acceptable.

1. artists

2. one or instructor

3. the animal, he

4. it

5. there

6. it

7. deficiencies

8. effort or work

9. there

10. courage

▼ EXERCISE 3

1. <u>To those</u> old allies whose cultural and spiritual origins <u>we share</u>, <u>we pledge</u> the loyalty of faithful friends. <u>United, there is little we cannot do</u> in a host of new cooperative ventures. <u>Divided, there is little we can do</u>—for we dare not meet a powerful challenge at odds and split asunder.

   <u>To those</u> new states whom we welcome to the ranks of the free, we pledge our word that one form of colonial control shall not have passed away merely to be replaced by a far more iron tyranny. <u>We shall not always</u> expect to find them supporting our view. But <u>we shall always</u> hope to find them strongly supporting their own <u>freedom</u>—and to remember that, in the past, those who foolishly sought power by riding the back of the tiger ended up inside.

   <u>To those</u> people in the huts and villages of half the globe struggling to break the bonds of mass misery, <u>we pledge</u> our best efforts to help them help themselves, for whatever period is required—<u>not because</u> the Communists may be doing it, <u>not</u>

because we seek their votes, but because it is right. If a free society cannot help the many who are poor, it cannot save the few who are rich.

(John F. Kennedy, "Inaugural Address")

2. "Call this a govment! Why, just look at it and see what it's like. Here's the law a-standing ready to take a man's son away from him—a man's own son, which he has had all the trouble and all the anxiety and all the expense of raising. Yes, just as that man has got that son raised at last, and ready to go to work, and begin to do suthin' for him and give him a rest, the law up and goes for him. And they call that govment! That ain't all nuther. The law backs that old Judge Thatcher up and helps him to keep me out o' my property. Here's what the law does. The law takes a man worth six thousand dollars and upwards, and jams him into an old trap of a cabin like this, and lets him go around in clothes that ain't fitted for a hog. They call that govment! A man can't get his rights in a govment like this. Sometimes I've a mighty notion to just leave the country for good and all. Yes, and I told 'em so; I told old Thatcher so to his face. Lots of 'em heard me, and can tell what I said. Says I, for two cents I'd leave the blamed country and never come anear it again. Them's the very words. I says, look at my hat—if you call it a hat—but the lid raises up and the rest of it goes down till it's below my chin, and then it ain't rightly a hat at all, but more like my head was shoved up through a jint o' stovepipe. Look at it, says I—such a hat for me to wear—one of the wealthiest men in this town if I could get my rights."

(from Pap Finn in The Adventures of Huckleberry Finn)

3. Four score and seven years ago, our fathers brought forth on this continent, a new nation, conceived in Liberty, and dedicated to the proposition that all men are created equal.

Now we are engaged in a great civil war; testing whether that nation, or any nation so conceived and so dedicated, can long endure. We are met on a great battlefield of that war. We have come to dedicate a portion of that field as a final resting-place for those who here gave their lives that that nation might live. It is altogether fitting and proper that we should do this.

But, in a larger sense, we cannot dedicate—we cannot consecrate—we cannot hallow—this ground. The brave men, living and dead, who struggled here have consecrated it, far above our poor power to add or detract. The world will little note, nor long remember, what we say here, but it can never forget what they did here. It is for us the living, rather, to be dedicated here to the unfinished work which they who fought here have thus far so nobly advanced. It is rather for us to be here dedicated to the great task remaining before us—that from these honored dead we take increased devotion to that cause for which they gave the last full measure of devotion; that we here highly resolve that these dead shall not have died in vain; that this nation, under God, shall have a new birth of freedom; and that government of the people, by the people, for the people, shall not perish from the earth.

(Abraham Lincoln, "The Gettysburg Address")

▼ EXERCISE 5

1. as; time

2. because; cause

3. after; time

4. when; time

5. furthermore; addition

6. despite; contrast

7. overall; summary

8. as; cause

9. until; time

10. to repeat; repetition

▼ EXERCISE 6

These are suggested responses, but others are also acceptable.

1. because

2. first, second, next, finally

3. unfortunately

4. consequently

5. because

6. even though

7. also

8. for example

9. although

10. therefore

▼ EXERCISE 7

1. (As a hobby,) gardening is not the tranquil, bucolic exercise that promoters claim. (Instead,) there are many problems and frustrations associated with "getting to know nature." (First,) Mother Natures does not smile and shed her warmth on the gardener during November and March, the prime months for planting bulbs and readying the soil. Spending hours on your knees digging in hard, cold soil is guaranteed to cause more arthritis than any tennis game ever could. (Second,) raking and hoeing the garden to prepare the soil are not the back-strengthening exercises recommended by the orthopedist. (In fact,) they are not recommended by anyone, other than your worst enemy. (Then,) once the soil is prepared and everything is planted, the real problems arrive: drought, flood, heat, and insects. There is nothing more frustrating than watching hours of back-breaking effort float away on a storm-produced stream or shrivel under record-breaking sunshine. (In short,) for tranquility, you should try a nice, quiet game of poker; at least *then* you can gamble away the proceeds of many hours of work in just two hours.

Dominant pattern: Importance

2. (Then) the man drowsed off into what seemed to him the most comfortable and satisfying sleep he had ever known. The dog sat facing him and waiting. The brief day drew to a close in a long, slow twilight. There were no signs of a fire to be made, and (besides) never in the dog's experience had it known a man to sit like that in the snow and make no fire. As the twilight drew on, its eager yearning for the fire mastered it (and) with a great lifting and shifting of forefeet, it whined softly, flattened its ears down in anticipation of being chidden by the man. (But) the man remained silent. (Later,) the dog whined loudly. (And still later,) it crept close to the man and caught the scent of death. This made the animal bristle and back away. A little longer it delayed, howling under the stars that leaped and danced and shone brightly in the cold sky. (Then) it turned and trotted up the trail in the direction of the camp it knew, where were the other food- providers and fire-providers.

(from Jack London, "To Build A Fire")

Dominant Pattern: Chronology

3. (While) the method of direct payments makes certain that those

suffering most from the anguish of unemployment will receive direct aid, its total effect may be less than public spending in the form of public works. (If) the individual is given a direct payment, the bulk of the payment is spent for consumption. This increases the level of economic activity to some degree, provided the funds received do not come at the expense of consumption and investment elsewhere in the economy. (Even if) the individual is employed on a simple project such as leaf raking for the sake of respectability, the total effect is not much greater. The capital needed to put a group of individuals on such a job is limited to rakes, shovels, wheelbarrows, and perhaps a few trucks. (Furthermore,) the spending of a direct income payment primarily for consumer goods may have no greater effect than decreasing excess inventories of consumer goods.

(from Thomas J. Hailstones, Basic Economics, *6th edition)*

Dominant Pattern: Addition

4. (One) of the many devastating effects of inflation on the middle class is the precipitous rise in tuition costs. (As) a direct consequence of annual tuition increases of fifteen to twenty percent, more and more students must combine schooling and working in order to be able to afford their education. Without the job, they cannot pay for school, yet, with the job, they have neither the time nor the energy required by school. (After) students have attended classes for five hours, and worked for another five hours, homework commands little, if any, interest or effort. (When) homework done in a slip-shod manner becomes the norm, grades suffer. (Then,) teachers must face students who do not know the material because they have not studied it. The final result is that the teacher becomes a remediator, a reviewer of basic skills, (instead) of an instructor in new materials. (Therefore,) despite the widespread belief in the value of working, there are instances (when) it is more advantageous for a student not to work.

Dominant pattern: Cause/Effect

5. More people should donate blood; giving blood is truly giving life. (Unfortunately,) too many adults have retained their childhood fear of needles, and so they refuse to face the blood technicians. (Or,) they don't understand the donating procedures, (and) this fear of the unknown prevents them from helping other human beings. (Perhaps) if the prospective donors knew all the uses to which their pint of blood is put and all the people who are helped by it, (then) they would be more willing to really give of themselves. The whole blood is used, (of course,) (but) so are blood products. The pint can be separated into its components, (and) each part given to an ill person.

Platelets help those whose respiratory systems do not function properly. In addition, the white cells are used to help leukemia patients, and the blood serum provides needed fluids. When adults realize the multiple recipients of their gift, each one will be eager to donate at least four times a year.

Dominant Pattern: Addition

▼ Writing Strategy: COMPARISON/CONTRAST

Model Paragraphs

I. "ORANGES: FLORIDA AND CALIFORNIA" BY JOHN McPHEE (READING LEVEL: 9.2)

1. Florida oranges have thin, tight-fitting skins and are heavy with juice. In contrast, California oranges have thick skins, are light-weight, have sweet flesh, are easily segmented, and are more beautiful.

2. He attributes the differences to water: Florida's water comes from natural rainfall while California's water is irrigation water from the Colorado River and other sources.

3. McPhee's personal preference for California oranges is clear. Even if Florida grows three times as many oranges as California, it doesn't matter to McPhee, since he attributes greater beauty to the western oranges.

II. "HIS TALK, HER TALK" BY JOYCE MAYNARD (READING LEVEL: 10.2)

1. They are characters from the television series *I Love Lucy*; Lucy is the title character and Ethel is her next-door neighbor.

2. Both males and females are "really talking about the same eternal conflicts."

3. Maynard says that men and women differ in their styles of talking. Men talk in direct, precise, and efficient style; they can summarize whole conversations in a single sentence. Women, in contrast, savor the telling itself, taking time and not worrying about direct routes to the point.

III. "TWO VIEWS OF THE RIVER" BY MARK TWAIN (READING LEVEL: 8.8)

1. Twain's main idea is introduced in the first three sentences of the first paragraph, and stated over them: "I had made a valuable acquisition. But I had lost something, too. I had lost something which could never be restored to me while I lived."

2. The first view focuses on Twain's perception of the romantic beauty of the river, "the grace, the beauty, the poetry", which he drank in "in a speechless rapture." The second view focuses on his valuing any feature of the river only by "the amount of usefulness it could furnish toward compassing the safe piloting of a steamboat." In each paragraph he furnishes a transition between the two views with the word "but."

3. He uses the rhetorical device of repetition. He repeats the same points about the river in explaining each view. Thus the "wonderful sunset" which at first signals only beauty later "means that we are going to have wind tomorrow." This repetition underscores the great contrasts between Twain's two views.

4. Twain became a steamboat pilot, and in learning "the language of the river" as a pilot must know it, he lost his previous innocent appreciation of the beauty of nature. After he became a pilot, he had only the memory of such a fresh, new world.

IV. "LIVES BEYOND THE BELTWAY" BY DOUG EPPLER (READING LEVEL: 6.3)

1. Eppler states his main idea in the last sentence of the first paragraph: "Daily glimpses of these distant points show me two different lives—mine." It controls the piece by indicating the types of details he will use—daily glimpses of each place— in order to show how his lives in each are altogether different and separate.

2. The first paragraph introduces the general topic, comparing his city life in Baltimore and his rural life in New Freedom, and it narrows to state his main idea. The second and third paragraphs focus on Baltimore only; the fourth and fifth paragraphs focus on New Freedom only. The last paragraph draws significant conclusions. This is an effective organization; separate discussions of each place underscore the separateness of his own lives and heightens the sense of difference or contrast.

3. The major differences are in population, appearance, pace, pastimes, and in personality. In order to illustrate these differences, Eppler details the constant growth of building in

Baltimore, its nationally famous people, the fast pace people must keep up with, and that people "rise and fall with the trends." In New Freedom, nature (rather than buildings and highways) dominates the scene. No famous people are there. Little change happens, and the pace slows.

▼ Coherence Checklist

1. Have you used pronouns to avoid needlessly repeating the same words?

2. Have you used synonyms to reinforce important concepts?

3. If the piece is long enough, did you repeat key structures to emphasize primary ideas?

4. If you repeated key terms or phrases, why did you? What was your purpose?

5. Do you have more than one type of sentence?

6. Did you coordinate ideas of equal value in compound sentences?

7. Did you subordinate ideas of lesser value in complex sentences?

8. Are there transitions between sentences and ideas?

9. Are the transitions appropriate? Do they represent the types of relationships you want to stress?

10. Can the reader easily follow the ideas presented in the paragraph?

▼ Comparison/Contrast Checklist

1. Does your paragraph offer readers an analysis of subtle, rather than obvious, points of comparison or contrast between the two items?

2. Did you organize your comparison/contrast effectively, presenting information about each item in the same sequence?

Chapter Seven
Diction

TEACHING OBJECTIVES

1. To use appropriate diction for achieving a specific purpose.

2. To avoid slang, jargon, regional expressions, clichés, and dead metaphors.

3. To be aware of a word's connotations and denotations.

4. To use context to define a word.

5. To recognize and create tone.

6. To explore composing through cause/effect.

Teaching Suggestions

Sensitivity to word choice is vital for any writer. Students need to practice levels of specificity and levels of abstraction; such exercises can be very useful in establishing the differences between general/specific and abstract/concrete. Further, learning about levels of diction enables them to select suitable vocabularies for different audiences. You could provide students with factual information from a newspaper article; they could then use the information as a basis for several paragraphs directed toward different audiences. To illustrate, the facts concerning a crime could be used in a police report, a letter to the editor calling for additional police protection, or a presentation to school children about crime.

Cause and effect analysis will probably be one of the writing strategies students will use fairly often, along with comparison/contrast. Again, it is a thought pattern that we practice daily in life, and showing students how they already use cause/effect can help them employ it in writing.

Additional Activities

1. Use groups of related words and have students arrange them in order from most general to most specific, or from most abstract to most concrete. Discuss when more specific or more concrete words would be desirable.

2. Bring in examples of "doublespeak" and have students try to decipher them; alternatively, you could have students bring in examples that they find.

3. Have students locate examples of jargon in their other text-books.

4. Distribute copies of journals from specific disciplines; have students identify the jargon and audience for each.

5. Brainstorm a cause/effect topic as a group and outline it on the board.

6. Have students write about why they made a particular decision (causes), or about the effects of that decision.

NOTE: As suggested for comparison/contrast, have students write two para-graphs on the same topic, so that they write one paragraph focusing upon causes and another focusing upon effects. These could form the rough draft body for a multi-paragraph essay, if the course includes essays as well as paragraphs.

Answer Key

▼ EXERCISE 3

The following clichés and dead metaphors are in the sentences. Students' revi-sion of these clichés and metaphors will vary.

1. stubborn as a Tennessee mule

2. sure as shooting, pleased as punch

3. pretty as a picture

4. dark as a bottomless pit

5. rained cats and dogs

6. ride the problem out

7. tough as nails, a kitty cat

8. she's a rock

9. Achilles' heel

10. let his hair down

▼ EXERCISE 5

1.

WORD	DENOTATION	CONNOTATION
a. politician	one who is in politics	negative, compared to an elected official
b. cronies	close friends	cohorts
c. bars	place where liquor is sold	here, a bar could be an unobtrusive place for a political deal
d. back rooms	literally, a room behind another	a private place for deals
e. goings-on	an occurrence	informal discussions and deals

Tone: informal
Probable audience: general reader

2.

WORD	DENOTATION	CONNOTATION
a. diplomat	one who works in international relations	positive; extremely tactful person, adept at the social and cultural graces
b. acquaintances	people one knows slightly	social or political contacts of the diplomat
c. reception	a gathering to receive guests	here, a social gathering with political overtones
d. manipulate	to deal with skillfully	to encourage tactfully and courteously to do one's request
e. undercurrents	currents below the surface	the tacit "give and take" of international relations

Tone: formal
Probable audience: this could appear in a political science book on international relations or in a pamphlet for new foreign-service employees

▼ EXERCISE 6   Answers will vary; these are only some possibilities.

1. An *amaneunsis* is a type of secretary.

2. *Phobias* are irrational fears.

3. *Paraplegics* are persons paralyzed in their lower bodies.

4. A *carnivore* eats meat.

5. The *ego* is the self.

6. *Neonatology* is the study of human newborns.

7. *Mammals* are animals like whales, dogs, and humans.

8. *Covert aid* is aid given secretly and its motives are usually questioned.

9. An *autarchy* is a form of government.

10. An *altruistic person* willingly sacrifices his or her own goals to help others.

▼ EXERCISE 7

1.a. *Tone:* pompous, pretentious
    Audience: the banker's peers
    Words contributing to tone: portly executive, regal stance, intimidate, insubordinate, awesome personage, disdainfully, sniveling nonentity, strode, petitioner, fear, wonder

 b. *Tone:* informal, colloquial
    Audience: general reader
    Words contributing to tone: fat, overwhelm, rebellious, cringing subordinate, fear-filled and wondering person

2.a. *Tone:* informal, uses jargon
    Audience: traders on the stock market
    Words contributing to tone: bottom fell out, plummeted an unbelievable forty points, scurry for their lives and pocket-books, tried to stonewall, shocking story, belittle the events, John Q. Public, looked for gold bugs

 b. *Tone:* factual
    Audience: newspaper readers
    Words contributing to tone: declined, fell, profit-taking, shaky investor confidence, less than five percent of the market's value, apprehensive, increased by twenty-five percent, gold futures rose by eighteen percent

▼ Writing Strategy: CAUSE AND EFFECT

Model Paragraphs

I. "THE ARREST OF ROSA PARKS" BY MARTIN LUTHER KING, JR. (READING LEVEL: 10.0)

1. Some of those who defend their civil rights are laborers; they have much to gain by their actions, though they also may suffer.

2. She was tired and wanted to sit on the bus rather than stand. Her ultimate reason may have been that it was her right to sit where she was.

3. Many people believe so, but the answer depends upon your definition of "heroic" and your view of the immediate consequences, as well of the circumstances.

4. The tone is very straightforward and matter-of-fact; it is reportorial.

II. "SEVERING THE HUMAN CONNECTION" BY H. BRUCE MILLER (READING LEVEL: 7.5)

1. The immediate cause was that people drove off from gas stations before they paid for the gas. The ultimate cause is that such behavior results in a significant loss of money and profit.

2. The police have other, perhaps more serious, crimes to deal with.

3. They adopted the pay-before-you-pump policy.

4. The following words are jargon: pre-pay (pay before you pump) and drive-offs (people who fill their tanks and then leave without paying).

III. "PRIMITIVE WAR" BY MARVIN HARRIS (READING LEVEL: 10.2)

1. Female infanticide is the deliberate, but usually covert, practice of killing or abandoning female infants.

2. Males are "reproductively redundant" because "one man can suffice to impregnate hundreds of females."

3. Harris asserts that women cannot be as proficient as men in armed combat that involves hand weapons. He believes that men have physical superiority—that they are taller, heavier, and more muscular; that they can throw farther and handle bigger weapons; and that they can run faster.

IV. "A PLACE TO COME HOME TO" BY RYAN BROMWELL (READING LEVEL: 10.0)

1. Bromwell's main idea is that home was a safe and nurturing place for him as he grew up. This idea is suggested from the first sentence in the first paragraph, but it is stated clearly and fully in the last sentence of that paragraph: "Over the years, my parents, my friends, and my neighbors have offered the safety and encouragement a growing boy needs along the way to young adulthood." This sentence controls the piece: it lists the three influences that made home safe and encouraging, and these three influences are each developed in a separate paragraph.

2. His parents encouraged him in what he tried, whether playing Little League baseball or traveling to Europe. Even if they were "a little apprehensive" about his desire to travel to Europe, they allowed him to do what he wanted, on the condition that he paid for the trip.

3. As an adult, he now finds his behavior and values reflect what they taught him, either through conditions imposed upon him, through play, or through direct example.

4. In paragraph 2, Bromwell the adult appreciates the lessons about responsibility which his parents fostered by making him pay for things he wanted, even if as a young boy all he wanted was "to run wild and free." In paragraph 3, he says that the harmless childhood games involving simple decisions about virtue and vice prepared him in their way for more complex decisions of morality. In paragraph 3, he traces his own adult generosity and trust to those older neighbors who showed him those virtues through their own examples.

5. His tone is one of reflection, gratitude, and perhaps amusement. His adult reflections on childhood and home reveal his gratitude to parents, friends, and neighbors in providing him with the "safety and encouragement a growing boy needs along the way to young adulthood." They also reveal his own adult amusement at his younger self.

▼ Cause and Effect Checklist

1. Does your paragraph begin with causes or effects?

2. Do the causes and effects go beyond the obvious ones? Did you include ultimate causes and effects as far as is reasonably possible?

3. In what order are the causes and effects presented?

4. Is that order effective in supporting the topic sentence? Why or why not?

5. Are the causes and effects verifiable by historical fact, statistics, or logic?

▼ Diction Checklist

1. Are your key concepts represented by carefully chosen words?

2. Can any word be replaced by a more specific word?

3. Have you eliminated slang, jargon, clichés, and dead metaphors from your paragraphs?

4. Does your paragraph achieve the tone you intended?

Chapter Eight
Style

▶ **TEACHING OBJECTIVES**

1. To develop a style suitable to your audience, purpose, and message.

2. To create a suitable style by effectively using voice, verbs, subordination, parallel constructions, and sentence variety, and by avoiding wordiness.

3. To explore composing through definition.

Teaching Suggestions

Students rarely have a developed sense of style. Often their concept of "good" style is formal, uses passive voice verbs, is wordy, and uses flowery or mannered vocabulary. That "good" style may sound more like their own voices probably seems unnatural to them. The more students learn about audience and purpose, the more they will understand how a writer's style should be shaped by these concepts.

Most students have a sense of the most basic of the three types of definition—dictionary definition; probably, they've had to memorize definitions for various classes. Those students who have had or are taking biology classes may be familiar with logical definitions. Some students may have written extended definitions in high school English classes. That this writing strategy has widespread application outside of English is clear to many students, so you might begin the discussion by asking students when and where definition is important; they can use their other classes and experiences to answer. As before, try to link this strategy with previously studied strategies, showing how extended definitions may be developed using other strategies. Both style and definition require a heightened sensitivity to language, so the link to the chapter on diction could be pointed out.

69

Additional Activities

1. Using common verbs like "walk," "drink," and so on, have students brainstorm other, more descriptive active verbs. This exercise also works well if you put up groups of related verbs, like "guzzle," "swill," "sip," and "gulp." Not only do students see the difference in action, but you can remind them of connotation—ask them what liquid each of these verbs implies.

2. Sentence combining exercises are ideal for practicing subordination and are easily constructed. Write a list of simple sentences about some recent campus or community activity; have students combine them, write them on the board, and discuss them.

3. An exercise similar to #2 would entail using other subjects for the groups of sentences that you write for the exercise. Soap operas are popular, so an exercise about characters or a plot line on a popular soap might be fun.

4. Students could work in groups and make up their own sentences, switch with another group, and combine each others' sentences.

5. You can also use sentence combining to focus on parallel construction or varying sentence type: simply direct students to combine the sentences using a particular structure.

6. Students can use a piece of their own work to analyze sentence types and then to rewrite those sentences using other types.

Answer Key

▼ **EXERCISE 1**

1. During the fall, Cheryl decided to join the army.

2. The gas occupies four cubic feet.

3. The snow fell quickly at 3 p.m.

4. Then Thomas decided to move to Oregon.

5. Mrs. James's student nervously paced the corridor as he awaited the principal's decision about his conduct.

6. The St. Patrick's Day parade attracted a large crowd dressed in green.

7. The four-wheel-drive Jeep climbed the steep, narrow, winding mountain road effortlessly.

8. The gymnast executed several difficult tumbling routines.

9. The newspaper journalist reported the latest developments of the Wall Street Stock Exchange.

10. After he had appeared in several television programs, the actor starred in a movie.

▼ EXERCISE 2

1. A well-known historian wrote the novel.

2. The network cancelled the television program after five weeks because of its poor ratings.

3. We washed the windows last week during our spring house-cleaning.

4. The priest opened the church doors as the newly married couple walked up the aisle.

5. Harriet, not Jason, gathered the information.

6. An expert artisan refinished the table.

7. acceptable use of passive-voice verb

8. acceptable use of passive-voice verb

9. acceptable use of passive-voice verb

10. acceptable use of passive-voice verb

▼ EXERCISE 3

1. The jogger paced down the street.

2. The football team huddles on the field.

3. The soprano expertly trilled "The Star Spangled Banner."

4. The bird flitted from tree to tree.

5. The wolf stalked the lamb.

6. St. Louis sprawls by the Mississippi River.

7. The skaters twirl on the ice.

8. The play excites the audience.

9. The child dashes around the playground.

10. The car's engine sputters strangely.

▼ EXERCISE 4

1. The topic sentence is the first one in the paragraph.

2. The controlling idea is "many reasons."

3. The following items support this controlling idea:
    a. Spring break is a well-deserved vacation for some students.
    b. Spring break is a time in which students can earn additional money.
    c. Seniors can use their spring breaks to apply for jobs.
    d. Students who procrastinated can complete assignments.

4. There are five supporting ideas located in dependent clauses (4 primary supports and 1 secondary support); only one secondary support is contained in an independent clause.

5. Yes, there is a problem with the focus since so many major ideas are buried in dependent clauses.

6. The following is a sample revision of the paragraph:
    College students appreciate their spring break for many reasons. First, spring break is a well-deserved vacation for some students who have worked diligently throughout the semester. These lucky students spend their vacation by relaxing at one of their favorite beach resorts. Second, students who work part-time during the academic year can work more hours during the break to earn additional money to pay for their college expenses. Also, many graduating seniors can use the time to apply for jobs and go on interviews. This extra time gives them an advantage over those students who do not apply for jobs until summer. Finally, those students who procrastinate can use this time to complete assignments and readings and to prepare for upcoming final examinations. Because spring break offers a welcome week away from academic pressures and schedules, college students are free to spend their time in several ways.

▼ EXERCISE 5

1. After he had purchased a sleeping bag, backpack, and hiking shoes, Gawain was prepared to camp and hike in the mountains.

2. Approaching the fence, jumping it cleanly, and landing gracefully, the rider received a round of applause from the spectators.

3. My grandmother enjoys cooking, reading, and singing.

4. The old cathedral with its stained-glass windows, high arches, and towering spires was impressive.

5. For the audition, she planned to sing a favorite aria but prepared it poorly.

▼ EXERCISE 6

The following is a sample revision; other revisions are possible. Types of sentences are indicated in parentheses:

The towns along the California coast have provided settings for many novels (Simple). John Steinbeck described Monterey in several of his novels, ranging from *Cannery Row*, which chronicles the adventures of the poor and a biologist, to *Tortilla Flat* (Complex). A little bit south of Monterey lies the small community of Big Sur (Simple). Situated on high cliffs overlooking the Pacific, this town provided the setting of Jack Kerouac's novel *Big Sur* (Simple). Portraying life in Los Angeles and its suburbs, Raymond Chandler wrote detective novels, such as *Farewell, My Lovely* and *The Big Sleep* (Simple). Other novelists also described Los Angeles and Hollywood (Simple). Nathaneal West explored the falsity of Hollywood movies in his novel *The Day of The Locust* (Simple). These novels all use California coastal towns as their settings (Simple).

▼ EXERCISE 7

Each sentence is labeled as loose or periodic. Sample revisions are included.

1. loose revision: Thus, not as men mainly, but as machines with their bodies, the mass of men serve the state.

2. loose revision: With remarkable schools, good libraries and not only major league baseball, but extensive concert series, second-run movie houses, expensive neighborhoods and a lovely rolling stretch of acreage called Prospect Park, Brooklyn had been a heterogeneous, dominantly middle-class community.

3. periodic revision: Plains felt peaceful and prosperous by comparison with meaner looking places with a gas station, barbecue shack, general stores, junkyard, empty lots and spilled gasoline, a redneck redolence of dried ketchup and hamburger napkins, splayed around thin-shanked, dusty trees.

4. loose revision: With more pomp and circumstance than Louisville ever knew before, in June she married Tom Buchanan of Chicago.

5. periodic revision: Give me truth rather than love, than money, than fame.

▼ EXERCISE 8

1. The tennis racquet Tom handed to Jill. (direct object)

2. Energetic and courageous, the captain boarded the alien vessel. (adjectives)

3. When he reached shore, the swimmer was exhausted. (dependent clause)

4. Joyfully, the children played at the beach. (adverb)

5. Clumsily but steadily, the bear climbed the tree. (adverbs)

6. Stripped of its finish, the desk was now ready for a coat of paint. (participial phrase)

7. With his briefcase filled with papers, the instructor faced several days of constant grading. (prepositional phrase)

8. Replete with ten rookies, the baseball team hoped for a better season than it had last year. (adjective)

9. On May 1, 1908, the city zoo first opened its doors. (prepositional phrase)

10. For its visual effects, the movie won an Academy Award. (prepositional phrase)

▼ Writing Strategy: DEFINITION

Model Paragraphs

I. "THE AMERICAN DREAM" BY BETTY ANNE YOUNGLOVE (READING LEVEL: 8.5)

1. Younglove uses extended definition (illustration) to define the American dream.

2. She defines the "original" American dream as "little to do with material possessions and a lot to do with choices, beginnings and opportunity."

3. She implies that the dream has now become a business, that people now make money off the dream itself.

II. "ON BEING A CRIPPLE" BY NANCY MAIRS (READING LEVEL: 8.0)

1. "Semantics" . . .

2. Mairs wants to be considered a tough customer because she wants them to see that she "can face the brutal truth" of her disease, that she does not feel sorry for herself nor does she want them to feel sorry for her.

3. cripple   disabled   handicapped   differently abled

   most real   least real

III. "BACKTRACKING" BY JACOB BOWERS (READING LEVEL: 5.7)

1. The title evokes the image of someone tracking prey, as a hunter does—doubling back over territory already traveled. It implies that this essay covers a topic Bowers has discussed before.

2. Bowers defines hunters as those who go because they must go, routinely leaving comfort and enduring hardship even with little hope of success. With these, "the animal hunted is not an opponent" and "hunting is decidedly not a game" but something "natural and real." In contrast, those who are only "going hunting" can quit it easily. It is something they do, like play sports.

3. Hunters rely only upon themselves when they hunt. Hunting is somehow part of their being, and when they hunt they are free to be themselves.

IV. "WAR GAMES" BY RAY STOLLE (READING LEVEL: 11.8)

1. Stolle defines war games as the "attempt to simulate realistically historical or fictional conflicts in a more or less conventional game format." His topic sentence is the second sentence: "The games played by war-gaming enthusiasts can typically be identified by their scope, method, and scale."

2. The paper is developed at first through dictionary definitions and then by extended definition through illustration by example and through comparison/contrast. Each primary support sentence supports the topic sentence by illustrating one of the ideas included—scope, method, or scale.

3. *Simulate* means to imitate.
   Subduing means conquering.
   Morale means someone's state, attitude, or spirits.
   Hordes means nomadic tribes.

▼ Definition Checklist

1. Does your paragraph use classification of types for an effective extended definition?

2. Can you use illustration by example for your extended definition?

3. Can you use comparison and contrast to define terms that are close in meaning?

▼ Style Checklist

1. Are any sentences needlessly wordy? Remember that you should not try to "pad" your writing.

2. Do your sentences use active-voice verbs?

3. If you are using passive-voice verbs, why are you? Do you have a valid reason for using that construction?

4. Look over your sentences. Can you substitute an effective, specific descriptive verb for a weaker one?

5. Are any of your sentences complex? Check their subordinate clauses. Make sure the less important idea is in the dependent clause.

6. Do any of your sentences have items in a series? Check them for parallel construction.

7. Are there any compound sentences? Check to be sure they are correctly punctuated.

8. Would any sentence be more effective if it were a periodic sentence?

9. Would any sentence be more comprehensible if it were a loose sentence?

10. Do you vary the beginnings of your sentences?

Chapter Nine

The Whole Essay

▶ **TEACHING OBJECTIVES**

1. To use the writing process to develop a coherent, organized, and unified essay.

2. To develop an effective thesis statement.

3. To develop an appropriate introductory paragraph

4. To write a clear summary.

5. To write a useful critique.

6. To make an informed evaluation.

Teaching Suggestions

This chapter applies the entire writing process and all of the writing strategies previously covered. Expanding all of the elements of an effective paragraph into a larger unit should be a logical move. The topic sentence of an entire paragraph, which has supporting primary statements that, in turn, have supporting secondary statements, clearly parallels the thesis statement of an entire essay. An essay has supporting primary statements that function as topic sentences themselves and that also have supporting secondary sentences to illustrate, explain, and otherwise develop those primary ideas/topic sentences. With the longer composition, students will need fuller and more detailed development of ideas.

Prewriting, also known as invention, still provides the necessary exploration of a topic, the discovery of ideas. Group work in brainstorming is useful here, especially with early essays; students may still lack confidence in their own abilities to "write that much," but may feel less threatened if working with others.

Many of the exercises in this chapter (1, 2, 4, 5, 6, 8, 11, 12, 14, 16, 18) can be analyzed in groups. Additionally, these exercises cover the entire writing process, from prewriting with brainstorming to proofreading.

Students also learn to summarize, critique, and evaluate additional pieces from other sources. In fact, some of this material could be used in earlier chapters if students seem ready; summarizing in particular fits in naturally with the reading process. You can link critiquing and evaluating to the work they've done in groups with each other's papers.

For proofreading, have students read the paper backwards to look for spelling errors. Also, students may find it helpful to read their papers aloud; often, they catch some of their errors this way.

Additional Activities

1. For summaries, with any earlier reading, you might have had students identify and underline main ideas (thesis), primary support (topic sentences), and secondary support (development) and then put these sentences together for a summary. If you've coached them through this type of summary throughout the semester, you can have them summarize other material on their own now. Use material from other textbooks, newspaper or magazine articles, and so on; either the students or you can provide the materials.

2. Students can try summarizing plots from their favorite television shows or movies.

3. Practice critiquing as a large group first, with any of the readings already studied. Use the checklist as a guideline. Then have students work in groups on another critique. Finally, have students critique a piece entirely on their own.

4. Have students examine articles using statistics and facts and discuss how those statistics might be interpreted more than one way.

5. When reading any assigned essay or articles, students can discuss the different types of introductions (why each is used, why it is or isn't effective, and so on).

6. Continuing from #5 above, students can also examine these readings' conclusions, again discussing the variety of conclusions, their appropriateness, their effectiveness, and so forth.

Answer Key

EXERCISE 3

1. thesis is adequate

2. thesis is inadequate: too vague ("great problem," "many urban areas")

suggested revision: Crime is a growing problem in my neighborhood.

3. thesis is inadequate: it is a statement of fact
suggested revision: Recruiting minority faculty members, especially women, has been difficult and not entirely successful at State College.

4. thesis is adequate

5. thesis is inadequate: too vague ("excellent" too broad; and for whom?)
suggested revision: Mountain climbing has been a rewarding and challenging hobby for our family.

6. thesis is inadequate: it is a statement of fact
suggested revision: Since only forty percent of all college students graduate in four years, our university has several new programs aimed at increasing its graduation rate.

7. thesis is inadequate: too broad
suggested revision: Keeping up with recent slang isn't always easy, but not knowing it has embarrassed me with my children and my students.

8. thesis is adequate

9. thesis is adequate

10. thesis is inadequate: too broad
suggested revision: Americans are known for their optimism because they have enjoyed steadily improving standards of living and health care.

▼ EXERCISE 5

1. Thesis: There were parts of the island which were as beautiful as I had expected, but there was an abundance of problems such as poverty and crime which contrasted sharply with my preconceived visions of the island.
Introduction needs revision; it is somewhat repetitive, but it does contain a thesis statement and suggested audience.
Type of introduction used: Anecdotal Introduction

2. No clear thesis.
Introduction needs revision; there is no clear thesis statement, no suggested audience, and the introduction does not develop the reader's interest.
Type of introduction used: "Focus-Down" introduction

3. Thesis: One of these people who displayed insurmountable supplies of hope, determination, and perseverance was my uncle.

Introduction is adequate: it contains a thesis, suggests an audience, and develops the reader's interest.
Type of introduction used: "Focus-Down" introduction

4. No clear thesis.
Introduction needs revision: no thesis, no suggested audience, does not develop the reader's interest.
Type of introduction used: Commonplace statement.

5. Thesis: Typical of these places was the Golden Nugget.
Introduction is adequate: it contains a thesis, suggests an audience, and develops the reader's interest.
Type of introduction used: "Focus-Down" introduction

▼ EXERCISE 7

Summaries will vary somewhat, but should include the thesis, the major supports (primary supports), and should paraphrase rather than quote. A short sample summary follows:

Americans vacationing in Europe are likely to find that their concept of friendship contrasts sharply with the concept in France, Germany, and England. In America, the word "friend" is casually used to refer to almost everyone from the closest confidante to the most casual acquaintance. In France, friendships tend to be between persons of the same sex, require an awareness of the person's intellect and interests, and are compartmentalized. These friendships fill different needs in a person's life and often increase each person's sense of individuality. In contrast, in Germany friends are brought into the family and friendship more clearly is based on feeling and loyalty. These friendships are designed to be lasting ones. In England, friends share activities from different stages of life. These friendships are based on continuity and the friends feel that they can pick up where they left off, even years later.

▼ EXERCISE 8

Students' critiques will vary, but they should all recognize that "On Friendship" clearly states its thesis, develops the thesis fully and clearly through specific examples about friendship in other countries, and includes ample evidence to convince the readers that the authors' assessment of friendship is accurate and valid.

▼ EXERCISE 9

If necessary, students could research this topic in a variety of ways. They could interview foreign students from different countries to find out how friendship is defined. They could talk to Americans who have lived or traveled extensively abroad. They could also talk to (or read findings from) sociologists, psychologists, or anthropologists.

▼ EXERCISE 10

Thesis: "As a boy in Mayfield, I learned through my school, my friends, my dreams, and my departure."

1. The author uses a "focus-down" introduction (general to specific) that includes a personal anecdote. The thesis is the last sentence in the paragraph, and it will be developed through examples focusing on school, friends, dreams, and his departure. The nostalgic (and somewhat regretful) tone of the introduction evokes a similar nostalgia on the reader's part.

2. In each body paragraph, the topic sentence is the first sentence. Each supports the thesis by focusing on a different idea from the thesis—Mayfield itself (paragraph 1), school (paragraph 3), friends (paragraph 4), and his departure (paragraph 5).

3. a. Paragraph 2:
   Topic sentence: In many ways, Mayfield *differed from other neighborhoods.*
   A. Sentence 2 is an admission that Mayfield was similar to other neighborhoods.
   B. Sentence 3 supports the topic sentence.
   C. One felt as if he or she were reading *Our Town.*
      1. Each family owned a house.
      2. The Protestant church sat on one corner.
      3. The Catholic church was a few blocks away.
      4. There was an ethnic mix in the area.
      5. His family was the only Asian family.
      6. People knew each other through the church, PTA, or gossip.

   b. Paragraph 3.
   Topic Sentence: St. Francis of Assisi School *initiated me into the life of Catholic education.*
   A. Sister Grace introduced him to math and reading.
      1. She did not scare him by remembering other siblings.
   B. Sister Edwards pinched his cheek.
      1. Youngest children learn to deal with such occasions.
   C. The first year of school amused him.
   D. By second grade Mrs. Young informed him he was no longer a child.
      1. He was a student.
      2. His eager attitude changed and he was overwhelmed.
   Concluding sentence: I wanted to go home.

   c. Paragraph 4.
   Topic Sentence: *When I got home from school*, I often spent my free time playing with the many kids in Mayfield.
   A. He envied and imitated big kids.
      1. He thought fifth grade kids could do anything.
      2. He practiced the things they did.
         a. He and Dave rode bikes without using their hands.
         b. The big kids elected someone to steal apples.
   B. He promised himself that he would never make smaller children endure what he had.

C. The big kids taught him important things.
Concluding sentence: Competing with the other kids, I often wondered about being big.

d. Paragraph 5.
Topic Sentence: At Mayfield I dreamed the usual *boyhood dreams that still exist in other kids.*
A. He believed he would play professional baseball.
B. He believed he would travel in space.
C. He believed he could save the president and win the Olympics.
D. He had more practical dreams later.
E. The other kids shared similar dreams.
Concluding sentence: Dreams change, and some die as kids grow older.

e. Paragraph 6.
Topic Sentence: When I *moved from Mayfield* on September 7, 1977, I *could not pack everything I wanted to take.*
A. Some items remained behind.
    1. He wanted to take his friends.
    2. He had to leave his bike.
B. He wondered if they would return home.
C. He believed he could still follow his dreams anywhere.
Concluding sentence: So I left most everything behind, but I packed away my hope, which remained after such a trauma.

Transitions between paragraphs have been italicized in the topic sentences.

4. The conclusion is a summary of the thesis, with comparisons made to the present. References to the Garden of Eden tie the conclusion to the introduction. Repetition of key words like *school (education), friends,* and *dreams* also links the two paragraphs.

▼ EXERCISE 13

The essay needs much revision. Students should read it carefully. In groups, they should revise it, paragraph by paragraph.

▼ EXERCISE 15

Here is a sample revision of the essay:

When I reflect on my life to understand which stage of development has influenced my attitudes the most, I see that my childhood had a major impact. The values and interests I developed during childhood have remained with me. My love of sports and athletic competition stems from my childhood experiences. Specifically, my family and childhood environment have caused, to a great degree, the intense competition and sometimes unsportsmanlike conduct that I exhibit when I play sports.

The intensity with which I play sports has been evident since my early childhood. As a young boy, I often played different sports with my father, and I can well remember our on-going rivalry in basketball. As I grew taller and more skilled, I was able to beat him almost every time. However, there were games in which the "old man" would get lucky and beat me. I never took defeat lightly, and I usually stomped off the court in anger after a loss. Maybe the fact that I seldom lost made defeat more difficult to accept.

My fierce competition in playing against my dad almost reached the point of being unsportsmanlike, but it certainly reached that point when I competed with my younger brother. Since we lived in a small community, my brother and I usually played games (such as football, baseball, soccer, and basketball) one-on-one rather than with other boys. When we played, I always won; my victories should not be surprising since I was three years older and several inches taller than my brother. Still, despite my obvious advantages, I never relented and prided myself on the fact that he had never beaten me in any of the sports we played. When he did come close to winning, I would usually go into a rage and double my efforts to defeat him. Sometimes I even resorted to cheating to keep from losing. I did whatever it took to win, and after winning, I would jump and shout in celebration as if I had just won the World Series or the Super Bowl.

When I play sports with people other than my family, I usually control my intensity, but still display much the same behavior. I always play to win, even if I am just playing in an intramural game, and sometimes I become quite depressed when I lose. Losing has also led me to some very childish acts, such as slamming down balls and bats, yelling unmentionables, and stomping off the playing field in anger. These actions mirror the behavior I exhibited playing against my father and brother, but others have now witnessed my conduct.

The three causes of this behavior are linked to my childhood. Foremost is the competition within my family, especially with my brother. Because of my need to dominate him since I was older, I behaved worse when I played against him. Because I never lost when I played against him, I never had to accept defeat. Second, my love of sports and the great importance I place on them have also led to the intensity I exhibit. Introduced to sports at a young age, I participated in them throughout my childhood. Finally, I need to be a sports superstar. Although I performed well on the teams I played on, I was never a superstar. However, when I played against my brother I was able to dominate him, and, in effect, become the star I never was otherwise. Even when I play against my peers now, I always strive to be the best.

My competitiveness has had unfortunate results. It has caused unnecessary tension and immature behavior that has, in turn, caused embarrassment. I have not set a good example for my brother, and, as a result, he has displayed similar actions. If I had played sports just for fun and not taken them so seriously, then I would probably have enjoyed playing much more.

▼ EXERCISE 17

The running craze has reached enormous proportions in recent years. One cannot help but notice the increase in the number of runners; the streets and sidewalks have been invaded by these fitness freaks. A number of them are serious competitors, entering any number of the countless races held every weekend. Of these racers, no two follow exactly the same training regimen; still, all routines are based on either high-mileage running or speed-oriented work-outs, or a combination of the two. Each method has its benefits and drawbacks.

Both training methods can be used to prepare for middle-distance and long-distance racing. Distance training consists of running at least a couple of miles at a steady pace and is used to develop stamina. Speed-oriented workouts, on the other hand, involve running short distances under one mile at a fast pace. This training is used to build speed and to simulate the final mile of a race in terms of pace and intensity.

▼ Thesis Statement Checklist

1. Is it located in the introduction?

2. Does it state your main idea?

3. Is it an opinion rather than a statement of fact?

4. Does it have a subject and a controlling idea?

▼ Introduction Checklist

1. Does the beginning paragraph contain the thesis statement?

2. Does it suggest an audience to establish your tone and opinion?

3. Does it attract the reader's attention and interest through "focusing- down," with a commonplace statement, with quotations or statistics, with an anecdote, or in some other manner?

Additional Checklists for Writing

▼ Critiquing Questions

1. What is the author's thesis?
   State the topic.
   State the author's viewpoint.

2. List the reasons given to support the author's opinion.

3. What details does the author provide to explain each reason?
   Are the details relevant to the thesis?
   Are the details factual and easily verifiable?
   Are the details based on subjective or objective experience?
   What are the sources of those details?

4. Does the author make a strong case to support his or her belief?
   Does the author provide enough evidence to convince a skeptic that the personal opinion is logical and valid? If you answer "yes" to the last question, then you can synthesize the essay's information because you have decided that it is worthwhile to incorporate that information into your store of knowledge.

▼ Evaluation Questions

1. What would be the most likely opposing thesis?
   State it.

2. How would opponents of the author's opinion support their viewpoint?
   What reasons would they give for their opposition?

3. Does the author refer to his or her opponents' views?
   Does the author try to refute their ideas?
   Is this refutation successful?

4. What facts, statistics, details, and so forth contradict the author's viewpoint?
   What facts, statistics, details, and so on weaken his or her case?

5. Are there acknowledged experts on the topic whose opinions differ from the author's?
   Who are they?
   Are their conclusions valid?
   Do they support their views with facts, studies, and so on?

▼ Revising Questions

I. Thesis
    A. Is there a thesis?
    B. Is the thesis accurate?
    C. How does the thesis define your opinion, predict the discussion, and control the essay?
    D. How could the thesis be worded more clearly?
    E. If there is no stated thesis, then what seems to be the main idea in the essay?

II. Organization
    A. What makes the final organization of the essay effective? If, for instance, you are narrating an event, then is the narration in chronological order?
    B. Would your paragraphs be better arranged in another manner?

III. Body Paragraphs
    A. Does each body paragraph in the paper have a topic sentence?
    B. How does each topic sentence refer to or support the thesis?
    C. How do these body paragraphs present the best ideas possible to support the thesis? Can you now think of other examples that might be more effective and interesting?
    D. Do you include specific details?
    E. How do the sentences in each paragraph support the topic sentence?
    B. Are these paragraphs unified?

IV. Introduction
    A. How does the introduction develop the reader's interest?
    B. Does the introduction supply enough information about the background of the topic?
    C. Is the introduction too short?
    D. Would another type of introduction be more effective?

V. Transitions
    A. What are the transitions between paragraphs?
    B. What makes effective transitions between the sentences within paragraphs?
    C. Can the reader easily follow the ideas presented in the essay?

▼ Editing List

I. Clarity
    A. Do all of your sentences mean what they say? Or are they ambiguous?

B. Have you used the correct words to communicate your meaning?

II. Coherence (See Chapter 6 in Part One)
   A. Did you use pronouns to achieve coherence? Are any pronouns ambiguous in their reference?
   B. Did you use synonyms? Are they accurate?
   C. Did you use limited repetition to achieve coherence?
   D. Did you use sentence combining to achieve coherence?

III. Diction (See Chapter 7 in Part One)
   A. Did you use specific words?
   B. Did you avoid slang, jargon, and regional expressions?
   C. Did you use clichés? Can you think of another way to express your meaning?
   D. Did you create a specific, identifiable tone through word choice? Is this tone appropriate for the intended audience?

IV. Style (See Chapter 8 in Part One)
   A. Are sentences wordy?
   B. Did you use active voice and descriptive verbs?
   C. Did you subordinate these ideas effectively?
   D. Did you vary your sentence structure?

V. Correctness
   A. Are there any fragments, run-ons, or comma splices? (See Chapters 4, 5, and 6 in Part Two)
   B. Do subjects and verbs agree in number? (See Chapter 7 in Part Two)
   C. Are there any unnecessary shifts in verb tense? (See Chapters 1 and 2 in Part Two)
   D. Are there any unnecessary shifts in point of view?
   E. Are your pronouns correct in case, number, and gender? (See Chapter 8 in Part Two.)
   F. Did you check marks of punctuation? Are commas, semicolons, colons, and other marks of punctuation used correctly? (See Chapters 9, 10, 11, 12, and 13 in Part Two.)
   G. Are words spelled correctly? (Check any good dictionary.)

▼ Proofreading Guidelines

1. Is each word spelled correctly?

2. Are words omitted? Or are words repeated?

3. Are there stray marks of punctuation?

Grammar Review

PART II

Introduction

TEACHING OBJECTIVES

1. To review the parts of speech.

2. To introduce identification of subjects and verbs.

3. To introduce four basic sentence formats.

Teaching Suggestions

This review could be done fairly early, in the first week or so of class. Students could use their own work to identify subjects and verbs; they could also use their own work to identify sentence formats.

You could put a sentence or two on the board at the beginning of class as a quick large-group exercise: get students to identify subjects and verbs and to identify sentence formats. This is quick and can provide continuity. You can have students rewrite their own sentences and/or the ones on the board to demonstrate other formats.

Sentence-combining exercises are particularly useful for creating sentence formats. You can give students a set of sentences and ask them to combine the same sentences to create different formats, adding material if they need to do so.

In general, drill work alone will not guarantee that a student will write well; it will not even guarantee that a student will write without grammar errors. Research shows that there is little automatic carryover from grammar drills to writing. Consequently, for grammar study to be meaningful and effective, students need to move from drill exercises to applications, study particular elements of grammar and then examine their own writing for those elements.

Nor will mastery of grammar and mechanics occur with one lesson, or even with two. For many students, it will take far longer than a single semester for such knowledge to be internalized. Instead, they will need to make a conscious effort to eliminate such errors—hence the need for true attention to editing and proofreading skills.

Chapter One

Verbs I: The Present, Past, and Future Tenses

▶ **TEACHING OBJECTIVES**

1. To recognize and use the basic verb tenses—past, present, and future.

2. To form correctly regular and irregular verbs in past, present, and future tenses.

3. To use a consistent and appropriate verb tense when writing.

Teaching Suggestions

Verbs can be very troublesome for some students. Verb tense forms can be particularly difficult.

     Copy exercises are very useful for these students. Give students a paragraph and direct them to rewrite it, changing tense all the way through (past to present, present to past). They don't have to generate any material; they have good models provided. You can generate class discussion from these exercises. Students will find that sometimes changing tense requires other grammatical changes, so you'll end up discussing some other element of grammar as well. They can also use their own work for this: you might direct them to write a narrative in the past tense, then to rewrite it in another tense.

Chapter Two
Verbs II: The Perfect Tenses and Progressive Forms

▶ **TEACHING OBJECTIVES**

1. To recognize and use the three perfect tenses correctly.

2. To recognize and use the six progressive verb forms correctly.

3. To use a consistent and appropriate verb tense when writing.

Teaching Suggestions

This chapter presents information that may be too advanced for some of your students. You may choose to assign it only as it is needed, or only as questions come up naturally in the course of their own writing. Once again, copy exercises might be a good idea with this chapter.

Chapter Three

Subjects, Verbs, and Prepositional Phrases

**TEACHING
OBJECTIVES**

1. To identify subjects, verbs, and prepositional phrases.

2. To recognize and write sentence patterns.

3. To identify and write the major classes of sentences.

Teaching Suggestions

As with the introduction to Part Two, this chapter could be covered early in the course and continued over time. Students can identify subjects, verbs, and prepositional phrases in their own work as well as in sentences you provide for them. Sentences on the board can be used with the entire class in large-group discussion.

Try using imitation exercises where students simply follow a pattern or type of sentence to create their own sentences; some students find this rote imitation helpful. However, don't stop there. Have them identify patterns and types in their own writing and then try to rewrite some of these into patterns or types they haven't used.

You'll find it natural to talk about sentence variety here, too. Students can begin to see that several sentences might be "right," but that each has a different effect; you can talk about the effects.

Chapter Four

Fragments

TEACHING OBJECTIVES

1. To recognize fragments, individually and in paragraphs.

2. To correct fragments.

3. To use the editing symbol for fragment (Frag) when proofreading.

Teaching Suggestions

Give a series of fragments to students. Have the whole class work as a group to identify what is missing in each fragment. Rewrite each into a complete sentence.

Give a series of fragments and sentences. Have the class break into small groups, identify which are fragments and which are complete sentences. Have groups rewrite the fragments.

Have students use their own writing, individually and in groups; this can be part of revising/proofreading.

Chapter Five

Comma Splices

▶ **TEACHING OBJECTIVES**

1. To recognize comma splices in individual sentences and in paragraphs.

2. To correct comma splices.

3. To use the editing symbol for comma splices (CS) when proofreading.

Teaching Suggestions

Commas splices are very common; indeed, most students have difficulty with commas in general. Consequently, you might want to use the first part of Chapter 9 on independent clauses at this point.

This is also a natural time to talk again about complete sentences and compound sentences. Students tend to remember more easily punctuation rules learned in context and to remember those rules longer.

You may find it useful to link this chapter with Chapter 6. Comma splices and run-ons are closely related, and students who make one of these errors may also make the other.

Chapter Six

Run-Ons

▶ **TEACHING OBJECTIVES**

1. To recognize run-ons, individually and in paragraphs.

2. To correct run-ons.

3. To use the editing symbol for run-ons (RO) correctly when proofreading.

Teaching Suggestions

As with comma splices, run-ons are very common. Students may know run-ons as fused sentences or run-together sentences, so talking about terms is beneficial.

You'll need to talk about complete sentences and compound sentences here, as with comma splices. You'll also find it helpful to use the section on independent clauses in Chapter 9 (Part Two) as well.

Chapter Seven
Subject-Verb Agreement

**TEACHING
OBJECTIVES**

1. To make subjects and verbs agree in number.

2. To correct problems in subject-verb agreement.

3. To use the editing symbol for subject-verb agreement (S-V Agr) correctly while proofreading.

Teaching Suggestions

Some students are particularly troubled by subject-verb agreement errors. Linking this chapter with the Introduction and Chapter 1 (both in Part Two) will be natural. Indeed, you might even have already previewed or reviewed that subjects and verbs have to agree in number. Have students proofread alone and in groups.

Chapter Eight
Pronoun Reference

TEACHING OBJECTIVES

1. To recognize pronoun-reference problems.

2. To correct pronoun-reference problems.

3. To proofread an essay for pronoun reference. The editing symbol for pronoun reference is pro. ref.

Teaching Suggestions

Pronoun agreement and subject-verb agreement are linked, and you can transfer the same principles from Chapter 7 here. Students with case problems may need additional practice; some popular usage often counters correct pronoun usage.

Some students find it difficult to find antecedents, so practice with locating antecedents might be useful. Chapter 6, Part One (Achieving Coherence) is related to this chapter, and you might link them for students.

Chapter Nine

Commas to Separate

<table>
<tr><td>► **TEACHING OBJECTIVES**</td><td>

1. To recognize the need for commas in sentences and in paragraphs.

2. To use commas correctly.

3. To proofread a paper for comma mistakes, and to use correctly the editing symbol for comma mistakes (P).

</td></tr>
</table>

Teaching Suggestions

Giving students paragraphs with no commas at all and having them put in commas is useful. Students also can look at their own paragraphs, circle commas, and apply these rules.

Chapter Ten
Commas to Enclose

▶ **TEACHING OBJECTIVES**

1. To recognize poorly punctuated sentences, in isolation and in paragraphs.

2. To use commas to enclose or set off words, phrases, and clauses correctly.

3. To proofread a paper for comma errors and to use the editing symbol for a comma error (P).

Teaching Suggestions

This chapter contains more complex uses of commas than Chapter 9 does, so you may want to cover each rule separately over several days. For commas in dialogue, you will need to talk about quotation marks. Give students a passage of dialogue that includes both commas and quotations. Discuss the punctuation used. Then have students write a similar dialogue. Depending upon the level of your students, you may or may not have luck with appositives. Restrictive and non-restrictive elements are particularly difficult, but you will need to discuss them.

Chapter Eleven

Apostrophes

1. To recognize the need for apostrophes.

2. To use apostrophes correctly.

3. To proofread a paper for apostrophe errors. The editing symbol for apostrophes is apos.

Teaching Suggestions

Deal with apostrophes as problems arise out of students' own work. Problems will probably arise with the first writing, since many people commonly misuse apostrophes to form plurals or omit them when they are needed.

Chapter Twelve
Capitals, End Punctuation, and Other Types of Punctuation

▶ **TEACHING OBJECTIVES**

1. To recognize the need for capitals in sentences and in paragraphs.

2. To recognize the need for end punctuation in sentences.

3. To use capitals and end punctuation correctly.

4. To learn how to use other types of punctuation correctly.

5. To learn to proofread for punctuation errors and to correct them.

6. To learn to use the editing symbol (P).

Teaching Suggestions

Deal with these individually as they are suggested by students' own writing. You'll probably talk about end punctuation marks fairly early in the semester. You can talk about different punctuation marks creating different emphases—dashes, for example; or semicolons as opposed to periods; or colons.

Chapter Thirteen

Confusing and Often Misused Words

▶ **TEACHING OBJECTIVES**

1. To recognize words whose spelling and usage are frequently confused.

2. To use these words correctly.

3. To proofread a paper for errors in the use of these words and to use the editing symbol (ww) correctly.

Teaching Suggestions

Consider covering this chapter throughout the semester. Assign a few sets of words each week; give a quiz every week that asks students to use the words correctly in context. You can give points for words being used correctly; you can also give points for correct sentences.

A Bibliography for Writing Teachers

Atwell, Nancie. *In the Middle: Writing, Reading, and Learning with Adolescents.* Portsmouth, NH: Boynton/Cook, 1987.

Calkins, Lucy McCormick. *The Art of Teaching Writing.* Portsmouth, NH: Heinemann, 1986.

Corbett, Edward P. J. *Classical Rhetoric for the Modern Student.* 3rd ed. New York: Oxford University Press, 1990.

D'Angelo, Frank J. *A Conceptual Theory of Rhetoric.* Cambridge, Mass.: Winthrop Publishers, Inc., 1975.

Donovan, Timothy R. and Ben W. McClelland, eds. *Eight Approaches to Teaching Composition.* Urbana, Ill.: NCTE, 1980.

Elbow, Peter. *Writing Without Teachers.* Oxford: Oxford University Press, 1973.

Emig, Janet. *The Composing Processes of Twelfth Graders.* NCTE Research Report No. 13. Urbana, Ill.: NCTE, 1971.
    The Web of Meaning: Essays on Writing, Teaching, Learning and Thinking. Portsmouth, NH: Boynton/Cook, 1983.

Fulwiler, Toby. *Teaching with Writing.* Portsmouth, NH: Boynton/Cook, 1987.

Gere, Ann Ruggles, ed. *Roots in the Sawdust: Writing to Learn Across the Disciplines.* Urbana, Ill: NCTE, 1985.

Graser, Elsa R. *Teaching Writing: A Process Approach: A Survey of Research.* Dubuque: Kendall/Hunt, 1983.

Graves, Donald. *Writing: Teachers and Children at Work.* Portsmouth, NH: Heinemann, 1983.

Graves, Richard L., ed. *Rhetoric and Composition: A Sourcebook for Teachers and Writers.* New edition. Upper Montclair, NJ: Boynton/Cook, 1984.

Hillocks, George Jr. *Research on Written Composition.* Urbana, Ill: NCTE, 1986.

Hirsch, E. D. Jr. *The Philosophy of Composition.* Chicago: University of Chicago Press, 1977.

Kirby, Dan and Tom Liner with Ruth Vinz. *Inside Out: Developmental Strategies for Teaching Writing.* Second ed. Portsmouth, NH: Boynton/Cook, 1988.

Knoblauch, C. H. and Lil Brannon. *Rhetorical Traditions and the Teaching of Writing.* Upper Montclair, NJ: Boynton/Cook, 1984.

Lindemann, Erika. *A Rhetoric for Writing Teachers.* New York: Oxford University Press, 1982.

Murray, Donald M. *Expecting the Unexpected: Teaching Myself—and Others—to Read and Write.* Portsmouth, NH: Boynton/Cook, 1989.

Prouett, Jackie, and Kent Gill. *The Writing Process in Action: A Handbook for Teachers.* Urbana, Ill.: NCTE, 1986.

Rico, Gabriele Lusser. *Writing the Natural Way.* Los Angeles: J.P. Tarcher, Inc., 1983.

Shaughnessy, Mina P. *Errors and Expectations: A Guide for the Teacher of Basic Writing.* New York: Oxford University Press, 1977.

Tate, Gary, and Edward P. J. Corbett, eds. *The Writing Teacher's Sourcebook.* New York: Oxford University Press, 1981.

Young, Richard E., Alton L. Becker, and Kenneth L. Pike. *Rhetoric: Discovery and Change.* New York: Harcourt, Brace, Jovanovich Inc., 1970.